AF520164

GIONALIZING PAN-ISLAMISM
CUMENTS ON THE KHILAFAT MOVEMENT

Regionalizing Pan-Islamism

Documents on the Khilafat Movement

Edited by

MUSHIRUL HASAN

MARGRIT PERNAU

MANOHAR
2005

First published 2005

ISBN 81-7304-593-3

Published by
Ajay Kumar Jain for
Manohar Publishers & Distributors
4753/23 Ansari Road, Daryaganj
New Delhi 110 002

Distributed in South Asia by
FOUNDATION
BOOKS
4381/4, Ansari Road
Daryaganj, New Delhi 110 002
and its branches at Mumbai, Hyderabad,
Bangalore, Chennai, Kolkata

Printed at
Lordson Publishers Pvt Ltd
Delhi 110 007

Contents

Introduction

The success which attended the Non-Co-operation and Khilafat movements in India is undoubtedly attributable to the Great War, for neither agitation could have attained the dimensions which it did but for the economic pressure to which the people were subjected in consequence of the prolonged and wide-spread hostilities. This pressure aggravated and magnified local grievances and spread it of unrest, thus making, for a time, the work of agitators easy.

Although the Khilafat movement ostensibly had the purely religious object of compelling the maintenance of spiritual and temporal Muslim control over the Holy Places of Islam, yet there is no doubt that the real aim of its most revolutionary and active leaders was the destruction of British rule in India: an aim which was justified on the ground that Britain is the most powerful rival to Muslim influence in the Near East. Gandhi quickly realized this and, appreciating the value of a common object for the Non-Co-operation and Khilafat movements, provided them with a common platform, i.e. the Punjab and Khilafat wrongs, from which to appeal to the feelings of people of all denominations. The annual Congress and Khilafat conferences were always held at the same time and place, and some of the personnel were generally common to the committee of both. These committees, during the period of their greatest activity in the years 1920 and 1921, were very closely associated.

P.C. Bamford, *Histories of the Non-Co-operation and Khilafat Movements*, Delhi, 1925, reprinted 1985.

Reports of a Turco-German conspiracy to incite Indian Muslims against the British coupled with the Khilafat and Non-Cooperation movements, sent shock waves across the colonial administration.[1] The British government responded in various ways. One was to strengthen and reorganize its police defence and the other to introduce legislations like the Police Disaffection Act of 1902. The government also pressed into service the Criminal Amendment Act and the Seditious Meeting Act. The Rowlatt Committee was the last straw. It recommended that the government be given powers to make arbitrary arrests and inflict summary punishments for the suppression of revolutionary activities. Accordingly, a Bill was introduced in the Imperial Legislative Council in February 1919 and was passed in the teeth of opposition from all the Indian members. On 24 February, Gandhi informed the Viceroy of his decision to launch a satyagraha against the Rowlatt Act. Two days later, he urged his countrymen to join the satyagraha. On 6 April, different parts of the country observed hartal.

National, provincial and local leaders were periodically rounded up, and put in jail, including some of the chief architects of the Khilafat campaigns like the Ali brothers, Maulana Abul Kalam Azad, Zafar Ali Khan, editor of *Zamindar*, and Hasrat Mohani, the poet-journalist. In November 1921, the Congress and Khilafat volunteer organizations were banned and, by January 1922, over 30,000 individual civil resisters had been jailed. Gandhi, their Mahatma, was arrested and convicted in March 1922.

P.C. Bamford's report of 22 June 1925 recapitulates these events in considerable detail. So do the annual series edited by the civil servant-historian Rushbrook Williams, and the *Indian Annual Register*, a vast compendium of information.

In addition to these sources, the provincial governments prepared, in response to the Secretary of State's request to the Government of India, their version of the Non-Cooperation and Khilafat movements. We have included the reports from Delhi, the United Provinces, the Central Provinces and Berar, Bengal and the North-

[1] For the political background to these developments, see H.F. Owen, 'Towards Nation-wide Agitation and Organization: The Home Rule Leagues, 1915-18', D.A. Low (ed.), *Soundings in Modern South Asian History*, California, 1969.

West Frontier Provinces.[2] For Sind, no report seems to have been prepared; instead, we have included the original weekly and fortnightly reports by the CID, produced under the authority of J.C. Curry, the Chief Civil Intelligence Officer for the province and author of a major publication entitled *The Indian Police*.

Although of a different category than the main corpus of the texts, the reports from the provinces, unlike the pan-Indian perspective provided by Bamford, enable us to plot the trajectory of the Khilafat and Non-Cooperation movements in much greater detail. They are useful to a historian for this, as also for other reasons. Sometimes, those reporting from a district or a *qasba* contest the claims of the Congress and the Khilafatists not infrequently exaggerated, over the success of their campaigns. On other occasions, their reports reinforce certain stereotypical notions about Islam and the Muslim communities. More often than not, they link the pan-Islamic upsurge to, for example, crime or, as in the case of the 'Silk Letter Conspiracy', to rebellion. Thus, a historian sympathetic to British rule could observe in the early-1930s: 'Mass civil disobedience means the opposition of all the people to the laws and institutions of a "Satanic" government. It appeals to baser motives because it offers the prospect of evading the payment of taxes and of looting and committing other crimes without the risk of punishment.'[3]

COLLECTION OF INFORMATION AND PRODUCTION OF COLONIAL KNOWLEDGE

From the beginning of British rule the collection of information and the surveillance of the semi-public and public spheres, in which collective opinion was being formed and expressed, was central to

[2] For Madras, see Home (Political), 4/5, 1937, National Archives of India, Delhi. Mohammad Waseem, Professor of Political Science at the Qaid-i Azam University in Islamabad, sent us photocopies of the reports on the North-West Frontier Province and Baluchistan. Sadly, though, their ink is too light to be read. The report on Bihar has disappeared from its archives in Patna. We have not been able to trace the report on Punjab, though we realize that it must be housed in some library or archives in Pakistan or the United Kingdom.

[3] W.R. Smith, *Nationalism and Reform in India*, New Haven, 1938, p. 123.

the empire's security.[4] These efforts were systematized after the revolt of 1857 by the weekly reports on native newspapers for every province. Moreover, policemen in civil clothes monitored the newly spreading world of associations and societies as well as public speeches, especially in religious settings. Delhi's separation from Punjab, necessitated by the transfer of the capital from Calcutta in 1911, brought about the reorganization of the Intelligence Department for both the provinces, allowing an insight into their organization and working.

From the 1857 revolt to Independence one preoccupation of both, the British and the Indians, has been the role of the police—'a metaphor for the colonial regime as a whole'. This volume carries a number of documents examining it from a variety of perspectives.[5] There are those, mostly colonialist writers like J.C. Curry and Percival Griffiths, who equate the police with the 'rule of law' and the 'firm establishment of law and order under the British'. Then there are professional historians like David Arnold who find the 'rule of law' to be a cliché that hid more than it revealed.[6] Finally, there are those who invoke the role of the police in suppressing the nationalist movement. In this respect, it is useful to turn to, besides the memoirs and autobiogaphies, the collection of articles produced by the Publications Division in 1971 entitled *1921 Movement: Reminiscences*. Let us, as an illustration, cite a lesser known but useful eyewitness description:

A few months later, the country was in the throes of the civil disobedience movement, and its impact was felt in our sleepy little town also. There were wild rumours and simmerings of trouble. In the evening a huge crowd had gathered at a public meeting to hear a local leader who had announced his decision to offer satyagraha. As the meeting progressed, the police came.

[4] C.A. Bayly, *Empire and Information: Intelligence gathering and social communication in India, 1780-1870*, Cambridge, 1996; for a case study of the Delhi region, see Margrit Pernau and Yunus Jaffry (eds.), *The Public Sphere in Early Colonial Rule: Three Persian Akhbarat firom Delhi, 1810-1830* (forthcoming).

[5] For a brief history of the police in the United Provinces, see Giriraj Shah, *Image Makers: An Attitudional Study of Indian Police*, Delhi, 1993.

[6] David Arnold, *Police Power and Colonial Rule, Madras 1859-1947*, Delhi, 1986, p. 3.

They were not the usual policemen with red turbans, but the armed police with their black regulation boots, lathis and evil-locking guns. The satyagrahi was arrested and was being taken away when the crowd lost control and made a concerted effort to prevent it. The police response was brutal. Standing on the edges of the crows, I could see little of the *mêlée*. Then the shots rang out and the crowd began to disperse in total disarray. I too ran for my life. The last I saw was of the policemen chasing, hitting and shouting and reveling in the display of their power and strength.[7]

The CID staff for Delhi consisted of one Deputy Superintendent, one Inspector, two Sub-Inspectors, 4 Head Constables and 16 Constables, who worked directly under the Superintendent of Police and who collected information of a political nature as well as kept track of 'wandering and criminal tribes, suspicious characters &c'.[8] From the daily confidential reports submitted to the Superintendent of Police, a weekly 'Secret Abstract' was compiled, after 'such reports as may require it have been previously "edited" by the responsible Gazetted Officer'.[9] This was the first level at which the editing of the information—its selection and interpretation—by the British took place. From these secret abstracts and other materials, correspondence, and the analysis of printed material, Delhi's Chief Commissioner compiled his fortnightly report on the internal political situation. This was the second level of editing. All the reports from the provinces were then collected at the capital and they, in turn, provided the basis for the weekly telegraphic reports to the Secretary of State as well as the weekly reports of the Director of the CID on the political situation—the third level.

While the reports were open ended, they constitute a first attempt at an interpretation from a historical perspective. It was no longer the gathering of information as a guide to necessary political action, which was the main aim, but making sense of the recent past, an attempt that found its conclusion in the report of Bamford on the histories of the Khilafat and Non-Cooperation movements. The

[7] S. Venugopal Rao, *Baton and the Pen*, Delhi, 1993, p. 4.

[8] Memorandurn Wallace, 18.10.1912, in: Constitution of a Criminal Investigation Department for the Province of Delhi, Home, Confidential, 1913, No. 14, Delhi Archive.

[9] Ibid., Memo to Hafley, no date, 1913.

Indian National Congress, too, produced its own version, a counter-perspective. The Civil Disobedience Enquiry Report represented a well-conceived effort to intervene in the collection and dissemination of information. Unlike the government reports that often dismissed the strong local and regional roots of popular outpourings against the British,[10] the Congress report documented the general awakening of the masses to their political rights and privileges, the government's failure to suppress them, and the ultimate lack of faith in its so-called good intentions. Indeed, Jawaharal Nehru had found 'the whole countryside afire with enthusiasm and full of a strange excitement'.[11] He spoke of the young Western-educated Indian when he wrote in his autobiography: '[after my return from England] the idea that we must not tamely submit to existing conditions and that something must be done began to obsess me more and more.... I felt that both individual and national honour demanded a more aggressive and fighting attitude to foreign rule.'[12]

BETWEEN THE GLOBAL AND THE LOCAL

For most of the nineteenth and twentieth centuries, history has been written and interpreted either from the perspective of the nation or, more rarely, from a global perspective, concentrating mostly on the expansion of empires, the Roman, the Islamic and the colonizations by Europe. The present wave of globalization, however, has brought about a renewed interest—which might well develop into a far-reaching change of paradigm—in processes transcending the boundaries of the nation-state, on encounters, entanglements and shared histories.[13]

[10] See, for example, the government of India's resolution on the Non-Cooperation movement, 1920, C.H. Philips (ed.), *The Evolution of India and Pakistan 1858 to 1947: Select Documents*, London, 1962, pp. 218-19.

[11] Jawaharal Nehru, *An Autobiography*, London, 1936, p. 51.

[12] Ibid., pp. 39, 43.

[13] Jürgen Osterhammel, *Geschichtswissenschaft jenseits des Nationalstaats. Studien zu Beziehungsgeschichte und Zivilisationsvergleich* [Historiography beyond the nation-state: Studies on relational history and the comparison of civilizations],

At the same time, this process raises important questions on the interrelations between empire, nation, and province, which had been debated for India in the 1970s and 1980s, notably by the Cambridge 'school',[14] focusing on the influence of local events in the shaping of imperial policies.

Gail Minault in her path-breaking study has already pointed out its dual nature, in so far as the Khilafat movement used pan-Islamic symbols in order to hold together locally fragmented movements by Indian Muslims, thus merging the transnational and the local.[15] It is this discussion that the publication of the provincial Khilafat reports wishes to revive and take further. Presenting a wealth of detail, they reveal not only the activities with which local leaders made sense of all-India developments within their own parameters, taking up directives by the national leaders, organizing the movement at the local level, and endowing it with popular support and money, all of which fed into the national movement.

The reports are particularly rich on those activities which threatened to disrupt the economy, especially when strikes were directed against the railways, the tea gardens, or the jute industry. Very often, issues that had been smouldering for a long time at the local level received impetus by being linked to nationalist slogans. In Delhi, for instance, some sections opposed the British-owned tramway from the turn of the century. Its boycott during the agitation, however, drew not on the arguments commonly brought forth in the Municipal Council and through petitioning, but on objections re-phrased them in non-cooperation terminology.

In a similar way, shifts in the leadership of the local Muslim

---

Göttingen, Vandenhoeck Ruprecht, 2003; Sebastian Conrad, Shalini Randeria (eds.) *Jenseits des Eurozentrismus. Postkoloniale Perspektiven in den Geschichts-und Kulturwissenschaften* [Beyond Eurozentrism: Postcolonial Perspectives in the study of history and culture], Frankfurt a.M., Campus, 2002.

[14] Judith Brown, *Gandhi's Rise to Power*, Cambridge, 1972; John Gallagher, *Locality, Province and Nation*, Cambridge, 1973.

[15] Gail Minault, *The Khilafat Movement. Religious Symbolism and Political Mobilization in India*, Delhi, 1982.

community were carried through by means of the Khilafat movement. In Delhi, the Muslim traders, notably the Punjabi community and the owners of the leather industry, had tasted on the fruits of prosperity from the 1870.[16] However, as they were converts from Hinduism, they were not considered equal to the *ashraf* in social standing. Though many of them had made it to the Municipal Council through British patronage,[17] the community's internal leadership was still in the hands of people like the Hakim-family of Sharif Khan. Patronage of religious and educational institutions had bestowed on the traders an image of community service and collective piety. They built on this image once pan-Islamic activities began to touch Delhi. Although the traditional leaders retained their position as far as mediation to the centre was concerned, the movement's control was wrested by the local traders. Here, then, is an example of multiple entanglements rather than clearly demarcated boundaries between the local, the national and the transnational. Similarly, we also find multiple entanglements between power politics and religious enthusiasm.

PRINCIPLES OF EDITION

As selection and language constitute central parameters for the production of knowledge, which this edition aims at showing, the texts have been reproduced integrally. Wording, spelling, paragraphs and headings are those of the colonial officers, unless indicated otherwise. This includes the reproduction of the British transcription of Indian names in the text. As far as possible, we have identified names and provided biographical notes on those included. In the biographical notes and in the index, we have standardized the transcription according to the Encyclopedia of Islam.

A parallel chronology of the events in the different provinces and on an all-India level completes the edition and allows a quick comparison between the provinces.

[16] Sultan Rafi (ed.), *Biradari ki marhumen ka tazkirah: Yadgar-e raftagan*, Karachi, Ilyas Press, 1996.

[17] Narayani Gupta, *Delhi between Two Empires*, Delhi, 1981.

We are grateful to Jan Peter Hartung who spent many hours on the correct transcriptions for the biographical notes appearing in this volume.

MUSHIRUL HASAN
MARGRIT PERNAU

1

History of the Non-Co-operation and Khilafat Movements in Delhi

ACTIVITIES. 1917, THE HOME RULE LEAGUE

Intensive political activity started in Delhi with the establishment of a branch of the Home Rule League on the 19th February 1917. A Delhi Congress Committee was already in existence but it did little more than hold occasional public meetings and nominate its members as representatives of Delhi at the Indian National Congress. In May 1917 in response to Mrs. Besant's advocacy of boy scouts' organisation it inspired the foundation of the first of the local volunteer corps, the Indraprastha Sewak Mandli. This was a Hindu corps. Its objects were stated to be to assist the management of large fairs and other gatherings. This corps still exists and to a considerable extent retains its desirable and distinctive characteristics. Not satisfied with this form of social service the Home Rule League at a meeting held on the 11th September 1917 decided to form a volunteer corps of its own, primarily and immediately to manage the Ram Lila celebrations, working if necessary under the Ram Lila Committee. This qualified and unwilling acceptance of the Ram Lila Committee is of interest as three years later in 1920 the volunteers succeeded in ousting the Committee and assuming control themselves. In 1917 the Ram Lila and the Moharram celebrations synchronised and much ill-feeling resulted in Delhi. Finally, the Hindu community decided to hold a hartal and on the 17th October 1917 the Indraprastha Sewak Mandli were active in enforcing general observance of this hartal.

In December 1917 Rai Bahadur Sultan Singh invited the Indian

National Congress to hold its next sessions in Delhi, and preparations were at once begun.

Mr. Horniman came to Delhi and on the 10th January 1918 he delivered an address in the Home Rule League reading room on political self-reliance. Asaf Ali, barrister, followed with an intemperate speech appealing for volunteers to work at the ensuing Congress. Another meeting was held ten days later at which it was definitely resolved to form and train a Home Rule League volunteer corps, to consist of Hindus and Muhammadans alike and to be employed for political purposes. A committee of management was appointed consisting of Asaf Ali, Dr. Ansari, Hakim Ajmal Khan, Shiv Narain Haskar [!] who became captain of the corps, Rai Sahib Pearey Lal and three others. It is noteworthy that at this stage Hakim Ajmal Khan refused to attend a garden party to congratulate Khan Sahib Aziz-ud-din and said he despised all such titles and no longer valued his own. In 1920 he was the first individual to resign his title in Delhi. The decision to raise the corps did not lead to much immediate activity. For some time national education occupied the stage. On the 20th March 1918 the Hon'ble Mr. Mazharul Haq at a public meeting derided the education supplied by the government and said that the foundation of national and independent universities was essential. A series of meetings held in April and May were not however a financial success. The audiences were small and payments fell far short of promises.

Meanwhile on the 20th April 1918 a swadeshi store managed by Shankar Lal was formally opened by Mr. Gandhi, who urged his auditors to refrain from buying foreign made goods, saying that if they would only combine to support the home rule movement no armies would be needed to bring Lancashire to its knees. In May 1918 Swami Shardhanand [!] founded a Hindu volunteer corps to work in the famine stricken Garhwal country. This body was shortlived as it was found that the conditions of distress had been much exaggerated. In June and the following months the Home Rule League worked an intermittent but comprehensive scheme of propaganda. A large number of public meetings were held and well-known lecturers from other provinces were imported lest public interest in politics might flag. On the 16th June 1918 Shankar Lal denounced the operations practised on Indians and appealed for 2,000 volunteers including students to register their names in the Congress Committee's office. Shiv Narain Haskar, captain of the Home Rule League volunteer corps, called for genuine workers as volunteers and worked himself up to such a state of indignation in arguing the necessity of crushing and destroying the tyrannical bureaucracy root and branch that he nearly fainted and had to be revived with water. Thirty volunteers were recruited at this meeting.

In July the Muhammadans became active. The Central Bureau for the relief of Muslim internees organised bodies of volunteers to raise funds in mosques and streets and to make 'pathetic appeals before and after the Id prayers on behalf of the brilliant personalities of the government's victims.' 'The nation,' it said, 'delights to honour those whom the government submits to disgrace since this is the only reply that a subject race can make to the tyranny of its rulers.' The Calcutta branch of the Bureau sent up posters declaring the existence of an organised conspiracy to destroy Islam. The volunteer corps formed at this time afterwards became the Muslim League volunteer corps. In August 1918 the Bureau issued stamps bearing a portrait of the Ali Brothers flanking a map of India and sold at three pice each. These reappeared in November 1920 as small change in connection with the Khilafat rupee note or receipt. On the 18th August 1918 a meeting was held to consider the reforms scheme. Shuaib Ali Qureshi condemned the proposals in fairly strong language and demanded total rejection. Abdul Rahman Sindhi made a somewhat forcible speech on the necessity for consulting Indian Muslims before sending them to fight a brother Muslim. On the 7th September 1918 a meeting was held to protest against the *Indian Daily News'* insult to the Prophet's tomb. Abdul Majid of Badaun [!] denouncing the inactivity of Muhammadan leaders got excited and declared that his religion was not dependent on the whims of Abdul Ahad or of the Imam of the Juma Musjid. The Imam was afterwards repeatedly persecuted and even assaulted by the extremists and did not regain his position until the Hindu-Muslim riots of 1924. Abdul Ahad's funeral in December 1920 was obstructed and scandalously insulted. On the 29th September 1918 the Home Rule League volunteers held a recruiting meeting and three days later paraded the streets headed by Shankar Lal and Shiv Narain Haskar waving a Home Rule flag and demanding subscriptions for the Congress. Unwilling subscribers were taunted with fear of the officials and of the C.I.D. On the 20th October 1918 Jaggannath Singh of the Indraprastha Sewak Mandli volunteer corps appealed for 500 volunteers for various duties connected with the Congress.

In November 1918 the Muslim League volunteer corps was organised as already explained and Hakim Ajmal Khan formed the Tibbia College corps from the students at his medical college to assist at the sessions of the Congress and the Muslim League. Activity became intense. The Muslim League held numerous preliminary and propaganda meetings. The Home Rule League met on the 25th November 1918 to recruit volunteers who, Shankar Lal said, would be used to beg for funds from door to door if necessary. Another recruiting meeting was held three days later at which Shankar Lal demanded self-determination for India and said that the internees were patriots innocent of all offence save that they had annoyed the C.I.D. On the 1st December Shuaib ridiculed the dream of expecting protection from a foreign Government which looked only after its own interests. Muhammadans, he said, could not help sympathising with Turkey and preferred internment to being false to Islam. On the 7th December Basharat Ali Jalib, editor, *Hamadam* [!] (Lucknow) declared that the European powers hated Islam but if the Muhammadans were united their joint forces would have to be respectfully considered. On the 11th December Qazi Abdul Gaffar [!] said that their Holy places were being handed over to the Jews. Maulvi Ahmed Said observed that the Quran forbade union with Christians and Jews or any intercourse with infidels. Nonetheless, he said, they were already passively subject to Christian rule. Abdul Majid more strongly declared that the Quran forbade Muslims to be ruled by or to become the slaves of an infidel king. Other speakers appealed for volunteers for the corps. Similar appeals were made at a Congress meeting on the 15th December. On the 18th Shuaib Ali Qureshi said that England was honouring the son of the Sharif of Mecca and intended to make his father Khalif of Islam although he deserved death for rebelling against the Khalif. On the 20th December 1918 the Imam of the Juma Musjid sought to speak in the mosque of the Kartarpur riots. Dr. Ansari, Shuaib, Qazi Abdul Gaffar, Abdulla Churiwala and other leaders accompanied by Muslim League volunteers and hooligans created a violent disturbance. Shuaib and Ansari mounted the pulpit and called the Imam a jackal of the English and made frenzied speeches about the Calcutta riots and the absence of Muhammadan representation at the peace conference. On the 23rd December at a Home Rule League meeting Gauri Shankar Misra said that Indians would not accept freedom from the hands of Montagu but would themselves achieve it. Soon, he observed, the farmers would rise with sticks in their hands and would tell the government that they intended to take possession of their own India. On the 24th December Abdul Aziz complaining bitterly of the authorities' veto on the proposed route of the Congress procession said that if it had been a marriage party they would have fought for their rights. (Shouts of 'We are ready'). Some, he said, advised them to have their procession in spite of orders but the result would be showers of bullets. (Shouts of 'We are ready to die'). Shankar Lal indignantly asked how long they would helplessly obey such oppressive commands. Had they no strength or spirit in them that their president's honour. . . . Here he was stopped by the chairman. Gokaran Nath Misra remarked that he wondered whether the officials ever considered who would reap the evil reward of their prayers and sentiments.

THE DELHI CONGRESS AND LEAGUE SESSIONS

The campaign of propaganda had admirably served its purpose of rousing popular enthusiasm for what was to be the most aggressive sessions in the history of the Congress. Messrs. Pal, Khaparde and others were first dragged in their carriages about the streets by volunteers to the Congress ground. There speaking on the 'petition of right' resolution Mr. Khaparde said, 'I am the owner of my house but I am expected to live in the stable and allow others to live in the house who have come here to make money. I must accommodate them in the central part of my house and starve but feed them and serve them'. Referring to the report of Rowlatt Commission Mr. Pal said, 'this much I will tell you that these recommendations if carried out will perpetuate a very pernicious and a very harmful and a very repressive provision of the Defence of India Act, perpetuate it in the permanent statute book. Are you going to allow it?' Dr. Kitchlew on the 'right of self-determination' resolution said, 'we should say that we are fit for the right, that we shall take it, that we shall not fear to take it. Our gospel should be, do whatever you like, we shall take it.' The president in his final remarks said that some Indians were ready to wait. 'Other brethren are a bit impatient. They in plain words say to the Government 'whether you give full responsible government willingly or unwillingly matters not to us. If you decline to give it to us as soon as we want it then we will take it from you. Now, gentlemen, we in this Congress are bent on helping the people who argue in this manner.'

The outstanding feature of the 11th sessions of the All-India Muslim League, which began on the 30th December 1918, was the special efforts made by the extremists who controlled the Council to introduce a religious element. Ulemas [!] and Maulvis were persuaded to come in fair numbers. The Maulvis held a private [me]eting at Fatehpuri on the 30th December at which they passed two resolutions, [the] first reminding His Majesty's Government of their solemn promise to respect [the] sanctity of the Muslim holy places, and the second impressing on Government [that] Jerusalem was regarded as a sacred spot by Muslim. Dr. Ansari's address[1] [as] president of the reception committee resembled the sermon of a fanatic more [tha]n the address of a politician, and amounts to a condemnation to death of the [Kin]g of the Hedjaz and an exhortation to Jehad if Mesopotamia, Arabia and [Pale]stine are not handed back to Turkey. It accuses Great Britain of breaking promise to respect the sanctity of the holy places, and demands the indepen[den]ce of the Muslims of North Africa and Central Asia. Dr. Ansari's demands [wer]e supported throughout by quotations from the Quran and the Hadis, and the [spee]ch, which was later on proscribed by the Punjab Government, had an extraordinary effect on the audience. The Muslim League of that period regularly [too]k its cue from the Congress and the methods employed to stampede

[1] Not printed in the report.

opinion of the ultra extremist camp met with as great success as in the Congress pandal. When they dispersed members were heard cursing the destroyers of Islam and strong [anti-]British feeling was evident.

JANUARY-APRIL 1919: THE ROWLATT BILLS AND SATYAGRAHA

At a Home Rule League meeting held on the 1st January 1919 Pandit Dev Narain Pandey of Allahabad declared that nothing could be achieved by mere talk. He pointed out that Gokhale had in vain tried to influence Government not to partition Bengal but that anything which had been gained was through the self-sacrifice of men like Khudi Ram Bose, the anarchist. This meeting marked the end of Congress week which was followed by a comparatively calm month. A movement was however at once instituted by Shiv Narain and Abdul Rahman pleaders and other supporters of the Congress to start a regular volunteer corps to be called the Delhi Volunteer corps to attend all Congress sessions and to take part in similar political work. On the contrary the businessmen were more in favour of establishing a social service league, but in this they were not successful and by February the Delhi Volunteer corps had been definitely established on a political basis with Shiv Narain as president. There were at that time said to be 29 members. Meanwhile on the 26th January at a garden party given to congratulate Hakim Ajmal Khan and Dr. Ansari on their Congress and Muslim League labours the former expressed the hope that the people would protest with firmness against the Rowlatt Committee Bills, and Rai Sahib Pearey Lal moved a resolution to request the Secretary of State to grant self-determination to India. On the 28th January Pandit Madan Malaviya delivered a lecture advocating the starting of Congress Committees in every city ward. On the 3rd February the agitation against the Rowlatt Bills definitely began. The bills were denounced by Rai Sahib Pearey Lal as repressive and unnecessary measures infringing on the fundamental rights of British citizens in India. It was rumoured at the time that an association would be formed to conduct passive resistance.

On the 14th February a very noisy Muhammadan meeting was held to denounce the proscription of Dr. Ansari's Muslim League address.[2] The speeches were somewhat violent but were for the most part drowned in the prevailing uproar. Maulvi Ahmed Said remarked that it was the quotation from the Hadis regarding the expulsion of Jews and Nazarenes from Arabia which offended the Government. He expressed a fear lest the order of proscription might extend further and Muhammadans might be forbidden to read the Quran. On the 7th March Mr. Gandhi attended a meeting to oppose the Rowlatt Bills. The Satyagraha vow was read out and also the names of fifteen subscribers to it including Dr. Ansari, Shankar Lal, Shiv Narain Haskar, captain of the Home Rule League volunteer corps and Miss Gmiener[!] its secretary, Shuaib Ali Qureshi and Swami Shardhanand. Hakim Ajmal Khan however refused to join. Shankar Lal asked those desirous of signing their names to do so in the Home Rule League office. Passive resistance and the taking of the vow were strongly urged and the number of signatories quickly rose to 120. On the 24th March another meeting was held and the tone of the speeches though still restrained was more heated. Swami Shardhanand said that the police arranged dacoities which were attributed to demobilised soldiers in order to secure the passing of the Rowlatt Act. The Act, he said, might secure the public from a few scoundrels but would hand it over to the mercies of the many scoundrels of the C.I.D. On the 27th and 29th March further meetings were held at which the speeches were distinctly violent. Maulvi Ahmed Said fanatically upbraided Muhammadans who were not prepared to die for their Khilafat and who by d[oing] good to Europeans did harm and evil to their country. Swami Shradhan[and] urged his audience to disobey any orders issued by the soldiers of whom the [gov]ernment had collected 4,000.

On the following day, the 30th March 1919, the disturbances broke out w[hich] lasted off and on until the 18th April. During this period most violent spe[eches] were delivered and reporters and suspected reporters were repeatedly ha[ndled] with great brutality by the crowds assembled.

[2] Not printed in the report.

On the 17th April 1919 the Sedition Meetings Act was extended to [last] for a period of six months. On the same day the Satyagraha Sabha diss[olved] itself.

A REPORT ON MR. GANDHI'S PLANS IN APRIL 1919

A quiet period followed. In the course of enquiries a most interesting r[eport] was received from a local informer who said that Mr. Gandhi had met Ma[ulana] Abdul Bari recently and had discussed the Satyagraha movement. Gandhi was said to have been most optimistic and to have told Abdul Bari that he had agents in every city and that the passive resistance idea would spread to the servants of the officials and to the army. Hindu-Muslim unity would be complete and the government would be paralysed. It was agreed that when agitation was at its height there would be a conference of Ulemas, Maulvis and Muhammadans generally, at which Abdul Bari should be elected Sheikh-ul-Islam and the Muslim demands regarding the Khilafat, the Holy Places, etc., should be formulated. The Hindus would support these demands which would be submitted to His Excellency the Viceroy with the warning that non-acceptance of them would mean jehad. In return for the assistance of the Hindus Abdul Bari in his capacity of Sheikh-ul-Islam was to issue a fatwa declaring that the animal originally slaughtered by Ibrahim was a sheep and not a cow and that cow sacrifice was prohibited in future.

(Delhi Secret Abstract for 1919, paragraph 321).

APRIL-OCTOBER 1919: THE SEDITIOUS MEETINGS ACT IN FORCE. MINOR ACTIVITIES

On the 13th May a meeting was held to express Delhi's loyalty in view of the Afghan invasion. A letter from Dr. Ansari was read to the effect that on an occasion of this nature it was the duty of the people to lay aside their grievances and assist the government to the best of their abilities. Swami Shardhanand however was at this time advocating the general boycott of British goods and of the law courts, and in June it was reported that Mr. Gandhi intended to renew his Satyagraha campaign on the lines approved by his more rabid followers. The all-India celebration in July of Tilak's birthday was not a local success. A thousand copies of the birthday card were obtained from Bombay and sold in the streets by members of the Home Rule League and of the Delhi Volunteer corps. On the 23rd July 1919 a meeting was convened by Hakim Ajmal Khan, Dr. Ansari and other leaders to thank the authorities for their handling of the situation in April. This was hotly resented by the younger party led by Asaf Ali and Shiv Narain Haskar, captain of the Home Rule League volunteer corps, and Arif Hasvi, at their instance moved an amendment explicitly reserving the right to criticise the authorities before the committee of enquiry. In August Hakim Ajmal Khan showed interest in what proved for 1919 an unsuccessful movement to prevent the sacrifice of cows on the occasion of the Baqr Id.

OCTOBER-DECEMBER 1919: THE HUNTER ENQUIRY AND THE KHILAFAT CONFERENCE

In October political activity increased. The Ram Lila and Moharrum celebrations were fully and quietly observed in spite of suggestions of a boycott. The Delhi Volunteer Corps then sixty strong wrote to Amritsar enquiring how many men would be needed for the 1919 Congress sessions. On the 17th October a Khilafat Day hartal was observed. There was evident anxiety as to its outcome, and the volunteers of all four corps—Muslim League, Home Rule League, Delhi Volunteer and Indraprastha Sewak Mandli—were widely used by the organisers of the demonstration to patrol bazars and discourage the formation of crowds. Dr. Ansari presided over a meeting at which most of the speeches were unobjectionable. On the 29th October a meeting was held to consider the preparation of the case to be submitted for the public before the Hunter Committee. Swami Shardhanand spoke of the need to cross-examine perjured police witnesses. Asaf Ali denounced the government for combining the parts of plaintiff, defendant, witness and judge. 'But the day of judgement,' he said, 'is at hand when murder will out. If the dagger is concealed the blood on the sleeve of the murderer will suffice.' Shankar Lal scoffed at the enquiry saying that the government was forming a habit a killing Indians like goats. Mr. Gandhi described the procedure which he wanted the committee to adopt. On the 31st October Shankar Lal as secretary of the Home Rule League volunteer corps invited numerous prominent politicians to a garden party given by the corps to demonstrate Hindu-Muslim unity. Meetings were held on the 1st and 2nd November at which subscriptions were raised to commemorate the 'martyrs' killed in the spring disturbances. Shankar Lal, Asaf Ali and Swami Shardhanand spoke violently on the atrocities committed by officials in the Punjab. Mr. Gandhi said he would persevere in Satyagraha against the Rowlatt Act and advocated the boycott of the peace celebrations in December and the simultaneous observance of a martyrs' memorial week as a counterblast. Actually this was observed earlier.

On the 5th November 1919 a private meeting was held at Hakim Ajmal Khan's house at which a local Khilafat committee was formed. It was also decided to summon an All-India Khilafat Conference to Delhi on the 23rd to obtain Hindu support for the boycott of the peace celebrations and of British goods. A public meeting was held on the 12th November to urge the boycott of the peace celebrations. Shankar Lal and Asaf Ali bitterly inveighed against government oppression and perfidy. On the 23rd Gandhi arrived for the Khilafat conference. A mass reception by the volunteers in uniform had been prepared but there was a misunderstanding as to the hour of the arrival and the function was a fiasco. The meeting of the subjects committee of the conference was distinctly stormy owing to Gandhi's opposition to the wilder proposals of Syed Hussain [!] of the *Independent* and of other United Provinces extremists regarding a general boycott of all British goods and of the government itself. He had not yet adopted non-cooperation and the only resolutions passed in public were to boycott the peace celebrations and to thank the Hindus and Mr. Gandhi for their sympathy. In private conclave further resolutions had been passed advocating the boycott of British goods, the surrender of personal titles and the despatch of a Khilafat deputation to England. Swami Shardhanand, Hasrat Mohani, Shankar Lal and others had further urged the definite combination of the Punjab issue with that of the Khilafat as being the only way by which to ensure Hindu co-operation, but had been overruled by

Gandhi. Immediately after the Khilafat Conference the Delhi Martyrs' Week began.

Meetings were held on the 25th, 26th, 27th, and 30th November. Very offensive and untruthful speeches were made, but financially the movement was not a success. An attempt to collect money at once broke up the meetings and although the Home Rule corps and the Delhi Volunteer corps spent much time in street collections and did not refrain from intimidation and insults to unwilling subscribers the funds raised were small. No accounts have ever been published, and open and repeated charges of perculation have received no reply whatever. Meanwhile an Anti-Peace Celebrations Committee had been formed and strenuous efforts were made to make the city join in the boycott, including the issue of posters entitled 'Mahatma Gandhi's orders and Maulana Abdul Bari's fatwa'. On the 4th December Neki Ram Sharma after thanking the Chief Commissioner for cancelling the order forbidding him to speak in public went on to denounce the peace celebrations in view of the tyranny practised in the Punjab. He described some of these atrocities with considerable heat including among other lies an account of the use of a machine gun and an aeroplane at the Jallianwala Bagh.

On the 11th December the Indraprastha Sewak Mandli and its Volunteer corps held its annual meeting at which speeches on semi-political social service were delivered by Mr. Gandhi, Indarjit, the son of Swami Shardhanand and other politicians. The anti-peace celebrations committee meanwhile issued numerous posters and leaflets, and its leaders accompanied by Home Rule, Muslim League and Delhi Volunteers, toured the neighbouring parts of the United Provinces, the Punjab and Ajmere [!] addressing meetings. In Delhi the Municipal committee succumbed to the agitation and withdrew its grant of money for illuminations and displays. The volunteer corps attempted with little success to enforce an evening hartal every day gave a plain hint of violent trouble to Rai Bahadur Sheo Prashad who wished to illuminate his house. The management of Juma Musjid received a similar warning from Abdulla Churiwala, then a prominent member of the local Khilafat and anti-peace celebration committees and later the patron of the disbanded Khuddam-i-watan volunteers. A meeting was held on the 15th December but was not of special interest as Shankar Lal and Asaf Ali had been officially warned to moderate their accustomed violence of language.

On the 23rd and 24th December large parties of the Home Rule and Delhi Volunteers left for the Amritsar Congress being followed in lesser numbers by members of the Muslim League volunteer corps. On the 25th a large crowd headed by Shankar Lal, Arif Hasvi and volunteers in uniform rushed the railway station premises in a disorderly manner to greet the late Mr. Tilak on his way through by special train. Similar but rather less noisy scenes took place on the 29th in honour of the Ali Brothers. A few days later a new volunteer corps called the Khilafat volunteers came into being and Asaf Ali suggested the combination of all local Muhammadan volunteers into the Askar-i-Islamia (literally the Army of Islam) afterwards proscribed.

JANUARY-FEBRUARY 1920: DEMONSTRATIONS

On the 7th January 1920 Lachhmi Narain who was convicted in the Benares conspiracy case returned home on release from jail. The people of his ward illuminated their houses and a few Hindu volunteers accompanied his carriage from the railway station. On the 9th January the volunteers turned out for their first mass operations on the occasion of the triumphal arrival in Delhi of the Ali Brothers. All the corps paraded and their total numbers amounted to about 250 including 40 horses. They took complete charge of the Chandni Chowk and endeavoured violently but unsuccessfully to control the assembled crowd. The crowd pushed through the volunteers at will and the noise and confusion were so great that the speeches were inaudible. Shaukat Ali briefly thanked the Hindus for their co-operation and emphasised that the Muhammadans were well wishers of the government. At the Juma Musjid Muhammad Ali explained that the time for the display of their faith in action had not yet arrived. On the 10th the brothers left for Lahore and were seen off by a small party of Muslim League volunteers. On the 16th January a Khilafat meeting was held at which Muhammad Ali urged the Muhammadans to sacrifice their health, wealth and life in the name of God. They should decide, he said, what they intended to do and announce it plainly, leaving the authorities to decide their own course of action as they pleased. Abul Kalam Azad said that the deputation to the Viceroy had no request to make. It would simply inform him of the nature of Islamic obligations. Saifuddin Kitchlew observed that the loyalty of Muslims to non-Muslim authorities was conditional. On the 18th January an unsuccessful meeting was held by Shankar Lal on behalf of the martyrs' memorial. On the 22nd he and Swami Shardhanand held a meeting on behalf of the Hindu rioters involved in the Kartarpur case. On the 30th January Hanwant Sahai who was convicted in the Delhi bomb case returned on release from jail. Shankar Lal and 25 volunteers of the Home Rule and of the Delhi volunteer corps with Swami Shardhanand escorted him through the streets in triumph. On the 2nd February a small swadeshi meeting was addressed by Swami Shardhanand. On the 8th February Messrs. Patel and Khaparde condemned the rumoured appointment of Lord Haig as Viceroy. Shankar Lal held two ineffective meetings to organise a reception for Lajpat Rai on the lines of the display of the 9th January. On the 22nd February Mr. Patel presided over a meeting at which he and Hakim Ajmal Khan, Dr. Ansari, Asaf Ali, Shankar Lal and Mr. Khaparde demanded the grant to Delhi of two seats on the reformed Imperial Legislative Assembly. Suggestions were made that taxes should not be paid if this request was refused. On the 23rd Lajpat Rai arrived and was met by Shankar Lal and a small crowd of Hindus. The next day a somewhat unsuccessful procession was organised by the Home Rule and Delhi volunteer corps. The Muhammadans displayed little interest as their volunteers were at this time employed in collecting subscriptions for the Ali Brothers' Purse Fund. Lajpat Rai lectured on self-help as contrasted with beggarly acceptance of gifts.

MARCH-APRIL 1920: THE LEADERS' MEETING AND THE KHILAFAT WORKERS

Early in March the local Khilafat committee began arranging for the Khilafat hartal to be observed on the 19th March. It wrote to Mr. Gandhi asking him to instruct the Hindus to co-operate and meanwhile bargained with the local Hindu leaders offering to show interest in the hartal for the 30th March, the anniversary of the outbreak of the riots in 1919, in exchange for Hindu participation in the Khilafat day. At the same time the committee put pressure on the leading gentlemen of its own community by demanding from them under threat of social boycott an immediate declaration in writing that the expulsion of the Turks from Constantinople would cause them acute personal sorrow. These demands were conveyed by uniformed members of the three Muhammadan volunteer corps—the Muslim League, the Khilafat and the Askar-i-Islamia—who were instructed to remain on the premises until a definite reply was vouchsafed. Several of the notables so addressed hurried in their perturbation to the authorities for advice. On the 16th a meeting was called to demand legislative representation for Delhi. On the 19th a very complete hartal was observed. Muslim League and other Muhammadan volunteers were posted in most of the bazars and were insistent and almost aggressive in discouraging the collection of even the smallest crowd. One Muhammad Ahmad Batla issued a very intemperate leaflet appeal to government servants on the line of that signed by Shaukat Ali but met with no response whatever. At a largely attended meeting the resolution involving conditional loyalty was duly passed. A special prayer composed by Maulvi Kifayatullah was read at all the mosques calling on God to annihilate the infidels and the enemies of Islam. On the 20th March, Mr. Tilak arrived by train and received a minor demonstration at the railway station. On the 21st almost every extremist leader of importance arrived in Delhi to attend a private conference. They were in most cases met by volunteers in uniform who aggressively disregarded the railway bye-laws and servants. On the same day Mr. Tilak was presented with an address by the orthodox Hindus. On the 22nd he was taken in procession through the streets. The Muhammadan volunteers were much in evidence, Ausaf [!] Ali of the Muslim League corps riding on horse back with a drawn sword in his hand. After speeches by Asaf Ali and Indarjit demanding legislative representation Mr. Tilak recommended watchful co-operation with the government in the matter of the reforms and the continuance of agitation.

Meanwhile the leaders were conferring in Hakim Ajmal Khan's house. They decided to press on with the Khilafat agitation by advocating the boycott of foreign especially British goods, progressive refusal to pay taxes, non-participation in government loans and subscriptions, and opposition to military recruiting. Some of the Hindu leaders had previously had a secret meeting in the house where Pandit Malaviya was staying. On the 23rd March two meetings were held: one by a trade union of clerks and accountants which was addressed by Mr. Tilak on labour organisation: the other by the Provincial Congress Committee which dealt with the representation of the Delhi province and with the meetings to be held in Ajmere. On the 24th parties of the Muslim League and of the Home Rule League volunteers went to Ajmere. At the same time the minor members of the local Khilafat committee founded the Khilafat Workers' Association and a volunteer corps called the Muslim Razakars. These gentlemen had been much annoyed at their exclusion from the leaders' conference on the 22nd and the repeated refusals of Hakim Ajmal Khan and of Dr. Ansari to attend public meetings. Chiefly they felt the loss by the committee of the position of prominence acquired at the time of the agitation against the peace celebrations. The Workers' Association was accordingly formed to force the pace.

On the 30th March an attempt was made to induce the city to commemorate by another hartal the anniversary of the first day of the 1919 riots. In the absence of most of the leading men who had gone to Ajmere this was not particularly successful. In the morning an objectionable speech was delivered to Muhammadans by Maulvi Ahmed Said who again in the evening at the Hindu burning ghats was virulent. The minor Hindu leaders however adopted an almost apologetic attitude and tone. No collections were made on behalf of the martyrs owing to the free circulation of charges of misappropriation. In this month of March Hakim Ajmal Khan wrote to the District Magistrate asking to be relieved of all his government titles and privileges. Mr. Gandhi's so-called National Week began on April 6th and was in Delhi a failure. The idea of holding any more hartals was scouted by the businessmen. The meeting on the 6th was a trivial affair noticeable only for the fact that Ram Chandra

Sharma, editor of the local *Congress* newspaper, was so grossly untruthful in relating the judicial scandals that had been perpetrated by means of the Rowlatt Act that Asaf Ali was stung into remarking that the Act had never been put into operation.

A Khilafat meeting on the 9th April was better attended. Dr. Ansari responding to the spur of the Workers' Association spoke of the need for practical work through commercial boycott and refusing co-operation with Government. Asaf Ali remarked on the danger of infuriating Indian Muhammadans and Shankar Lal vouched for Hindu support. The meeting on the 13th called to collect subscriptions for the martyrs' memorial was attended only by a few loafers whose obvious poverty safeguarded them from appeals for cash. Shankar Lal announced that at meetings and by street collections by volunteers Rs. 27,000 had been raised. This figure is probably false. It certainly conflicts with other public announcements made by Shankar Lal and the money may be regarded as misappropriated for there is no pretence that any memorial exists in fact. The Pataudi House was bought, but no new building was constructed. On the 14th April at a Khilafat meeting Abdul Majid of Badaun encouraged by Hakim Ajmal Khan in person delivered a wild speech including such remarks as 'the sword of Mustapha Kemal Pasha and the weapon of Enver Pasha will brighten the Muslim glory. Are you waiting to see the Union Jack flying over Macca [!] and the keys of the Holy Places in Christian hands? A Muslim who is loyal to the Government curses God. Liquor is freely sold in Macca under British rule which makes pilgrimage of no avail.'

The culmination of such wild talk was seen at the Khilafat Workers' Conference on the 18th and 19th March 1920. The Association declared that its purpose was to carry into execution the resolutions passed at the Khilafat conference at Calcutta and elsewhere. About 500 delegates attended the Conference, mostly men from the United Provinces and the Punjab of little social standing. The violence of the language in the meetings and in the association's special newspaper, the *Hurriyat*, exceeded all previous local records. Hasrat Mohani in his presidential address called for immediate practical action without awaiting the return from Europe of the Khilafat deputation. He insisted on unflinching application of the commercial boycott, wholesale resignation from Government service and boycott of the law courts. In the meeting of the Subjects Committee Ataullah of Benares and the Bhopal extremists frankly stated that they had come to Delhi in anticipation of a declaration of jehad and not a mere policy of hijrat as recommended by Maulvi Ataullah of Amritsar.

The public meeting on the 19th began by Maulvi Bashir Ahmad praying for the downfall of the British. Maulvi Ahmed Said as first speaker said that God would give them strength to conquer their enemies. He favoured the idea of boycotting British goods and said that personally he was prepared at once to preach *jehad* and *hijrat* to the army and to Government servants. He called for the surrender of personal titles and honours especially attacking the Imam of the Juma Musjid for retaining his title and recommended a refusal to pay taxes. Maulvi Muhammad Daud Ghaznavi of Amritsar was equally violent. He implored them to have no fear. The Czar of Russia had learnt his lesson and the British Government would soon meet the same fate. Accusing Indians of having murdered Turks by helping the British he called on them to do their best to ruin the Government. Other speakers advocated hijrat, refusal to pay taxes and withdrawal from co-operation with the Government. In the evening sessions Ataullah of Amritsar said that begging was useless. What they wanted could only be obtained by hijrat or jehad. He advocated hijrat and the boycott by domestic servants of individual Europeans. Maulvi Muhammad Daud Ghaznavi, the chairman, casually remarked that unless a few Europeans were murdered no satisfaction would be obtained from the Government.

Consequent on these meetings a hijrat office was established in the city by Ghulam Muhammad Aziz of Amritsar and a scuffle took place on the 23rd in the Juma Musjid in the course of which a shoe was thrown at the Imam striking one of his relations who was supporting him. On the 28th April Asaf Ali presided over a meeting summoned ostensibly to elect a new Imam. Asaf Ali announced that they would first give the Imam a last chance and send a deputation to him demanding the immediate surrender of his title. Dr. Ansari offered to lead the deputation and declared it unlawful to pray behind the Imam as a title holder. Many other speakers continued the attack and finally Ghulam Muhammad Aziz advocated hijrat. On the 29th the deputation visited the Imam and secured his resignation of his title. The Seditious Meetings Act was then applied to the province for a period of three months which was subsequently extended by another three months.

MAY-JULY 1920: THE SEDITIOUS MEETINGS ACT IN FORCE. CONTINUED ACTIVITIES

On the 8th May Shaukat Ali paid a flying visit to Delhi and roundly abused the most extreme agitators for their premature activities which he declared had afforded the Government their long awaited opening for a counter stroke. On the 13th a female Milad Shariff or religious reading meeting was held under the auspices of the Khilafat Workers' Association and proved to be of the usual Khilafat propaganda type under a religious cloak. The association also issued forms of allegiance for signature by persons ready to observe and advocate the boycott of foreign goods, surrender of titles, resignation from Government service, refusal to pay taxation, rural propaganda and religious migration. On the 13th May Shankar Lal with two Muslim League volunteers went on tour to Biawar. On the 16th, 17th and 18th May Neki Ram Sharma held thinly disguised political meetings under the pretence of reading extracts from Hindu religious books. Ghulam Muhammad Aziz meanwhile made many tours and issued many posters on behalf of his religious migration, but without much resutlt locally. Names were registered freely but these appear to have been mostly pseudonyms and false addresses.

On the 12th June the late Maulana Mahmud-ul-Hassan arrived in Delhi but at Dr. Ansari's instance no public demonstration was made. Maulvi Ahmed Said however delivered a fiery speech to his religious students exhorting them to do all in their power to harm the English. Every child was to be taught that English-men were his enemies and were to be driven out of India. He prayed that God would destroy their kingdom. At this period the local syces, largely at the instigation of Asaf Ali, formed a trade union an demanded increased pay. The development of this movement will be noted later.

On the 18th June Maulvi Ahmed Said again delivered a sermon

urging the instruction of children in their duty of exacting vengeance from Englishmen. On the 19th some Hindus with a number of volunteers distributed drinks to the Muhammadan worshippers at the Id celebrations. On the 22nd June a meeting was held by permission to protest against the Hunter Committee Report. Dr. Ansari, Asaf Ali and Shankar Lal spoke as usual on martial law in the Punjab but the proceedings were dull. The Khilafat Workers' Association in June issued leaflets calling for a boycott of British goods and for intensive rural propaganda and appealing for funds. On the 4th July Maulvi Ahmed Said left for a propaganda tour in the Rohtak district accompanied by 15 Khilafat volunteers. He also began to make arrangements for the summoning of a conference of Ulema at Delhi. This meeting did not however take place until November. On the 17th July the workers at the Government Press went out on strike. Asaf Ali gave them much verbal but little pecuniary encouragement and became their official spokesman. The Khilafat Workers' Association issued leaflets entitled, 'Do jehad for the sake of Allah; do jehad in the path of God; do full jehad if you are faithful to God'. The leaflets appealed for funds and advocated the boycott of foreign goods and non-co-operation with Government. The association also issued appeals for membership of the Jamiat-ul-Ulema-i-Hind. Shankar Lal, Ahmed Said and Asaf Ali made numerous propaganda tours in the Punjab and the United Provinces accompanied by volunteers usually in uniform. It was decided to extend the application of the Seditious Meetings Act by another three months.

AUGUST-OCTOBER 1920: THE SEDITIOUS MEETINGS ACT IN FORCE. NON-CO-OPERATION

Meanwhile the Khilafat agitation was at its full swing and on the 1st August a hartal was well but not completely observed, the volunteers being as usual active in persuading shops to shut and in patrolling the bazars. A meeting was held just outside provincial limits at which resolutions were passed adopting non-co-operation, calling for the return of all Indian troops and condemning the application of the Seditious Meetings Act, the imposition of special taxation with respect to the 1919 disturbances, and the decision of the House of Lords in the Dyer debate. The death of Mr. Tilak led to another hartal on the 2nd. A meeting called by permission to deplore his death was raided and dispersed by Abdulla Churiwala and Khilafat volunteers. An extremist meeting was held at Ghaziabad to which 400 men travelled by train. Encouraged by volunteers they rushed to the railway premises on both journeys, travelling in all four classes of carriage and buying no tickets. A meeting held on the 8th by the clerks' trade union to deplore the death of Mr. Tilak who had lectured to the members a few months earlier and to protest against the rise in house rents was raided by Shankar Lal and Home Rule volunteers who however failed to disperse it and were themselves ejected. On the 9th August Shankar Lal and Arif Hasvi organised an indifferently successful hartal and conducted an extremely minor procession of volunteers and loafers in honour of Mr. Tilak. On the 10th another meeting was held at Ghaziabad, a large crowd headed by Shankar Lal and Asaf Ali truculently refusing to buy railway tickets. Meanwhile the Khilafat Workers' Association issued poster inviting intending religious emigrants to assemble in Delhi in September.

On the 19th August the local Khilafat Committee decided to obstruct the flower sellers fair at Mahrauli. All the volunteer corps were mobilised to picket the roads leading out of the city to prevent traffic. Carriages were held up by volunteers in uniform and persons insisting on continuing their journey were assailed with gross insults. Those who hoped to set up wayside booths for the sale of sweets, etc. were plainly informed that their wares would be looted. In consequence, few people reached Mahrauli. A last effort was there made by the Khilafat party forcibly to prevent the performance of the religious rites associated with the fair. The procession carrying the 'punkhas' was obstructed by a hooting crowd of loafers and volunteers who were with difficulty persuaded to stand aside.

Encouraged by this success the Khilafat Committee decided to prevent the slaughter of cows at the Baqr Id, a move very close to Hakim Ajmal Khan's heart. Tajuddin, Qutbuddin, Aziz Hasan and Abdulla Churiwala were especially active. Muhammadan members of the volunteer corps brought most of the butchers over to their side, and then picketed the slaughter house and approaches. Parties were even sent out on the roads leading to Delhi with instructions to tell drivers of herds that the sacrifice of cows had been forbidden. Numerous posters and leaflets were issued including one declaring the slaughterer of a cow to be an enemy of the Khilafat and a traitor to his faith. In consequence few cows were brought to slaughter and fewer still were sacrificed, for until the police interfered animals were forcibly released and 'bought' by Abdulla Churiwala from their owners, the money offered being generously 'returned' to the Khilafat Committee. Those who succeeded in slaughtering their cows were subsequently subjected to a partial social boycott which was only ended by the imposition of a counter boycott by the Ahl-i-Hadis and other orthodox Muhammadan parties. At the slaughter house Abdulla Churiwala, temporarily infuriated by an unsuccessful attempt to intimidate the police, announced that he would form an association to deal once and for all with such rascals. In September he formed the afterwards proscribed Khuddam-i-Watan volunteer corps of selected holigans one at least of whom displayed by his correspondence a strong inclination towards personal violence. Meanwhile special taxation was imposed to meet the costs of the additional police and of compensation in connection with the 1919 disturbances. A storm of opposition arose and the volunteers conducted a house to house canvass in favour of passive resistance to the assessments.

At the special sessions of the All-India Congress Committee held at Calcutta in September 1920 it was decided that there could be no contentment in India without redress of the Khilafat and the Punjab wrongs and that the only effectual means to vindicate national honour and to prevent a repetition of similar wrongs in future was the establishment of Swaraj which would be obtained by a policy of progressive non-violent non-co-operation inaugurated by Mahatma Gandhi.

Among the items of non-co-operation sanctioned by the Calcutta special sessions were the boycott of the reformed councils, hand-spinning, hand-weaving, boycott of foreign goods, renunciation of titles, boycott of Government aided schools and the boycott of the British law courts. Asaf Ali sent a press message to the special sessions of the Congress recommending the evolution of institutions to work parallel with the Government and in pursuance of this policy adopted from Sinn Fein began working to increase the membership of the volunteer corps and to unite these corps into one general organisation to supplant the police. This line had already been indicated by the formation of the Askar-i-Islamia in January 1920.

The increasing lawlessness of these volunteer bodies and the danger of their arming themselves with swords were brought to the notice of the Government of India who decided to demand licenses for the possession of these weapons in Delhi. There are indications that the strengthening of the volunteer movement was directly inspired by the Central Khilafat Committee. On the 17th September Hakim Ajmal Khan and other leaders with a dozen volunteers went to Agra to settle the Hindu-Muhammadan disputes in that city. On the 22nd Asaf Ali and a similar party went to Jagadhri for a similar purpose.

The Muharram celebrations were performed with great splendour. Large numbers of Muhammadan volunteers in uniform on horseback and on foot behaved excellently and in full co-operation with the police. During this month was formed the Sadr Bazar or Pahari Dhiraj Sewa Samiti, a Hindu volunteer corps devoted to political propaganda on behalf of non-co-operation in rural areas. It had as its drill instructor an ex-chaprassi of the Chief Commissioner. Daily parades and infantry drill were for some time practised. The Askar-i-Islamia commanded by Asaf Ali held similar daily parades. On the 3rd October Qutbuddin went on tour to Sonepat with seven Askar-i-Islamia volunteers. Recruiting for the volunteer corps went on briskly especially among young boys.

On the 7th October 21 volunteers received Mr. Gandhi at the railway station. On the same day the local Congress Committee met somewhat indecisively to consider the details of non-co-operation. Asaf Ali sent to the press a complete scheme of national courts and national administration conducted by volunteer forces on the basis of an intensive social, economic and religious boycott of opponents. He also established a national court in the Khilafat office, serving summons by Khilafat and Askar-i-Islamia volunteers.

On the 10th October posters issued demanding that the Ram

Lila committee be publicly elected and not self-constituted and that the management of the ceremonies be conducted by national volunteers and not by the police. The Ram Lila was celebrated on the 14th to the 23rd October and the arrangements were made by different volunteer corps, the maximum number of volunteers on duty being 282 on the 20th October. It was decided that the volunteers would in future force their way into control despite the Ram Lila committee and would prevent any garlanding or honouring of the officials. On the 19th the Muhammadan and the Home Rule volunteers invaded the enclosure practically by force and in numerous instances molested police constables on duty. On the 20th the protest of the orthodox Hindus kept the Muhammadan and the Home Rule volunteers outside the enclosure. On the 21st the Ram Lila committee interviewed Hakim Ajmal Khan and asked him to stop these political demonstrations at a religious ceremony. Their reception was discouraging and the enclosure was again invaded by volunteers encouraged by a poster issued by the Indraprastha Sewak Mandli stating that the volunteers should be in charge of the Ram Lila procession and the police should be only a helping hand. On the 22nd Shankar Lal and his Home Rule volunteers fled before a crowd which burst into a part of the enclosure, leaving the police to restore order. In consequence on the 23rd he did not turn out but about 150 volunteers of other corps were similarly put to flight by the crowd at the Clock Tower.

Meanwhile on the 16th October Qutbuddin and six Muslim League volunteers went to Panipat. On the 20th Iqbal of the Khilafat corps with twenty Muslim League volunteers and Shiv Narain and 32 Delhi volunteers went to Bhiwani to attend the Ambala Divisional conference. On the 21st Abdulla Churiwala and three others went to Muzaffarnagar, and Inderjit and the Home Rule volunteers left for Bhiwani. On the 22nd Shankar Lal rallied 19 Home Rule volunteers and went to Bhiwani. On the 22nd Maulvi Ahmed Said delivered a sermon in the Machhliwalan mosque discussing all the chief topics of current political controversy and advocating non-cooperation. A C.I.D. officer taking notes was subjected to the grossest personal insult and roughly handled. On the 26th Maulana

Saadat Hussain delivered a sermon recommend-ing religious migration.

On the 26th October a provincial Sikh League was formed and the raising of a Sikh volunteer corps was discussed inconclusively. On the 27th and 28th a rival and more moderate Sikh Young Men Association was constituted which decided to form a Sikh volunteer corps to work on days of religious ceremonies and a social service corps to work continuously. On the 28th Shankar Lal, Asaf Ali and five Home Rule volunteers went to Muzaffarnagar. About this time Principal Gidwani of the Ramjas High School resigned his appointment in pursuance of non-co-operation. At this stage the local Khilafat Committee was arranging a boycott both of the Council elections and of the census operations.

On the 29th Maulvi Ahmed Said delivered a sermon advocating the immediate withdrawal of students from schools regardless of interruption to their education. He went on to abuse the C.I.D. On the 30th October Asaf Ali dressed as colonel of the Askar-i-Islamia, Abdulla Churiwala, colonel of the Khuddam-i-Watan, Nur Muhammad, a dismissed drawing master, and six uniformed volunteers went to the Anglo-Arabic school and though refused admission by the head master succeeded in getting a number of boys to come out ostensibly on strike. At a meeting held later in the day Gidwani speaking strongly in favour of non-co-operation said that he had declared war against the Government and needed the students as his sepoys. Shankar Lal urged Delhi to recapture the position it obtained by contributing the first martyrs in 1919. On the 31st in the Fatehpuri mosque Asaf Ali and others explained their ideas on national schools. Nur Muhammad read out a strong fatwa signed by Maulvi Kifayatullah in favour of non-co-operation and a fiery one by Maulvi Ahmed Said justifying non-co-operation and even resistance.

In the afternoon Asaf Ali and Gidwani endeavoured without success to convert a meeting of Hindu students to their views. At a mass meeting in the evening Asaf Ali voiced his sympathy with Sinn Fein. Shankar Lal said that their work had not been stopped by the Seditious Meetings Act. They had successfully refused to pay the special tax for the disturbances and had arranged to eject the flatterers of the officials from the municipal committee. They had prevented the Ram Lila committee from garlanding officials and had persuaded all nationalist candidates to boycott the council elections. Now, he said, they were successfully tackling the schools. Hakim Ajmal Khan spoke of the treachery of the Aligarh college trustees. Dr. Ansari asked students to abandon their books as was done in England during the war. Shankar Lal recommended a boycott of the Duke of Connaught's visit. Qazi Abdul Ghaffar denounced the Aligarh trustees. Resolutions were passed congratulating Zafar Ali [Khan] and other convicts.

Another meeting was held on the 2nd November at which Asaf Ali in a long address reviewed the history of the British in India, finding it wholly and without exception vile. There were many other speakers of whom perhaps the most violent was Sher Singh of Muzaffarnagar who was in favour of beating the English monkeys with sticks out of the land into which they had mischievously intruded. Throughout the meeting actual and suspected members of the C.I.D. were surrounded by students using filthy language and inflicting such insults as the puffing of tobacco smoke into the face of a Sikh. At this and a later meeting on the 4th resolutions were passed in favour of boycotting the Government, the schools, the courts, the census, the councils, candidates, voters, officials and opponents generally. There was much exited talk such as that of Sundar Lal of Muzaffarnagar who said that minor details of personal inconvenience were trivial as they were engaged in a war of independence, and of Sher Singh who appealed not for workers who drank milk but for those who were ready to give their blood. A national school was opened by the local Khilafat committee but the few boys who attended did not take this seriously. It was arranged to hold a conference of ulemas on the 19th November. In anticipation two new volunteer corps were founded affiliated to the Askar-i-Islamia. These were the Bhojla Pahari volunteer corps and the Khuddam-ul-Islam corps of Ganda Nala. The former body held daily parades under Lotan, the *ex*-chaprassi already mentioned. The Askar-i-Islamia for a time employed two *ex*-soldiers to teach infantry work but these men soon went away.

Minor propaganda meetings were held on the 9th, 17th and 18th. Asaf Ali spoke of Indian soldiers as void of shame, enemies to their country and objects of universal hatred. Gurbakhsh Singh as an extremist Sikh repeated several old lies about the dishonouring of Sikh girls at the time of the Amritsar riots. Dr. Abdul Rahman recommended the social boycott of opponents in which he was enthusiastically supported by Shankar Lal. At this stage the Khilafat rupee note or receipt made its appearance and an effort was made to revive the Central Bureau Ali Brothers stamps as small change. An interesting feature was an Arya Samaj revolt against the excessive use for politics of religion. Master Lakhshman headed this movement undeterred by Asaf Ali's counter stroke of employing the national courts to initiate and to decide ex-parte numerous civil suits against his interests.

The ulemas' conference was held from the 19th to the 21st November. The main resolution declared all relation and connection of friendship and co-operation especially in military matters with the British Government to be religiously unlawful. Eleven minor resolutions on details of non-co-operation were also passed. The language used though strong was not as violent as at the Khilafat Workers' Conference in April largely owing to the marked undercurrent of opposition which centered on such points as unity with the Hindus, the sacrifices to be made to secure this unity, the propriety of manipulating the Quran to provide texts for political purposes and the desirability of non-co-operation generally. Azad Subhani typically voiced the prevailing tone by asking that there be no examination of and disputes over details but that a broad line be drawn between the faithful and the infidel. Non-co-operation would first destroy sinful edifices and then erect perfect structures, thus obtaining self-government. Only on the last day did the heat increase. Maulvi Sultan Hassan of Ajmere spoke regretfully of the impossibility of declaring jehad. Asaf Ali said that the English came as guests but remained as vampires. Aqil-ul Rahman raved against the C.I.D. reporters for not destroying the papers on which national leaders would be imprisoned.

On the 21st Mr. Gandhi addressed a zenana meeting on the demoniac [!] nature of the British Government and Dr. Kitchlew asked the united Indians to save India from the unholy feet of the British. On the 23rd and 24th an uninteresting Delhi-Ajmere-Merwara political conference was held. Muhammad Ali explained with apparent glee the innuendo conveyed by the Sinn Fein alteration of the recruiting poster 'join the army and see the world' into 'join the R.I.C. and see the next world'. Asaf Ali expressed unbounded admiration for Sinn Fein. Dr. Ansari tried without much success to reconcile Mr. Gandhi's extensive railway journeys and telegrams with perfect non-co-operation. Mr. Gandhi regretted that subscriptions did not come in as fast as he would like, a subject on which Shaukat Ali subsequently lost his temper. Mr. Gandhi also opened the national school and unsuccessfully addressed the students of St. Stephen's college. Shiv Narain Haskar proposed that the aid of the police be refused at public functions and be replaced by the national volunteers. Minor meetings were held on the 19th, 21st and 25th at which the boycott of the councils and of the army were advocated. On the 30th Maulana Mahmud-ul-Hassan died at Dr. Ansari's house.

Muhammadan volunteers leading a huge crowd escorted the body to the railway station. A hartal was observed. On the 1st December a meeting was called to mourn his death. Dr. Ansari said that the Maulana had in 1914 refused to sign a fatwa justifying Indian participation in the war, had denounced the Shariff [!] of Mecca as a rebel and had been the motive force in inducing the Maulvis to adopt non-co-operation. Asaf Ali added to his repertoire of lies by stating that since 1840 London had grown from a collection of huts into a city of palaces while India had been looted by tyrants into a state of abject ruin. On the 2nd December Khan Bahadur Maulvi Abdul Ahad died and his funeral on the 3rd was obstructed by Abdulla Churiwala of the Khuddam-i-Watan corps, Muhammad Ishaq of the Askar-i-Islamia, Arif Hasvi and Aziz Hassan with other volunteers in undress uniform until the relatives in despair falsely announced that the Maulvi had on his death bed surrendered his titles and adopted non-co-operation. A criminal case was taken up in connection with this obstruction which ended in the conviction of Abdulla Churiwala and Aziz Hassan Naqshbandi. On the 5th Shankar Lal and other extremists conducted a disgraceful demonstration before the house of Rai Bahadur Sheo Pershad who was ill.

A C.I.D. officer was served with an eviction order by his landlord accompanied by an alternative demand that he resign the service while another was approached by Moulvi Ahmed Said with an offer of enhanced pay in the national C.I.D. Enquiry disclosed the interesting fact that most of the volunteers were paid and that Asaf Ali as 'General Officer Commanding, Delhi' was endeavouring to obtain a salary of Rs. 250 per mensem. On the 3rd Maulvi Ahmed Said had threatened opponents with the fate that had befallen Abdul Ahad, and on the 5th, the date before the council elections, Shankar Lal demanded a rigid social boycott of candidates and voters. Asaf Ali declared that such people were on the side of the devil and must expect to suffer the natural consequences. On the 6th all the polling stations were picketed by volunteers on horse and foot with numerous flags who did everything except use physical force to discourage intending voters. In the evening at a public meeting Arif Hasvi called for the social boycott of Mr. Nur Ahmed one of the candidates who was described as a national enemy and Asaf Ali demanded the professional boycott of Mr. Raj Narain a lawyer who had also stood for election. Mr. Nur Ahmed was later unable to perform the marriage ceremony of his child until he had apologised to Hakim Ajmal Khan. Abdul Hamid, a sweet meat vendor of Delhi was subsequently returned as a member of the Legislative Assembly as representative for Delhi, the object being to bring ridicule on the new Councils and on Government. It was also intended that Abdul Hamid should later resign his seat at the instigation of the Congress, but this he refused to do as he found his post a lucrative one and he held it for the full term of three years.

At this stage the Seditious Meetings Act was again imposed on Delhi, and the Askar-i-Islamia, the Khuddam-i-Watan, the Muslim League volunteers and the Khilafat volunteers were proscribed under Act XIV of 1908. The dissolution, outwardly at any rate, of the Askar-i-Islamia immediately followed. The Home Rule League volunteers however took up the running and on the 13th December following on a dispute between a clerk of the Swadeshi stores and the staff of the railway octroi post Shankar Lal and 30 volunteers invaded the post using abusive language and threatening all who opposed them. On the 14th the procession of the Guru Granth

Sahib was accompanied by many members of the disbanded corps in plain clothes escorting in triumph the four men under trial in the burial case.

About this time Asaf Ali organised a strike of the men working for the electricity company in pursuance of his new policy which he outlined to the volunteers. This consisted of encouraging the formation of every kind of communal and functional panchayat or union and of establishing friendly relations therewith and fomenting thoroughly successful strikes. When the unions were in real working order they would be used to conduct social boycott which Asaf Ali found almost impracticable owing to the absence of labour solidarity. He especially emphasised the necessity of concealing the ultimate object from the men until full preparation had been made.

The local Khilafat committee published a report dealing with the period November 1919 to December 1920. This put the number of volunteers—presumably of the Askar-i-Islamia and affiliated corps—at nearly 500, and the number of the members of the committee at 59. The Jain community had a religious procession on the 28th December and under great persistent pressure permitted the Home Rule volunteers to assume control.

JANUARY-JUNE 1921: THE SEDITIOUS MEETINGS ACT IN FORCE

In January 1921 arrangements were made to enforce the boycott of the ceremonies connected with the visit of His Royal Highness the Duke of Connaught to Delhi. The decorations in the Fort attracted huge crowds of women and children until volunteers of the Home Rule League and the Khuddam-ul-Islam in plain clothes were sent to picket the approaches and warn off visitors. In February the royal visit was almost entirely boycotted by the public. Shankar Lal organised the Home Rule League volunteers and to a lesser extent the Khuddam-ul-Islam volunteers to preach hartal and to picket the bazaars. Members of the proscribed Muslim volunteer corps were also active. On the 13th February Mr. Gandhi went in procession through Delhi to open the Tibbia College and was escorted by an immense crowd controlled by volunteers on horse and foot.

On the 27th February a large crowd of all communities attended the Sisganj Gurdwara to protest against the slaughter of Sikhs at Nankana Sahib. Gurbakhsh Singh, leader of the extremists, spoke on the use of kirpans of unlimited dimensions. Asaf Ali and other minor leaders freely accused the government officials stationed in Sheikhupura of being privy to the murders. A procession was formed and was escorted by mixed volunteers.

About this time the Education Department reviews the progress of non-co-operation in Delhi as affecting the schools and reported that only 298 students out of 9839 had joined the movement since its inception. Most of these were gathered into the National School and the Dayanand national school.

From this stage the volunteer movements degenerated. New corps were founded, merged and dissolved in a bewildering way and with the obvious intention of bewildering. For the most part officers and uniforms were abolished and it was clearly intended that this should render impossible any controlling or repressive action by government. As instances of such vague corps may be quoted the National College corps, the Masoom corps, and a particularly invertebrate [!] body formed from the men employed by the electricity company who were on strike in March.

During the early part of the summer the Sikh agitation increased largely. The local Sikh hotheads accompanied by 15 volunteers left on the 21st March for the Sikh Educational Conference in Hoshiarpur returning a few days later much inflamed and eager to spread the new fashion of wearing kirpans and black clothing. In their absence Shankar Lal with 26 volunteers succeeded after a wordy quarrel in intimidating the manager of the Chhatri Circus into giving one day's earning to the Delhi martyrs' memorial fund. This fund from its inception in April 1919 was almost exclusively devoted to the maintenance of the two martyrs Shankar Lal and Maulvi Ahmed Said.

The 30th March was the second anniversary of the outbreak of the riots. The demonstration projected to celebrate the memory of the martyrs was not a great success. A half-hearted hartal took place and also a meeting at Ghaziabad when Gurbakhsh Singh spoke offensively. The volunteers of this occasion assisted in the collection of the railway tickets. Gurbakhsh Singh at this period addressed the congregations daily at the Sikh gurdwaras in the most advanced extremist style but on the whole with singularly little effect. In April Gurbakhsh Singh founded a Sikh female society to run extremist meetings for women and issued a Sikh rupee note receipt book. Both efforts were still born. In the same month appeals for volunteers were made by the Bharat Sewa Samiti; while 29 members of the Saraswati Sewa Samiti, the Home Rule corps and the Pahari Dhiraj Sewa Samiti were noticed collecting recruits for the local Congress committee. The subscription was four annas, and donors of one whole rupee earned the privilege of being inscribed in the books as four separate members. On the 6th April Qutbuddin, Arif Hasvi and Asaf Ali took 18 members of the Khuddam-ul-Hind corps to the Khilafat Conference in Meerut.

A series of hartals projected for the 5th (for the Nankana affair) the 6th, 10th, 13th April (for the national week) proved an abject failure. The only notable event was the statement made by Shaukat Ali on the 13th that the army and the police might soon be expected to join their Indian fellow country men. On the 12th a threatened visit by a party of Amritsar Akalis to take possession of the Tila Majnun gurdwara was averted by the leading well disposed Sikhs. On the 17th the managers of the Ram Naumi procession succumbed to pressure, invited the Police to withdraw and handed over control to 25 volunteers of the Home Rule League corps and of the Indraprastha Sewak Mandli, officered respectively by Mohania and Bishamber Nath. Meanwhile the non-co-operators persuaded the washermen, water carriers and sweeper communities to pass prohibition resolutions. Membership and subscriptions for the Tilak Swaraj Fund were also collected with moderate success.

On the 4th May Master Lakhshman with two Sewa Samiti volunteers left for work in the famine area of Chhatisgarh. His social labours were discouraged by the politicians. During May the Sikh agitation waned. There was some picketing of liquor shops by Bharat Sewa Samiti volunteers but this was short lived. The Indraprastha Sewak Mandli declined to co-operated, as the movement was political. The Seditious Meetings Act ceased to apply to Delhi on the 8th June.

JUNE-OCTOBER 1921: NON-CO-OPERATION AND THE PROSCRIBED FATWA

On the 14th Arif Hasvi and Shankar Lal addressed a meeting of cab drivers, water carriers and other menials and urged them to form unions so that, when required, they should be able to apply a lightning [!] boycott of loyalists. A general Congress election was announced and a very large number of ward meetings were held for this purpose and to raise money for the Tilak Swaraj Fund. The establishment of a parallel system of administration, intensive social boycott of loyalists, of the police and the army, and refusal to pay taxes were frankly explained as the objectives of the Congress organisations. The elections received a fair show of public interest among the lower classes. The meetings were controlled by volunteers noticeable among whom were men of the Khuddam-ul-Hind, Khuddam-ul-Islam and Home League [!] corps. In July it was announced that the Delhi Province had obtained Rs. 1,44,000 for the Tilak Swaraj Fund or exactly twice its allotted quote. Three months later—in October—another announcement was made with equal effrontery that Delhi was considerably in arrears with its allotted quota. The money really obtained [?] by October is believed to have been Rs. 18,000 odd. On the 5th July Arif Hasvi was arrested on a Warrant under section 124 A issued from Muttra. This raised the general temperature for a time and public meetings became more violent. Rural propaganda received increasing attention. Police officers were repeatedly hustled and insulted. On the 7th July the procession of Rathjatra of Jaggannathji was escorted by volunteers.

On the 16th July the election of five Delhi members to the Shiromani Gurdwara Parbandhak Committee was held. Only one moderate was elected but there is reason to suspect the polling officers sent down from Amritsar of considerable mal-practice. The extremist Sikhs locally had long lost all influence and their success in this election in no way restored it. Towards the end of July Congress activity turned towards the cloth boycott. An organisation alternatively called the Gandhi corps and the Congress corps was founded. This was really an attempt to amalgamate all the corps and to secure unity of command. Membership was large and free to all who could obtain enough khaddar to make an armlet. Even this qualification was not rigidly insisted on. The average age of the volunteers was about 15 years, a large proportion being children aged about 6 years.

An attempt was made to enlist young men by the formation of a Young Men's Hindustani Association on behalf of which on the 25th July particularly anti-British and mendacious speeches were delivered by members of the National school at the Pataudi House public meeting. The association was however a failure and nothing more was heard of it.

Early in August orders were issued proscribing an abstract of one of the resolutions (Appendix I) passed by the Ulemas' Conference in November 1920 which directly aimed at provoking soldiers and policemen to fail in their duties. The local Khilafat office was searched and 812 copies were confiscated. This was a signal for very intense Muhammadan agitation. Maulvi Ahmed Said arranged for an early meeting of the Ulemas in Delhi and meanwhile wired to Mr. Gandhi for permission to start civil disobedience. Mr. Gandhi was to acute to fall into the trap but gave a non-committal reply.

On the 15th August the Bakr Id was celebrated. The extremists found it convenient to modify their campaign against cattle slaughter by a compromise under which 25 cows only were to be sacrificed. Actually 36 cows were sacrificed. Hakim Ajmal Khan, following his invariable custom, absented himself from Delhi on what might, in his view, be a critical occasion. At the Id prayers Congress and Khilafat volunteers distributed badges to the wearers of khaddar cloth and generally made such a nuisance of themselves that many regular attendants at the prayers kept away.

On the 19th August a meeting of chamars was held under non-official inspiration and loyal resolutions were passed by acclamation. The extremists were much disconcerted by this episode, trying, but in vain, to wreck the gathering. On the same day 80 volunteers attended a public wrestling tournament held to raise funds for the Congress organisation. Syed Mubarik Hussain, Secretary of the Congress corps, was in general charge of the arrangements.

On the 22nd August a dozen extremist maulvis of the Punjab and United Provinces but headed by Abul Kalam Azad arrived in

Delhi and consulted the local ulemas in secret conclave. Instant disobedience of the proscription of the fatwa was advised but a decision was deferred until the special meeting of the Jamiat-ul-Ulema-i-Hind to be held the following month. On the 23rd and 26th large public meetings were held and very fiery addresses were delivered by Mufti Kifayatullah, Syed Hussain Ahmad Madni Muhajir, Maulvi Ahmed Said, Maulvi Sanaullah, Abul Kalam Azad and others. They exhorted all Muhammadans to resist this attack on their faith and described the fatwa as equal in sanctity with the Quran itself. They proposed to print copies of the fatwa and distribute them broadcast [*sic*] to see what action government would take. At the latter meeting an unfortunate individual, wrongly suspected of being a member of the C.I.D., was severely beaten by the crowd until Abdulla Churiwala and his volunteers at length interposed to prevent what was likely to develop into murder.

On the 23rd the *Fateh* published an abominable article announcing the alleged discovery in Meerut of an English soldier who had been living by drinking the blood of Indian children of whom he had killed about fifty, and who, on detection, was protected from punishment by the authorities and given a pecuniary allowance as a mad man. The security of the *Fateh* was in consequence forfeited under the Press Act. Throughout August and September daily meetings were held in the non-co-operation interest in streets and wards. Shankar Lal and Balwant Singh made a point of taunting Muhammadans for their passive endurance of insults to their religion. These two men were in September forbidden under section 144, C.P.C. to make any speeches in public for two months or to attend any public meeting. The order was never served on Balwant Singh as that individual, mistakenly believing that he was to be arrested, fled from the province.

Meanwhile the Muharram was celebrated peacefully. On the earlier days Muhammadan volunteers were out in a large numbers [!] and on the last day the escorting of the procession was entrusted to them, the authorities contenting themselves with placing at strategic points strong police pickets. During this week Shaukat Ali and other leaders were arrested and sent for trial in connection with speeches on the sinfulness of service in the Army and Police. From the 21st to 24th September meetings of the Jumiat-ul-Ulema-i-Hind and of the Central Khilafat Committee were held. They decided to maintain the doctrine that service in the army and the police was a sin and to propagate the doctrine by word of mouth and by reprints of the proscribed fatwa. This was followed up on the 29th September by open and wholesale distribution of reprints. There was much excitement and wild speeches were delivered. In consequence security was demanded for the press which printed the leaflets. Deshbandu was forbidden under section 144, C.P.C. to attend any more meetings for two months and Maulvi Ahmed Said and Abdul Aziz Ansari were prosecuted under section 107 and 108, C.P.C. The arrests of the two last named were effected through the instrumentality of Abdulla Churiwala who with his volunteers succeeded in keeping some semblance of order among the huge crowd that gathered at nightfall round the central police station. After further public meetings on the 30th September and 2nd October at which foreign cloth was burnt, the leaders became alarmed at the excitement of the unruly crowds and announced that no meetings would be convened in October. Meanwhile insults and intimidation of police officers and loyalists redoubled. The witnesses against Ahmed Said and Abdul Aziz Ansari were marked out for special torment and there was daily danger of riot and assault. In order to avoid precipitating a conflict it was decided to entrust the management of the Ram Lila celebrations entirely to volunteers. When the Ram Lila concluded a tea party was given in honour of the volunteers in[!] part of the Juma Masjid. The volunteers arrived and departed with much show, marching in procession with flags and bands up the Chandni Chouk and halting before police station to cry out that the police were condemned to hell for service which was a religious sin.

NOVEMBER-DECEMBER 1921

During November Delhi was visited by most of the more prominent leaders of non-co-operation, and a number of public and private committee meetings were held. The result was remarkably infructuous. The first of these was a meeting of the subjects committee of the Khilafat Committee on the 3rd November which had been advertised as the date of a public meeting subsequently abandoned. The Khilafatists found themselves much embarrassed by the question of the grievances of the Hindus in the disturbed Moplah area, and confined themselves to resolving to leave the adoption or postponement of civil disobedience to the Congress Committee. A scheme to subsidise two presses in London and Paris for propaganda purposes at a monthly cost of £ 1,200 was also adopted without much regard to its financial practicability.

The proceedings on the 4th and 5th November of the All-India Congress Committee did not arouse much local interest. The following resolutions were passed: (1) sanctioning civil disobedience in those areas where the great majority of the inhabitants wore khaddar, (2) entire boycott of foreign cloth, (3) asserting the inherent right of appealing to soldiers and civilians to sever their connection with the government and (4) congratulating convicted non-co-operators.

Even Gandhi's presence failed to arouse the enthusiasm he evidently hoped for. The local leaders were constrained to walk delicately over the troubled matter of the Tilak Swaraj Fund concerning which from time to time they had issued many false and contradictory reports. The khaddar campaign was certainly not a success, and Gandhi's personal address to the cloth merchants was a fiasco, only bringing down ten out of some hundreds, and these doubtfully, on his side of the fence. Faced with this public apathy the working Congress committee decided on nothing more dramatic than forming its own members into a Civil Disobedience Sub-Committee charged with the duty of distributing spinning wheels to enable the prospects of disobedience to be tested. Civil disobedience was to commence when a sufficiency of spinning wheels had been distributed.

The Hindu Maha Sabha held two public meetings on the 6th and 7th November attended by Gandhi and most of the Chief leaders. There was a remarkable output of untruths more or less connected with the history of the cow in India, and resolutions were passed supporting non-co-operation and exhorting the pandits to prove from the Hindu scriptures that police and army service is heretical. The pandits who have hitherto inculcated loyalty to the Crown as an essential feature of the Hindu religion were to be regarded as out of date and old fashioned. On the 17th November a general hartal was engineered by the non-co-operation party to keep Delhi in line with the other towns were the landing of His Royal Highness the Prince of Wales at Bombay was celebrated in this fashion. The hartal was outwardly very complete in the City. During the course of the day as many as fifteen meetings were held in the various wards of the City after which a mass meeting of non-co-operators and their 'volunteers' took place at Pataudi House. The language used at the latter was restrained, but the tone of the speeches at the ward meetings was very different, abuses of the Government and of service in the police and the army being interlarded with references to practically every possible topic calculated to excite the religious and political feelings of the audiences. Most of the meetings were small and attended by less than 100 persons each. The detailed reports of this deluge of poisonous oratory convinced the Authorities that the time had arrived to exercise the authority granted by the Government of India for the reintroduction of the Seditious Meetings Act when necessary. The next few days were occupied in holding 'Congress' elections in each of the City wards and in a few of the small towns in the rural area. This general election was more than ever in the hands of the controlling caucus, with the consequence, as far as could be judged, that general public interest in them waned considerably. The elections having been held, the leaders formed themselves into a civil disobedience sub-committee, prepared a budget for the ensuing three months with an expenditure of Rs. 1,65,450 against funds in hand amounting to Rs. 21,500, and set out to raise some at least of the balance by organising picketing of all cloth shops with the intention of extorting blackmail from the dealers and merchants, though ostensibly to persuade them to deal only in swadeshi goods. This picketing began on the 21st November with some 60 'Volunteers' stationed in the cloth market section of the Chandni Chauk. The intimidation as witnessed by the Deputy Commissioner, Police Officers and the Chief Commissioner fell short of any actual violence. Picketing was continued on the 22nd and 23rd and a much larger number of 'volunteers' was employed. Orders under section 144, Criminal Procedure Code, were therefore issued by the District Magistrate to the eight persons known to be mainly responsible for directing the actions of the volunteers forbidding any further picketing. At the same time the Chief Commissioner issued notifications declaring the 'volunteers' bodies unlawful associations under the Indian Criminal Law Amendment Act XIV of 1908, and enforcing the Seditious Meetings Act for a period of six months. On the 24th November, in order to provide for the possible contingency of the orders issued the previous day being disobeyed, a strong force of police was drafted into the Kotwali in the Chandni Chauk, and a squadron of cavalry was stationed in the Queen's Gardens with infantry in reserve. There was some hesitation and division of counsel among the agitators, but this show of force decided them in favour of obeying the orders. No attempt to send out pickets was made, and the volunteers were told to doff their uniforms and keep clear of the Chandni Chauk. The aspect of the City at once changed to one of peace, the magistrates, police officers and troops being greeted respectfully wherever they went. The only incident that might have disturbed the general harmony was the appearance in the Chauk of a fanatically minded Muhammadan with a knife anxious to effect the release of the Ali brothers! His arrest was quickly effected by a police piquet, and he and his companions were subsequently convicted.

The more vain-glorious of the agitators were unable to stand for long the strain of total eclipse involved in obedience to the orders proclaiming the various gangs of 'volunteers' and re-imposing the Seditious Meetings Act. After a few days' discussion of civil disobedience two of them (Shankar Lal and Hanwant Sahai) issued, apparently on their own authority and not on that of the local Congress organisation, posters calling on the young men of Delhi to join a new body called the Swarajya Saina (Army) in defiance of the orders. The day after the posters appeared warrants were issued for the arrest of these two men. This was effected on the 9th December without trouble, and on the same date the office of the local Congress Committee was searched and some recruiting forms were seized. Shankar Lal and Hanwant Sahai were sentenced to three years and four months' rigorous imprisonment respectively. On the

9th December another man Suraj Bal, whose prosecution under section 124-A, Indian Penal Code, the Chief Commissioner had sanctioned for a seditious speech delivered at the outlying township of Najafgarh, was arrested. His trial was held by the District Magistrate on the 13th at Najafgarh where several of the local leading men readily gave evidence, and he was subsequently convicted. On the 11th the District Magistrate received an impudently worded letter announcing that 'in the cause of men's rights' 50 volunteers in uniform would parade on the 12th under Asaf Ali, the non-co-operating Barrister. This they duly did in the Jama Masjid. Adequate police arrangements having been made their intention to march in demonstration round the City was frustrated, and the gang were arrested on issuing from the mosque. Next day they were all convicted and sentenced, Asaf Ali to 18 months' simple imprisonment under section 17 (2) of the Act and the rest to terms of three to six months' simple imprisonment under the first part of the section. The action taken by two of the eight signatories of the manifesto mentioned above being sufficient evidence of the intentions of the 'leaders', notices under section 107, C.P.C. were issued on the 12th to the remaining six (Muhammad Taqi Vakil, Deshbandhu, Shiv Narain Haskar, Dr. Abdul Rahman, Nanak Singh and Abdulla Churiwala). On declining to furnish security to keep the peace they were ordered to undergo simple imprisonment for one year each. On the afternoon of the 13th December owing to the state of excitement prevalent in the city and the uncertainty as to the conduct of the unruly mobs which gathered and dispersed with surprising rapidity, military assistance was requisitioned. The General Officer Commanding moved a squadron of Indian Cavalry into the Queen's Garden, and a company of British Infantry to the Fort, another company of Indian Infantry being located in the police lines. It did not, however, become necessary to bring the troops into contact with the rabble and they were dismissed by 4 p.m. But the knowledge of their presence on the spot was undoubtedly the main factor in preventing a badly organised demonstration developing into a riot. On the 14th 21 volunteers were arrested, of whom 19 were duly convicted and sentenced the following day. In the early morning of the 15th a band consisting of 29 Muhammadan, five Hindu and three Sikh volunteers headed by Sunder Singh, a tailor employed in the police lines, demonstrated outside the Kashmiri Gate police station. They were arrested by the police. On the 16th when it was rumoured that huge mobs were to accompany several demonstrating bands of volunteers after the Juma prayers, the authorities determined upon a change of tactics, so that the police might take the offensive earlier in the proceedings. The congregation at the Fatehpuri mosque reported to be 5,000 in number waited after prayers to accompany 30 volunteers in uniform in their procession. Meanwhile some 4,000 men from the Jama Masjid congregation collected in front of the Kotwali to watch and shout. Three Magistrates were sent out with strong bands of police, and ordered the crowd to disperse, but only met with abuse and derision. After giving the crowd due warning that they would be dispersed by force the police were ordered to charge with their batons and lathis. This manoeuvre was completely successful, the crowd dispersing in all directions in a very few minutes. No serious casualties were reported.

The total number of arrests in Delhi during the period of 'civil disobedience' was 154. These steps taken by the authorities had a good effect, and an instructive lesson was afforded by the holding of the annual Jain procession on the 17th—one of the largest functions of its kind in Delhi. Influential Jains applied to the District Magistrate for permission to carry out their ceremonies under the usual police arrangements. Sanction was readily accorded, and the old fashioned procession came off with all its former pomp and ceremony.

1922

On New Year's Day a proclamation parade is always held in Delhi on the ground in front of Juma Masjid. The parade was held on the 2nd, the 1st being Sunday, and on the previous day small parties of Congress volunteers went about the bazars announcing that it would be sinful to watch the proclamation parade. On the 2nd from an early hour the approaches to the parade ground were picketed by volunteers of whom 105 were removed to the central police station. Otherwise no overt acts of non-co-operation or civil disobedience were witnessed in Delhi during January and the 'volunteers' kept themselves in the background. There was a great output of offensive booklets sold in the streets for one or two pice. These pamphlet had only one theme, creating and exasperating [!] racial hatred. Two men were prosecuted under the I.P.C. for issuing a pamphlet filled with insults aimed at British private soldiers. The non-co-operators also issued instructions to the ward Congress secretaries inviting them to disobey the Prevention of Seditious Meetings Act. In February the policy of hartal and boycott was preached with much fervour in the press, by posters and by word of mouth. On the 5th February and for seven ensuing days a small party of women volunteers made daily marches through the city. Under shelter of these women, groups of loafers made and listened to speeches, but the demonstrations were very trivial and the police were instructed not to interfere. At the last moment the leaders, alarmed by the Gorakhpur murders, tried to recant and call off the hartal. In this they were unsuccessful and as far as the shutting of shops was concerned the formal hartal on the 14th was absolute and complete. There was, however, no picketing by volunteers.

His Royal Highness the Prince of Wales arrived in Delhi on the 14th February. The zamindars of Delhi and neighbouring districts came in large number to see His Royal Highness' procession and other functions, and the Prince's arrival was an immense success. It is impossible to estimate the numbers of sightseers who came out of the City and crowded behind the zamindars, or of the spectators all along the route in the Civil Lines. A modest computation gives a gathering of at least 100,000 people gathered to welcome His Royal Highness. There were no disturbances or unpleasant demonstrations. This was attributable to the completeness of the police and military precautions in the City and Suburbs, and the unruly elements must have realised that any attempt to disturb the peace could be immediately suppressed. Private meetings of the All-India Congress and Khilafat Committees were held on the 24th and 25th February. The proceedings were at times rather tumultuous. In the Congress

Committee meeting Gandhi's Bardoli resolution suspending mass civil disobedience was only reaffirmed in a modified form permitting individual civil disobedience, and mass disobedience at the discretion of provincial committees. The Bengal and Punjab delegates led the opposition to Gandhi, with whom the Delhi delegates sided throughout. Pandit Malaviya received very scant courtesy in the Committee. The Khilafat Committee headed by Hasrat Mohani and M. Abdul Qadir of Kasur definitely rejected the Bardoli programme, on the ground that if religion enjoined violence a policy of non-violence could not be adopted at the bidding of a dictator.

The postponement of civil disobedience caused a sudden collapse among the 'volunteers' undergoing imprisonment. They had for sometime been grievously disappointed by finding that their numbers were not being daily augmented by fresh arrivals in large batches, and in the beginning of March 49 volunteers applied to be conditionally pardoned and signed the undertaking to refrain from 'volunteer' activities if released.

The news of Gandhi's arrest, having possibly been discounted by previous rumours, was received with complete apathy. But the local agitators celebrated the 18th of every month as Gandhi Day by holding meetings, which however later on lost all attraction. A very half-hearted hartal took place on the 30th March in memory of the 'Martyrs' of that date in 1919. Traffic in the streets was not impeded, and among the shopkeepers as many objected to the demonstration as a nuisance as took part in it. In April a Muhammadan preacher (Maulvi Abdul Halim) was arrested for a breach of the Prevention of Seditious Meetings Act and sentenced to six months' rigorous imprisonment.

The period for which the Seditious Meetings Act was put in force expired on the 22nd May and from that date till after about a month little political activity was noticed. In the middle of June some violent speeches began to be delivered in the ward meetings and one of the vigorous speakers, Qutbuddin, a native of Azamgarh, who had been editing the *Congress* newspaper for some time was prosecuted under Section 124-A, I.P.C., and sentenced to three years' rigorous imprison-ment. This step put a stop to the frantic efforts to arouse enthusiasm by daily meetings in the city wards, and signs of healthier state of affairs began to appear. In this month complaints of defalcation of the money deposited by the litigants with the officials of the national courts established in connection with the programme of non-co-operation, were received, and the reader of the 'court' was successfully prosecuted and convicted. This practically closed the national court. By November such surface unity as there was in Delhi between Hindus and Muhammadans had worn very threadbare and was officially dead.

A complaint was also made to the Police against the secretary of the Delhi Khilafat committee for misappropriation of Khilafat funds. The secretary was sent up for trial in November but was discharged on some technical law point. This, however, destroyed all faith of the public in the Khilafat workers, and Hakim Ajmal Khan and Dr. Ansari for fear of losing their prestige owing to defalcation in the Khilafat funds did not like to hold any office in the Khilafat committee.

1923

The year 1923 proved to be more peaceful than the previous two years which were full of troubles.

The Proclamation Day parade on the Champs-de-Mars was a great and significant success, and was attended by a huge crowd of people from the City, estimated at something like 50,000. No attempts, such as those of last year, were made to prevent the people enjoying the military display, even 'volunteers' being seen in the crowd evidently relieved at being off duty and able to take part in the tamasha.

The disorganisation produced by the Gaya conference was reflected in Delhi, where of the two prominent Khilafat 'leaders' Ansari remained with the 'no-change' party while Ajmal Khan ranged himself with C.R. Das. An agitation was started against Ajmal Khan for daring to say that mere majority of the Ulemas in favour of a fatwa against entry into Councils is not the last word on the subject. The Central Khilafat Committee called upon Delhi to collect Rs. 20,000 and enlist 1,500 'volunteers' for the first stage of the civil disobedience programme. The local Committee however put

Delhi's proper proportion at Rs. 4,300 and 250 'volunteers', but proposed to double these figures. The local working Congress committee as well in pursuance of the Gaya Congress programme for starting civil disobedience proposed to collect Rs. 24,000 towards the Tilak Swaraj Fund and enrol 500 volunteers, but owing to lack of enthusiasm and differences of opinion between the leaders both the Khilafat and Congress committees utterly failed either to enlist the volunteers or to raise the necessary funds.

In the beginning of February a meeting of the Jamiat-ul-Ulema-i-Hind was held and was attended by about 100 maulvis from various places. The results of their private meetings on the 9th and 10th were mainly negative. The Jamiat discussed the appointment of an Amir-ul-Shariat and decided to leave the appointment to the Khilafat-ul-Muslamin [!]. The question of the attitude to be adopted by Muhammadans in the event of war between Turkey and the Allies was shelved by deciding that the Muslim public should await and obey the orders of the Khilafat-ul-Muslamin or the Amir-ul-Shariat. Hakim Ajmal Khan and Abul Kalam Azad were able to bring sufficient pressure to bear on the meeting to have a resolution passed in favour of entry into the Councils.

In March public interest in the preparations for the 'national' week was so feeble that the programme had to be frequently altered. The idea of having a hartal on the 18th was abandoned when it was discovered that the butchers had no intention of closing the slaughter house that morning. The celebration of the anniversary was therefore shifted to the 16th, which being a Friday was a day on which the slaughter house is always shut and most of the Muhammadan shops do not open after the Juma prayers. Even this transparent device to show an outward semblance of Hindu-Muhammadan unity was not very successful and the hartal was a partial failure and practically confined to Hindus. At this stage Muhammadan feeling was being worked up against the Arya Samaj on account of the Shudhi movement started by Swami Shardhanand and the bitterness between the communities went on increasing and reached such an extent that it was apprehended that any small incident might lead to a local fracas.

In April a charge of embezzlement of funds was brought against the local Congress committee and was investigated by the Delhi Criminal Investigation Department. The Committee's office was searched in this connection. Though sufficient evidence for the prosecution of any of the office bearers could not be obtained it was proved beyond doubt that funds were actually misappropriated and this gave a severe blow to the Congress activities.

In May a branch of the Swaraj or pro-Council entry party was established with Ajmal Khan as its president. Opinion on this matter was divided. Ansari being in the other camp, but the stupidity committed at the last election of leaving Delhi to be represented for three years on the Legislative Assembly by a small sweetmeat seller was being seriously realised. Both the Khilafat and Congress committees were on the verge of bankruptcy. The latter had only a balance of Rs. 150 in hand at the end of April, while the expenditure of the former during the month was Rs. 637 against an income of only Rs. 81.

Considerable apprehension had been aroused as to the outcome of events on the day of Baqr Id, and applications were received from respectable citizens for guards of British soldiers and machine guns! Careful police arrangements were made with the co-operation of the military authorities, who moved in some cavalry and infantry from New Cantonments to points nearer the scene of possible disturbances. The three sacrificial days, however, passed off perfectly peacefully. The number of cows slaughtered was 190 as compared with 131 in the previous year.

The meeting on the 1st August to celebrate the anniversary of Tilak's death was poorly attended. The celebration of the Turkish peace was indefinitely postponed for want of funds.

A special session of the All-India Congress Committee was held in Delhi in the middle of September. Very little interest was taken in the Congress or its proceedings by the people of Delhi. An attempt by the local Congress Committee to force their nominees on the Municipal Committee to vote an address from that body to the 'leaders' on their arrival, resulted in an amusing fiasco. On receipt of a formal requisition signed by a majority of the Municipal Commissioners for a meeting to discuss the advisability of presenting such an address, the President fixed the morning of the 7th

September for the purpose. At the appointed hour, though a few of the signatories to the requisition attended, they remained outside the meeting room seeing no chance of a quorum and still less of a favourable majority, and the President finding himself the only member present had to declare the meeting off. Apparently most of the members who lent their signatures trusted that the authorities would veto any such meeting and others had no intention of supporting the proposals if it came to the point. This backsliding on the part of their nominees naturally seriously disturbed the local Congress Committee. They hurriedly got up an address of welcome on behalf of 'the Citizens of Delhi' which was duly presented to the 'leaders' on the morning of the 13th September. The address represented no one except the writer, our briefless lawyer, Asaf Ali, and the small caucus of which he was Secretary. In this connection a serious blunder was made in omitting, apparently intentionally, the name of Madan Mohan Malaviya from the list of honoured leaders. This caused considerable umbrage to the Hindus. It had been announced by posters that after the presentation of the address, the 'leaders' would be taken through the City in a grand procession, and appeals were made to the citizens to decorate houses and shops in the main bazaars in their honour. This procession was abandoned at the last moment, ostensibly because such rejoicings were out of place while the supreme leader, Gandhi, was unable to be present, but really because the appeal for decorations met with no response whatever. All this marked a very significant difference between the situations in 1923 and in December 1918 when Pandit Madan Mohan Malaviya as President of the All-India Congress of that year, was escorted daily from his house to the Congress pandal with much enthusiasm by a bodyguard of mounted volunteers.

Another proof of the public apathy to forms of agitation which had only resulted in fraudulent waste of funds collected for religious or political purposes, was afforded on the evening of the 16th September which was appointed for illuminations to celebrate the Turkish peace. A few of the mosques including the Jama Masjid and the Fatehpuri were lit up, but hardly a single private house. It was noticed that even Ajmal Khan had not taken the trouble to illuminate his house.

A very noticeable feature of this Congress session was the abstention of a large number of prominent politicians generally found on the platform at such gatherings. None of the 'moderate' party put in an appearance. Only about a dozen really prominent 'leaders' from outside Delhi attended the sessions. From Bengal delegates turned up from both the 'no-change' and the 'Council-entry' parties. The problem of which set of delegates was entitled to be recognised was the first of the thorny matters a sub-committee had to decide. This decision in favour of C.R. Das' supporters practically settled the view to be taken by the special session on the 'Council-entry' question. In his terribly lengthy presidential address delivered at the opening meeting on the 15th September Abul Kalam Azad naturally took the same line. The large pandal erected to accommodate 6,000 persons was never really full.

The motion permitting individuals to exercise their discretion as to standing as candidates for the Councils was proposed on the 16th by Muhammad Ali and seconded by C.R. Das. It was opposed by a Madras delegate named Vardachari while other speakers such as V.J. Patel took up a neutral attitude in order not to disturb the unity aimed at by the 'compromise'. After a heated and acrimonious discussion, the resolution was eventually declared carried by a show of hands.

The sitting of the 17th was taken up by the discussion on Kitchlew's proposal to form a committee to organise a campaign of civil disobedience. This also met with opposition, notably from Madan Mohan Malaviya and some Punjab delegates. It was apparently intended to leave the Punjab out of the scheme. After much discussion and a good deal of confusion a slightly amended resolution on the subject was passed by a majority. This was perhaps due to many of the delegates having been carried away by the excitement of the moment, as the general feeling appeared to have been against the restarting of civil disobedience, a sentiment which was quite in accord with public opinion outside Congress circles. The meeting on the 18th September was mainly occupied by the discussion on the *khaddar* and the boycott resolution. In the end a committee was appointed to arrange for the issue of directions to secure the universal use of Indian made goods and the complete boycott of all foreign goods, especially those of British and colonial manufacture. Though supported by several virulent speeches, some of which justified the use of violence to secure their object, the resolution met with vigorous opposition, the boycott clauses being regarded as unpractical and unsound. The meeting of the 19th September was chiefly devoted to the Hindu-Muslim question. No agreement having been found possible in the subjects committee, the main issue was conveniently shirked. The necessity for unity was reiterated, and a small committee appointed to prepare a draft of a national pact. Another larger committee was nominated to visit places where communal disturbances had taken place to allot the blame to the proper parties and suggest measures for restoring confidence. Another resolution exhorted newspapers to exercise restraint and threatened with boycott those that continued to stir up strife. The two other resolutions suggested the appointment of mixed district committees to enquire into and remove grievances or causes of friction, and the formation of local corps of civic guards to maintain peace and order. A sixth resolution professed to deal with the burning question of conversions by appointing a small committee to enquire into and report to the December Congress on any cases in which proselytes were alleged to have been gained by coercion or intimidation. The results were purely negative in relieving Hindu-Muhammadan tension, and the relations between the two communities remained as strained as ever. A public Khilafat meeting was held on the 21st September to explain the results and shortcomings of the Lausanne Treaty and give Muhammad Ali a change of clearing the air as regards Khilafat funds. After expressing his conviction that there was nothing dishonest in Chotani's inability to produce 17 lacs of rupees at a moment's notice, Muhammad Ali had the effrontery to make a further appeal for subscriptions on behalf of distressed Turks, and added that needy workers like himself were worthy of their hire, stating that he would be the first to accept a small monthly stipend if offered. A private meeting of the executive of the Jamiat-ul-Ulema-i-Hind was held on the 20th and 21st September to discuss the withdrawal or modification of the fatwa against council entry. Maulvi Hussain Ahmed of Deoband strongly opposed any alteration, and finally left the meeting in annoyance.

To the great disappointment of Muhammad Ali and his Congress friends, the prolonged discussion only ended in the formation of a sub-committee to look into the matter further. On the 8th November (after several failures to obtain a quorum) a private meeting of the working committee of the Jamiat-ul-Ulema-i-Hind was held and after a long discussion it was decided that the original *fatwa* declaring the entry into councils, etc., as *haram* should stand but the ulema would not enforce any of its items.

At the close of the year the various local extremist committees fell on evil days. Internal dissensions regarding election of office bearers threatened to split the Khilafat committee into two factions. The Congress committee was practically bankrupt and unable to pay its office rent; it was therefore suggested that all the 'national' committees should combine in one office and share the rent. The only apparent function of the Delhi Congress committee was to furnish its secretary, Asaf Ali, with a precarious means of subsistence.

1924

In January the split in the Khilafat Committee reached the stage of the institution of criminal proceedings against its secretaries by one of the opposing factions. Another interesting event was the resumption of practice by the only Delhi lawyer of any position, a pleader named Muhammad Taqi who ceased practising when the non-co-operation movement was at its height: in December 1921 he preferred under-going a year's simple imprisonment to furnishing a bond to keep the peace in connection with organising unlawful associations of 'volunteers'.

On the 5th February a largely attended public meeting was held at Pataudi House to celebrate Gandhi's release. The speakers generally confined themselves to expressions of gratitude at the generosity and statesmanlike wisdom of Government in ordering his unconditional release. The Chairman, Mr. Jinnah, promptly suppressed an Allahabad Pundit who sought to introduce party propaganda.

Several meetings were held to advocate the uplift of the untouchable classes. After one of these presided over by Pandit Madan Mohan Malaviya, who urged the Hindu public to allow the untouchables to enter their temples and draw water at their wells, the ineffable Swami Shardhanand led a procession of members of depressed classes round the City on the 13th February visiting a number of the public wells. The Muhammadan users of one well objected to the proceedings, and a small affray took place resulting in injuries to several of the Swami's followings. The untouchables apparently became a bone of contention between the Hindus and the Muhammadans as to which fold was entitled to receive them.

On the 12th February the Ali brothers paid a short visit to effect a compromise between the factions in the Khilafat Committee. Their efforts were unsuccessful and the defamation case against the secretaries of the committee ended in the discharge of the accused.

The celebration of the 18th February as a day of rejoicing over Gandhi's release fell very flat. In the afternoon a *charkha* procession accompanied by about 80 volunteers went through the bazars. They failed to attract any notice, and the only interesting feature was that the Hindu volunteers did not shout the *jais* of the Muhammadan leaders and *vice versa*. In the evening a meeting attended by about 3,000 persons was convened in Pataudi House, and speeches on Hindu-Muslim unity, use of *khaddar* and the enlistment of volunteers were made. In the evening a few shops in the main bazars were illuminated, but their sparseness was very noticeable.

News of the deposition of Abdul Majid and the abolition of the Khilafat was received by the Delhi Muslims with sullenness, and the action of the Turks was generally condemned although the feeling of resentment was not outwardly shown. Shaukat Ali sent to the Jamiat-ul-Ulema, Delhi, to say that he intended to cable to Abdul Majid, the late Caliph, saying that he and the Indian Muslims continue to acknowledge him as their true and real Caliph and that his name will be read in India in the *Khutba* at the Juma and other prayers. He urged the Jamiat-ul-Ulema to issue a similar *fatwa*. On this a private meeting and discussion was held by Ajmal Khan, Kifayatullah, Ahmed Said and Dr. Ansari. They decided that it was not advisable to condemn the Turks for the deposition of the Caliph and they should await further particulars from the Angora National Assembly. It was pointed out that by their support of the Turkish cause they had incurred the displeasure of the British Government, and if they now turn against the Turks they would make themselves a laughing stock before the world.

In March the local Congress committee became quite bankrupt and was unable to repay a loan of [Rs.] 330 for want of funds. In a meeting Hakim Ajmal Khan and a few other well-to-do members decided to subscribe Rs. 100 each for necessary expenses. In a meeting held on the 4th March by the Congress committee great disappointment was expressed at the Secretary of State's speech refusing further reforms and a resolution calling upon the elected members of the Legislative Assembly either to obstruct the passage of the Budget or to withdraw from the Assembly, was passed. It was also said that in the event of the Budget being rejected by the Assembly the Government would have no right to realise taxes and if it did it would be acting like a pickpocket. In a speech delivered on the evening of the 14th March in the Hindu College on 'Parties and politics in India' Mr. Jinnah deplored the lack of uniformity and unity between the different political parties in India. He believed only in the party which meant to exhaust the stages of constitutional struggle for the attainment of their goal. Government was watching them and knew that there were not many statesmen in India and also the weak points of Indians. The Government will not yield, and they have to attain their object by unity, character and discipline. If the Government persistently continue a policy of indifference and injustice and the constitutional party fails then those who believe in direct action must come into prominence. The Government which has the experience of Ireland, he trusted, will not compel India to resort to direct action.

In April the activities of Hindus and Muslims were confined to a few meetings advocating the boycott of the shops of the other community and though the Muslims did not take any practical step in this direction the Hindu chamars refused to sell shoes to the Muslim shoe merchants and at the instigation of Arya Samajists contemplated the opening of their own shops. In the local Hindu fairs of Budho Mata and Kalka held on the 2nd and 12th April 1924 the services of Muhammadan water carriers which had been utilised in previous years were dispensed with in favour of those of the Hindus. Muhammad Ali who was staying in Delhi owing to the illness of Shaukat Ali told a few friends of his that Madan Mohan Malaviya and Lajpat Rai had prejudiced the mind of Mr. Gandhi against him and his brother Shaukat Ali and had convinced Mr. Gandhi that the Ali brothers were fanatic Muslims. The views of Muhammad Ali expressed by him in his letter to the *Times of India* in reply to his Hindu critics, that he was a Muslim first and an Indian afterwards were not looked upon favourably by the Hindu Press. They accused him of changing his former views that one should be an Indian first and a Hindu or Muslim afterwards. They further attacked him by quoting the example set by Angora. Muhammad Ali appeared to be disappointed with his Hindu friends.

In the end of April the local working committee of the Congress discussed the starting of civil disobedience on the lines of the Bardoli resolution in certain parts of the city; but the movement totally failed.

In May the Idul Fitr passed off quietly, but the refusal of the Muslims to take refreshments offered by Hindus in pursuance of a custom started by the advocates of Hindu-Muslim unity in 1919 made the feelings of the communities more bitter. Both the communities accused each other in their meetings of adopting unfair means and stratagems to get hold of the unclaimed children of the other community.

The adverse criticism made by Mr. Gandhi on the Arya Samaj, *Vedas* and *Shudhi* led to several emphatic protest meetings by the Aryas and it was said that Gandhi who was esteemed and regarded as a national leader, was lost to the nation. The Sanatanists on the other hand supported Gandhi's views.

Meetings of the Central Khilafat Committee were held on the 24th and 25th June at which resolutions on the organisation of the Muslim community, the opening of schools and banks, and the supervision of Waqf property, the collection of zakat and expenditure of the proceeds on proper objects, were passed. A resolution declaring Sharif Hussain unfit for the office of Caliph was also passed. The conference did not attract much interest or enthusiasm from the Muslim population of Delhi. A few speeches made by Shaukat Ali and other leaders on Hindu-Muslim unity did not have any good effect and the proceedings throughout were marked with grave interruptions, each community accusing the other of being the cause of all the trouble.

The strained relations of the Hindus and Muslims had made the Delhi atmosphere very troubled. The timely intervention of the Police averted riots on several occasions. In the morning of the 11th July riots occurred quite unexpectedly over a minor and in itself insignificant incident, and continued till the 19th. There was much loss of life and property. It is noteworthy that during the investigation into the riot cases each community accused innocent persons of the other side including even the most respectable persons who could never have taken part in the riots.

APPENDIX I

Clear injunctions of the Book of God and the Hadis of the Prophet

1. It is unlawful to be member of Government Councils.
2. It is unlawful to plead in Government Courts.
3. It is unlawful to read or teach in Government or aided schools.
4. It is unlawful to possess honorary magistracies, honorary offices and other titles conferred by Government
5. All Government services helping Government are *haram*, particularly services in the Police and the Military are the most sinful, for men serving in these have to fire at their brethren.

God says: He who murders any Musalman intentionally will be sent to hell where he will be subjected to eternal tortures, and will remain under God's curse and anger; and God has prepared a very severe torture for him.

The Prophet has said, 'He who has raised his arms against a Musalman is no longer a Musalman.[']

The above is an abstract of the Fatwa issued by the Jamiat-ul-Ulema unanimously. The original fatwa is signed by about 500 ulema.

2

The Khilafat Movement in the United Provinces (1919-1924)

PART I. EARLY GROWTH OF THE KHILAFAT MOVEMENT

At the annual meeting of the Muslim League held at Delhi in December 1918 Dr. Ansari expounded publicly in a speech, which was immediately proscribed, the claim that the countries of the Turkish Empire, in which the Holy Places of Islam are situated, should be left intact. Resolutions were passed to this effect, and protest was made against the occupation of Jerusalem and Najaf. Speeches, full of religious fervour, created strong anti-British feeling, which the members of the audience made no attempt to conceal. The speakers were drawn largely from the United Provinces, among them being Qazi Abdul Ghaffar, Muhammad Shuaib Qureshi, Khwaja Abdul Majid, Dr. Abdur Rahman Sindhi, Hasrat Mohani, Abdul Bari and Azad Subhani, who had already acquired notoriety as pan-Islamic or pro-Turkish agitators.

There was however little outward indication of pro-Turkish agitation in the United Provinces until March 1919 when there appeared in the press a letter from Abdul Bari to the Viceroy, supporting, with the approval of sixty maulvis whom he had consulted, the claim made by Dr. Ansari and declaring that the Muhammadans were bound to expel Christians from Arabia and, if necessary, to assist the Khalifa in retaking the Holy Places. Mr. Gandhi, who was trying at this time to foster Hindu-Muslim unity, visited Abdul Bari at Lucknow on the 10th March with the result that Abdul Bari published a newspaper article recommending the *satyagraha* movement to his Muslim brethren. In April, during the time of the Punjab disturbances, Abdul Bari was attending an important religious fair at Ajmer where he collected signatures for a memorial in favour of Turkey and endeavoured also to promote Hindu-Muslim unity. The memorial was subsequently circulated for signature in the United Provinces, and in other parts of India. There were also circulated at this time many copies of a printed letter to the Viceroy from the Ali Brothers (who had been interned since 1915), protesting against the proscription of Dr. Ansari's address, stating *jihad* and *hijrat* as the only alternatives open to them, and declaring their adherence to Mr. Gandhi's Passive Resistance movement. They referred to Abdul Bari as their spiritual preceptor and to Mr. Gandhi is their guide, philosopher and friend. In July Abdul Bari wrote to the Viceroy saying that he and others were not in favour of the policy of the Ali Brothers and had disapproved of the publication of the above letter.

On the 3rd July 1919 Yakub Hasan wrote to Mr. Chotani, President of the Khilafat committee of Bombay, describing the activities of the Muhammadan delegation then in Europe and the propaganda work which was being carried on with money obtained from His Highness the Aga Khan. He suggested the creation of a network of Khilafat committees in India which should pass resolutions whenever suitable occasion offered and cable them to London.

During the period May to August the enthusiasm of educated Muhammadans appears to have been considerably damped by the lessons which were to be drawn from the Punjab disorders. Mr. Chotani in fact found it difficult to get replies to invitations to join a deputation to the Viceroy in connection with the Khilafat question.

In September the receipt of news regarding the proposals of the Peace Conference for the partition of Thrace, the assignment of Smyrna to the Greeks and the creation of mandates for other portions of the Turkish Empire was the signal for agitation. Meetings were held in the towns and a conference of the All-India Muslim League at Lucknow on the 21st September was attended by 3,000 persons including 300 delegates from other provinces. Resolutions were passed declaring the dismemberment of Turkey to be an intolerable interference with the Khilafat (the word 'intolerable' was interpolated at the insistent request of the audience), and the proposed internationalisation of Constantinople, and the uniting of a portion of Thrace to Greece to be a direct violation of a pledge given by Mr. Lloyd George on the 15th January, 1918. Saiyid Sulaiman Nadwi, a divine from Azamgarh, discoursed in elegiac strain on the passing of the last remnant of Islamic splendour. The conference approved of the establishment of a Central Khilafat committee at Bombay and recommended the formation of branch committees all over the country. Friday, the 17th October was fixed upon as a Khilafat Day or day of prayer on behalf of Turkey and Mr. Gandhi called upon the Hindus to share in the observances of the occasion. Fervid exhortations were circulated. One of the bulletins of the Khilafat committee recommended a progressive boycott of English goods and institutions. Opinion was divided as to the advisability of having a *hartal*, and on the day itself shops were generally closed only in Allahabad, Gorakhpur and a few smaller places. Meetings were held after prayers but the attendances were small save in Cawnpore and Allahabad, where about 10,000 persons, and in Agra where about 3,000 persons assembled. The response of the important Muhammadan cities in the north-western portion of the provinces was decidedly weak and the participation of Hindus in the observances was noticeable in a few towns only. At Allahabad members of the Nehru and Malaviya families identified themselves with the proceedings. Bitter feeling was stirred up by the speeches. At some places the members of the audience were moved to tears.

The formation of local Khilafat committees was now taken in hand and the first action of the Lucknow committee was to send a violent telegram to the Secretary of State for India and to the Islamic Bureau which had been started by Indian agitators in London. This telegram charged the British Government with trampling on religious sentiment and disregarding pledges given during the war.

On Khilafat Day, 17th October, resolutions were passed at a few centres to the effect that the Muhammadans could not participate in the forthcoming Peace celebrations. A few days later Mr. Gandhi published his approval of this view. The matter was taken up with enthusiasm by the agitators of Allahabad and the extremist daily newspaper the *Independent* embarked on a campaign of lurid propaganda in favour of a boycott of the celebrations. During November large meetings were held at Lucknow and Allahabad and Hasrat Mohani, one of the most irreconcilable agitators of the United Provinces, presided at a meeting of 10,000 persons held at Delhi on the 16th November at which an anti-Peace Celebration Propaganda committee was appointed.

On the 23rd November an All-India Khilafat conference was held at Delhi. There were 161 delegates present from the United Provinces and only 20 from the Punjab. The first resolution was one of gratitude to Mr. Gandhi for his support of the Muhammadans. The second urged that the Peace celebrations should be boycotted. The third recommending a progressive boycott of British goods and institutions was referred to a sub-committee. Raza Ali who spoke on this resolution expressed strong resentment at the evidence given by General Dyer before the Hunter committee and said that the Muhammadans should give a taste of their fury to the man who had goaded them. Saiyid Husain, editor of the *Independent* of Allahabad, apparently at the suggestion of Mr. Gandhi, moved a resolution to the effect that if the Khilafat question were not settled in accordance with the wishes of the Muhammadans it would be incumbent on them progressively to withhold co-operation from the British Government.

On the following day, the 24th November, at a joint meeting of Hindus and Muhammadans, Mr. Gandhi urged that the Peace celebrations should be boycotted on the Khilafat issue alone.

Three weeks of feverish propaganda followed. The events in the Punjab were described in an inflammatory strain at numerous meetings throughout the provinces and more eloquence was expended on them than on the grievances of the Muhammadans. Agitators from Delhi were prominently active in the western districts and bellicose speeches were delivered notably at Agra on the 8th November when with the Hon'ble Saiyid Ali [?] in the chair, Babu Prag Narayan denounced the British to an assemblage of 4,000 persons for having, in the fashion of the Huns, fired on and bombed innocent persons in the Punjab. Asaf Ali compared Turkey to a heap of bones around which dogs were fighting and said that the Indians were being asked to rejoice over the breaking of English promises. Islam had been trampled on and the Indian Muslims had been betrayed; if their wishes were not respected they should dissociate themselves from Government and abandon Government service. At another meeting on the 16th December violent speeches were delivered to 8,000 people by Neki Ram Sharma of Delhi, Muhammad Fakhir of Allahabad and Dr. Monji of Nagpur. At Meerut on the 28th November Maulana Ahmad Sa'id of Delhi said that if Government played football with Islam the Muhammadans would play football with the British *raj*.

At Lucknow on the 12th December Abdur Razak Nadwi delivered a fervid speech to about 4,000 people.

Allahabad was a centre of considerable activity. Meetings were held in mohallas and villages. At one these on 1st December Muhammad Fakhir cursed the Indian soldiers and police for the manner in which they had performed their duties in the Punjab. At another meeting, two days later, he praised the martyrs of the Punjab, said it was incumbent on a Muhammadan to kill any one who insulted the Prophet, and, if necessary he would relieve his own feelings by the use of his hand, but he wished to incite people not to commit murder but merely to offer themselves to be massacred.

In spite of this opposition the Peace celebrations were held successfully at most places, the only regrettable feature being the absence of a large number of Muhammadans from the functions in the cities.

The closing days of 1919 brought the Royal assent to the Reforms Act and an amnesty to persons guilty of political offences. In the United Provinces seven internees and eleven prisoners were released.

During Christmas week the annual meetings of the Congress

and Muslim League were held at Amritsar. Most of the speakers strongly condemned British rule and, by allusions to the Amritsar tragedy, aroused excitement in their audiences. The Congress decided not to boycott the Reforms. The Muslim League accepted them as a step forward. Dr. Ansari, Hasrat Mohani and Muhammad Ali failed to persuade the Muhammadan delegates to pass a resolution recommending the abandonment of cow-sacrifice. A resolution recommending non-co-operation was defeated but Hasrat Mohani secured the acceptance of an amendment threatening a boycott of the British Army if employed for anti-Islamic purposes.

The All-India Khilafat conference held at the same time sent a message of faith in and allegiance to the Sultan and resolved to open a Khilafat fund to provide for the despatch of a Muhammadan deputation to England and to meet other expenses.

After the meetings at Amritsar the extremist leaders took up with great earnestness the cultivation of Hindu-Muslim unity. They brought about shallow demonstrations at some places but achieved nothing permanent.

The extremist leaders and particularly those recently released from jail had been lionised at Amritsar and in January it became apparent that popular excitement had been kindled to a dangerous degree. Visits of the Ali Brothers to Moradabad, Aligarh, Cawnpore and Lucknow and of Mr. Gandhi to Meerut drew from the excited populace demonstrations of unusual magnitude and undisciplined confusion. Carriages were dragged by lusty admirers; volunteers in a semblance of military uniform headed disorderly processions of citizens; and chairmen of municipal boards presented addresses of welcome. It was estimated that 50,000 persons took part in the proceedings at Cawnpore. Shaukat Ali could with reason boast that on his release from internment he had found a fire in the land.

This adulation was not bestowed on agitators only. The youths who had been convicted in the Mainpuri conspiracy case and released under the amnesty were on their arrival in their native town given an ovation in which the chairman of the municipal board and other leading townsmen took prominent parts. It was evidently forgotten that they had been responsible for two murders and that one of their victims had been a helpless serving maid.

In January an influential Khilafat deputation waited on the Viceroy and received a most conciliatory reply to an address but this had no effect on agitation.

During February the attitude of the leaders stiffened. The second Sindh Khilafat conference declared that Muhammadans should not enlist in the army. A Khilafat conference in Bombay which was attended by more than twenty delegates from the United Provinces demanded the removal of British troops from Turkish territories. The Bengal Khilafat conference at Calcutta on the 28th February threatened the severance of all relations of loyalty to the Government, and the boycott of English goods; made an appeal to Muslims in the army; and outlined the obligation on Muhammadans to assist the Khalifa in the event of an unfavourable settlement. A protest was entered against the hostile attitude of British statesmen and churchmen towards the decision to leave Constantinople to the Turks and Friday, the 19th March was appointed for the suspension of business and the despatch of a final message to the King-Emperor and the Viceroy threatening the withdrawal of secular loyalty.

The resolutions of the Bengal Khilafat conference became the basis of a movement to secure the general observance of the 19th March. Posters and leaflets containing the resolutions (which had been proscribed by the Government of Bengal) were circulated in profusion. A notice was issued by Shaukat Ali, Abul Kalam Azad, Hasrat Mohani and others to the effect that whoever wavered an inch from the obligation of Islam and from allegiance to the Khalifa and died in that condition would die the death of an infidel. In Mainpuri a resolution was carried sentencing to religious ostracism any one who did not observe the rules for Khilafat Day. At Lucknow on the 12th March Maulvi Muhammad Shafi of Firangi Mahal assured his audience that the soldiers who had fought against the Turks were no longer Muhammadans. Some days later a Khilafat zealot named Zafar-ul-Mulk was more explicit and said that these soldiers would go to hell. By means of violent declarations that the Powers meant to obliterate Islam, emissaries from the big cities worked on the feelings of their brethren in outlying places and on the actual day it became apparent that an increased number of small towns had been affected. *Hartal*, or shutting of shops, was carried out as generally as on the 6th April 1919.

References were made to the Punjab troubles at seven or eight meetings only. Attention was directed almost exclusively to Turkish affairs, and the Calcutta resolutions were adopted in most districts. The Hindus, though they closed their shops, did not, at most places, identify themselves conspicuously with the public meetings. Objectionable speeches were delivered at Pilibhit, Meerut, Budaun [!] and Gorakhpur, and a prayer of remarkable fervour describing the Turks as men who had sacrificed themselves in the cause of God was circulated and read aloud in Lucknow and neighbouring districts.

The meetings in the larger cities were well attended. At Mirzapur about 8,000 persons were present at the public meeting, three-quarters of them being Hindus.

Abul Kalam Azad had advised Abdul Bari to hold a United Provinces Khilafat conference at any place where the people were prepared to go 'some steps' further than the Calcutta people or at least to keep pace with them. This was duly held at Meerut on the 21st to 23rd March. Volunteers in Turkish and Arab uniforms and wearing colours symbolic of martyrdom were conspicuous. Among the delegates were some from the Muhammadan Anglo-Oriental College at Aligarh. Resolutions were passed expressing indignation at the anti-Turkish attitude of the British bishops, statesmen and press, refusing to accept the findings of Lord Bryce's committee regarding the Armenian massacres, asking for a commission of inquiry into the atrocities committed by the Greeks in Asia Minor and protesting against the temporary occupation of Constantinople by the Allies.

Mr. Gandhi visited the meeting with other leaders and announced that they had decided at a conference at Delhi that in the event of an unfavourable settlement of the Turkish question three steps should be taken:

(1) Resignation of honorary posts.

(2) Resignation of Government servants.
(3) Refusal to pay taxes.

PART II. ADOPTION OF NON-CO-OPERATION BY THE KHILAFAT PARTY

During the next three months agitation was carried on almost without a check. The Khilafat leaders went from excess to excess in their efforts to rouse popular fanaticism and to bring its full force to bear on Government. Agitation was carried gradually into all the small towns in the provinces and into many villages. Meetings became frequent and subscriptions were collected for the Khilafat fund. The several points which emerged in the course of the peace negotiations, such as the opposition in certain quarters to the proposed restitution of Constantinople to the Sultan, or the conferment of Smyrna with its outlying plain on the Greeks, were quickly seized upon as fuel for agitation. By the time provincial Khilafat committees had been established at Meerut, Lucknow and a network of branch committees provided an organisation capable of being used with great effect. Propagandists from Delhi, Meerut, Budaun and Lucknow were moving about freely.

The week from the 6th to the 13th of April was observed as a National week in accordance with the instructions issued by Mr. Gandhi. Public meetings were held to ask for the repeal of the Rowlatt Act and to urge Government to take effective steps to render a repetition of the Punjab tragedy impossible. Friday was set apart for Khilafat meetings.

The proceedings seemed to disclose a slackening of enthusiasm, save at Agra where Shaukat Ali and Muhammad Fakhir were taken in procession escorted by volunteers armed with swords. The former delivered a speech threatening adherence to the Sultan, while Muhammad Fakhir denounced as treacherous and dishonest the Muhammadans who had fought against Turkey and said that the time for action had come and soldiers and policemen should resign. He prayed God to crush the enemies of Islam.

The attendance at one meeting at Agra was 7,000 but only fourteen other meetings during the week drew audiences of 1,000 or more. The speakers indulged in highly-coloured narrations of the occurrences in the Punjab and of the misfortunes of Turkey. Muhammadans were told that they had to choose between the Government and their God.

In Cawnpore, Benares and a few other places the Hindus declined to commit themselves to the threat of non-co-operation and the committee of the Cawnpore Hindu Sabha expressed the opinion that some of the resolutions passed by a conference of *ulama* on the 4th and 5th April had overstepped the limits of constitutional agitation.

Things were, however, moving fast. On the 18th and 19th April a Khilafat workers' conference was held at Delhi. The speakers denounced Government in the most violent terms and expressed their readiness to spread the doctrines of *jihad* and *hijrat* among Government servants and soldiers. Some went as far to suggest, under a thin mask of disapproval, the murder of Europeans. Their fieriness communicated itself to their hearers and the latter would probably have taken any violent action proposed to them at the time.

Hasrat Mohani presided at this conference and among the violent speakers were Shanti Sarup of Farrukhabad and Nazir Husain of Muzaffarnagar.

One of the important results of this conference was the popularisation of the idea that *hijrat* or emigration on religious grounds was now obligatory on Indian Muhammadans.

This Khilafat workers' association was founded at Delhi about 25th March for the purpose of executing the resolutions of the Bengal and other Khilafat conferences. Nine residents of the United Provinces were members of the subjects committee which met on the 18th April. Hasrat Mohani from Cawnpore and Zafar ul-Mulk from Lucknow were given places on the committee of management. Many delegates from the United Provinces and particularly from Meerut and Aligarh attended the conference on the 18th and 19th April.

A branch of the association was started at Lucknow and about 300 workers were enrolled before the end of May. The enrolment forms asked for information as to the amount of work the applicant could do under six heads of a non-co-operation programme including village propaganda.

There was also in the field an association of *ulama* the members of which were much more extreme than their secular brethren. This association had been formed at the same time as the original Khilafat committee. Meetings held under its auspices at Cawnpore on the 4th and 5th of April attracted as many as 15,000 persons to whom inflammatory speeches were delivered by Salamat Ullah, Azad Subhani, Muhammad Fakhir, Nisar Ahmad and Abdul Majid, members of the association, and also by Mushir Husain Qidwai, a member of a well-known family of Oudh. The resolutions of the Bengal conference were reiterated and others added urging the adoption of every means for securing the release of Khilafat workers in trouble, the prevention of recruitment of Indians for the army and the boycott of elections under the Reform Scheme.

On the 24th and 25th April a Khilafat conference was held at Shahjahanpur. Abdul Majid of Budaun presided. The resolutions passed at the *ulama's* conference at Cawnpore were adopted. Hasrat Mohani said that the principles of Bolshevism were the same as those of Islam. Azad Subhani delivered a perfervid[!] oration in which he threatened with hell fire any Muslim who remained faithful to English rule if the Khilafat problem were decided against Muslim wishes.

On the 1st and 2nd May a Khilafat conference for Oudh was held at Fyzabad. The resolutions passed

(a) thanked the Amir of Afghanistan for his attitude towards the Khilafat cause and for having offered a home to Muslim emigrants from India;
(b) said it would be impossible for Indian Muslims to welcome the Prince of Wales;
(c) requested the Central Khilafat committee to put non-co-operation into practice.

A resolution welcoming the Khilafat workers' association was rejected by ten votes. Shaukat Ali entered a protest against the too rapid advance made by the hot heads under Hasrat Mohani and also against the extremism displayed at the conference of *ulama* at Cawnpore on the 4th and 5th April, but he made a pronouncement to the effect that if Muslims' demands were not satisfied the Muhammadans should no longer consider themselves subjects of the King-Emperor.

The attendances at the meetings varied from 2,000 to 5,000 of whom about one-tenth were Hindus.

On the 5th May Shaukat Ali delivered a reckless speech at Shahjahanpur in the course of which he said:

'To lay down our lives in the way of God for righteousness and to destroy the life of the tyrant who stands in the way of righteousness are both very great services to God.'

On the 6th May Hakim Ajmal Khan, Shaukat Ali, Hasrat Mohani, Azad Subhani, Muhammad Fakhir and Salamat Ullah visited Budaun. A procession of about 4,000 persons escorted them and at a meeting of 7,000 persons Shaukat Ali spoke of a time when the non-co-operation programme having been carried out without success Mr. Gandhi would stand aside and say 'Brothers! You may now do what you like.' On the 7th May at Friday prayers Muhammad Fakhir abused the police as sons of pigs and dogs and as dishonest rogues.

On the 8th May very objectionable speeches were delivered by Shaukat Ali and by Ahmad Sa'id of Delhi to large audiences at Amroha in the Moradabad district.

The terms of the Treaty of Sèvres were announced on the 16th May and the Khilafat agitators agreed at once that they were disgraceful and that non-co-operation was necessary. The All-India Congress committee which met at Benares on the 29th May recorded its opinion that the terms were a flagrant violation of the solemn promises of His Majesty's Government, but the majority of its members were strongly opposed to the adoption of non-co-operation and no resolution on the subject was recorded either at Benares or at Allahabad where a joint conference of the Hindu and Muhammadan leaders was held on the 1st June. It fell to Mr. Gandhi to report this result to a meeting of the Central Khilafat committee at Allahabad on the 1st June when he put forward a printed manifesto of the committee proposing recourse to non-co-operation with regard to

(1) honorary offices and titles, and
(2) civil employment under Government

only. It appears that a majority of the Muhammadans present led by the Hon'ble Saiyid Raza Ali were opposed to the proposal but the violence of Shaukat Ali and the bitterness of Abdul Bari silenced open opposition and the proposal was carried.

At a subsequent meeting Mr. Gandhi said that the first stage could include the boycott of schools and colleges and the surrender of their practices by lawyers. He would get through the stages one by one in four or five months and then if the Muhammadans wished to go further he would stand aside. The following sub-committee was appointed to give practical effect to the movement without delay:

Mr. Gandhi
Abul Kalam Azad
Muhammad Ali
Ahmad Haji Siddiq Khatri
Shaukat Ali
Dr. Kitchlew

The meeting also appointed a sub-committee to direct the *swadeshi* movement and resolved to organise a Khilafat volunteer corps, to collect subscriptions for the Khilafat fund, and to prepare the public for non-co-operation.

At private meetings of the *ulama* on the 2nd and 3rd June the peace terms were repudiated as an insult to Islam and a resolution was adopted that it was the duty of the Muhammadans to try to drive away from the Holy Places the enemies of Islam and particularly the British. *Hijrat* was pronounced to be optional.

Mr. Chotani presided at a public Khilafat meeting held on the 3rd June and explained the wishes of Mr. Gandhi with regard to non-co-operation.

PART III. WAITING FOR CONGRESS (JUNE TO AUGUST 1920)

The Allahabad conferences were followed by three comparatively quiet months during which Mr. Gandhi, having secured the leadership of the Khilafat movement, was largely engaged with the growing embitterment of Hindu feeling. Special collections of the *'Id,* the 19th June, gave poor results, and after the *'Id* little money was forthcoming. The boycotting of two loyalist *pesh imams* was the only sign of vigour recorded in June. The difficulty of giving practical effect to the non-co-operation programme was felt everywhere, and on the 18th July the provincial Khilafat secretary found it necessary to send a circular to district committees asking them to abandon the idea that the programme was impracticable. At his time the programme was extended so as to cover the boycott of courts, schools and council elections.

The unfortunate *hijrat* movement in the middle of the year induced very few residents of the United Provinces to abandon their homes.

The 1st of August was appointed for observance as a Khilafat Day. Districts were flooded with leaflets advertising it and warning the people against friendship with the enemies of Islam. A call to *hijrat* by Abul Kalam Azad was widely circulated. The day was observed in a somewhat half-hearted manner in most places. There was little coercion in connection with the shutting of shops. The meetings in the large towns were fairly well attended and strong speeches were delivered at Aligarh and Lucknow. One orator at Lucknow threatened the soldiers serving in Mesopotamia with consignment to the worst part of hell. A resolution asking for the recall of such soldiers from Mesopotamia had been included in the programme for the day issued by the Oudh Khilafat committee at the suggestion of Mushir Husain Kidwai who cabled from England that the Khilafat deputation had failed to accomplish anything.

The provincial propaganda bureau at Meerut was now reorganised, and authorised to spend Rs. 1,000 a month.

On the 3rd August Shaukat Ali published a pronouncement in favour of non-co-operation by Maulana Mahmud-ul-Hasan of

Deoband who had recently returned from Malta where he had been interned in connection with the Silk Letter conspiracy.

The Central Khilafat committee on the 10th August appointed a committee of seven *ulama*, five of them resident of the United Provinces, to select preachers for every province of India.

On the *Bakr-Id* festival, 26th August, Mr. Willoughby, Deputy Commissioner of Kheri, was assassinated by three fanatical low class Muhammadans. The murder was directly traceable to Khilafat propaganda working on ignorant and fanatical minds. One of the murderers said that he had been affected by the *ulama's* conference in Cawnpore in April. The resolutions passed at this conference had been read out at a meeting in Kheri on the 8th April when also a boy had recited a poem on the downfall of Islamic countries entitled 'Tears of Blood'. The opening lines were

> 'We would drink the blood of our enemies as if it were a cup of red wine; we require the skull and not the cup of wine.
>
> Swords should clash instead of the tunes of musicians, regarding a general massacre as a marriage gathering.'

Offensive speeches had also been delivered on the 9th and 10th May at Kheri by Abdul Samad, a maulvi of Budaun, and one Ram Narayan, a low class agitator. General Dyer had been referred to as a black dog and swine and European officers held up to ridicule as whitefaced treacherous monkeys.

Furthermore, one of the assassins had attended the Khilafat workers' conference at Delhi, one of the most fiery meetings in the whole history of the movement.

Considerable efforts were made to induce the Muhammadans to refrain from cow sacrifice on the *Bakr-Id*, but they met with no success worthy of note.

There was an outburst of activity when the time for the special Congress meetings at Calcutta drew near. The provincial Khilafat leaders toured in the Meerut and Rohilkhand divisions and attended large meetings at which several violent speeches were delivered.

In August, the Khilafat leaders at Bombay issued a special

whip to the provinces calling for the attendance of a large number of Muhammadan delegates at Calcutta, armed with certificates of Congress membership, so as to enable them to influence the proceedings of the Congress.

During the special Congress meeting at Calcutta at which non-co-operation was adopted there were also held meetings of the Khilafat and *ulama's* associations and of the All-India Muslim League. On the 5th September the Khilafat conference declared non-co-operation to be a religious obligation.

On the 6th September some sixty *ulama* met, with Abdul Majid of Budaun in the chair, and registered decisions with regard to propaganda, the appointment of a Shaikh-ul-Islam for India, private tribunals, participation in a proposed deputation from the Muslim League to Afghanistan and the appointment of representatives to threaten with boycott those Muslims who had so far refrained from participation in the Khilafat movement.

About one-third of the persons present at the private meetings of the subjects committee of the All-India Muslim League were agitators from the United Provinces. Shaukat Ali displayed considerable annoyance on account of the attitude of Messrs. Fazl-ul-Haq (Bengal) and Jinnah (Bombay) towards non-co-operation. When the former was proposed as chairman at the public meeting on the 8th September cries of protest came from the audience. On this Fazl-ul-Haq assured the audience that he had been opposed to non-co-operation merely because he considered it impracticable but as there was a majority in favour of it he was now with them. He left the meeting however and Hakim Ajmal Khan took his place. Shaukat Ali delivered a speech condemning the Anglo-India press for having represented that the assassination of the Deputy Commissioner of Kheri was due to the Khilafat movement.

The non-co-operation resolution passed by the special Congress was adopted with the addition that persons who did no support the movement should be boycotted socially. Propaganda for the stoppage of recruitment was also agreed upon. A stirring prayer offered by Abdul Majid for the victory of Kemal Pasha evoked great enthusiasm from the audience.

PART IV. KHILAFAT AGITATION (SEPTEMBER 1920 TO FEBRUARY 1922)

The Khilafat-Congress alliance may be said to have lasted from September 1920 to February 1922. A general account of the part played by Khilafat agitators in the non-co-operation movement during that period will be found in parts IV and V of the separate note on the non-co-operation movement.[1] What follows is a more detailed account of the distinctively sectarian side of the movement.

(A) Course of Agitation

In October and November 1920 many of the Khilafat agitators were engaged in the campaign against schools which was part of the non-co-operation programme. On the 23rd November 1920, a conference of 500 *ulama* was held at Delhi. Muhammad Ali was present. Resolutions were passed declaring it *haram* or religiously unlawful to maintain relations of love and co-operation with Government; urging abstention from military service and educational institutions of the enemies of Islam as a religious obligation; and disowning such *ulama* as had failed to recognise their religious duty.

This naturally encouraged platform orators to speak in a more intolerant and inflammatory strain. At large meetings held in Moradabad from the 10th to the 14th December, Husain Ahmad Madni of Deoband accused the British of having bombed wounded soldiers sheltering in mosques in the Holy Land. Ahmad Sa'id of Delhi, speaking objectionably on the Smyrna atrocities and the events in the Punjab, said that a time was coming when the wives of loyalists would leave them and they would not be allowed the use of Muhammadan graveyards.

In January 1921 the provincial Khilafat committee circulated a pamphlet *Tark-i-Mawalat* (non-co-operation) containing *fatwas* by various maulvis to the effect that co-operation with infidels was irreligious, but especially so with those who were still openly tormenting the Muslims. Great Britain was represented as the principal enemy of Turkey.

[1] Not printed here.

In January and February 1921 much activity was shown by the Khilafat agitators who were trying to collect subscriptions for the Central Khilafat fund and particularly for the Muhammadan sufferers at Smyrna. A provincial deputation toured in Hamirpur, Jhansi, Cawnpore, Fatehpur, Mirzapur, Benares and Etawah where inflam-matory speeches were delivered and appeals made to lawyers and students. On the 27th of January a meeting of 10,000 persons was held at Jhansi in honour of a local agitator who was being tried for seditious speaking. In February several objectionable speeches were delivered by *ulama* and Khilafat leaders in the Bijnor district, and at a conference of *ulama* in Bareilly on the 24th and 25th of March Muhammad Ali said that though the Sultan had declared *jihad*, the Holy Places had been taken by the British with the help of Indians, and Indian Muslims were still serving there; they would not obtain salvation on the day of judgement. A resolution was passed declaring the modification of the Treaty of Sèvres, then under contemplation, to be inadequate. Ahmad Sa'id of Delhi described the Smyrna atrocities in the most revolting terms possible. Abul Kalam Azad announced that it was forbidden by religion to enlist in the army. The effect of these speeches on large audiences (there were on one occasion 10,000 persons present) must have been considerable. Muhammad Ali had also spoken objectionably at the Oudh Khilafat conference on the 26th and 27th February, and at a Khilafat conference in Shahjahanpur at the end of March he reproached the local Muhammadans with having murdered their co-religionists and with thus having helped the Cross to crush the Crescent.

In March and April a false newspaper report that Najaf had been bombarded caused several large demonstrations by the Shias of Lucknow. Muhammad Ali and Jawahir Lal Nehru attended an All-India Shia conference at Lucknow on the 30th April and 1st May. The Government had issued a *communiqué* explaining the facts which had led to the inaccurate report but the conference resolved to send a deputation to make enquires at Najaf.

Objectionable speeches were delivered at a provincial Khilafat conference at Meerut from the 7th to the 9th April. On the

10th April, at a conference of *ulama* at Moradabad, Hamid Ahmad, an ex-convict of Allahabad, expressed approval of the conduct of the murderers of the Deputy Commissioner of Kheri. He had already spoken in similar terms at a gathering held in honour of his release from jail, when he had been received by a guard of honour of 80 men and boys armed with swords. He was eventually transported for life for these speeches.

In the first fortnight of May the leaders toured the United Provinces and objectionable speeches were delivered by the Ali Brothers. Their prosecution was contemplated, but was deferred in consequence of Mr. Gandhi's interview with the Viceroy and the subsequent public apology made by the Ali Brothers. This involved them in some discredit, but in June development in Anatolia revived interest in the Khilafat agitation. It was feared that England would side actively with the Greeks against the Turkish nationalists and warnings were issued by Abul Kalam Azad, Abdul Bari and Abdul Majid that if she did so she would immediately find herself in a state of war with Islam. It was explained that the Muhammadans had never committed themselves to constant adhesion to the policy of non-violence. These sentiments were uttered at public meetings and the inflamed state of Muslim feeling was shown by prayers in mosques for the success of Mustafa Kemal Pasha, by the subscription of Rs. 10,000 for the Smyrna fund on the occasion of the *'Id* and by the boycott of two loyalist *pesh imams*. The All-India Congress Working committee passed a resolution on the 14th June to the effect that the Indian soldier class should decline to serve in connection with the hostilities against the nationalist Turks.

(B) Defiance of Government

The All-India Khilafat conference held at Karachi from the 8th to the 10th July threatened to start civil disobedience and establish complete independence, and declared that service in the army and police was religiously unlawful. The Ali Brothers, Husain Ahmad Madni of Deoband, Nisar Ahmad of Cawnpore and others delivered seditious speeches on this resolution. Leaflets containing a *fatwa* of the leading *ulama* (including Azad Subhani and Abdul Bari) to the effect that Government service, and especially service in the army and the police, was religiously unlawful were now being very widely circulated and sent by post to soldiers. These leaflets were proscribed by Government and the proscription was immediately challenged as an intolerable interference with religion. Protests were made at meetings held throughout the provinces. On the 21st of September the *ulama* decided to disregard the order of proscription. Their decision was re-affirmed in a stronger form by the Central Khilafat committee. Ahmad Sa'id of Delhi, the secretary of the *ulama's* association, issued a notice calling for the names of persons willing to distribute the *fatwa*. At this juncture came the arrest of the Ali Brothers and of those who had spoken seditiously along with them at Karachi. Husain Ahmad Madni was the only member of the party to be arrested in the United Provinces. Drums had been placed on the minarets of the Juma Masjid at Saharanpur to apprise the people of his arrest if it were effected there. He was, however, arrested in Deoband after a show of opposition by a party of volunteers, armed with spears, who assaulted a police inspector.

Meanwhile from July onwards there had been a considerable increase of Muhammadan bitterness owing to the reverses sustained by the Turks in Anatolia. On the 28th of July Abdul Bari wrote to the *Independent* saying that a body of sympathisers was required who would be prepared to give up their lives for Islam. An address presented to Mr. Gandhi by Salamat Ali of Lucknow on the 1st of August contained a statement that owing to the situation at Angora the Muhammadans did not consider non-violent non-co-operation sufficient and volunteers should be enrolled to help the Turks. A few weeks later at a Khilafat meeting in the Unao district a message from Abdul Bari was read out to the effect that if the Greeks defeated the Turks, *jihad* would be obligatory. At Nagina in the Bijnor district a congregation of 2,000 persons prayed that the members of the Aman Sabha, the local loyalist association, might go to hell. Muhammadan feeling was affected also by the news of the Moplah rebellion which the

Government was accused of misrepresenting, with the design of weakening Hindu-Muslim unity. The extremists at Aligarh and Saharanpur were trying to bring about a stoppage of the *Muharram* celebrations as religiously unlawful owing to the unfortunate condition of Muhammadan affairs.

The arrests therefore came at a bad time but they did not produce any immediate outburst of violence. Meetings of protest were held in most districts but only at seven did the attendance exceed 1,000. In Meerut it was 15,000; in Aligarh 5,000. The general line taken was to re-state the Karachi resolution, to condemn the action of Government and to threaten civil disobedience in the near future. Hindu agitators rallied to the support of their Muslim colleagues. Jawahir Lal Nehru addressing 30,000 peasants in the Gorakhpur district said that every Indian should declare his readiness to follow Muhammad Ali's example. The Government, he added, was nearing its end and its atrocities would soon be finished. He appealed to the religious passion of his Hindu auditors by reminding them of the thousands of cows slaughtered for the British army. This speech was repeated to 5,000 persons in the Basti district on the 19th September.

It now became the fashion to re-state either the Karachi resolution or the proscribed *fatwa* at public meetings. The agitators seemed to be resolved to fill the jails. No action was taken by Government to gratify their wishes.

Khilafat organisations were also active in other ways. On the 21st of September the provincial committee resolved to select mujahidin for Angora, but it finally decided that money, not men, was required, and preachers were appointed to tour the districts in order to collect money. Large amounts were collected in October: Rs. 21,000 in Saharanpur, Rs. 8,400 in Agra and Rs. 3,000 at one meeting in Cawnpore. In November there were further large collections. New Khilafat committees were formed in various districts and Khilafat workers were enlisted.

On the 4th October the All-India Congress Working committee passed resolutions declaring the Karachi prosecutions to be an undue interference with religious liberty, authorising qualified civil disobedience by individuals, calling for a *hartal* on the arrival of the Prince of Wales, and declaring that the Government of India in no way represented Indian opinion. The leaders issued a manifesto calling on Government servants to resign their posts.

A direct challenge was now being offered to Government from almost every platform. Open sedition had replaced vituperation of Government. On the 1st of October at a meeting in Benares 1,000 signatures were taken on a declaration re-stating the Karachi resolution. It was also re-stated at the Tanda Khilafat conference on the 3rd October. On the 25th October Abul Kalam Azad, presiding at the provincial Khilafat conference at Agra, declared openly that one could make peace with snakes and scorpions, but not with the British. Resolutions on the lines laid down by the Congress Working committee were passed at district conferences and at the provincial conference on the 23rd and 24th October the audience of 5,000 people stood up by request and affirmed that it was sinful to serve Government. Speeches gradually became more bitter and more violent, especially in Saharanpur, Jhansi, Aligarh and parts of Oudh.

The income of the provincial Khilafat committee from the 1st April 1921 to the 1st October 1921 was Rs. 1,14,957 of which Rs. 26,660 was collected for the Smyrna fund and Rs. 45,000 for the Angora Government.

The growing embitterment of Muhammadan feeling in the autumn of 1921 gave place to enthusiasm when news of Mustafa Kemal's success over the Greeks was received. Attention was concentrated on making the Angora fund collections a success, and by the 6th December Rs. 35,000 had been remitted from these provinces. Further large sums were remitted in December, notably from Azamgarh, Benares and Lucknow; and in January 1922 at least Rs. 29,000 was collected on an Angora Day, half of the amount coming from Aligarh. In the first week of February about Rs. 65,000 was collected. A conference of *ulama* including at least seven prominent representatives of the United Provinces was held at Lahore from the 18th to the 20th of November. Service in the Police and Army was proclaimed to be sinful, but Shabbir Aḥmad of Deoband gave offence to the Hindus by stating in a speech that Muhammadans could not abandon cow-sacrifice. A committee of seven *ulama* was appointed a elect an *Amir-us-Shariat* for the whole of India. Some members of the committee duly met in Budaun but owing to differences of opinion the appointment was not made.

The action of the Congress with regard to the proscribed *fatwa* and the subsequent introduction of civil disobedience with regard to the Criminal Law Amendment Act strengthened the alliance between the Congress and Khilafat parties, though the Muhammadans appeared at first to be reluctant to take up a position of open defiance towards Government. Nevertheless one of the first acts of civil disobedience in the United Provinces was a violent speech delivered by one Ahmad Mukhtar at Meerut in defiance of an order under section 144, Criminal Procedure Code. In the middle of January the Central Khilafat committee appointed a working committee consisting of Hasrat Mohani, Abdul Majid, Suleiman Nadwi and Azad Subhani, all of the United Provinces, and Shaikh Haji Abdul Harun to act in consultation with Mr. Gandhi on the subject of civil disobedience. This committee was invested with practically all the powers of the central committee. Resolutions were passed by the committee congratulating the Egyptians on their struggle for independence, and arguing that the freedom of Egypt from non-Muslim control was essential for Khilafat purposes. Mr. Chotani announced that 25 lakhs of rupees had been collected for the Angora fund. From January onwards the Muhammadans may be said to have pulled their full weight in the civil disobedience campaign, notably at Bara Banki, where no fewer than 43 Khilafat committees had been formed and where the fanaticism of the local Muhammadans was a dangerous feature of the demonstrations.

The sudden suspension of civil disobedience in February was less welcome to them then to the Hindu agitators and in some quarters Mr. Gandhi was denounced in private as a traitor. The Cawnpore Khilafat committee decided to ask the central committee to carry on civil disobedience, irrespective of the Congress decision. The provincial Khilafat committee then ordered the cessation of all non-co-operation activities but explained a few days later that it had not meant to suspend agitation with regard to *swadeshi, panchayats* and educational institutions. At a meeting held on the 23rd of February it was resolved to bring pressure to bear on Mr. Gandhi with a view to the reversal of the Bardoli decisions. The state of mind of the Muhammadan agitators at this time was shown in a circular letter issued by the provincial committee to branch committees suggestion the separation with mutual good-will of the Congress and Khilafat organisations.

PART V. DECLINE OF KHILAFAT AGITATION (FEBRUARY TO DECEMBER 1922)

The hostility of the Muhammadan extremists to the Bardoli resolutions was one of the factors which led to the decision of the Delhi meetings of the 26th of February permitting individual civil disobedience. Nothing, however, could undo Bardoli, and from February onwards the Muhammadans may be said to have had but little share in the general non-co-operation agitation. The central Khilafat committee, it is true, made a show of working in accordance with the constructive programme of Mr. Gandhi but its efforts were faint-hearted and, as time advanced, were increasingly hampered by local disagreements between the Congress and Khilafat workers and by disagreements between the Khilafat workers themselves, while the cause also suffered from a growing and well-grounded suspicion that the Khilafat funds had been mishandled.

The publication in March of the memorandum of the Government of India supporting certain demands of the Muhammadans, while it led to the resignation of the Secretary of State, must have convinced a great many Muhammadans that the Government of India was a more powerful ally than Mr. Gandhi. It undoubtedly had a considerable effect in the United Provinces, though the extremists, particularly those of Cawnpore, were not led by it to regard with any favour the results of the Near East conference which were published at the beginning of April. In this connection a meeting of 4,000 persons was held at Cawnpore and Azad Subhani prophesied, not for the first time, that a time would come when violence would be resorted to. Some indignation was displayed at the attitude of Ajmal Khan and Dr. Ansari, who showed a disposition to accept certain modification of the Muhammadan demands. On the political side it must be remembered that the Muhammadan extremists of the United Provinces had little genuine leadership, their champions being Hasrat Mohani, a poet of Cawnpore, Moazzam Ali and Muhammad Husain, a barrister of indifferent standing. On the religious side they still had Abdul Bari, whose feelings on the subject of the Bardoli resolutions had recently betrayed him into violent incoherence, and Abdul Majid of Budaun who was constantly threatening *jihad.*

Hasrat Mohani was arrested in April on account of a seditious speech delivered in Bombay. His arrest provoked but one small and ineffective meeting of protest. During April and May there was little Khilafat agitation. The few meetings which were held drew small audiences. Azad Subhani of Cawnpore visited Madras to organise relief for the distressed Moplahs and he was reported to have preached contingent violence to the young men of that presidency. On his return from Madras he toured in the Oudh districts for the same purpose. In June a Khilafat meeting at Lucknow presided over by Moti Lal Nehru and addressed by such prominent speakers as Madan Mohan Malaviya, Sarojini Naidu and Abdul Majid, who was now vice-president of the Central Khilafat committee, attracted an audience of 800 people only. They were assured that the Bardoli decision was not a retreat but a prudent move. Abdul Majid condemned the proposed Turkish peace terms, and indignation was expressed at the appointment of a committee to investigate the alleged Turkish atrocities in Greece, and at the non-inclusion of Khilafat representatives in the commission. In July Azad Subhani presided at a meeting of the Jami'at-ul-Tulba (or students' association) at Lucknow. This meeting was very badly attended. Few big meeting were held between March and July, the most noticeable being one of 4,000 persons at Khurja in the Bulandshahar district in June when Mazhar-ud-din delivered a speech in which he described the Khilafat wrongs, the Punjab atrocities and the burden of slavery as the three sores of India. He said that the money earned by the posts, railways and other means was not used for the public good but was used to burn the covering of the Ka'aba, or was lent to the Greeks to enable them to burn mosques and to put Muhammadan women and children mercilessly to death.

But on the whole Khilafat agitation was at a very low ebb during this period and there seemed to be little prospect of a revival when Muhammad Husain, Masud Ali, Abdul Majid and T.A.K. Sherwani were selected by the Central Khilafat committee to serve on deputation with the Civil Disobedience Enquiry Committee. In July the Central Khilafat committee finding that the Angora fund alone was attracting any appreciable subscription decided to take one lakh from it for Khilafat purposes.

The Turkish victories over the Greeks in September occasioned considerable elation in the provinces and demonstrations took place for about a fortnight. The negotiations between the Allies and the Turks were followed with close attention. Several Khilafat conferences were held in conjunction with district conferences, and at some places dissatisfaction was expressed at the attitude of the British who were represented as withholding from the Turks the full fruits of their victory. Money came in freely for the Angora fund, the Saharanpur district alone giving Muhammad Ali's mother Rs. 11,500 in October. On the 14th of November six *ulama*, including Abdul Majid, Mazhar-ud-din and Muhammad Anwar Shah of the United Provinces issued a *fatwa* to the effect that the British had been most hostile to the Turks and helpful to their enemies and that it was religiously unlawful to assist them. The Mudania agreement had a soothing effect. The deposition of the Sultan was on the whole accepted calmly, the general disposition being not to question the actions of the Kemalists.

The report of the Civil Disobedience Enquiry committee caused much diversity of opinion, but the *ulama* opposed it steadily with a *fatwa* declaring entry into the councils to be *haram*. The Khilafat-Civil Disobedience Enquiry committee, six of seven members of which were residents of the United Provinces, submitted a report to the effect that the council entry controversy was premature.

PART VI. KHILAFAT AGITATION DIES OUT

The All-India Khilafat conference at Gaya passed resolutions threatening immediate civil disobedience in the event of war with Turkey, appealing for ten lakhs of rupees and fifty thousand volunteers within three months, and whittling down the boycott of courts by excepting cases involving serious issues.

The deadlock at Lausanne which had led to the talk of war at Gaya provoked intemperate and threatening speeches at Meerut, Bara Banki, Saharanpur and Bijnor and at small meetings elsewhere during January and February. A report which may be taken as indicative of the style of the stronger speeches at this time runs as follows:

> The mother of the Ali Brothers spoke to 10,000 people at Cawnpore on the 3rd February on the slackness of the country in 1857; had the people helped the army the 'traders' would never have become rulers of the country; sacrifice, fearlessness and unity were required in order to start civil disobedience for which volunteers and money should be collected; they should subscribe also to the national university as they could expect nothing from their king who was a murderer; no one had been hanged over the Punjab, Bareilly, Cawnpore and Moplah affairs but 172 men had been sentences to death in the Chauri Chaura case. ... The people would have to mix their blood with that of the Turks as well as to subscribe to funds.

The worst and happily the most infrequent type of speech is shown by the following extract from a report of a small meeting at Allahabad on the 15th February:

> ... Mohi-ud-din, ex-political convict of Allahabad, spoke of his endurance in the cause and appealed to Muhammadans to make sacrifices in the cause of Islam; he described Englishmen as monkeys, dogs, dishonest and cowards, and asked if it were not possible to kill or dispose of these two lakhs of English people to bring them to their senses so that the danger to Islam might be removed. He said 'if you will show me that by my annihilation the goal will be achieved, then by God, I am ready at this time to give up my life and take that of others;' he said he did not ask them to draw the sword (or to)

prepare bombs or guns, but they should be ready to come out when the *ulama* ordered *jihad.*

Most of the speeches on the possibility of war were delivered to congregations after prayers at the mosques. It was noticeable that lasting fervour was not aroused and it was not always easy to get an audience. Abdul Majid spoke in a carefully inflammatory way at a meeting in Budaun in January but though notices had been issued saying that war with Turkey was inevitable, the attendance was only 150.

The ladies of Muhammad Ali's family, however, touring as a Khilafat deputation with Abdul Majid of Budaun and T.A.K. Sherwani of Aligarh, drew large audiences in Bijnor, Saharanpur, Fatehgarh, Benares, Jaunpur, Ghazipur and Azamgarh. They collected for the Turkish aeroplane fund, about Rs. 3,000 in Bijnor, Rs. 5,000 in Saharanpur (where the town of Sakraoda furnished Rs. 3,600), Rs. 5,000 in Cawnpore, and about Rs. 600 at each of the smaller places.

Scarcely anything was done in the United Provinces to supply the provincial quota of Rs. 1,60,000 and 8,000 volunteers. In January the Central Khilafat committee met at Aligarh and appointed a working committee and three touring parties for the provinces; also two commissioners to enquire into the working and expenditure of the Khilafat Press at Bombay. The committee admitted its inability to provide funds for the National Muslim university any longer. This had been apparent for a considerable time. The provincial committees were instructed to support the university directly. There were now dissensions at many centres, and talk of peculation and embezzlement quickly closed the purses of the public. In March Dr. Alam's report on the unsatisfactory condition of the central Khilafat accounts (though it was said to have been prepared in the absence of the office superintendent and accountant and its accuracy was immediately denied) completed the undermining of public confidence in the Khilafat workers.

In the spring an attempt was made to revive the Muslim League. A meeting was held at Lucknow on the 31st March and 1st April. A resolution of Mr. Jinnah's recommending entry into the councils was rejected in the subjects committee meeting by 12 votes to 9. The public proceedings were interrupted at an early stage when Zahur Ahmad, a non-co-operating barrister of Allahabad, raised the objection that a full quorum of 75 *bona fide* members of the League were not present. The objection was upheld and the meeting was adjourned *sine die*.

There was little unanimity among the Muhammadans on the subject of standing for the municipal elections in March. A party headed by Salamat Ullah of Firangi Mahal was definitely opposed to it. The resultant paucity of the Muhammadan share in the general success of the extremists helped to weaken the alliance between the two great communities.

Salamat Ullah at this time resigned the presidentship of the Oudh Khilafat committee which had come to the end of its financial resources.

The arrival of the 'Khalifa's flag' in Meerut attracted little attention. The Muhammadans of the United Provinces were now alarmed by the Arya Samajist campaign, led by some of their former supporters, for the re-conversion to Hinduism of the Muhammadan Rajputs of Agra, and they gave but little indication of interest in foreign affairs until the end of July when the announcement of peace with Turkey was greeted with jubilant demonstrations. The extremists still tried to create discontent by pointing out that the Jazirat-ul-Arab had not been liberated from non-Muslim influence, but their efforts met with little success. They made a show of preserving the Khilafat organisation, but its lack of influence was clearly seen in December when the provincial Khilafat conference at Benares, with the prominent leaders Shaukat Ali, Azad Subhani, Husain Ahmad Madni, and Abdul Majid amongst the speakers, drew an attendance of 700 persons only. Agitation had reached its lowest point and it remained only for the Turkish leaders to stultify the whole movement by abolishing the Caliphate in March 1924. The Muhammadans of India then realised that their religious conservatism had been exploited in favour of a country in which conservative Islamic institutions had lost all their political power.

3

History of the Non-Co-operation and Khilafat Movements in the Central Provinces and Berar

1. The year 1919 opened in comparative calm. The people were exhausted after the effects of the combined visitations of influenza and the famine of 1918, and the situation was aggravated by high prices. Politically, the atmosphere was peaceful. Outside the educated classes and the professional agitators the population at large took little interest in politics. The news of the termination of the Great War was greeted with a spontaneous outburst of enthusiasm, and local celebrations were held everywhere, though a small section of the educated classes tried to induce the public not to participate.

2. The publication of the Rowlatt Bills in February 1919 roused a chorus of protest from the local press, and meetings were held at various centres in the Maratha country to urge that the bills be dropped. The elected members of the Provincial Legislative Council sent in a protest against them and commissioned Dr. Munji, an extremist leader of Nagpur, to forward it to the Viceroy. The people at large, however, took little notice of this agitation or of the *Satyagraha* that was started as a protest against the passing of the bills into the Rowlatt Act. The Maratha extremists also appeared to be generally lukewarm in their attitude towards the passive resistance movement, and the hostile attitude of Mr. G.S. Khaparde, the Berar leader, prevented the movement from making any headway in the province.

3. Concurrently with the agitation against the Rowlatt Bills, attempts were made from outside the province to organise meetings

amongst Mahomedans in connection with the fall of Constantinople. The local Mahomedans had not, however, begun to trouble themselves about the peace terms to be imposed on Turkey, and except in Chhindwara, where the Ali brothers were in internment, Mahomedan feeling was unperturbed.

4. Events outside the province moved with rapidity in the spring of 1919. The seriousness of the Delhi disturbances of the 30th March was overshadowed by the Jallianwala Bagh tragedy on the 13th April. The local press waxed bitter over the Rowlatt Act and moderate and extremist organs alike joined in protesting against the action of the authorities of Northern India 'in firing on unarmed and unoffending crowds'. The province as a whole was not, however, ruffled, and the political atmosphere was one of comparative calm in the remaining six months of the year. A few political agitators, notably W.G. Joshi, a fire-brand of Amraoti, carried on desultory speech-making in support of *Satyagraha* and during the Ganpati celebrations in September there was the usual orgy of political speeches. The apathy of the general public was exemplified by the fact that a meeting called at Nagpur on the 17th of August with the object of raising funds for the relief of the Punjab sufferers fell through for want of support. Nor was there any real feeling in the matter of the probable severity of the Turkish peace terms. The removal of the Ali brothers to the Betul Jail created no excitement even at Chhindwara, where their presence had been a disturbing element. The efforts of Maratha Brahmin extremists in the southern districts of the province to secure the observance of 'Khilafat Day' met with very little success, the Mahomedans as a rule holing aloof from the movement, or if they took part in it, insisting on watering down the draft resolutions sent from Bombay and Lucknow. Organised attempts were made by the extremists in many parts of the province, to induce people not to participate in the peace celebrations, the initiative coming, significantly enough, from Hindu extremists. The attempts met with a limited measure of success in a few places, but in the province as a whole the celebrations aroused enthusiasm, especially at Nagpur, thanks to the efforts of the local moderates led by Sir Bipin Bose.

5. During the first six months of 1920 the Khilafat agitation

outside the province evoked little response in the province. Attempts made from outside to induce the local Mahomedans to form a branch committee of the Khilafat were infructuous. At a meeting held at Nagpur on the 12th March which was addressed by Shaukat Ali on the invitation of the Hindu leaders, the Calcutta resolutions were reaffirmed, and although he undoubtedly stirred Mahomedan feeling, the Khilafat day, the 19th March, passed off without any untoward incident. Hartal was observed in most of the towns of the province, the completeness of this observance varying according to the activity of the local Hindu extremists. In the north of the province it was observed much less generally than in the south, although the former contains a larger proportion of Mahomedans. As a reaction from the worked up excitement of Khilafat day, the national week evoked little enthusiasm. A few poorly attended meetings were held in Nagpur, but the interest in the Turkish question appeared to be on the wane. Well aware that unless worked up from outside the local Mahomedan feeling on the Khilafat question was one of apathy, Government had all along pursued the policy of abstention from interference, and the expectation that the declaration of the Turkish peace terms would be received quietly in the province was justified when the terms were announced on the 14th May. Although the local Mahomedan leaders were lukewarm, manifestations of the activities of a few fire-brands were not wanting. A District Moslem League was formed at Jubbulpore by Tajuddin, an emissary of Dr. Ansari, and the Secretary of the Provincial Moslem League, and several Khilafat Committees came into existence. Shaukat Ali, who had come to the province to preside at the Raipur District Conference from the 12th to the 14th June, went away distinctly disappointed with the progress of the agitation and wrote reproaching the Nagpur leaders for the lukewarmness of the Central Provinces' Mahomedans. Many Mahomedans realised that the practical acceptance of the peace terms by the Sultan had put them in an awkward position, and there were indications that the Hindu extremists preferred a boycott of British goods to the forms of non-co-operation laid down by the Khilafat Committee.

6. Apart from the Khilafat agitation, the main political pre-occupation of the Hindu extremists during the last six months of 1920 was the coming elections in November and the preliminary

arrangements for the meeting of the Congress at Nagpur in December. They carried on an active propaganda in the form of pergana and district Conferences and electors were urged to vote only for candidates who accepted the full Congress resolutions. In marked contrast with the activity of the extremists was the inertia of the moderate leaders who made no effort in the way of organisation for the elections. Moreover, several of the politicians whose views were really moderate were afraid to break with the extremists as they recognised the difficulty of securing seats if the extremist organisations worked against them. Canvassing for the elections started in June and extremists dominated the meetings, the moderates contenting themselves with issuing an appeal to the electorate through the Central Provinces National Liberal Association to elect only those men who had faith in the Reforms and who were willing to work with them in the true spirit of co-operation.

7. In the meanwhile the non-co-operation programme was receiving the attention of the press. While the moderate organs dwelt on the absurdity of the non-co-operation movement, the extremist section appeared to find it difficult to grasp Gandhi's policy. Some of the extremist papers gave a vague support to the non-co-operation movement, but the leading paper of Nagpur definitely appealed to Gandhi to abandon his programme as impracticable and to substitute for it a boycott of British goods.

8. Such was the political situation in the provinces prior to the 1st August 1920, the date on which the non-co-operation campaign was formally launched. The 1st of August 1920 was also the date on which Tilak, whose personality and influence dominated the Maratha country, died. Tilak's death, occurring as it did on the evening before the hartal which was to inaugurate the non-co-operation campaign, completely overshadowed it. The manifestations of grief at his death were genuine and universal, and Mahomedans joined with Hindus at the meetings of condolence. His death removed the one influence that could have stemmed the tide of non-co-operation, at least in the Maratha country. It was however destined to revive and play an important part in the struggle between the discredited non-co-operation party and this school of obstructive co-operation that was to occur two years later.

9. For the time being, however, non-co-operation was in the

ascendant and was gradually espoused by the local extremists who had long been doubtful about its efficacy. This change of attitude was perhaps facilitated by the grant of independence to Egypt, which the extremist section of the press described as a triumph for the policy of systematic non-co-operation. The Central Provinces Provincial Congress Committee met on the 22nd August and passed a resolution accepting the principle of non-co-operation, but stipulating that for the time being Nagpur was only prepared to boycott British goods. At a special meeting subsequently called on the 25th August at the instance of the more advanced elements of the Committee to reconsider this decision, a resolution to bring the entire scheme of non-co-operation into force was put to the vote, but was lost. The three leading extremists of Nagpur Messrs. Munje, Alekar and Bobde announced their resolution not to stand for election, although this action was said to be due to a split in the extremist party. That non-co-operation in its extreme form did not receive whole-hearted support in the province at this stage was clear from the voting at the Special Congress at Calcutta, where the Central Provinces and Berar stood alone in providing majorities against Gandhi's resolutions. In the end, however, the extremist party accepted the mandate of the Congress and withdrew their candidature at the approaching elections. The visit of Mr. V.J. Patel to Nagpur at this juncture probably influenced the decision. The leaders subordinated their personal views to loyalty to the Congress in the hope that complete Home Rule would be achieved within one or two years of non-co-operation. There is no doubt, also, that the example of Egypt and Ireland considerably influenced extremist opinion. In the north of the Province the news of the success of the non-co-operation resolutions was received without enthusiasm, as it was felt that two items of the programme at any rate—the boycott of the Councils and the withdrawal of students from Government schools—were inexpedient.

10. The immediate manifestation of non-co-operation in the province was the withdrawal of extremist candidates from the forthcoming elections. The only leader of note who had the courage to dissent was Mr. Khaparde, who announced his decision to stand for the Council of State and who held out in spite of threats of

social boycott. Extremist opinion was strongly divided as regards the other forms of non-co-operation and there was much irresolution due to a belief that some alternation in the programme would result from the Nagpur Congress. A campaign of political meetings and lectures was organised in order to expound non-co-operation to the people, resulting in an outburst of violent talk. The extremist leaders toured the province to collect funds to meet the expenses of the Congress and with their appeals mingled denunciation of Government and advocacy of the doctrines of non-co-operation.

11. The progress of the movement was, however, slow. The pleader fraternity, with one or two exceptions, who relinquished practice to become paid itinerant preachers, fought shy of resigning practice, with the result that they lost much of their political power over the masses and the movement tended to fall into the hands of irresponsible mob-orators of no status. By December 1920 only about seven title-holders and half a dozen Honorary Magistrates had resigned their titles or posts and some of these had been forced to do so under threats of social boycott, a weapon the evil potency of which in the hands of the agitators began to be manifest at this juncture. Volunteer organisations known as Sewa Samitis and the Khilafat volunteers showed increased activity in a few districts, but not of such a nature as to give any grounds for alarm. At Nagpur some Khilafat volunteers picketed liquor-shops and were warned by Government against interfering with consumers. Some half a dozen arbitration courts were established at different centres, but did little work. There was no sign of serious trouble yet among college students and school-boys, although in November unrest developed among the schools at Jubbulpore. A few national schools were started, but an attempt to nationalise the Anjuman High School at Nagpur met with no success.

12. The elections for the Council were completed by the third week of November. More than half the number of constituencies were uncontested, and in all constituencies strong efforts were made to induce good candidates to withdraw and to persuade voters not to exercise their franchise. In many places dummy candidates were set up with the double object of opposing good candidates and of facilitating their substitution by extremist leaders in the event of the

Congress rescinding the non-co-operation resolution. The voting in the urban areas was undoubtedly affected by the non-co-operation movement; in the Nagpur-Kamptee constituency, for instance, only 25 per cent of those on the roll voted. In the rural constituencies there were probably large abstentions due to the same cause, but here the exact effects were more difficult to gauge. On the whole the boycott of the Councils was more successful in the province than was thought to be probable.

13. The situation prior to the Nagpur Congress may be characterised as one of suspense. The attitude of Government was one of watchfulness. In accordance with instructions received from the Government of India and in anticipation of some modifications of the non-co-operation programme in the Nagpur Congress, Government had so far pursued a policy of non-interference. The only political prosecution undertaken was that of Tajuddin, a firebrand journalist of Jubbulpore and the editor of the *Taj*, for a particularly dangerous article, under section 153-A of the Indian Penal Code. The position was however full of evil potentialities which awaited a lead from the Congress to materialise. A spirit of unrest was abroad. The infection was spreading on the one hand to immature school-boys, and, on the other, to the rural population, now faced with the prospect of a serious deterioration of the crops owing to the premature retirement of the monsoon.

14. The Congress passed off peacefully, save for an affray in the Bengal Camp, resulting in injuries to about fifteen delegates. The outstanding feature of the Congress was the personal domination of Gandhi over all political leaders and followers alike. He carried through the policy that he had decided for the Congress without any material modification. All opposition to his views was overcome owing to his stronghold over the bulk of the delegates and visitors, with whom his word was law. Direct opponents of non-co-operation were all silenced without difficulty. Gandhi made some concessions to opposition in regard to certain details of the non-co-operation programme by whittling down the boycott of schools and the surrender of practice by lawyers. The moderates were not heard and the extremist opponents under Mr. Khaparde and Dr. Munje were brushed aside. A striking proof of Gandhi's power was the change

in the presidential address, which as printed had contained views opposed to Gandhi's in several respects. In the Subjects Committee there was considerable opposition to the change in creed as formulated by Gandhi, *viz.*, 'the attainment of Swaraj by the people of India by all legitimate and peaceful means', but those who, like Messrs. Das, Pal and Malaviya, favoured the retention of the British connection, as well as those who, like the Ali brothers, made violent proposals in favour of complete independence were overruled. The Congress resolution for the organisation of Committees of propaganda in all districts, towns and tahsils foreshadowed an intensive propaganda throughout the length and breadth of the province.

15. The Moslem League and Khilafat Conferences came into line with the Congress and passed the usual resolutions. Of the other conferences—for no less than 17 different bodies held their conferences at Nagpur during the Christmas of 1920—that of the depressed classes was of some interest. At this conference the leading Mahar explained that his community was opposed to the policy of non-co-operation, but if Gandhi could induce the higher castes to remove the ban of untouchability, he would earn the dignity of Mahatma even among Mahars. Gandhi in reply suggested the non-co-operation of Mahars with the higher castes by refusing to serve them in any way till they were admitted to equality.

16. Gandhi and the Ali brothers left Nagpur on the 8th January. Before his departure Gandhi addressed a meeting of students and schoolboys in the Congress pandal on the subject of national education. The Ali brothers addressed several meetings at Nagpur, Seoni and Jubbulpore before they left, at which Mahomed Ali was conspicuous for the violence of his language. The result of the intensive propaganda pursued prior to and after the Congress was to familiarise the masses in the towns and in the larger villages with the idea of non-co-operation, and the political situation rapidly became worse. The Mahomedans were roused to a considerable state of excitement. The attitude of defiance to the authority of Government servants which was hitherto latent now became pronounced. Petty local grievances were magnified. Every possible difficulty was placed in the way of touring Government officials,

who found it difficult to obtain supplies, labour and means of transport. A good deal of pressure was exercised upon members of the Legislative Council, holders of titles and Honorary Magistrates to induce them to resign their seats, titles or offices. The knowledge that Government had decided to depart from the policy of non-interference pursued so far and to institute prosecutions for seditious speeches or speeches inciting to violence produced a certain amount of moderation, but the gospel of non-co-operation was preached all the same all over the province. By the middle of February 33 legal practitioners (out of a total of 903 [?] for the province) had withdrawn from practice in order to devote themselves to the cause of non-co-operation; three members of the Legislative Council resigned their seats, eight title-holders their titles and about a dozen Honorary Magistrates their offices. Arbitration Courts and Panchayats multiplied and there was a considerable development of volunteer organisations. The effect of the propaganda on schools and colleges was, for the time being disastrous. Students were told that their services were required by their country for carrying on a propaganda for Swaraj in the villages, and the news of the action of the Calcutta students gave strength to the attack. But perhaps the most serious effect of the non-co-operation movement was in a direction not anticipated by the originator of the movement, *viz.*, that of anti-liquor agitation. In order to give a correct idea of the extent to which non-co-operation affected the province during the six or seven months following the Nagpur Congress, it is necessary to describe in some detail its more important developments.

NON-CO-OPERATION AND EDUCATION

17. During the early part of the academic year 1920-21 there had been a certain amount of unrest among the students, which had manifested itself in spasmodic outbreaks of indiscipline, but the first direct effect of non-co-operation was seen in Jubbulpore in November 1920, when a number of students left the local high schools. No greater headway had, however, been made till the Congress meeting and the concurrent meetings of the All-India Students' Conferences. The definite adoption of the boycott of all

Government and Government-recognised educational institutions by both these bodies had an immediate effect. There were many absentees from the Nagpur schools and colleges when they reopened after the Christmas vacation and withdrawals continued almost daily during the whole of January. The vocational institutions, *viz.*, the Engineering and Medical Schools and the Agricultural College did not escape, but they recovered later and by the end of March 1921 had a better attendance than the two Arts colleges at Nagpur. During February and March students continued to dribble away from the Nagpur institutions: by the end of March the Neill City High School had only 150 students on the roll against nearly 600 at the beginning of January. The boycott of colleges in Calcutta in the beginning of February was reflected in the strengthening of the movement and the disturbances at Nagpur, to be referred to later, also affected the Nagpur institutions. The efforts of the non-co-operators in Jubbulpore were to a great extent concentrated on the Hitkarni High School, whose managing body, the Hitkarni Sabha, resolved in February to nationalise the school and its branches. The Jubbulpore colleges and some of the other Jubbulpore schools were affected early, but the position got no worse and in one or two cases even improved. Outside the large towns the movement spread more gradually. Schools in nearly all the towns in the Nagpur and Berar divisions were affected during the latter part of January and during February, English schools being affected worse than Vernacular schools. Village schools were affected in certain districts, but on the whole escaped much more lightly than town schools.

18. No educational significance could be attached to this exodus from the schools. The disapproval by non-co-operation leaders of the Government system of education was an afterthought. In the early days after the Congress meeting when nearly all students were inoculated with the non-co-operation virus many of the best students joined the movement. Later, when patriotic ardour had cooled and there was time for reflection, there was a marked tendency for the better type of students to stay and for the inferior to leave. There was an equally marked tendency for students who were to appear at University examinations in 1921 to continue their studies. Another feature was the greater success of the movement among the sons of

illiterate and backward parents than among those of educated parents, and also its success in some of the more backward parts of the province such as the Chhatisgarh division. Economics as well as political causes contributed to the decline in attendance at schools and colleges. The students most affected were those who or whose parents desired their education to be as cheap as possible. The attitude of parents towards the movement was on the whole distinctly unfavourable. The inspecting and teaching staff behaved well under extremely trying circumstances and the movement would have made much greater headway but for their exertions. Only 12 teachers in Government Anglo-Vernacular or Normal schools, 12 teachers in aided Anglo-Vernacular schools, and 22 primary school teachers either resigned or had their services dispensed with for reasons connected with the movement.

19. The general effect of the movement on the discipline was slight. In colleges work continued in spite of unrest and severe pressure from outside. In certain cases the collateral activities of student life suffered from the apathy of reaction, but the actual damage done to college discipline was small. A certain amount of deterioration in manners, dress and general deportment was also noticeable. On the other hand, some intellectual improvement was visible in some schools as a result of the desertion of the weaker students. It was significant that the High School entrance examination results showed a marked improvement on those of former years.

20. A large number of 'national' schools sprang into existence within the six months after the Congress meeting and at the close of April 1921 some 38 Anglo-Vernacular schools and 85 Vernacular schools had been established. As in the case of the non-co-operation students, numbers were by far the greatest in the Nagpur Circle. Most of the boys who left the schools in Nagpur City joined the Tilak Mahavidyalaya High School, which had about 1,000 pupils and 20 teachers. The staff consisted of pleaders, who had suspended practice or failed to obtain any, or non-co-operating students from colleges and secondary schools. In most of the schools the courses prescribed were the same as in recognised schools, but lectures on politics and classes in spinning were generally arranged. National

songs were taught and in some, *e.g.*, the Nagpur Asahyog Ashram, students were put through an intensive training for propaganda work. Discipline and organisation were conspicuous by their absence; accommodation and equipment were of the poorest; and regular teaching hardly took place. None was based on a secure financial foundation and almost all led a hand-to-mouth existence on funds raised by subscriptions. Run by amateurs on unbusinesslike lines and with no definite educational purpose they were doomed to failure and the attempts to start and maintain these national schools could only be described as pathetic.

THE ANTI-LIQUOR MOVEMENT

21. The combination of industrial and agricultural distress at the close of the year 1920 facilitated the agitation against the consumption of liquor. Non-co-operation first came into serious contact with the excise department in September 1920, when the adherents of a temperance movement in the Nimar district sought to enforce temperance by the picketing of liquor shops and assault on the consumers. The movement received an impetus from the Nagpur Congress, and the picketing of liquor-shops which had begun just before the Congress met was renewed with vigour and in some cases with violence. Individual consumers and sellers were assaulted, insulted or intimidated. Some shops were burnt and some liquor contractors' houses were defiled. Excise consumption was already on the decline on account of the *Sisghast* [?] synchronising with the early indications of a crop failure, and the non-co-operators congratulated themselves on a facile victory. A further field for this activity was provided by the public excise auctions held in January and February to dispose of shops for the year 1921-22. The Raipur district sales were stopped by a body of hooligans from the town. In Nagpur the auctions were accompanied by a riot, followed a month later by a more serious disturbance in which nine men were killed. Auctions had also to be abandoned at Durg, Bhandara, Nimar, Hoshangabad, Damoh and Seoni and were a partial failure at Balaghat, Chhindwara, Betul, Nagpur and Jubbulpore. By this time it became apparent that the working of the excise department

depended upon the exercise by Government of its primary function of maintaining law and order. Prompt action to suppress any further tendency towards intimidation, violence and arson was taken in a number of districts both by prosecution under the Penal Code and by utilising the preventive sections of the Criminal Procedure Code. An improvement at once became visible, which was maintained steadily throughout the last quarter of the excise year 1920. Economic depression remained, but political aggravation weakened.

22. A significant feature of the movement was that the consumers and the sellers of liquor only were attacked. Consumers or purveyors of solid intoxicants were not molested. The instigators of the anti-drink campaign were primarily influenced by the consideration that only alcohol and fermented liquor are proscribed by the Hindu Shastras. The use of opium and hemp drugs or even of intoxicating drinks made from the latter is no offence to the most orthodox Hindu. Besides, the bulk of Government revenue came from liquor, and drink was a European habit. Therefore, from the point of view of arousing religious and racial prejudice and of causing the maximum loss to Government with the minimum disturbance of the social habits of the literate classes, whose support was essential to success, expediency pointed to an anti-liquor campaign.

23. The influence of non-co-operation in keeping people from intoxicants was small as compared with the influence of economic causes such as scarcity and high prices. The decline in Berar was no greater than in the adjoining areas of the Hyderabad State where non-co-operation had no hold at all.

24. In spite of its intemperate aims and intemperate methods, the political crusade against liquor drew strength from two respectable sources, *viz.*, (i) the religious prejudice both among Hindus and Mahomedans in favour of total abstinence, and (ii) the social aspirations of the backward classes. But the non-co-operators employed dishonest methods. They taught the people that distillery liquor was filthily polluted; the Gonds of Mandla were urged on this ground to get their liquor from the outstills or by illicit distillation. Elsewhere people were told that if they held out and won *Swaraj* they would be allowed free distillation as in 'the good old days'. A propaganda which rested on misrepresentation for its

support was foredoomed to failure, and with the return of normal conditions the futility of intimidation and deception as factors in social progress became apparent.

25. This general account of the effects of non-co-operation on the administration of the excise department during the first six months of the year 1920 would be incomplete without some reference to the two Nagpur disturbances. Details of the first disturbance on the 23rd February are contained in the local Government's Press Communiqués, dated 28th February 1921, and the 9th March 1921, and those regarding the second on the 23rd March, in the Press Communiqués, dated the 29th March 1921, and the 1st April 1921 and in the report of the Committee appointed to enquire into the firing on the 28th March, together with the Resolution on the report published in the *Central Provinces Gazette* (extraordinary), dated the 23rd March 1921.

26. On the 21st February the District Magistrate, Nagpur, issued an order under Section 144 of the Criminal Procedure Code restraining the general public of Nagpur from obstructing and annoying persons lawfully resorting to liquor-shops. One of the principal leaders of the movement, Dr. Paranjpe, was also served with an order to refrain from inciting to picketing and other interference. On the 22nd Dr. Cholkar, a medical practitioner and Vice-President of the Nagpur Municipal Committee, was arrested by a warrant under Section 124-A and 153-A of the Penal Code on account of a speech made by him at a public meeting at Nagpur some short time previously. The district excise auctions were fixed for the 23rd. On the 22nd a large meeting had been held in the town and there had been some excitement, chiefly on the part of youths and schoolboys, over the trial of two Mahomedan volunteers for assaulting a native Christian returning from a liquor-shop. On the 23rd a hartal was observed in the city and a meeting in connection with the anti-liquor movement was held by its leaders in a bungalow close to the District Court. A crowd of about 5,000 people collected at the place where the sales were held and on the adjoining roads and a riot soon started. Excise contractors who had bid at the sales were attacked by the mob, and stone-throwing was freely indulged in, during the course of which the District Magistrate

was hit. The Civil Surgeon who happened to drive into the middle of the crowd on his way to his office was heavily stoned, but fortunately received no serious injuries and was rescued by the police. The crowd was pushed back gradually by the available police force and eventually dispersed towards the city. Their attitude was defiant, but no further collision with the police took place. Seven policemen and two European officers were injured in the stone-throwing and one of the crowd had his leg broken by being knocked down by a police sawar. The military had to be called in to preserve the peace of the city and an order prohibiting meetings in the municipal area for a period of one month was issued by the District Magistrate.

27. During this period matters appeared to have quieted down. The term of the District Magistrate's order prohibiting public meetings expired on the 23rd March 1921, and on the next day meetings began to be held where speeches were made in support of the temperance movement. The excise sales which had been interrupted on account of the riot on the 23rd February were fixed for the 30th March. On the night of the 29th March a mob collected in Nagpur City and looted some liquor-shops, burning their contents. A police force dispersed the mob and effected thirty arrests. The following morning a European Magistrate with a force of 25 armed and about 15 unarmed police proceeded to the quarter inhabited by Koshtis (weavers) in order to effect the arrest of other individuals accused of taking part in the riot. They made a few arrests, when they were attacked by a large mob with sticks and stones and two arrested persons in their charge were rescued. The crowd grew more and more threatening. Warnings had no effect and ultimately the Magistrate ordered fire in self-defence. In the collision nine men from the crowd died and several were injured. On the side of the police, one constable died, a Sub-Inspector of Police and four policemen were seriously injured and about 20 others suffered more or less severe injuries. A small police party which was proceeding on the road back to the City Police Kotwali was also followed and stoned heavily by the mob. Some individual shots were fired to keep back the mob, but no casualties occurred. A small police guard at the tahsil building was also beaten by the mob. Military had again to be requisitioned to preserve peace, and on the

31st March the District Magistrate passed an order prohibiting meetings and assemblies in Nagpur and within a radius of ten miles for a period of two months.

28. It was a significant commentary on the non-violent nature of the non-co-operation propaganda that the looting of liquor-shops started a week after Gandhi's visit to Nagpur, where he addressed a large meeting, condemned the previous riot and exhorted the people to avoid violence.

29. A committee consisting of an Indian Judge of the Judicial Commissioner's Court, a Commissioner and an Indian Advocate of the Judicial Commissioner's Court made a thorough enquiry into the circumstances of the riot and in their report fully endorsed the action taken by the Magistrate and the police. A rival committee was set up by the Provincial Congress Committee, who decided that in accordance with the principles of non-co-operation people should neither recognise nor give evidence before the Government Committee. The Congress Committee was presided over by Mr. Baptista of Bombay and took some evidence, a good deal of which was deliberately manufactured by the local non-co-operators. The report issued by the Committee was palpably one-sided and attracted very little notice.

THE VOLUNTEER MOVEMENT

30. Prior to non-co-operation, the volunteer movement in the province was of comparatively recent origin. A few Sewa Samitis were started in 1917 with the object of performing various kinds of social service such as attendance on the sick, and the widespread influenza epidemic of 1918 gave the movement a considerable impetus. In 1919 the activities of the United Provinces volunteers at the Kumbh Mela at Allahabad attracted notice in the north of the province, where various societies were formed on the United Provinces model. The *Gaorakshana* movement in connection with the Ratona tannery scheme and the Saugor slaughter-houses was also responsible for the formation of a number of societies in the Saugor, Damoh, Hoshangabad, Khandwa and Narsinghpur districts.

31. Sewa Samiti volunteers had on occasion rendered useful help to the public at fairs and similar gatherings and had also done

valuable work during epidemics. With the spread of the non-co-operation cult, however, the societies lost their distinctive character as social service organisations and came under the control of the extremist party. Several formed in 1920 added to their objects some such aims as 'to spread political education' and 'to work for Swaraj'. Members of the societies were prominent at political gatherings and on the arrival and departure of political agitators helped to organise hartals. Another development of the movement was the formation of National volunteer corps in one or two districts for the definite purpose of rendering assistance at political meetings.

32. In the Mahomedan community two organisations (the Khilafat volunteers and the Namaj [!] volunteers) came into existence as the outcome of the Khilafat agitation and the Mahomedan revival. Only in Nagpur where 50 youths were drilled by a demobilised sepoy, was there any real attempt at organising the Khilafat volunteers. The principal duty of the Namaj volunteers was to keep the faithful in the straight path of religious duty and one of their favourite activities was the picketing of liquor-shops and forcible interference with Mahomedan drinkers.

33. All classes of volunteers wore some distinguishing badge or sash and carried sticks. Uniforms were scarce, though most 'officers' had something approaching a uniform with a Sam Brown belt. Only in Nagpur, Akola and Jubbulpore were drill parades at all regular. The majority of the volunteers were drawn from the student class.

34. The movement never developed in the province to the extent of causing any anxiety regarding the maintenance of peace. The organisation was extremely loose. Grandiloquent schemes were advocated from time to time, but little practical progress was made. Volunteers made public appearances at all fairs, conferences, public meetings, processions of popular leaders and similar functions. On special occasions the local volunteer corps was invariably swelled by temporary enlistment. At public meetings and conferences volunteers made their own arrangements. During processions they endeavoured to deal with traffic, an activity which involved them in minor collisions with the police. At the end of 1920 the idea of employing volunteers on police duties was openly mooted by public speakers. In certain districts, notably Jubbulpore, Mandla and Nagpur more

definite attempts were made in this direction. In February 1921 at a village in Amraoti district a National Police Station complete with staff and a National Tahsildar was appointed, but never functioned, and generally, anything definite in the way of a National Police Force failed to materialise. In several districts local Sewa Samitis interfered with police investigations. In Berar the movement to change the site of weekly bazaars with a view to avoid the payment of bazaar dues brought volunteers into conflict with the police. Other forms of activities in which volunteers indulged were in connection with the cow-protection movement, the 'national' cattle-pounds [!] and the arbitration and Panchayat courts.

NON-CO-OPERATION AND THE LAW COURTS

35. Mention has already been made above of the general disinclination of pleaders to resign their practice. It is computed that the maximum number of pleaders who suspended practice for reasons connected with non-co-operation was 93, *i.e.* a little over 10 per cent of the total number of legal practitioners in the province. Many more made open profession of their political faith, although continuing practice, by wearing the Gandhi cap in courts, an action of which Government, in consultation with the Judicial Commissioner, decided to take no notice. The desirability of taking steps against non-co-operating pleaders was carefully considered by Government, but as the decline of the movement became apparent by the middle of 1921, the matter was dropped. Most of those who had withdrawn from practice resumed it towards the end of the year or the beginning of the next.

36. The attempt to establish national institutions for dispensing justice was a dismal failure. In the Jubbulpore, Nerbudda and Berar divisions the numerous arbitration courts and panchayats that came into being were either still-born or ceased to exist after showing some faint signs of activity. In the Chhatisgarh division the only real working non-co-operation Panchayat court was that at Raipur, which had 14 quorums each presided over by a pleader. This court made no attempt at enforcing decrees or penalties. A few courts in the Nagpur division transacted a certain amount of business. There

was a Panchayat court at Nagpur, promoted by Dr. Munje, Dr. Cholkar, Mr. W.G. Joshi and non-co-operating members of the local bar, which decided a few petty civil cases. There was another court started at Nagpur, ostensibly for deciding suits by private arbitration, but really as a formal court for hearing original cases as well as appeals from the Panchayats, but it transacted no business. In the Wardha district, where the non-co-operation movement prevailed in an accentuated form owing to the presence of Seth Jamnalal, a leading disciple of Gandhi, about 16 arbitration courts came into existence. The court at Wardha met at Seth Jamnalal's house and was an appellate court, presided over by three legal practitioners and a few merchants. The court at Arvi (a tahsil headquarters in the Wardha district) presided over by 30 panchas, five of whom were pleaders, was perhaps the most active court in the province. By the end of August 1921 it had taken on its file some 141 Civil cases, including rent-suits, of which 130 were decided. The highest money-value dealt with was Rs. 2,000. These arbitration courts wisely refrained, as a rule, from meddling with the Criminal Law. As dispensers of Civil justice they had little influence in the absence of power to enforce decrees. In most places the courts were self-elected and inspired no confidence and by the middle of 1921 most of them had ceased to function.

RESIGNATIONS

37. Altogether about 33 Government servants in the Central Provinces and Berar resigned their posts on political grounds in the year 1921. Among these were one Police Inspector, three Sub-Inspectors of Police, six Head Constables, four Constables and seven Clerks, eight Teachers, one Deputy Ranger of Forest and three others. The number of Honorary Magistrates (out of a total of about 410 in the province) who resigned their seats was 29 out of whom 7 were Mahomedans. Nine title-holders (out of nearly 200 holders of Indian titles conferred by Government) renounced their titles, between September 1920 and March 1921, and about 23 persons resigned their seats in the Central Provinces Legislative Council, their durbar seats and other miscellaneous offices.

38. The general survey of events during the first six months of the year 1921 may now be resumed. The arrest of W.G. Joshi on the 28th March, led to a demonstration at Amraoti by a crowd consisting mostly of youths who broke open a liquor-shop and did about Rs. 1,500 worth of damage, but dispersed immediately on the appearance of the police. In the same month Bhagwandin, a favourite disciple of Gandhi, who had conferred on him the title of Mahatma, was sentenced to 18 months' rigorous imprisonment at Seoni under Section 124-A of the Indian Penal Code. Gandhi arrived in the province on the 17th March and visited the districts of Wardha, Nagpur, Amraoti, Seoni and Jubbulpore. He made the usual speeches, promising Swaraj in seven months, provided no violence was used and no Indians wore foreign cloth. He also expressed disapproval of the practice of social boycott. His main interest lay in collecting money for the Tilak Memorial Fund, in which he was fairly successful. His visit stimulated the non-co-operation movement in the Wardha district and elsewhere, but by the end of March there were distinct signs of reaction among the more sober elements of society. The prosecution of some of the principal orators had also a moderating effect. Arjunlal Sethi, a virulent agitator, was sentenced under Section 124-A and Section 153-A, Indian Penal Code, to one year's rigorous imprisonment on each count. W.G. Joshi, who had been a very mischievous influence in Berar, was convicted under Section 124-A and sentenced to 18 months' rigorous imprisonment. Sundarlal, the editor of the Allahabad paper, *Bhavishya*, was sentenced at Wardha under Section 124-A, Indian Penal Code, to one year's rigorous imprisonment. In a few other cases prosecutions were instituted under Sections 124-A and 153-A, Indian Penal Code, and extensive use was made of the preventive sections of the Criminal Procedure Code. By the middle of 1921 altogether 9 prosecutions under Sections 124-A and 153-A, Indian Penal Code, and 13 under Section 108, Criminal Procedure Code, had been instituted, as a result of which six persons were sentenced to periods of imprisonment and four were bound over. In addition 35 orders under Section 144, Criminal Procedure Code, were passed at various times. Prosecutions against volunteer pickets under the ordinary sections of the law were most useful and the measures taken led to a distinct improvement in the towns.

39. The lesson of the Nagpur riots, which showed how quickly a mob gets out of hand, was not altogether lost on the local non-co-operation leaders. No violence of any magnitude took place during the four months from April to July. The hartal of the 6th and 13th April passed off peacefully on the whole. A few minor incidents in the Bhandara district and some grain dacoities in Berar made it clear that the non-co-operation movement had affected the masses in town mainly on account of the unfavourable economic conditions. In the districts, the agriculturists, busy in preparing their fields for the monsoon, ceased to attend public meetings and moreover a change in attitude towards the Government took place as a result of the famine relief measures, particularly in Berar. The suspension of land revenue, the relief works and especially, the distribution of *taccavi* on a liberal scale convinced the people that the Government was their best friend, while the non-co-operation movement had done nothing for them. The firm attitude of Government heartened the moderates, who had bowed their head to the storm, and a Liberal League was successfully launched at Saugor in June. In Berar the anti-Brahmin agitation among the Mahars, under the auspices of *Satya-Shodhak* organisations, further weakened the non-co-operation movement. People were also getting tired of paying subscriptions for the various national causes and in spite of the efforts of itinerant agitators, appeals at public meetings and house-to-house visits collections for the Swarajyya Fund were disappointing, although the enrolment of members for the Congress was fairly large. In the extremist camp itself signs of differences began to be manifest. The breach between the non-co-operation pleaders who had not resigned their practice and the rest of the party widened and it was significant that one of the resolutions passed at the Central Provinces Provisional Conference at Jubbulpore between the 13th and 17th May was that practising lawyers should not be elected to any office in Congress Committees. Further, there were signs of scepticism in the Maratha country, which had never been whole-heartedly in favour of Gandhi's policy.

40. By the beginning of July the cumulative effect of all these causes of decline became apparent. Arbitration courts ceased to function. The *charkha* movement, which had always been a failure,

made no advance. The numbers of boys in schools and colleges rapidly recovered, the recovery being more complete in Government schools and colleges than in private and municipal institutions. National schools in a few towns had still a fair number of students, but in most places they collapsed through financial difficulties or lack of organisation. In the excise department the crisis had already been passed in April 1921. The leaders were piqued at the readiness with which the vendor class had taken up excise contracts. They had hoped that the disturbances at the auctions would paralyse the department and vented their spleen on individual licensees. Liquor consignments were stolen, prospective purchasers were kept from the shops by intimidation, 'peaceful' pickets consisting not infrequently of hired *badmashes* were established, house-owners were induced to refuse contractors sites for their shops, Kalars were socially boycotted and so forth. The rank and file however showed a characteristic infirmity of purpose and before six months of the new excise year (April 1921 to 31st March 1922) were over, non-co-operation was a spent force as a disturbing element in the administration of the excise department. In the succeeding months the temperance campaign was pursued spasmodically and half-hearted picketing was carried on in a few centres. A few local bodies lent it their support and it received a temporary stimulus from the arrest of the Ali brothers in September, but for the general public it had lost its interest. One of the effects of the campaign was an outbreak of illicit distillation on an extensive scale in certain of the Satpura districts, where the Gonds had been advised not to use Government liquor.

41. The general political situation in the last six months of the year 1921 was marked by a growing split between the Tilak and Gandhi schools of thought. The first open rupture took place at the Maharashtra Conference at Akola on the 1st December, which was followed by a Conference of the Central Provinces and Berar Marathi-speaking districts on the 2nd and 3rd. The most important resolution passed by the Conference was in favour of a policy of 'obstructive co-operation' to replace Gandhi's original programme. The failure of that programme was generally admitted and many of the items came in for scathing comment. Boycott of schools, law-

courts, and Councils did not find a place in the new programme, the most important item of which was the decision to oppose Government in a constitutional way through the Councils. The revolt against Gandhi's supremacy did not however meet with universal approval and public meetings were immediately held in Nagpur and Akola to protest against any change in his programme. The repressive action taken in other provinces temporarily checked the revolt against Gandhi's doctrines and the Nagpur leaders returned to their original support of the Gandhian programme.

42. Mahomedan feeling was quiet at the beginning of this period, and the arrest of the Ali brothers on the 17th September caused little excitement. Meetings of protest and processions were held at a few centres, but the attempts made in some places to organise hartals met with a half-hearted response. The Muharram celebrations naturally evoked a certain amount of political oratory, and it became necessary to take action under the preventive sections of the Criminal Procedure Code against a few speakers who exceeded the bounds of moderation. At meetings held to condemn the arrest of the Ali brothers audiences were called upon to re-affirm the Karachi resolutions and the speeches made there roused an under-current of excitement in some Mahomedan centres. Little was however done to give effect to the Karachi resolutions. The only resignations that could be attributed to the Gandhi manifesto were those of a Mahomedan head constable and two clerks. With the arrival of the open season the number of meetings increased. The speeches took on a more definite religious tone, the proscribed *fatwa* was freely circulated. The agitation undoubtedly created a feeling of bitterness among the Mahomedan community. They were stirred by the confiscation of the *fatwa* and also by the speeches of Mahomed Ali at the Karachi trials, while agitators sedulously strove to create an impression that Government was hostile to their community. A conference of Jamiat-ul-Ulemas [!] held at Raipur on December 20th and 21st was broken up on the seizure by the police of copies of the proscribed *fatwa* which were being circulated at the meeting on the 21st. The action taken in other provinces under Part II of the Criminal Law Amendment Act, 1908, and the consequent wholesale

arrests added to the excitement and gave some impetus to Khilafat volunteer recruitment.

43. The main political activity during this period was in the direction of the boycott of foreign cloth. In August meetings were held to advocate the boycott and efforts made to persuade merchants and the public to sign a pledge neither to trade in nor to use foreign cloth. A demonstration at Nagpur on the 1st August to give a fillip to the movement was a failure. In some places merchants were persuaded to promise not to trade in foreign cloth when their existing stock was sold. A few Swadeshi shops were opened, but the rise in the price of this cloth was an obstacle in the way of progress and made people sceptical. The President of one Municipal Committee passed an order that the masters and students of municipal schools should wear only Swadeshi cloth. There was a substantial increase in the number of wearers of Gandhi caps, and in some towns of *khadi* cloth. The Hindustani Central Provinces Congress Committee held at Raipur on the 24th of August voted Rs. 25,000 for an industrial school at Burhanpur, and also sums varying from Rs. 2,000 to Rs. 6,000 to districts for the encouragement of handweaving. The movement for the complete boycott of foreign cloth, however, made little headway. Merchants who had large stocks agreed not to buy any more, but no merchant agreed to burn his stock or get rid of it in any but the ordinary way. Picketing of cloth-shops was started in a few places and it was understood that the Congress Committee had allotted a sum of Rs. 500 for forming a Volunteer corps for Swadeshi propaganda. Picketing was however a failure, once the shopkeepers had received an assurance that Government would deal strictly with any indications of violence. On the whole there was little public opinion behind the movement. The request of the Provincial Congress Committee that local bodies should insist on their servants wearing *khadi* was not taken seriously. The *khadi* cloth was also becoming unpopular as it took much washing to make it look decent, which counteracted its cheapness. Indeed in Berar some of the merchants were towards the end of October said to be laying in large stocks of foreign cloth in anticipation of good business owing to the excellent cotton crop.

44. Civil disobedience made little progress in the province. A meeting of the Provincial Congress Committee was held in November 1921 where the Delhi resolutions were upheld. There was much discussion regarding civil disobedience, but it was decided to take no action till the result of Gandhi's measures in Gujerat was known and till the matter was considered by the general Maharashtra Conference. In the Wardha district, where Seth Jamnalal had considerable influence, some activity was shown in enlisting volunteers for the scheme. The news of the Bombay riots, however, spread consternation in the extremist ranks and although the Hindi District Congress Committee selected the Saugor district for the first experiment in civil disobedience, the Saugor party itself was anxious for the honour to be transferred to some other district. Three tahsils were selected by the Provincial Congress Committee for the inauguration of civil disobedience, but in each case the local representatives opposed a trial in their districts, declaring that the conditions were not fulfilled. It became apparent towards the end of the year that an appeal for civil disobedience would not meet with much response in the province.

45. Throughout the latter part of 1921 the visit of the Prince of Wales was a subject of carping criticism in the press and on the platform, the expense of the visit being made a special point of attack. Propaganda for the boycott of the visit started in October and the Provincial Congress Committee issued instructions for a general hartal on the 17th November, the date of His Royal Highness' arrival in India. The hartal, though not uniformly successful throughout the province, was, on the whole, more effective than any previous one. The effect was however secured by means of misrepresentations and fear of social boycott, the exact purport of the hartal not being understood by the mass of the people. Some local bodies also took part in the movement by closing their schools. The boycott continued to be preached and orders for a general hartal on the 30th December 1922 were issued by the provincial leaders. In spite of this persistent campaign the visit of His Royal Highness to Nagpur passed off most successfully. He received a cordial reception at the railway station and the processional route was lined by a crowd numbering between 40,000 to 50,000. The durbar held

at midday was a most successful function and His Royal Highness' departure was a scene of remarkable enthusiasm. His charming personality won the hearts of all with whom he came into contact and the only regret expressed in connection with the visit was that it was too short.

46. Ahmedabad was another notable triumph for Gandhi. The local leaders on their return busied themselves with explaining to the people the meaning of the Ahmedabad resolutions and made a special point of the enlistment of volunteers and disobedience to any orders of Government which might be issued, prohibiting meetings or notifying volunteer corps. A good deal of activity was in evidence in the Chhatisgarh division in the matter of enrolment of volunteers and Congress members. Elsewhere spasmodic efforts were made to put existing corps on a better footing and in one district instructors from Allahabad were secured. Generally, however, the response was not enthusiastic and the refusal of Government to put into force the Criminal Law Amendment Act had evidently knocked the bottom out of the campaign for the enrolment of volunteers.

47. The first attempt at civil disobedience occurred in the Raipur district and took the form of unlicensed plundering of Government forests by the people of four villages in the jungly Sihawa tract. The attempt was quickly nipped in the bud and a number of offenders were prosecuted and punished. It was unfortunate, however, that the non-co-operation leaders who had undoubtedly instigated the movement, using as a lever certain petty grievances in regard to the local forest administration, escaped scot-free. The non-co-operation party in the province had however no real enthusiasm for civil disobedience, and the Chauri Chaura affair was a great set-back to the party advocating its introduction particularly in the northern districts. The Bardoli decision was generally welcomed in the province, although Gandhi's *volte-face* increased the dissatisfaction of the Maharashtra leaders with his leadership. This party had no faith in the doctrine of non-violence and feared that the new programme of social reform drawn up by the working committee at Bardoli would damp the political fervour of those who expected early and effective results from the campaign of civil disobedience.

48. Picketing of liquor-shops was revived at a few centres as a result of the Ahmedabad Congress and one Municipal Committee passed a resolution appointing two men for this duty. The picketing was not however effective and the consumers were beginning to show active resentment against any interference with their habits. The excise sales passed off successfully and in spite of an increase in the duty rate the license fees rose. No obstruction to the sales was experienced, although at a few places bidders were too timid to come forward for some town shops. The Bardoli decision did not affect the results, which were due to the improved economic condition of the people and also to lack of fixity of purpose among the non-co-operation party.

49. The boycott of foreign cloth shops languished, no picketing being seriously attempted. Many cloth merchants insisted on ordering foreign cloth on the ground that the period of their vow had expired and they could not face any further loss of business. In the Jubbulpore district some attempt was made to stimulate picketing and at some centres dealers were persuaded to adopt a system of fines for those ordering fresh stocks. Dealers, generally, however, were becoming restive under the terrorism which it was sought to impose upon them.

50. The reaction against non-co-operation continued to gather strength throughout the year 1922. At a meeting held in Nagpur on the 2nd March 1922 to explain the Delhi resolutions, the local extremist leaders severely criticised Gandhi's methods and programme as impracticable and the criticisms were not received unfavourably by the audience. The news of Gandhi's arrest was calmly received throughout the province. There were no hartals and no demonstrations, saving a few meetings held to congratulate Gandhi on his arrest. This lack of interest was not due to the control exercised by the non-co-operation leaders in pursuance of Gandhi's advice, but to the fact that Gandhi's influence had already largely disappeared in the province. The Maharashtra leaders began to look to Mr. C.R. Das as the only possible successor to Gandhi. The meetings held during the 'national week' were poorly attended and the audience was apathetic, while the hartal on the 13th April was only partially successful.

51. The Hindi Provincial Conference was held at Chhindwara in April and was presided over by Mrs. Naidu. The Provincial Khilafat Conference, the Central Provinces Students' Conference and a Municipal Conference were also held. Mrs. Naidu's presidential address mainly consisted of an appeal in favour of the carrying out of the constructive programme comprised in the Bardoli resolutions. Resolutions on the lines laid down by the All-India Congress Committee were passed and the enrolment of three lakhs of Congress members and the collection of Rs. 1½ lakhs for the Tilak Swaraj Fund by the end of June were adopted as the immediate programme. The Khilafat Conference dealt with the Turkish situation on the usual lines. The Municipal Conference afforded an interesting instance of the political inclinations of an extreme type prevailing among local bodies during the year, it being resolved that the Provincial Congress Committee should create and organise a board in order to control municipal administration along non-co-operation lines. The object of the resolution was to avoid even such co-operation with Government as the recognition of the authority of the Minister would involve. The important municipality of Nagpur had already been captured by the non-co-operators in the preceding year, and the municipal elections which took place in the beginning of the year had proved on the whole a triumph for the non-co-operation party, which was better organised and was not averse to using methods of canvassing to which the moderate party would not descend.

52. A jarring note was struck at the end of the Hindi Provincial Conference by the resignation of the office-bearers and members of the committee in protest against criticism levelled against some of them in the vernacular papers, and a new committee was elected, the President being Sundarlal of Allahabad, then recently released from jail and among the members being Makhanlal Chaturvedi who had also completed a term of imprisonment. The management thus passed into the hands of the more extreme followers of Gandhi's programme. The release of these two men and that of Arjunlal Sethi led to a considerable stiffening of the opposition to the campaign against Gandhi's programme initiated by the Maratha leaders.

53. The report of a sub-committee appointed by the Central

Provinces Congress Committee (Marathi districts) to suggest modifications in the non-co-operation programme was forcibly opposed by the more fanatical section of the non-co-operation party headed by Seth Jamnalal Bajaz and Sundarlal and other agitators released from jail. The sub-committee's main recommendations were the development of national education; the organisation of volunteers on new lines; the revival of foreign propaganda; the abandonment of the boycott of Government courts by litigants and lawyers; the abandonment of the boycott of defence in Government courts; the abandonment of the boycott of Councils; concentration on the boycott of foreign cloth, particularly British cloth, and the cult of the *charkha*, but not so as to interfere with modern industrial development; it finally declared that mass civil disobedience was an impossibility. The followers of Gandhi intended to concentrate their energies on the use of *khaddar* and the *charkha* and were in favour of organising small Committees at different centres to push on the work. Sundarlal was constantly on the move in the Hindi districts trying to revive enthusiasm for the Gandhian programme. A novel idea of his was to bring the aboriginal Gonds within the Congress fold, and at a Gond Conference in the Nerbudda division he persuaded them to pass resolutions in favour of Gandhi's programme. Generally speaking, the pro-Tilak party had a majority in the Marathi districts and the Berar Provincial Congress Committee recommended by an overwhelming majority that the Congress programme should include 'flooding the Imperial and Provincial Councils and the representative bodies with nationalists' representatives'. The committee appointed a sub-committee of eleven members to report by the 1st August 1922 on the working of non-co-operation. In Nagpur itself public feeling in the middle of 1922 was against the local Maratha Brahmin leaders, and the Gandhi-ites generally carried the meetings held by Sundarlal and his friends with a view to preparing the ground for civil disobedience. Notwithstanding this some waverers openly joined the Tilakites by the middle of the year. It was significant that with the close of the hot weather vacation the majority of the members of the Nagpur bar who had suspended practice, resumed it on the ground that the Bardoli and Delhi resolutions absolved them from continuing suspension.

54. The Civil Disobedience Committee arrived in the province

at Jubbulpore on the 9th July. The Municipal Committee, which had been captured by non-co-operators in the beginning of the year, presented an address to them and hoisted the 'national' flag on municipal buildings. Hakim Ajmal Khan and Dr. Ansari in their reply to the address dwelt mainly on the necessity of Hindu-Muslim unity for the attainment of Swaraj. The evidence of the Provincial Working Committee (Hindi districts) and about 20 other witnesses was taken *in camera*. The Working Committee, while approving the constructive programme of Bardoli, favoured civil disobedience against Section 144, Criminal Procedure Code. The Congress Committee expressed themselves disappointed with the progress made in the Central Provinces and complained that the witnesses would not give accurate information regarding the number of Congress members, volunteers and *charkhas* or the progress of *khaddar*. The visit aroused some temporary enthusiasm in the city, but had no permanent effect. The committee arrived at Nagpur on the 11th July, where two meetings were held; Ajmal Khan, Motilal Nehru, V.J. Patel and Dr. Ansari, whose speeches were moderate in tone, appealed to the audiences to carry out the Bardoli programme by enlisting Congress members, collecting for the Swaraj Fund and popularising the use of *khaddar*. The bulk of the evidence of Mahratta leaders was against the early introduction of civil disobedience while the Gandhiites pressed for immediate action. The Khilafat Committee also heard evidence at Nagpur, but their proceedings attracted little attention. The party left on the 12th for Akola, where as there were two parties and the time available was short, one spokesman was appointed for each party. Both parties agreed that Berar was not ripe for mass civil disobedience; they were united in supporting the constructive programme of the Congress, but were divided on the question of entry into the Councils. This last question was indeed the one to which the committee gave considerable attention, the question of the introduction of civil disobedience being hardly treated with any seriousness as the evidence was distinctly against it. The committee left the province thoroughly disappointed with the position in the province. Their visit did nothing to compose the differences between the two rival factions and its effect was purely transitory.

55. The succeeding months witnessed some recrudescence of

political agitation, particularly in Chhatisgarh, and the non-co-operation party, reinforced by the release from jail of some of their old leaders, against attempted to rouse enthusiasm for their programme. Demonstrations were held to welcome the leaders released from jail, including public meetings, and in some cases the presentation of addresses by Municipal Committees and the flying of the Swaraj flag. Some of the speeches were objectionable and prosecutions were instituted under Section 108, Criminal Procedure Code, against the principal offenders, including three leaders released from jail. In the north of the province Sundarlal, the President of the Provincial Congress Committee, revived agitation at some of the places visited by him on tour. The efforts of the non-co-operation party were however, not attended with much success. In several parts of the province, notably in Jubbulpore, the party suffered from internal dissensions and accusations were rife regarding the mis-appropriation of funds. The enrolment of Congress members was not large except in the districts of Raipur, Saugor, Bilaspur, Jubbulpore and Chhindwara. There were signs of some small revival of the volunteer movement and at a few centres some revival, of a spasmodic nature, of the picketing of liquor-shops occurred. The movement for the boycott of foreign cloth, however, made no progress, save in centres like Burhanpur, where the large weaver community had found the manufacture of *khaddar* profitable. The collection of funds was disappointing: the accounts of the Tilak Swaraj Fund showed that as against Rs. 45,500 received by the Provincial Congress Committee in 1921-22, during the year 1922-23 the collections had only amounted to Rs. 897 by the end of October. In Berar attempts made by the politicians to use the levy of a Jaglia and Mahar cess as a new focus for agitation against Government were a failure, owing to an effective counter-propaganda by Government.

56. The main interest of the last six months of 1922, however, lay in the struggle between the pro-Council and the anti-Council factions. The struggle centred round the Congress elections, re-criminations were bitter about the electioneering methods adopted and appeals to the All-India Congress Committee to have the elections set aside were made on either side. In Berar the Tilakites

secured a large majority in spite of the efforts of W.G. Joshi, who had since his release assumed the rôle of the political leader of Berar and declared himself in support of the Gandhi programme. At a meeting held on the 10th September the newly elected Provincial Congress Committee accepted the statement submitted by their President, Mr. Ane, to the Civil Disobedience Committee as the official pronouncement of the committee, thus indicating a definite decision in favour of entering the Councils. In November Mr. C.R. Das visited Amraoti, and, after conferring with the Maharashtra party leaders of all shades of opinion, including the Hon'ble G.S. Khaparde, W.G. Joshi and others of Berar, Dr. Munje and others of Nagpur, and N.C. Kelkar of Poona, issued a political manifesto advocating entry into the Councils. At public meetings and conferences, however, the Gandhi party still held sway and in the Central Provinces the preliminary Congress elections pointed to the success of the Gandhiites. While Sundarlal and his followers publicly expressed their loss of faith in Das and Nehru, W.G. Joshi of Berar veered round to the Tilak party, and at a meeting in Nagpur in November stated that, though not himself in favour of entering the Councils, he would not oppose the party who wished to enter. The election of delegates to the All-India Congress at Amraoti was the scene of violent difference between the Tilak and Gandhi parties; eventually the Tilak party withdrew and the Gandhi party delegates were elected.

57. The Maharashtra Home Rule League held its annual conference on the 9th and 10th December at Yeotmal under the presidency of Mr. Joseph Baptista of Bombay. The delegates numbered about 250, mostly from Berar and Nagpur and included the Hon'ble G.S. Khaparde and Mr. N.C. Kelkar of Poona. In his presidential address Mr. Baptista made a strong appeal on behalf of responsive co-operation. He described Gandhi as an excellent guide to the Kingdom of Heaven, but preferred Tilak as the architect of a Kingdom on Earth. The resolutions carried included the following: 'that efforts should be made to impress upon the voters the rights given to them according to the Reform Act in order to obtain their real assistance to get more rights'. It was significant that this resolution was supported by W.G. Joshi. As was anticipated, the

Central Provinces Marathi Congress Committee and the Berar members of the All-India Congress Committee solidly supported Council entry at the Gaya Congress, while the vote from the Hindi districts was divided.

58. During the last six months of 1922 the interest of the Mahomedan community in events outside India was on the wane. Although the Turkish victories were celebrated by the community with thanksgiving services and illuminations at all important centres, little real excitement was aroused. The Khilafat party was perturbed at the announcement of the Angora Government and the press was puzzled over the Khilafat question and the effect of depriving the Sultan of his temporal powers. The election of the new Khalifa at Constantinople was, however, generally accepted by Mahomedans in the province.

Mahomedan interest in the Khilafat was, however, of less political importance at this stage than the state of Mahomedan feeling in regard to the Hindus. In some towns of the Jubbulpore division the Hindu-Moslem unity was imperilled by disputes over the election of Municipal office-bearers and the building of mosques, and in Berar the coincidence of the Muharram and Ganpati festivals exposed the hollow nature of the Hindu-Mahomedan entente, for in several towns dissensions broke out, two small riots occurred and in several cases preventive action had to be taken by the police. As the year progressed it witnessed the growth of the antagonism between the two communities, which was destined to break out in open dissensions in the following two years.

59. In Berar, the anti-Brahmin movement, which has been noticed before, continued to grow and one of the non-Brahmin castes decided to dispense with the services of Brahmins altogether at their religious ceremonies. The political significance of the anti-Brahmin movement lay in the fact that the hostility to Brahmins extended to the extreme political theories professed by the intellectual class, which was composed almost entirely of Brahmins.

60. Finally, mention must be made of the state of the Liberal party at the close of 1922. The Indian Liberal Federation held its annual session at Nagpur, under the presidency of Mr. Sastri, whose presidential address met with general approval. On the whole the

session was a success, the attendance (500) being larger than anticipated. On the conclusion of the conference at Nagpur, Mr. Sastri visited the Amraoti, Akola and Yeotmal districts of Berar. The main theme of his speeches throughout his visit to the province was the urgent need for the Liberal party to organise itself and to take a vigorous part in the education of the electorate. His ridicule of the non-co-operation programme was not always to the taste of his audience, but it was significant of the change in public feeling that his meetings were never seriously interrupted.

61. The return of the local delegates from Gaya led only to a small revival in political activities. The meetings held to convey the Congress message to the public roused little or no enthusiasm, and the people were more interested in the prospects of a good harvest and a fall in prices than in the progress of the non-co-operation movement. There was an almost complete restoration of the old cordial relations between Government officers and the people, and the annual district darbars were well attended. The visit of Mrs. Gandhi to the province in January fell very flat, although she received an address of welcome from one small municipality. The two main items in the Congress programme, enlistment of volunteers and collection for the Tilak Swaraj Fund, made little progress. In the north of the province Sundarlal presided over a few sparsely attended meetings at which he put the Central Provinces' contribution at 2,000 volunteers and Rs. 50,000, but the appeals met with little response. Subscriptions were very hard to get as the people were suspicious over the fate of previous collections. The Nagpur Congress Committee issued an appeal in support of the boycott of British goods and liquor-shops, with the result that a few volunteers were enrolled for picketing purposes. The movement was not however taken seriously. In Berar W.G. Joshi, who for tactical or other reasons rejoined the Gandhi party, found it difficult to secure a president for his meetings. The public were puzzled by the existence of two parties within the Congress and did not understand what the Congress programme really was. Owing to internal dissensions the various district Congress conferences failed to arouse enthusiasm and vague appeals regarding preparation for civil disobedience fell flat on a apathetic public. The Provincial Congress meeting at Betul

was a dismal failure and ended in a split between the pro-council and anti-council factions. The jealousies of the rival leaders of the Central Provinces Congress organisation (Hindi districts) led to the resignation of Sundarlal and the appointment in his place as president of a member of his own party, Sundarlal being elected vice-president.

62. There was some increase in political activity during the latter half of March owing to the Gandhi week and the tour in the province of a party of Congress leaders, headed by Raja Gopalchariar [Rajagopalachari], Rajendra Prasad, Devidas Gandhi (Gandhi's son) and Muazzam Ali. The meetings addressed by them were not large and the speeches were generally mild, consisting mainly of appeals for volunteers and money to carry on the Congress programme. At Jubbulpore the Municipal Committee tried to celebrate the visit of the deputation by flying the 'national' flag, as in July 1922, but on a protest by the leading citizens of the town, the Deputy Commissioner suspended the Municipal Committee's resolution and took action to prevent effect being given to it. On the 18th March an attempt was made to carry the national flag in procession through the Civil Station and the Cantonment; the procession was prohibited from proceeding into the Cantonment without a license under Section 30, Police Act, and the leaders were informed that one of the conditions of licence would be that the 'national' flag should not be carried. A small party persisted in attempting to enter the Cantonment area in defiance of these orders and ten persons including one woman were arrested; but they were released the next morning.

63. In the meantime the Das party was gaining strength at the expense of the Gandhi party. The Central Provinces (Marathi) pro-Council party was led by Dr. Munje and Mr. Abhyankar, barrister of Nagpur, who resumed his practice. The Central Provinces (Hindi) party was led by Raghavendra Rao of Bilaspur. In Berar the supporters of Mr. Das opened their campaign at a meeting in Yeotmal when a resolution was passed appointing a committee to educate the voters with a view to swamping the Councils at the next election with nationalist members. In Amraoti the leaders of the Das party formed a voters association and similar preparations were made in other constituencies.

64. It was becoming increasingly clear that non-co-operation was a lost cause and the non-co-operation leaders attempted to utilise the Jubbulpore flag incident as a means of reviving enthusiasm in their creed. National flag flying incidents occurred at Bilaspur and Seoni of which Government took no notice. On the 12th April, however, Sundarlal, who had been active in connection with the Jubbulpore flag incident and who had delivered some objectionable speeches at Katni, was arrested at Jubbulpore under Section 108, Criminal Procedure Code. On the 13th April (the anniversary of the Jallianwala Bagh affair) at Nagpur, a small procession of volunteers was organised to carry the 'National' flag in procession through the Civil Station; the procession was not interfered with until it attempted to proceed in the direction of the European club, when it was stopped by an order under Section 30 of the Police Act. Some volunteers refused to obey the order, and four leaders were arrested and the rest dispersed. On the following day these four men were convicted and fined Rs. 60 each. As they refused to pay the fines they were sentenced to two months' simple imprisonment in default.

65. Thus started the Nagpur flag agitation, which overshadowed all other forms of non-co-operation activity in the province in the succeeding four months. A connected account of the principal events in the course of this agitation is to be found in the Resolution of the local Government (Political and Military Department) No. 1262-1057-II, dated the 8th September 1923, while the local Government's Press Communiqués, dated the 1st May 1923, the 28th June 1923 and the 1st September 1923[1] also refer to certain aspects of the movement. For the sake of preserving the continuity of this report, however, it may be useful to outline the course of the Nagpur flag agitation and its exact political bearing.

66. Prior to the incident described in paragraph 64 little had been said or heard in Nagpur of the national flag. Thereafter, however, the local leaders sought to justify lawless and disorderly

[1] A reference may also be made to the local Government's (Political and Military Department) Letter No. 163-I, dated the 1st October 1923 to the Secretary to the Government of India, Home Department, together with enclosures.

conduct under the pretext of asserting the dignity of the national flag. On the 1st May, when a procession under Seth Jamnalal Bajaz sought to enter the purely residential area of the Civil Lines, the District Magistrate stopped it by the issue of an order under Section 144, Criminal Procedure Code, prohibiting processions without his permission within that area on the grounds that such processions were likely to cause annoyance to the residents and lead to a disturbance of the public tranquillity. The procession was induced to turn back, but the next day a third procession crossed into the prohibited area. Thereafter day after day parties of varying numbers sought to enter the prohibited area with the object of breaking the District Magistrate's order, and forcing their own arrest. Numerous volunteers of all ages and castes were brought to Nagpur for the purpose of defying the District Magistrate's order and when local sources began to fail, volunteers were enlisted from outside, chiefly from Bombay and Madras. The leaders maintained their defiant attitude unchanged until the end of June, asserting that *Satyagraha* was justified by 'the denial of the elementary right to exhibit the flag, and carry it in peaceful and orderly procession on public roads'. The sinister origin of the disturbance was suppressed and the disorder and civil disobedience organised and sustained by Awari, Seth Jamnalal and Bhagwandin and others was transmuted into the harmless right to carry a flag in peaceful procession.

67. Seth Jamnalal was arrested on the 18th June and thereafter the Working Committee of the Congress took charge of the movement, and disavowals were made of any intention to insult the Union Jack or to cause annoyance to the European residents. Negotiations for a settlement of the agitation were initiated with the Home Member of the Government by Mr. V.J. Patel before the meeting of the Legislative Council at the beginning of August. The position of the Government was explained by His Excellency the Governor in his address to the Legislative Council of the 6th August. He made it clear that Government regarded the agitation as civil disobedience and an attempt to overcome lawful authority. On the 15th August His Excellency the Governor granted an interview to Mr. V.J. Patel and Mr. V.B. Patel and after subsequent negotiations the Government communicated to Mr. Patel the conditions under

which a procession would be permitted within the prohibited area upon application to the local authorities. On the 16th August Mr. V.B. Patel issued a statement as the authorised representative of the Working Committee of the Congress that they did not claim the unrestricted right to take processions along the public roads, that the processions were not intended to annoy any section of the public, and that the national flag was not carried with any intention to insult the Union Jack. The order passed by the District Magistrate expired on the 16th August and on the 17th August an order under Section 30 (I) of the Police Act was promulgated by the District Superintendent of Police, Nagpur, prescribing the routes for processions in the City of Nagpur. Subsequently a procession organised by Mr. Patel proceeded, with the permission of the District Superintendent of Police, through the Civil Lines. The route prescribed did not include the strictly residential portion of the Civil Station, the numbers were limited to one hundred and orderly conduct was required. The conditions were duly observed and thereafter the leaders declared that *Satyagraha* had ceased. No procession entered the prohibited area after that date.

68. Having satisfied itself that the agitation had ceased, the local Government, as an act of clemency, decided to release the 'Flag' prisoners, except these convicted of offences against the Prison Act. Most of these were misguided youths with no real knowledge of the movement.

69. Throughout the agitation the policy of the Government had remained unchanged. It insisted on the maintenance of two principles—the first, was submission to lawful authority and the second that no procession could be permitted within the prohibited area without application to the local authorities and due observance of the conditions imposed.

70. The agitation throughout received little local support in Nagpur; it failed to appeal to the uneducated, while the more responsible political leaders regarded it from the outset as entirely unjustified; the Swaraj party of the Congress considered the agitation as an astute political move directed against themselves and threw its influence against the agitation. The view that the flag movement was successful was mainly confined to the extreme section of the

Congress, who grossly misrepresented the circumstances in which the procession was permitted. Moderate opinion considered that the local Government had successfully vindicated its authority, while the Swaraj press bitterly attacked the civil disobedience party and considered that Mr. Patel had surrendered abjectly to Government.

71. While the no-change party was thus preoccupied in a futile struggle with constituted authority, the Swaraj party was consolidating its position by quiet and steady work. In the Berar and Central Provinces Provincial Marathi Conference held at Buldana on the 8th May and presided over by Mr. C.R. Das, it was resolved to contest all seats in the Legislative Councils and Assembly. Canvassing for the elections started in June and the organisation of the Swaraj party was in marked contrast to the aimlessness of the no-change party on one hand, and to the inactivity of the moderate party on the other.

72. The anti-Brahmin movement in the province steadily gained ground during the year 1923 and a Mahar Conference in Chanda was the occasion for a violent attack on Brahmins by the president, a gentleman from the Kolhapur State. Of greater political significance was the spread of the movement under the auspices of the Satya Shodhak Samaj in Berar, which seemed likely at one time to have a considerable influence on the approaching Council elections. At Yeotmal and Buldana meetings of non-Brahmins were held in September to promote the cause of non-Brahmin candidates, and an intense non-Brahmin propaganda was carried on in connection with the elections.

73. As the year progressed relations between Hindus and Mahomedans became distinctly worse. The *shuddhi* and *anti-shuddhi* movements gave rise to a certain amount of friction between the two communities, but in spite of this the Muharram passed off fairly quietly, although what might have been a serious disturbance was averted in Jubbulpore. The formation of branches of the Hindu Mahasabhas [!] on the one hand and of Mahomedan 'Akharas' as a counterblast to the *Sangatham* movement on the other considerably strained the relations between the two communities, and the vexed question of cow-slaughter aggravated the position. Disputes between Hindus and Mahomedans at Nagpur, centring round the playing of

mu! [music] in front of mosques assumed a very serious turn during the Ganpati festival and culminated later in several minor collisions, followed by desecration of Hindu temples. Much of the trouble at Nagpur was attributed to electioneering tactics on the part of the local Swarajists and it was remarkable that as soon as the local elections were over the quarrel subsided.

74. Apart from the Hindu-Mahomedan question the main political interest in the last quarter of the year centred in the elections. Very little interest was taken in the special Congress sessions at Delhi and the number of delegates from the province was small. The Central Provinces Committee met on the 29th and 30th September at Jubbulpore and there was a heated discussion on the subject of Council elections, which finally resulted in the no-change supporters forming an independent party to contest the seats against the Swaraj party. The policy of the Swaraj party was then still undefined, considerable indecision prevailing regarding the choice between responsive and obstructive co-operation.

75. The resolutions of the special Congress had little effect on the situation in the province, and no steps were taken to organise a campaign of civil disobedience, although Sundarlal Sharma was active in trying to revive interest in the movement. A few bombastic speeches were made by leaders of the 'no-change' party, and in one district some progress was made in enlisting volunteers for the corps of civic guards. The first Maratha Central Provinces volunteers' Conference was held at Gondia on the 12th and 13th November under the presidentship of Radha Mohan Gokulji and was attended by about 60 volunteers. It was decided that only those who had signed the Ahmedabad Congress pledge and had been convicted for participation in the Nagpur flag agitation were eligible to represent the Central Provinces volunteers at the All-India Volunteers' Conference at Cocanada. The chief aim of the conference was stated to be to 'concert measures to give effect to the Ahmedabad Congress resolution'. Several resolutions connected with *Satyagraha* were carried, and a Committee was appointed to make arrangements for opening a Volunteer Training School at Gondia. The progress made in the collection of subscriptions and the enlistment of volunteers willing to sign the pledge was however negligible.

76. The polling in the elections for the Legislative Assembly and the Council passed off without incident. Considerable interest was taken in the elections, especially in the towns, and a fairly heavy vote was given. A feature of the election was the excellent organisation of the Swaraj party, which was responsible among others for the defeat of Rao Bahadur Kelkar, Minister of Education. The organisation of the Liberal party was defective. There was carelessness in filling up nomination papers, leading to their rejection, and a splitting of the Liberal vote in most constituencies between several candidates. For the Legislative Assembly five Swarajists and one Independent who was supported by the Swaraj vote, were returned. In the elections to the Council, out of the 54 elected seats, 41 were secured by Swarajists, 4 by Liberals and 9 by Independents, with uncertain leanings.

77. The victory of the Swarajists at the polls signalised their triumph over the no-change party. The doings of the Swarajists in the Legislative Council in the year 1924 are outside the scope of this report. The non-co-operation party proper continued to show fitful signs of life, especially in the Mandla district, where unsuccessful attempts were made to set up the Gonds against the district administration. As a force in politics non-co-operation has long been dead in the province. Beyond half a dozen national schools struggling for life and a dozen volunteer associations leading an inactive and inglorious existence, it has left little trace of its course in the province. Its influence on local bodies has been unfortunate in that it has fostered a tendency to intrude politics into the sphere of parochial affairs. In the mass of the people it has perhaps stimulated political consciousness, which right guidance may turn to useful account.

History of the Khilafat Movement in the Central Provinces and Berar

1. The first Khilafat Committee to be formed in the province was the District Khilafat Committee organised at Khandwa on the 28th January 1920, mainly through the efforts of Hindu agitators. In the beginning the movement made little progress, a fact which was

brought to the notice of Shaukat Ali, Abul Kalam Azad and others when they passed through the Central Provinces on their way to Benares from the Khilafat Conference held at Bombay in the middle of February 1920. A fortnight later Shaukat Ali, on his way back from the Calcutta Conference, broke his journey at Nagpur, Burhanpur and Khandwa and addressed meetings at which the Calcutta resolutions were reaffirmed. In appealing for funds for the organisation of local Khilafat Committees at a crowded meeting at Nagpur, Shaukat Ali made a violent speech, in the course of which he threatened that the entire body of Mahomedans in India would throw of their allegiance to the British Government, should the Peace Conference disregard the views of Indian Mahomedans as put forward by the Khilafat deputation. The effect of his speeches was undoubtedly to stir Moslem feeling, and Khilafat Committees came into existence at Nagpur, Akola and Buldana. Although much intemperate language was used in the meetings held on the Khilafat day, *i.e.* the 19th March, it was clear that the agitation found little favour with the real leaders of Mahomedan opinion. In a Khilafat Committee of fourteen formed at a town in the Akola district in March, the President, Vice-President, a Secretary and three members were Hindus, and at two Khilafat meetings held in Berar in April, the only speakers of note were Dr. N.S. Paranjpe, and Ramalal Vyas, two extremists of the Tilak school.

2. Three representatives of the Central Provinces attended the meeting of the Central Khilafat Committee held at Bombay on the 11th April, in which owing to Gandhi's influence, the Calcutta programme was considerably modified, but no important representatives from the Central Provinces appear to have been present at the meetings of either the All-India Workers' Conference at Delhi or the Conference of Ulemas [!] at Cawnpore held in the following April. No representatives of the Central Provinces are also known to have attended the Madras Khilafat Conference. In writing to Chhotani, a Central Provinces correspondent lamented the apathy of the local Mahomedans. At Jubbulpore, owing to the influence of a local follower of Maulana Ahmad Razak Khan of Baus Bareilly, who held that the King of Hedjaz was the rightful claimant to the Khalifat, no Khilafat Committee could be formed for some time.

3. At the second Berar Mahomedan Conference held at Khamgaon in the Buldana district in May, the Khilafat question was banned, and an attempt to hold a separate Khilafat meeting failed as the local Mahomedans were not prepared to adopt either *jehad* or *hijrat*, the only two logical courses opened to Khilafatists. Early in May information reached the Nagpur Khilafat Committee that directly the peace terms were announced, two maulvis would be sent from Fyzabad to carry out the policy decided on by the Central Khilafat Committee. The news greatly perturbed the more responsible members of the Nagpur Committee, and Mr. Samiulla Khan, a leading pleader of Nagpur, and Secretary of the local Committee, wrote to the Central Committee, pointing out that Nagpur leaders were unwilling to accept the progressive non-co-operation programme. Chhotani replied that the Central Provinces Mahomedans must accept the Central Committee's decisions, but later wrote that modifications of the programme would be considered at the All-India Khilafat meeting. Two Central Provinces delegates were present at the meeting which was held at Bombay on the 12th May and which passed the full non-co-operation programme.

4. The publication of the Turkish peace-terms caused no excitement in the Central Provinces in spite of the efforts of Hindu extremists to misrepresent the intentions of the British Government. The Nagpur leaders were, however, finding their position increasingly difficult, being spurred on by the Central Committee against their convictions. Shaukat Ali summoned Samiulla Khan and Abdul Hasan Natik, a Nagpur maulvi, to a conference at Allahabad in June, and finally both suc-cumbed to pressure. On the 5th of June they addressed a Khilafat meeting at Jubbulpore organised by Tajuddin, the editor of the Urdu paper *Taj*, and a fire-brand, and advocated the first step in the non-co-operation programme, namely the boycott of British goods. Khan Bahadur Malak, the President of the Nagpur Khilafat Committee, was obstinate and avoided Shaukat Ali when he stopped at Nagpur on the 12th June, on his way to Raipur. In other parts of the province the movement made little headway. The Khilafat question remained in the background in the 8th Provincial Conference held at Saugor on the 17th - 20th June,

scarcely 50 out of an attendance of 2,000 being Mahomedans. At meetings held by Shaukat Ali at Raipur to explain the Allahabad decisions, with one exception, the speakers were Hindus. Indeed, at this stage there were a few influential Mahomedans who were openly opposed to the movement. Abdul Salaam, the leading maulvi of Jubbulpore, after an hour's interview with Shaukat Ali, declined to alter his views and refused to help the non-co-operation movement or to assist in organising a Khilafat Committee or to help in raising funds. Seth Kamruddin, who had been one of the Central Provinces delegates to the 12th session of the All-India Moslem League at Amritsar in December 1919, resigned his post of Secretary to the Khandwa Khilafat Committee in June 1920 on the ground that he could not sympathise with non-co-operation.

5. The Khilafat question was one of the planks in the platform of the Extremists, who were at this period preparing for the November elections to the reformed Council. In July, Khan Bahadur Malak issued a circular to all districts enquiring what attitude Mahomedans proposed adopting towards the non-co-operation programme. Only four districts replied, and all replies were to the effect that the scheme was unworkable. Tajuddin, who had been sent to Nagpur by Shaukat Ali to inform the Nagpur Mahomedans that the boycott of the Councils was part of the non-co-operation scheme, was told that they were opposed to this part of the programme and that Samiulla Khan and Khan Bahadur Malak intended to stand for the Legislative Council and Legislative Assembly, respectively. A meeting of the Provincial Khilafat Committee held at Nagpur on the 25th July, at which Khan Bahadur Malak presided, ended in a vote of 18 against 12 against full non-co-operation, and in favour of Samiulla Khan's amendment that though the full non-co-operation programme was agreed to in principle, owing to local conditions in the province, only the portion relating to the boycott of British goods could be up into operation. On the day after this meeting, Khan Bahadur Malak severed his connection with the Khilafat agitation, resigned his post as president of the Provincial Khilafat Committee and withdrew his offer to contribute Rs. 20,000 to the Khilafat funds. This abrupt desertion

by an influential leader was a great set-back to the agitation, and although the *hartal* of the 1st August was fairly complete in most towns in the province, no district reported any progress towards putting non-co-operation into practice.

6. Previous to the special session of the Congress at Calcutta pamphlets signed by Shaukat Ali, Dr. Kitchlew and others had been received by Samiulla Khan from the Central Khilafat Committee, urging that Mahomedan representatives be sent to the Congress, and to the simultaneous All-India Khilafat Conference. Accordingly, out of the 57 persons of the Central Provinces who attended the Conference, 16 were Mahomedans, including Samiulla Khan. Although at the Khilafat Conference the Central Provinces delegates voted against the non-co-operation resolution, as at the Congress meeting, the leaders decided to abide by the decision of the Conference and the Khilafat candidates withdrew their candidature from the elections to the reformed Council.

7. In the report on the non-co-operation movement, reference had already been made to the results of the Khilafat and Moslem League Conference held at Nagpur during the Congress week of December 1920. The Central Provinces and Berar Khilafatists did not take a prominent part in the deliberations of these bodies, but were prompt to take exception to the rumoured misuse of the Khilafat funds. In the following January, Abdul Hasan Natik and Karim Khan, Secretary and Assistant Secretary to the Provincial Khilafat Committee resigned their posts on the ground that they suspected the Ali brothers of misappropriating the Khilafat funds. The effect of the Nagpur Conferences was to give a stimulus to the Khilafat agitation, and several more Khilafat Committees were formed and corps of Khilafat volunteers were organised, which took part in the pseudo-temperance campaign. The Khilafat agitation, however, formed but a small part of the general agitation during the first four months of 1921, when non-co-operation was at its height. Many of the newly organised Khilafat Committees never functioned, and after the first few months of the year it became apparent that interest in the Khilafat agitation was on the wane. Tajuddin, who had been prosecuted under section 158-A of the Indian Penal Code, though acquitted, damaged his reputation as a

non-co-operator, by defending himself in court, like Dr. Cholkar in similar circumstances. In Jubbulpore Maulvi Abdul Salaam carried on a vigorous anti-non-co-operation campaign with success. The apology published by the Ali brothers in the press in May gave rise to considerable comment, and Samiulla wrote to Shaukat Ali for an explanation threatening to sever his connections with the Khilafat movement if he were convinced that the apology had been made in order to avoid a prosecution. Although in May, Shaukat Ali during a tour in Berar collected more than Rs. 15,000 for the Smyrna Fund, his visit created no lasting impression. The efforts of Khilafat lecturers in the province were now devoted to appealing for subscriptions for the Khilafat and Smyrna Funds, in which they were assisted by some 24 students sent by Mahomed Ali from the Aligarh College.

8. The boycott of foreign cloth occupied at this stage a prominent place in the non-co-operation programme and accordingly received some attention from Khilafatists. At a private meeting of the Central Provinces (Hindi) Conference at Raipur, held on the 23rd August, which was attended by Tajuddin and half a dozen other Mahomedan delegates, it was decided to start an intensive campaign against foreign cloth and a Committee was formed to organise Swadeshi industries in the province. The scheme, which was estimated to cost Rs. 1½ lakhs, never materialised. The Karachi resolutions and the proscribed Delhi *fatwa* made a stronger claim on the attention of the Khilafat party and in accordance with the resolution passed by the managing committee of the Central Khilafat Committee on the 22nd September, Samiulla Khan, A.K. Siddique, Abdul Rauf Shah (of Akola) and others openly circulated the proscribed *fatwa* and advocated its contents. During the last three months of 1921 Khilafat agitation in the Province increased in intensity; it was accompanied by a kind of religious revival among Mahomedans and the propaganda became more bitterly anti-British and anti-Christian. The British Government was said to be on the verge of a collapse, and people were told that mass civil disobedience would soon complete its overthrow. The Khilafat speeches of the period were frankly inflammatory and full of deliberate misrepresentation of the intentions and actions of the British Government. 'We must disregard the authority of Government', said A.K. Siddique at a crowded

meeting at Nagpur early in November, 'and break its laws. The day we accomplish this will witness the funeral of British rule'. Action under section 107 or section 108 of the Criminal Procedure Code was taken against several Khilafat lecturers, the number of such prosecutions during the year amounting to 13.

9. On the 26th of October 1921, eight so-called maulvis, including Tajuddin, A.K. Siddique, Hamid Ali (of Bilaspur), Muhammad Yasin (of Raipur) and others, held a secret meeting at Jubbulpore and established, it is believed, a branch of the Jamiat-ul-Ulema with a view to spread amongst Mahomedans a spirit of hatred against the Government, to preach *jehad* secretly and to prepare Mahomedans for civil disobedience. On the 4th November Samiulla, Tajuddin, A.K. Siddique and other Khilafat delegates attended the special All-India Congress session at Delhi, at which it was decided to start civil disobedience only in places which could be shown to be ready for it. On the 17th November A.K. Siddique and Tajuddin attended a private meeting of the executive of the Central Provinces Congress Committee at Jubbulpore at which three places in the Provinces were selected for the inauguration of civil disobedience. Nothing tangible, however, emerged out of the Delhi resolutions, except increased activity in the enrolment of volunteers and an increase in the number of Khilafat Committees in the Province, which by the end of 1921 numbered 68.

10. After the Ahmedabad Conference in December 1921, Khilafatist propaganda in the Province was concentrated on the enrolment of volunteers and the collection of funds preparatory to the introduction of civil disobedience. At a meeting in Nagpur held on the 3rd January, Samiulla Khan stated that civil disobedience would be started directly and orders were passed prohibiting meetings or the formations of volunteer corps. The Chauri Chaura tragedy and Gandhi's subsequent declaration that the country was as yet unfit for civil disobedience, however effectively arrested the progress of this part of the programme and henceforth commenced a definite reaction in the Khilafat agitation.

11. Another factor which helped the reaction was the split between the anti-Council and pro-Council parties, which was gradually

widening. The removal of the boycott of the Councils was at first opposed by all the Khilafat leaders of note, *viz.*, Abdul Rauf (the Berar leader), Samiulla and Natik (the leaders in the southern districts of the Central Provinces) and Tajuddin (the most energetic of the leaders in the northern districts of the province). Meetings were held by the Khilafat Committees of Amraoti and Akola in June to protest against the resolutions of the Berar Provincial Congress Committee on the 25th May, advocating the removal of the boycott on the Councils. Similar meetings were held in Buldana and Yeotmal, in July. The results of the elections to the local bodies, which took place at the time, strengthened this attitude of the Mahomedans. Non-co-operators had swept the board in these elections, but the expectations of Mahomedans had not been fulfilled. In nearly all cases the office-holders in the newly elected bodies were Hindus. Tajuddin actually resigned his post as President of the Jubbulpore District Congress Committee because the vice-presidency of the Municipality, which he coveted, had gone to a Hindu. Mahomedans apprehended that what occurred in the local bodies would be repeated in the new Council.

12. This mutual distrust between Hindus and Mahomedans which now emerged to an increasing extent and which correspondingly weakened the Khilafat agitation, was also exhibited in the matter of cow-protection. The cow-protection agitation had affected the Mahomedans in general and the butcher community in particular, but notwithstanding this Khilafatists had supported it in order to enlist the help of the Hindus. So long as the question of cow-slaughter remained optional, no differences arose, but when in May, the local Government introduced rules under which the slaughter of cattle in municipal limits could be restricted at the option of the Municipality, Mahomedans protested strongly. The new Municipal Committee, with Hindu majorities, were not slow in applying the new rules and many protest meetings were held, at which the misuse by Hindus of the power secured by them with the help of Mahomedans was the theme.

13. In the Khilafatist camp itself, the knowledge or suspicion that funds were being misappropriated was the cause of disruption.

In a few cases definite embezzlement of funds was exposed. Accusations of misappropriation were rife amongst the workers. In August Samiulla Khan was asked by the local Khilafat Secretary to produce the Khilafat accounts, as no receipt for a sum of Rs. 7,000, said to have been sent to the Central Khilafat Committee, Bombay, could be traced. Samiulla Khan refused to comply and later stated his intention of resigning.

14. The local Khilafatist leaders were, however, reluctant to acknowledge defeat. They were among the minority which gave evidence favouring the introduction of civil disobedience before the Civil Disobedience Committee. The evidence was, however, unsupported by facts and at Akola, Abdul Rauf, as the spokesman of the Berar Khilafatists, was constrained to admit that Berar was not prepared for civil disobedience. Although the Turkish victories against the Greeks resulted in a temporary increase in propaganda, it was obvious that the Khilafat question had no longer any interest for the Mahomedan community, who accepted without demur the decision of the Kemalists deposing the Sultan and appointing Abdul Majid in his place. Tajuddin, Samiulla Khan, A.K. Siddique, Abdul Rauf and five other prominent Khilafatists attended the Gaya Congress and the first three definitely declared in favour of Council-entry; Abdul Rauf's attitude was undecided, but after the Congress he openly joined the anti-Council party. This party now confined itself to making preparations for civil disobedience, the original Khilafat grievances being seldom mentioned. Their efforts, however, met with little success. Economic conditions were improving, and there were signs that the public was tiring of political agitation. This lack of interest was most noticeable among Mahomedans. In the Hindi districts, Tajuddin and one Abdul Ghani alone displayed any zeal; the former was too obviously working for himself to have any influence and the latter was without any status. A.K. Siddique had left the no-change party and in Nagpur Samiulla Khan was thinking of resuming practice. On the 14th March 1923, the Berar Provincial Khilafat Committee held a private meeting at which it was decided to try and revive interest by systematic touring. Nine Berar Mahomedans volunteered for the work, including Abdul Rauf, the president. The propaganda, which consisted chiefly of an appeal

for funds, met with a poor response. The rumour that Rs. 15 lakhs of the Central Khilafat Funds had been embezzled only added to the difficulties of collection.

15. The breach between Hindus and Mahomedans was further widened by the reports of the conversion of the Malkana Rajputs by the Arya Samaj. An effect of this was the dissociation of Mahomedans from the National Flag agitation at Jubbulpore and Nagpur. The appeals of Abdul Subhani of Bombay, who toured the province in June 1923 to enlist Mahomedan support for the Nagpur *Satyagraha*, met with no response and at the meeting of the All-India Khilafat Committee held at Nagpur in July Subhani's proposal to support the movement was defeated by 17 votes to 6. As the *Shuddhi* movement progressed, the friction between the Hindus and the Mahomedans increased. The Hindus, on the one hand, formed branches of the Hindu Maha Sabha in various districts; the Mahomedans, on the other hand, made strenuous efforts to organise counter propaganda and to collect funds for the purpose. In October the Amraoti leaders prepared a declaration of rights, demanding

(1) adequate representation in the various elective bodies and in the public services;
(2) adequate provision for Mahomedan education and religious instruction;
(3) guarantees against anti-cow-killing legislation; and
(4) prevention of the playing of music in front of mosques.

16. For the time, however, communal trouble subsided, the coming council election engrossing public attention. The Berar Khilafatists opposed the decision of the Delhi Conference in September in favour of Council entry. Others, like Tajuddin, joined the Independent party formed by those Gandhi-ites who were in agreement with the Delhi pact. Tajuddin stood for the Jubbulpore Mahomedan Rural Constituency, but was defeated by a Liberal. Samiulla Khan, who stood as a Swarajist candidate for the Central Provinces Mahomedan Constituency of the Legislative Assembly, was returned unopposed. The result of the elections to the Legislative Council was as follows:

Name of constituency		Name of elected member	Name of party
1. Jubbulpore	Mahomedan Rural	Maulvi Syed Mahomed	Liberal
2. Chhatisgarh	Do.	Mahomed Masud Khan	Swarajist
3. Nerbudda	Do.	Syed Hifazat Ali	Independent
4. Nagpur	Do.	M.K. Siddique	Swarajist
5. Berar	Mahomedan Urban	Khan Bahadur Syed Abdur Rahman	Liberal
6. East Berar	Mahomedan Rural	Syed Muzafar Hussain	Swarajist
7. West Berar	Do.	Muhammadali Khan	Liberal

Nos. 1 and 3 were opposed by Swarajist candidates. No Swarajist candidates were nominated for constituencies Nos. 5 and 7.

17. With the close of the year 1923 Khilafat agitation in the Central Provinces may be said to have ceased. The resolutions of the All-India Khilafat Conference at Cocanada in December 1923 caused no appreciable increase in Khilafat activity. The decision of the Angora Government to abolish the Khilafat came as a shock but the local leaders awaited developments and a lead from outside.

18. The antagonism between Hindus and Mahomedans again became acute in the third quarter of the year 1924, the bone of contention being the playing of mu! [music] before mosques. The differences culminated in riots at Saugor and at Jubbulpore, where the aid of the military had to be requisitioned, and minor incidents at Nagpur and Kamptee. Another matter which has accentuated the cleavage between the two communities had been the question of the restoration of Berar to the Nizam, retrocession being generally supported by the Berar Mahomedans and opposed by the Hindus.

19. Recent Khilafat activities in the province are only of academic interest. On the 5th of September the Berar Provincial Khilafat Committee met at Yeotmal, with Abdul Rauf as president. The balance in hand was said to be Rs. 1,100 and it was decided to retain two local men as paid preachers. In the same month, Shaukat Ali ordered the Central Provinces Provincial Committee to remit the balances in hand to the Central Khilafat Committee, and Rs. 100 is said to have been sent. On the 18th November Shaukat Ali attended the Central Provinces Khilafat Conference at Raipur. He appealed for unity and for funds and is believed to have made an impression. The office of the Central Provinces Provincial Khilafat

Committee, which was transferred to Seoni in January 1924, has since been moved to Raipur, with Vakil Ahmed Rizvi as president. The new office has issued a circular, calling on all districts to reorganise their Khilafat Committees. It included a list of Committees at 17 out of 22 Central Provinces districts and appeals for funds in aid of the deputation to Arabia. The recent developments in that country have not evoked any real interest or definite opinion in the province.

20. In all, about Rs. 1,32,000 is believed to have been collected in the province for the various Khilafat funds.

As a result of the Khilafat agitation one honorary Magistrate resigned his office in 1920 and six in 1921; nine Mahomedans renounced their titles in 1921. Out of a total of thirty-three Government servants, who resigned during the non-co-operation agitation, fourteen were Mahomedans, of whom eight belonged to the police and included two Sub-Inspectors. Five Mahomedan pleaders out of a total of 39 suspended their practice, but all of them have since resumed it.

The following is a statement showing the number of Mahomedans prosecuted during the Khilafat agitation:

	[?]	Convicted		Discharged or acquitted or cases withdrawn		Compromised	
		Cases	Persons	Cases	Persons	Cases	Persons
Cases connected with the liquor boycott	27	17	33	6	22	4	3
Assaults on Government servants	4	4	4	—	—	—	—
Social boycott	6	5	8	1	10	—	—
Section 107 and Section 108, CPC in cases of seditious speeches	15	8	15	3	4	—	—
Section 124-A, IPC	1	2	1	—	—	—	—
Section 153-A, IPC	2	1	1	1	1	—	—
Section 504, IPC. Defaming of Govt Servants	1	1	1	—	—	—	—
Total	56	38	63	11	37	4	3

A NOTE ON PROSECUTION FOR SEDITION

1. The following figures show the results of sedition cases during the non-co-operation movement:

Section	Prosecutions	Convictions	Discharged, acquitted or withdrawn
124-A, IPC	10	8	2
107, CPC	27	19	8
108, CPC	38	33	5

2. M.R. Cholkar, a Maratha Brahman medical practitioner of Nagpur, aged 38, has been an extremist of the Tilak School since 1908, and declared himself as a non-co-operator in 1919, ostensibly as a protest against the Rowlatt Bills. In reality he is of the many who thought that Gandhi's pacific policy might pave the way for a revolution in which the use of force would be possible. In 1920 he was regarded as the most dangerous agitator in Nagpur and had for some time been an advocate of a republic completely separated from the British Empire. In October 1920 the Deputy Commissioner in recommending his prosecution for a seditious speech delivered at a public meeting in Nagpur on the 23rd September 1920, remarked as follows:

'To my mind only one construction can be placed on what Cholkar said, *i.e.*, that he meant to incite the people to prepare for a rebellion. Hitherto the most irresponsible speakers have defined the national ideal as complete Home Rule within the empire and urged that India is fit for a full measure of Home Rule. Cholkar explicitly states that the ideal should be complete independence without the British connection.'

However no action was taken, as the Legal Remembrancer recorded the following opinion:

'I agree with Government Advocate that this speech is seditious. It not only brings the established Government into contempt, but it purports to outline a scheme which, if successful, will utterly paralyse it in all its functions. Dr. Cholkar says:- When it comes to pass that this foreign authority, this foreign power, fails to get a single reporter, a single policeman for service, a single soldier to carry a rifle, or a single postman, rest assured that our fight is won on that day and at that time. He even goes further, and urges those policemen who remain in service to become supporters of their nation, *i.e.*, to intrigue against the interest of the Government that employs them, and after the Russian pattern, to turn against that Government when the opportunity arises.'

'I agree with the view of the Deputy Commissioner that the speaker advocates non-co-operation at present, under the leadership of Mahatma Gandhi with a view to a final shaping of the contest under a later warrior Mahatma. I understand this to mean that Government should be weakened first by means of non-co-operation and finally destroyed by military force.[']..."It is now the policy of Government not to prosecute in these seditious cases except "in cases in which there is incitement to violence".' ... 'As regards the speech now under consideration, I can find nothing that can be construed as incitement to violence. The only way in which violence is introduced is in the vague promise of a future military Mahatma who will complete the work begun by the non-co-operation movement. This is not an incitement. There is mention in several passages of "fighting" and struggling but these words could reasonably be said in a figurative sense, and may mean no more than a fight or a struggle, for instance, in a Civil Court.'... 'On the basis of the present policy, we cannot launch a prosecution, in my opinion.'

Cholkar continued his speeches and was finally arrested for a speech made at Nagpur in February 1921. The situation in Nagpur was becoming critical, and the Deputy Commissioner wrote as follows in forwarding his recommendation for prosecution:

'For some time past we have been having speeches everyday, chiefly aimed at the students. Closely connected is a violent so-called temperance agitation. The boys are to be got out of school, and used to picket the liquor shops. Attempts are also being made to intimidate the Kalars. The non-co-operation propaganda is being extended to the villages, and as soon as enough boys can be collected as emissaries the intention is to endeavour to stop all touring by Government officers. Progressively the impression will be given that Government has broken down, with the danger of the result we have seen in Northern India. The speechifying is being spread all over the district, and is not confined to headquarters. The main body of Maratha Brahmans under Munje have now come completely round to the full Congress programme.'

'The most virulent speaker as might be expected is Dr. Cholkar. He

* Passage left out in the original.

has let himself go pretty well during the last few weeks, but generally moderates his tone when he finds reporters are present. The dangerous part of his speeches are [!] that they are calmly reasoned out, and although he lefts fly occasionally at the 'Satanic' Government his appeal is more to the reason of his audience. As when I proposed to send him up for prosecution before Christmas he is now openly setting up the ideal of an Indian republic.'

'The movement among the students is gaining ground. The Hislop College is said to have only three students, and those Christians, left. Unless something is done to turn the tide we shall soon be faced with a very dangerous situation.'

'On the 3rd instant a meeting was held with Ogale, the editor of the *Maharashtra*, in the chair. Dr. Cholkar was the speaker of the evening. He addressed himself principally to students. His text was paragraph 2 of the non-co-operation resolution of the Congress, applying to students, and he stated that he proposed to set forth the "line of political agitation" to be adopted in the future. In reading his text, he laid stress on the words "irrespective of any consequence". He proceeded to set out his definition of *Swaraj*. "I interpret *Swaraj* as absolute independence, a republic." For this it would be the pleaders' duty to give their blood as well as their practice if Congress should so decide. The analogy of the French defending their liberties against Germany followed. "The history of France is the history of liberty, and remember that it is written in letters of blood shed by the gallant soldiers and heroes of that nation." If the people cannot make any kind of sacrifice they must be prepared to be slaves. Pleaders in Germany and England during the war abandoned practice and went out to fight. As the pleaders have failed, the students, the second line of troops, must come forward and "fight the national war". Students must "follow the order of the National Congress without the least care for their future fate just as soldiers obey the commands of their general".

'The speaker then went on to define the goal of political agitation. "The very basis of the line of our political agitation" is a republic. Government must then proceed upward from the village "Sabha Mandal" to the main Government of the republic, and not downwards from a central Government to the villages as now. Land should belong to the tenant not to the King. The President must be elected. The republic so constituted need not sever connection with England at once. But it is to be an alliance on equal terms, and liable to "undergo a change".'

'The way the students should work for this ideal is for two to volunteer to live in each village, learn all about the village and the views of the people in it, and do propaganda work. Eventually they "ought to set up a Government carried on by Congress, similar to, and within, the system or the wheel of the administration of the present Government". They are no longer to pay homage, or extend patronage to the British Government, the Government of India or the Central Provinces Government either". Their "sarkar" is now not the British Government, but the Congress.'

'Throughout the speech we have expressions thrown in probably with a view to the Government reporters, to show that the British connection is not altogether to be severed, but the whole thesis is that the present order must be upset by the creation of general unrest, the ultimate ideal being an independent republic. (For republic the English word is used.)'

The papers were sent to the Legal Remembrancer, Home Member and Governor, all of whom agreed that the speech was seditious.

After the case was over a 'co-worker' wrote as follows about him in the local paper, the *Hitavada*:

'I know that when his friends and co-workers were attempting to dissuade him from talking so loud of Independence and Republic he maintained his attitude as the dauntless champion of an absolutely independent Republic and advised his younger friends to suffer and die for that ideal.'

Unlike most non-co-operators Cholkar fought the case, and after a long trial he was discharged, as a shorthand reporter of the speech broke down in cross-examination. Cholkar's defence was an evasion of what he had actually said, and his reputation suffered accordingly. The *Hitavada* in a leader on the case wrote as follows:- 'Mr. Slaney (the Magistrate) has found him innocent of sedition against the King but public opinion declares him to be guilty of high treason, against the Kingdom of truth.'

3. The only other prominent member of the Tilak party who were prosecuted for sedition were N.S. Paranjpe of Yeotmal and W.G. Joshi of Amraoti.

The former, a Chitpavan Brahman, aged 48, is a doctor by profession and has been a prominent agitator since 1907.

The latter, a Kokanasth Brahman, aged 43, has since 1907 been a professional agitator.

Both were convicted under section 124-A, Indian Penal Code, in 1921 for seditious speeches. Paranjpe was sentenced to 15 months' and Joshi to 18 months' imprisonment. Neither made any defence, in accordance with their creed as non-co-operators. Both are irreconcilably anti-British, and both probably thought with Cholkar, that Gandhi's policy was only a preliminary step to enable India as a united nation to turn out the British by force.

Speaking at Kurankhed in the Akola district, on the 31 January 1921, Joshi said:

'It is quite likely that we will have to take arms, but nothing can be told with certainty. For the period of a year, the movement is to be carried on non-violently. The fact that the English are armed matters but little. The police and military are our brothers and once they join hands with us, the English people will find India too hot for them. It would be hardly possible for them to cope with such an overwhelming majority of 30 crores, who might perish, but 10 crores of us will at least knock them down, striking a heavier blow.'

Prior to Paranjpe's prosecution the District Superintendent of Police, Akola, wrote as follows:

'His speeches have varied little: on each occasion he has compared the miserable present with the glorious past and the worthless idlers of today with the fighting men of former days: abused Government; and urged his hearers to fight for Home Rule by non-co-operation and drive the Government out like dogs.'

The speech for which he was prosecuted was delivered at Kuram in the Akola district, on the 10th March 1921. After comparing India's miserable condition, mental, physical and moral, with her glorious past he went on to give his reasons for the change.

'The only answer to this can be that India is being ruled by foreigners—by the English—in whatever way they please. An Englishman having carried lakhs of rupees goes back to England. The result of this is that the wealth of India is being wrested from us. What blood is to a body, so wealth is to a nation. India is getting worn out. The English during the period of these two years (1919-1920) have committed acts of the greatest injustice and tyranny.' (Here follow statements about atrocities at Jallianwala).'They have already started devastating the holy places of the Mahomedans. This is the compensation we get for our assistance (in the war).' 'This all goes to prove that the English and the British Government are not merely foreigners, blood suckers or absorbers of wealth, but in their dealing with us, are even devils. How are we to put an end to this foreign rule? We should not give any help whatever to the British Government.'

4. On the 20th June 1919 W.G. Joshi in one of his first speeches after Gandhi had begun his *Satyagraha*, stated that *Satyagraha* was the moral discipline necessary to prepare the present generation which had grown effeminate, for the fight of *Swaraj*. The speech for which he was prosecuted was addressed to an audience of students at Murtizapur in the Akola district, on the 1st February 1921. The following are extracts:

'I say the present Government is not only like the Government of Rawan, but it is more satanic than Rawan's Government. It has no scruples about massacring the innocent and the poor. This Government must be destroyed. They have reduced this country to poverty—they have rendered you feeble. The mind of the nation had become slavish. The Indians are seven times as much as the English. In the act of killing, how many Indian could they kill? The most they may kill may be 20 crores. The remaining 10 crores of people are sure to overpower them. You boys ought to leave your houses and go to the battlefield. Three generations have rotten in slavery. It matters not if boys meet death. There is virtue in such state. This is my country, I shall rule over it. I will not permit it to be ruled by others. Tell the Government that our mutual friendship cannot continue. I am not afraid of being put into prison. I will tell my sons when I go that this Government has to be destroyed in one year. This Government is an enemy of this country and you should therefore consider it as your enemy.'

5. The only other two residents of the Province who were prosecuted for sedition were the 'no-changer', Makhan Lal Chaturvedi and the Khilafatist, Maulvi Hamid Ali. Both came into prominence for the first time during the non-co-operation movement.

The former is the son of a village schoolmaster of the Hoshangabad district. From sub-editor of the *Karmavir*, an Extremist paper of Jubbulpore, he developed into a professional agitator and toured the province advocating the non-co-operation programme. He was arrested in June 1921, for an objectionable speech made at the Bilaspur District Conference, on the 13th March 1921. He made no defence and was sentenced to eight months' rigorous imprisonment under Section 124-A, Indian Penal Code.

The following are extracts for his speech:

'Our predecessors were wiser then we, that they, finding the British oppressions intolerable, tried to decide their fates on one and only one particular day, that is, in the year 1857, they broke out into Mutiny. ...The English cut down the thumbs of these weavers to destroy the Indian industry. ... We must now turn out these enemies from the country.... We should all cut off our connections with such a Government.... The Government is treacherous, so we should also be the same to them.'

6. Maulvi Hamid Ali of Akatara [?] in the Bilaspur district, carried on active propaganda in the north-western half of the province throughout 1921 and the beginning of 1922.

He was prosecuted in April 1922 under section 124-A and sentenced to 18 months' rigorous imprisonment for a speech delivered at Raipur on the 21st April 1922 accusing Government of trying to destroy the Mahomedan religion and inciting the police to resign.

7. The remaining five persons prosecuted under section 124-A did not belong to the province. Four of them had previous records as political agitators. The most notorious are Sundarlal Kaynath of Mirzapur, United Provinces, and Arjunlal Sethi, a Jain, of Jaipur.

Sundarlal is a product of Lajpat Rai's influence at the Dayanand Arya Vedic College at Lahore. He studied law, but was debarred from taking the final examination owing to violent Swadeshi speeches in 1907. He was suspected in the Delhi conspiracy case and is the author of proscribed and other objectionable literature. Both he and Arjunlal Sethi came to the Central Provinces at the invitation of Jamnalal Bajaz, a Jain of Wardha, and one of the foremost no-changers of the Central Provinces. In 1921 Sundarlal was placed in charge of the National School at Nagpur, and in addition to advocating the full non-co-operation programme he was suspected of trying to seduce the loyalty of Indian troops. He was prosecuted and sentenced to one year's rigorous imprisonment for an objectionable speech at Wardha on the 13th May 1921. After his release he continued his propaganda unabated. He became president of the Hindu Central Provinces Congress Committee and the leader of the no-changers in the Central Provinces. At the Lucknow

* Passage left out in the original.

Conference on the 7th June 1922, he advocated violent measures, and was elected a member of the Civil Disobedience Committee, and the All-India Congress Committee. Later in 1922 he resigned his post of president when the policy of Civil Disobedience was rejected, but continued as vice-president and made objectionable speeches, for which he was prosecuted and sentenced to six months' rigorous imprisonment under Section 108, Criminal Procedure Code, in default of furnishing security. The following are extracts from two speeches made by him after his first conviction:

'Non-violent non-co-operation is a war started against the British Government.'

'Empires are born and killed just in the same way as men are born and killed. Empires are subject to maladies in the same manner as men are. I am prepared to say before you in the capacity of a student of history that the British Government whom you are considering the mightiest, is now showing the signs of a slack pulse. Its days are numbered. It has been surrounded by so many maladies that no physician on earth can save it—the stump of the tree under whose shadow you are thinking to pass your days has been eaten up by white ants and will be uprooted by the weakest wind ... Civil Disobedience means non-payment of taxes and disregard of certain laws. The real war will begin when you refuse to pay taxes and that time is drawing near. I shall consider that I have done my duty if Civil Disobedience is started from one of 14 districts (in my charge). (Turning to the reporters) The power under whose patronage you are playing the traitor to your nation will prove totally unfit to protect you from a mighty typhoon.'

'If anyone asks me if I wanted Swaraj within the British Empire, I have only one reply and that is *never*. Is there any mother who would entrust her babe to any ayah rotten with disease...?'*

'A day will come when Civil Disobedience will be passed. Government will use force, big guns and machine guns. At that time Government does not discriminate between the loyal and disloyal. All are treated in the same way. All are fired at. The same thing at Jallianwala Bagh. Amongst the killed and wounded there were title-holders and men whose breasts were adorned with medals for having served Government. Prepare yourselves for the Great War that is inevitable.[']

* Passage left out in the original.

8. Arjunlal has an infamous record dating from 1906 which includes complicity in more than one political murder.

As a result of the Delhi conspiracy enquiry he was detained as a State prisoner until 1920, when he was released under the general amnesty on his accepting the condition of good behaviour in future. Soon after his release he visited Jamnalal Bajaz and began to [?]. He became one of the most notorious advocates of non-co-operation. His lectures are characterised by violent and filthy abuse of the English.

In June 1920 he received a warning from the Government of India, advising him to moderate his language.

Both he and Bhagwandin were arrested and prosecuted at Seoni for a speech made on the 5th February 1921. Both were convicted. On his release Arjunlal continued to advocate non-co-operation, but the tone of his speeches was milder.

The following are extracts from his speech at Seoni:-

['] In 1857, attempts were made to drive out these white-skinned tyrants....*

These indigent beggarly Europeans came here to fill their bellies as well as that of their hungry countrymen....

These conquerors were rubbing their nose before the Emperors of India....

In this bureaucratic Government we are looked upon as even worse than dogs....

Such was not our condition during the Moslem Rule.[']

In asking how a few English could govern India he said:

['] Do they do so by means of military force....

Their trick lies in the fact that they closed our industries and introduced their own country-made goods....

We cannot find any country-made thing....

People are starving in India while wheat is exported from the Punjab. The bellies of Englishmen are being filled....

Rule, Britannia rule always, Britannia never shall be slaves: But who will be slaves? Indians. The results of this education has been that our countrymen are serving in the police and prepared to cut the throats of their fellow countrymen....

* Passage left out in the original.

After passing you will enter service, polish the boot of the sahib and after leading the life of a slave die in the end....

At the time of the Bengal partition there came forward several youths who were prepared to either kill or die and who would not tolerate these unjust persons committing atrocities on India. But when such a power which is ready to sacrifice itself comes into existence, the tyrants try to win it over to their side by other means. They accordingly created the phantom of the Reform Scheme....

To co-operate and assist the unjust, the sinful and the murderous and to bow one's head before them is a great sin....

The Khilafat has been abolished, religion has been uprooted....

Instruct the women to advise their husbands and turn these Government slaves out of their houses till they adopt non-co-operation. O students, imitate Pralhad, that India, which has been turned into a hell by the injustice of this bureaucracy, will put an end to the oppression of these tyrants.[']

9. Bhagwandin Jain of Aligarh appears to have come to the Central Provinces as an assistant to Arjunlal. He is an ex-Railway employee who took first to religion [*sic*] and then finally in 1919 to politics. Gandhi, for some reasons, conferred on him the title of Mahatma. The following are extracts from his Seoni speech:

Can any, except these white-skinned people, ever think of committing such a great sin as cutting off the thumbs of the workmen? ...*

We became disunited during this white (British) regime....

How long could the subjects bear such hardship? It was not a mutiny but a struggle for independence....

Indians had the best opportunity during the war. They could have risen in rebellion and driven them out. We, however, thought that it was not the time as they were in difficulties, descendants, as we are, of the rishis (sages)....

The British assured that in case they came out victorious out of the war, they would not dismember Turkey, and would not occupy the sacred places. But on the termination of the war they brought about the dismemberment of Turkey. The sacred places of Arabia were bombarded....

There are three aspects of the Turkish question. The first is that the Sultan is the spiritual leader of the Moslem[s]. The British therefore resolved

* Passage left out in the original.

to smash that centre with a view to crush their religion. They therefore instigated the Arabs to become independent....

Secondly, they thought that if Turkey, Arabia, Persia and Afghanistan were to fall into their hands, then India would remain for ever in their possession....

He made a pretence of hunger striking in jail, and then submitted an abject apology (subsequently withdrawn) with a view to getting released.

He was reconvicted in 1923 under sections 143/114 of the Indian Penal Code for taking part in the Nagpur Flag *Satyagraha*.

10. Two other prosecutions under sections 124-A, Indian Penal Code, were sanctioned, one against Narayan Swami Khattri of Amritsar and the other against Radha Ballab, *alias* Som Dutt Sharma, a Brahman, of the Muttra district. Both were political agitators prior to 1919. Narayan Swami being a religious fanatic and Som Dutt a professional agitator of lesser importance. Both prosecutions were withdrawn as Narayan Swami left the province for the time being and Som Dutt tendered an apology.

11. Section 108, Criminal Procedure Code, was used for the most part in the case of seditious speakers of minor importance. The accused included six pleaders who had given up practice to become paid agitators for the time being; one Secretary of a Khilafat Committee; a student sent down as a Khilafat agitator from the National College, Aligarh; two doctors; three national school teachers; nine landowners or cultivators and others of no particular status.

Non-Co-operation and the Press

When Mr. Gandhi first published his doctrines of non-co-operation even the extremist papers refused to subscribe to all its details. The Moderate Press was against it from its very inception and continued to denounce it in varying degrees of bitterness. But when the Calcutta Special Congress eventually passed the non-co-operation resolution, some of the nationalist papers, like the *Karmavir*, which were originally against it began to advocate its acceptance by the whole country. On the other hand, there were others like the *Maharashtra* and *Young Patriot* which continued to be suspicious of the utility of the non-co-operation programme as a political weapon on account of its impracticability and desired to substitute for it responsive co-operation and the boycott of British goods.

The *Karmavir*, Jubbulpore, in its issue of the 11th September 1920 says:

'The National Assembly has now passed its verdict in favour of non-co-operation which has been taxing everybody's brain for long. It is the dutiful sons of India on whom now devolved the responsibility of successfully carrying out the national mandate and thereby creating an impression on the whole world. India is now passing through the period of transition. Her pace has been quickened by the recent Dyerian deeds and it is the duty of her sons to execute the will of the nation to help her in reaching the goal.'

The *Maharashtra* of Nagpur, dated the 30th June 1920, in the course of its leading article says:

'Regarding the lines of non-co-operation as laid down by Mr. Gandhi there cannot be an unanimity of opinion, but barring the Moderates, all others believe that some sort of non-co-operation must be resorted to in order to bring home to the British Government the indignation of Indians and also their loss of confidence in the British sense of justice. The successive methods of non-co-operation as set forth by Mahatma Gandhi do not appear to us to be practicable. At any rate, we do not think that they will be effective. We should therefore like to suggest to him to set aside his non-co-operation movement and take up the boycott against British goods.'

Later on, on the 7th July the same paper observes:

'Mahatma Gandhi's faith in non-co-operation appears to be ill-placed, as on the announcement of the recent titles in honour of the King-Emperor's birthday none of the recipients has refused to accept them or throw them either. The title-hunting class in India has such a peculiar psychology that it is sure to baffle and vanquish Mahatma Gandhi. Regarding the aspect of non-co-operation in giving up Government service, who is going to solve the bread problem of its dependants. Again, if Mahatma Gandhi were to try and induce Indian soldiers to give up military service he would be instantly court-martialled and hanged and none would venture to try one's hand that way. Thus, on all counts, the non-co-operation scheme being impracticable will be a failure.'

The *Young Patriot* of Nagpur in its issue of the 13th September 1920 says:

'For our ownselves we think that Mr. Gandhi's resolution of non-co-operation is highly impracticable barring his programme of Swadeshi; we are honestly of opinion that responsive co-operation as propounded and put before the nation is the only right course to be adopted by the people.'

But in view of Mr. Gandhi's increasing influence even papers like the *Maharashtra* began to give a qualified approval to his programme and agreed to give it a fair trial. Accordingly at the beginning of the year 1921 the Nationalist press united in supporting Mahatma Gandhi's policy.

The *Praja paksha* (Akola), dated the 16th January 1921, observes:

'Now that the non-co-operation resolution has been unanimously passed by the Nagpur Congress with its all-embracing character, it is highly surprising to find a vacillation or halting attitude on the part of the people in translating it into practice with all promptness! The pleaders and students, for instance, are still hanging back, apparently on account of misgivings in their minds. India needs the services of all her sons of any rank or station in life to attain her goal of *Swaraj* in the near future as assured to them by Mahatma Gandhi. To achieve that end, a whole generation in India must behave itself in a spirit of complete self-surrender, and the present generation can as well glorify itself by coveting that honour. We, therefore, call on all the sons of India to take the solemn vow of carrying out bravely and honestly the non-co-operation programme and marching speedily onwards to *Swaraj*.'

The *Sankalpa* (Nagpur) in its leading article, dated the 22nd January 1921, says:

'The tremendous progress made by the non-co-operation movement within less than a month's time from the last session of the National Congress amply testifies to its potential force. The whole nation is agitating with unexampled zeal and fortitude. Every section of the population is doing its level best to make the whole scheme a success, as is evident from the evacuation of the existing schools by students in sweeping numbers, the establishment of national institutions in their stead, the renunciation of practice by lawyers on an increasingly larger scale, and the resignation of Government service by those who have now come to regard it as a source of poison! Foreign fashions are now being given a gradual go-by, and those who were long fondly clung to them have come to prefer the country-made coarse *khadi* to foreign cloth. There has been a vast change in their vision, so much so that the Gandhi cap has become an article of general use and an instrument of national awakening. The "Gandhi spinning wheel" has at the same time been a source of maintenance to many a starving family! The former has at places evoked official disapproval and resentment as being the badge of non-co-operation. Such things, petty and life-less though they may be, are the embodiments of great principles, *e.g.*, patriotism and self-reliance, that are sure to be crowned with success.'

The first non-co-operation campaign lasted up to the end of March 1921. During this time the Nationalist press undertook an intensive propaganda to familiarise the masses with the idea of non-co-operation and the agitation was principally directed towards the boycott of schools and colleges and against the excise sales. The local press supported the temperance campaign and bitterly condemned Government for 'perpetuating the vice which is ruining thousands of Indians with the sole object of raising revenue for the maintenance of a costly administration.' Social boycott of liquor contractors was generally suggested in the press to dissuade them from bidding at the sales. Some of the papers made no secret of the fact that the main object of the campaign was to embarrass the Government by causing the reduction of revenue, as will appear from the following extracts.

The *Lokmat* (Yeotmal) in its second serial on 'Excise licenses and non-co-operation' dated the 28th January 1921, observes:

'The people in the Central Provinces and Berar have already made some efforts to check the evil of the drink habit among the masses, and in the providential dispensation it seems to be fortunate that just at this opportune time a fresh and vigorous stimulus is imparted to those efforts by the inspiring message sent by Mahatma Gandhi to Jamnalal Seth of Wardha in the matter of creating such a keen and strong volume of public feeling against the use of liquor as to secure total abolition of the drink traffic in the province. It is, indeed, alarming to contemplate that the Excise Department has trebled its income within the last twenty years which nearly rivals that from the Land Revenue and which has been feeding fat high-salaried officials? Education ought to have found far more favour with Government than liquor, but unfortunately the number of liquor shops in the Yeotmal district alone outstrips that of primary schools by over one hundred! Though Government are responsible for the growth of the drink habit among the masses, it is an imperative necessity for the people now to get rid of the harmful Excise Department and banish for ever the use of liquor. Meetings ought to be held everywhere, deputations sent to the liquor contractors inducing them not to bid for Excise licenses any more and caste meetings held to make stringent regulations to prohibit altogether the use of liquor.'

The [*Chhatra S ...*] (Jubbulpore) of April 1921 observes:

'The Government of the Central Provinces, for instance, has, till very recently, viewed with regret the indifference on the part of the public leaders and moneyed classes towards the temperance activities, but it has now taken to imprisoning the reformers of the society on the ground that they have prevented the thekedars from bidding for the Excise licences or have reduced the Government revenues. The shrewdness and duplicity of this policy of Government have awakened us by shaking off its credit. The nation would, at any rate, be benefited inasmuch as it would be in a position to stop the waste of its money on intoxicants and paralyse Government by stopping its income. Our country has been reduced to an impoverished condition by a continuous drain into the treasury that has served to fatten Government. Now that this is not possible and that the interest of the temperance movement clash with those of Government, the latter is appearing in its true colours; its sinister designs and inner "blackness" are brought to light. The result is that an attempt to check drunkenness is regarded as an offence against the State, the offender being dealt with under section 144, Criminal Procedure Code.'

The non-co-operation programme changed with the changing outlook of its author, and in April the press was busy giving the widest possible publicity to the Bezwada programme of Charkhas, the Tilak Swaraj Fund and the registration of Congress members. The Moderates regarded the change in policy as an admission on the part of the non-co-operators of the failure of the original non-co-operation programme. Some of the Nationalist papers were jubilant over it and made an impatient appeal to the people to make the use of the Charkha universal.

But the Berar papers were lukewarm in their support and regretted the omission of a national strike from the programme, which they regarded as 'the most effective way to humble down the bureaucracy and completely clog the wheels of Administration.'

The *Udaya* (Amraoti) in its leading article, dated the 17th May 1921, observes:

'As Germany, before the Great War broke out, had fixed upon for her world empire, India too must settle the day for a great national strike to make non-co-operation a full success. All classes and interests in India must from now begin to prepare themselves for that grand strike. The Mulshi Peta affair has vindicated the power of *Satyagraha* and the Chittagong affair has demonstrated the terrible power of non-co-operation by compelling the District Magistrate of the place to withdraw his order under section 144, Criminal Procedure Code. If all Indians unite in going on a national strike, the bureaucracy in India being quite helpless will be in the hollow of their hands. It cannot carry on the administration without their help. It is hoped that the Congress will do its duty of fixing and announcing the day for the national strike.'

Later when Mr. Gandhi charged the Maharashtra politicians with lack of faith, the Berar papers began more openly to withdraw their support from Mr. Gandhi's policy and started attacking it vehemently with a view to discredit it as impracticable. For instance the *Udaya* (Amraoti) in its issue of the 26th July 1921 remarked:

'Though during his recent visit to Poona, Mahatma Gandhi paid compliments to Maharashtra, he found fault with its lack of "faith". Does the Mahatma mean by "faith" taking anything and everything on trust? There are impracticable details in the programme of non-co-operation for which he is responsible. As for the people of Maharashtra, they have up to now carried out the programme as far as possible, though they did not believe in some of its details, but it is now high time that they should unanimously speak their mind frankly on the question and vigorously embark on their programme of work. Mahatma Gandhi had better carefully bear in mind that the Maharashtra people will yield to none in their ardour for *Swaraj*.'

The subsequent investiture of Mr. Gandhi with the powers of a dictator at the Ahmedabad Congress was strongly criticised by the Marathi papers, which started an intensive propaganda to prepare the ground for the scheme of 'obstructive non-co-operation' formulated by the Maharashtra Conference at Akola. While this was the attitude of the Press towards non-co-operation, the Extremist papers were keenly solicitous about the development of the Khilafat movement and endeavoured to show that Government was hostile to Islam.

The *Taj* (Jubbulpore), dated the 3rd March 1921, says:

'The dismemberment of Turkey is due to the action of British Ministers who have systematically shown a cynical disregard for the Moslem sentiments. It is difficult to understand why England has determined to destroy the Moslem world. Britain has now the last chance to comprehend the self-interested policy of her Ministers.'

As the non-co-operation movement progressed, the press regarded Mr. Gandhi's experience of launching civil disobedience involving non-payment of taxes with varying degrees of favour. The Moderate papers expressed grave doubts as regards the possibility of its success, the Nationalist Marathi papers looked at it with mingled curiosity and distrust, while the Hindi papers acclaimed it with joy. But Mr. Gandhi's sudden *volte-face* after the Chauri Chaura tragedy alienated the sympathy of some of the Extremist papers, which began to attack his programme on the grounds of impracticability. The papers that remained loyal to Mr. Gandhi justified his action as statesmanlike and suggested that the movement might be launched again when circumstances permitted.

The *Rajasthan Kesari* (Wardha), dated the 26th February 1922, observes:

'The Bardoli decision has greatly upset the minds of the pessimists in the country. For, they regard the decision as highly prejudicial to the interest of the nation, the national agitation and the National Congress. The followers cannot realise the manifold difficulties of the leader. It is, therefore, but natural for them to be disappointed. But if they only care to ponder over the views expressed by their great National Leader during the days of his "fast" and try to understand the difficulties that come in his way of leading the nation, they will find that they have no cause for disappointment. We are not concerned with idlers and their idle criticism. The *Satyagraha* campaign has only been postponed so that by the time it is brought into use, we should have established a peaceful atmosphere all over and assimilated the value of non-violence. We hope that the All-India Conference Committee, now sitting at Delhi, will, while confirming the Bardoli decision, chalk out a practical scheme for carrying out the constructive side of the programme and lay a particular stress on the item of National education which will provide the Congress with a number of able workers.'

The Bardoli Working Committee's resolution suspending every activity of an offensive nature and advising the adoption of more social work for the sake of self-purification and national education chilled the enthusiasm of the whole Nationalist press.

The *Udaya* (Amraoti), dated the 21st February 1922, observes:

'The resolutions passed by the Working Committee of the Congress at Bardoli on the 12th February 1922, have, indeed, sounded the death-knell of the current politics in India. They have converted the great political body of the National Congress into an organisation for doing a mere social service. This altered form of the Congress runs counter to the chief aim of the body, *viz.*, devotion to Indian politics, as settled in its third session. Now politics will be replaced in the Congress by social activities such as the organisation of the temperance campaign, elevation of the depressed classes, promotion of unity and mutual good-will among all classes and races, etc. It has revived the old controversy whether the social reform should precede or follow the political reform. Lokamanya Tilak convincingly proved in his life-time that the question of political reform ought to have the first claim on the attention of the country. And if the people diverted their energies in the channel of mere social service to the exclusion of politics and political reforms, the nation is sure to receive a serious political set-back for about quarter of a century. Further, if the non-co-operation movement was primarily started to cut off our co-operation with the Britishers and paralyse the existing system of British administration in India, it has now ended in advising the people to promote and emphasise unity among all classes and races (even Europeans and Indians, etc.) and cultivate mutual good-will! Thus the movement has now completely eschewed politics and become one of self-purification. What a conflict between the definitions and scope of non-co-operation.'

The *Maharashtra* (Nagpur), dated the 22nd February 1922, observes:

'The resolutions recently passed at Bardoli by the Working Committee of the Congress have cast a deep gloom over the nation. They have politically benumbed and paralyses the people. Whatever faith the Mahatmaji pins on the divine revelations of his mind, quite a large number of people will not be prepared to blindly accept his oracles. They may even find therein another Himalayan mistake, though they may not choose to call it openly as such. It is high time for Mahatmaji's friends and admirers to speak out their mind candidly in India's interests. Though the recent Bardoli decision has brought to a dead stop all the political activities, it has violently agitated the thinking minds. It now entirely rests with the All-India Congress Committee to be held at Delhi on the 24th instant to discriminate between the acceptable and unacceptable part of the Bardoli programme and decide upon a programme which ensures the progress of the national cause.'

The Berar papers became increasingly convinced of the impracticability of the Gandhian programme and suggested a modification of it in favour of Council entry which gave rise to bitter recriminations. The majority of the Hindi papers denounced any modifications as 'inopportune, unwise and treacherous'.

The *Rajasthan Kesari* (Wardha) in its issue of the 30th April states:

'We have already shown that the present is the most inopportune moment for effecting modifications in the existing programme of the National Congress. Our view has not only been borne out by eminent and experienced men like Shrinivas Ayengar, but it is also supported by the general public in the country as is evident from the proceedings of the Conferences held at Pen, Chittagong and other places. The people of Wardha, in a public meeting, while vehemently condemning the idea of altering the present programme and rejecting a scheme to that effect, formulated by the Nagpur Congress Committee, have rightly expressed their view that any alterations in the current National programme, especially at a time when the country is passing through a period of storm and stress, will mean nothing but treachery towards those who have already gone to jails in the cause of the country. The people from almost all the quarters are thus raising their voice against the destructive policy adopted by our Maharashtriya brethren and that to rightly. For, the former know full well that Councils are a mere farce and that the only way to attain their goal of *Swaraj* is to steadfastly adhere to the non-violent non-cooperation programme and carry it out to the finish.'

The findings of the Civil Disobedience Committee that the country was not fit for a national strike enraged the orthodox non-co-operators, who insisted on loyalty to Mr. Gandhi and strict adherence to his constructive programme, which, they said, provided training for civil disobedience. The split in the Extremist party widened and led to the creation of two sections of the Congress which were now known as pro-Council and anti-Council parties. The following extract is given as an illustration of the spirit in which the more extreme section viewed the decision of the Civil Disobedience Committee.

The *Rajasthan Kesari* (Wardha) in its leading article on the report of the Civil Disobedience Enquiry Committee dated the 26th November 1922, says:

'The Committee has by its recommendations not only damped the courage of the country, but has also exhibited that the nation woefully lacks in leaders consistent in their views, conduct and ideals. Besides failing to give a clear lead to the nation, the Committee has unnecessarily caused a schism in the people and has, by upholding the cause of responsive co-operation, created false hopes in the country. The natural result of the differences of opinion between the leaders and the people will be to undo the entire work of the great sage who has been incessantly toiling all these years for the uplift of the nation. The pro-Council party argues that it insists upon the change with a view to wrecking the Councils and causing a split between the Moderates and the bureaucracy. We fail to see what useful purpose will be served by giving undue importance to the Moderates. The best course under the circumstances would be to leave them alone. If the people honestly work out the constructive programme, as has been laid down by the Congress, we are sure the day will soon dawn when the power of the Moderates will disappear along with that of the bureaucracy. It is, indeed, a thousand pities that those who are attempting this day to alienate the sympathies of our Moderate brethren from the bureaucracy, should themselves be desirous, be it with any motive, of gracing the Council chairs and sitting shoulder to shoulder with the bureaucrats. To advocate entry into the Councils at a time when the greatest man of the world and a true son of mother India is rotting in the Yervada Jail is to cast a stigma on his fair fame. It must be remembered that while the Councils stand for evolution, *Satyagraha* stands for revolution. A beneficent rule may be secured by recourse to evolution, but *Swaraj* is impossible without revolution. The people should, therefore, beware of the snare and delusion of the Councils, for once they take to evolution they cannot hope to see prosperous days in the near future.'

Matters came to a head at the Gaya Congress in December 1922, where the pro-Council party found themselves in a minority. The Majority party opposed the resolutions regarding Council-entry and passed the resolution on civil disobedience.

The *Prajapaksha* (Akola), dated the 31st Dec. 1922, says:

'If there is anything that has lent importance to the Gaya Congress, it is distinctly the eminent and self-sacrificing personality of Mr. C.R. Das, the president of that body. Undoubtedly, his speech must be acknowledged as the best of all other Congress addresses delivered by the presidents up to now. A glance, however, at the resolutions passed by the Congress only serves to bring disappointment. The Congress expense at Gaya is, indeed, a huge waste from the view-point of national progress, since the resolutions only confirm the political mistakes of the two or three years past! One would easily bear out this remark when one finds that the resolutions on contesting elections to the Councils and on boycotting the British goods were negativated, while the resolution on civil disobedience was recklessly passed! What next is the question that now faces the pro-Council party? Why, it must steadily maintain itself in the Congress and try to win the majority eventually to its side.'

The split in the Congress received considerable attention from the press, and papers like the *Karmavir* and *Pranavir*, which were originally opposed to the policy of Council-entry, gradually changed their attitude as they realised which way the wind was blowing. Regarding the Gaya Conference the *Karmavir* wrote as follows:

'The whole country will feel a sense of relief and pride that the Congress has risen to the occasion of the grave crisis in the national movement. The resolution is in the nature of an honest compromise. It is an expression of the national will and few who are alive to the complexity of the political situation will question its wisdom.'

The *Swatantra Hindusthan* and the *Taruna Maharashtra*, papers representing the orthodox non-co-operation school of thought, were however, scathing in their comments. 'It is doubtful' the *Swatantra Hindusthan* said, 'how far this compromise will establish a lasting peace in the Congress. From the non-co-operators' point of view the compromise is a bitter pill which the nation is called to swallow as a preventive against the collapse of the Congress.'

To keep up this show of unity in the Congress the All-India Congress Committee, which met at Bombay, decided that the two wings of the Congress should work in harmony. Therefore, the papers belonging to both parties carried on a vigorous election campaign with a view to keeping the Moderates out of the Council, and in this they succeeded beyond expectation.

In spite of this show of unity between the two wings of the Congress, the No-changers were smarting under a sense of injustice, inasmuch as they believed Council-entry to be repugnant to the principle of non-co-operation. So after Mr. Gandhi's release they made a final attempt to exclude the Swarajists from the Congress organisations and also to revive the old controversy on Council-entry; but when as a result of continued deliberations between Mr. Gandhi and the Swarajists a policy of 'live and let live' was adopted by both the wings of the Congress and the three boycotts which had already failed were formally called off to placate the Swarajists, the Extremist press applauded Mr. Gandhi's decision.

The *Maharashtra* (Nagpur), dated the 28th May 1924, in its leading article observes:

'From the two statements it is clear that the two political parties stand as poles asunder with regard to the meaning and objective of non-co-operation. While with Mahatma Gandhi non-co-operation is a mere mental attitude, with the Swarajists it is a real political weapon. When the Swarajists in accordance with their political programme entered the Councils, it was a question as to what attitude the orthodox non-co-operationists should assume towards the former. It was apprehended that Mahatma Gandhi would even indirectly help the bureaucracy in defeating the Swarajists. It was even rumoured that he and his party would enter the Councils and co-operate with Government in beating down the Swaraj party. But thanks to the good sense of Mahatmaji that he has belied the expectations of the enemies of India's interests by his declaration of the principle "live and let live". Since the Gaya Congress the Swarajists had been impressing the same principle upon the orthodox non-co-operationists, and it is now gratifying to find that Mahatmaji has accepted it. Now if beyond the application of the same principle to the Swarajists' entering the Councils and resorting to obstruction there, it is faithfully extended and carried out in the case of other matters too by the non-co-operationists, the bureaucracy can be effectively attacked on all sides. As regards civil disobedience, both the non-co-operationists and the Swarajists agree in holding that the country is not yet prepared for it. In the meanwhile, while the former will set themselves to work out their "constructive programme", as decided upon by the Mahatmaji, the latter will extend the range of non-co-operation and start such activities as will, in their opinion, be conducive to the growth and fighting power of the country to carry on a successful struggle against the bureaucracy and to win their way to *Swaraj*.'

4

History of the Non-Co-operation and Khilafat Movements in Bengal

NO. 1. LETTER NO. D. 3374, DATED THE 21ST OCTOBER 1924, FROM THE GOVERNMENT OF INDIA, HOME DEPARTMENT

Hon'ble Member has seen. Start collecting information at once (it is probably available in Calcutta) and show to Mr. Birley on arrival.

A.N. Moberly—29. 10. 1924

Our papers are being collected and a note will be put up later. Meanwhile it is for consideration whether we should forward copies to the Commissioners of Divisions, Inspector-General of Police and the Commissioner of Police for an early note. Local Self-Government Department may also be asked to furnish us with information with regard to the effect on local self-government.

B.N.M.—4. 11. 1924

This seems to need the attention of one officer for a considerable time, it is a Herculean task if it is to be done in detail. Probably, however, the Government of India do not require a detailed comparison of speeches and examination of propaganda for the provinces, so much as a review of the progress of the movement and its political effects, of the nature of, but somewhat fuller than Part I of the Administration Reports.

It is for orders how we are to deal with the case, whether by consulting the different departments of Government only or perhaps by asking selected District Officers for notes. In the present circumstances we should wish to avoid putting any additional burden on the Calcutta Police's and Intelligence Branch offices.

R.H. Hutchings—4. 11. 1924

We are concerned only with the history of the movement in Bengal and with speeches, etc., delivered in Bengal. I think we have most of the information on record; we had periodical accounts of the movement drawn up under the Intelligence Branch, I think, and at various times we have made reports to the Government of India. I do not think we need worry other departments, and at the present stage I would not ask districts; let us get together all the material we have available. As the Secretary of State want [!] it in a hurry, I think we shall have to put a special man on to read the material and draft. Please consider who is available for this. I should like to consult with Mr. Birley as soon as he arrives; he had a personal knowledge of the material available.

H.L. Stephenson—6. 11. 1924

Mr. K.C. Chunder, who is now at Mymensingh, is being brought in from there for the Administration Report. He might also take up this work. Mr. Porter can do a good deal of the preliminary routine work for Part II of the Administration Report.

R.H. Hutchings—10. 11. 1924

Taken up. I think that more materials can be found. Did not the Intelligence Branch submit quarterly reports? If not, we had better have the weekly confidential reports from the Deputy Inspector-General from January 1921 to April 1922. There was also an enquiry by Government from District Officers about non-co-operation in relation to chaukidars. Also there must be paragraphs in Annual Administration Report. When further materials have been collected I will suggest the lines on which the report should be prepared.

L. Birley—13. 11. 1924

Extracts of the notes have been sent to the Intelligence Branch as directed. It may be noted that the Intelligence Branch published a monthly report on the non-co-operation movement from February to December 1920 and from January to June 1921. They then stopped publishing them as separate reports. These are all put up together with the subsequent weekly reports up to April 1922 as directed by Chief Secretary....

2. The three Annual Administration Reports for the years 1920-21, 1921-22 and 1922-23 are put up.

3. The file regarding non-co-operation in relation to chaukidars is put up.

4. Discussions about the formation of Swarajya Party is contained in the Intelligence Branch weekly reports for the weeks ending 16th and 23rd November, and 7th, 14th, and 21st December 1922, and 14th January and 1st March 1923. They are also put up.

5. Files containing (1) notes for the moral and material progress report for the years 1921 and 1922, (2) list of specific instances of non-co-operation in the districts of Bengal, and (3) notes on the development of arbitration courts are put up.

6. Besides these, office has collected all the files in connection with the non-co-operation movement generally and is preparing a statement grouping them under various heads, such as incidents of the movement, situation in districts, prosecutions, etc. They will be put up when required.

B.N.M.—14. 11. 1924
W.H.A.—14. 11. 1924

Perusal. Chief Secretary has told me that Mr. Lyne is destined for this work with the assistance of Mr. Porter.

R.H. Hutchings—14. 11. 1924

[...]*

NO. 2 NO. 1266 P, DATED 31 JANUARY 1925

A history of the Khilafat movement is put up for approval.

H.W. Lyne—13. 2. 1925

I think this will do very well. Hon'ble Member has approved, but

*One or more pages of the original missing.

would be glad if the Hon'ble Sir Abdur Rahim would examine the first two and a half pages.

L. Birley—16. 2. 1925

The office of Caliph (successor) or as otherwise called the *Imam*, combines spiritual functions as well as the duties of the chief executive head or Magistrate of the Islamic Commonwealth. Among his purely spiritual and ecclesiastical duties, are the leading of Friday prayers, the delivering of sermons and the enforcement of religious injunctions relating to prayers, fasting, and *zakat* or obligatory alms corresponding to the tithe in the Christian Ecclesiastical Law. Another most important duty of his is the protection of the holy places of Islam and the safeguarding of the Islamic Commonwealth from hostile attacks. This latter function of his invests the office with great political importance and accounts for the allegiance and attachment which it invokes from the Musalmans generally.

It is not the aim of Muhammadan religion or the Muhammadan Constitutional Law to seek domination of the world through the office of Caliph or otherwise. There is not one word throughout the *Koran* or in the vast theological-legal literature of Islam which would warrant such a supposition, though it is often put forward by ignorant or prejudiced writers. It is quite true that Moslem peoples such as Arabs, Turks, Persians, Moghuls, Africans, etc., ruled for centuries in Asia, Europe and Africa just in the same way as the Christian nations are now dominating the world.

It would be as true to ascribe the political power attained by some of the Moslem peoples to any direct teaching of Islam as it would be to attribute the political ascendancy of the English, the French, and the Germans to any direct teachings of Christianity. Not am I aware of any Khilafatists or Pan-Islamists who entertain any idea of domination of the world by Moslems. What they desire is that the holy places of Islam should remain in the custody of a Moslem power able and willing to protect them from non-Moslem attacks and that the countries which are entirely or predominantly inhabited by Muhammadans should be allowed to remain as independent and self-governing States. On this point all Muhammadans are agreed, but when we come to the methods adopted by the 'Khilafatists' or at least by many of them, there is a wide divergence of opinion. The 'Khilafatists' by joining the non-co-operation Swarajist movement seek to put pressure on English opinion by weakening or threatening to weaken the position of the British in India. The other Muhammadans strongly object to undermining British position in India and would keep separate the question of Khilafat from that of constitutional progress of India and the protection of Muhammadan interests in this country.

As regards what Sultan Abdul Hamid [II] did, I cannot say whether the statement at page 1 of the draft is correct or not, but I have heard of such allegations.

The first two and a half pages should be considerably modified and I shall be glad to discuss the matter further with the Hon'ble Member (Political) or the Chief Secretary if thought necessary.

I have also looked into the rest of the draft and though my opinion is not asked on it, I feel it my duty to record my opinion that the picture presented is one-sided, and does considerable injustice to the Muhammadan community of Bengal. The fact that the Muhammadans of Bengal, in spite of the inflammatory speeches of some men mostly if not all hailing from places outside Bengal, have kept aloof as a body from the anarchist crime and revolutionary and anti-British propaganda is not even mentioned nor is any notice taken of the great efforts which have been made by the leaders of Muhammadan community to stem the really dangerous movements headed by Mr. C.R. Das and his anarchist and Swarajist followers. The authority of a man like Mr. J.M. Sen Gupta is in fact invoked to paint as black as possible the character of the Muhammadans some of whom he and Mr. C.R. Das have all along done their best to mislead into paths of non-co-operation. What I object to, is the whole tone of the draft which suggests that the Muhammadans of Bengal are enemies of the British, an entirely unjustifiable suggestion; while the fact is that it is they who in spite of a wide-spread feeling that their interests have been repeatedly sacrificed to please some clever Hindu agitators and schemers, have consistently supported British regime in Bengal. I should like to see the draft again before it is finally adopted.

Abdur Rahim—23. 2. 1925

This should be sent to Mr. Lyne at Barisal. He is requested to revise the first two and a half pages, and to make the latter part so that it cannot be understood to refer to the attitude of the whole Muhammadan community.

L. Birley—26. 2. 1925

The first two and a half pages have been modified and alterations made throughout so as to make it clear that the draft does not discuss the general Muhammadan attitude, but is simply a history of the Khilafat propaganda. It is meant to be read in close connection with the history of the non-co-operation movement, in which the extent to which the Khilafat propaganda affected the Muhammadan community as a whole is given more attention. The action taken by Muhammadan leaders with regard to the Anarchist and Swarajya movements does not fall within the period to which the draft refers, but a final paragraph had been added in which reference is made to it.

H.W. Lyne—7. 3. 1925

Mr. Lyne had revised his report in the light of the remarks of the Hon'ble Sir Abdur Rahim, who has asked to see it again before it is finally adopted. I think that it does not now give a wrong impression. It may be shown again to the Hon'ble Sir Abdur Rahim.

L. Birley—12. 3. 1925

This should be submitted to His Excellency who has not seen it.

H.L. Stephenson—13. 3. 1925

Lytton—17. 3. 1925

I think Hon'ble Member will find that Mr. Lyne has revised this so as to meet his objections.

L. Birley—17. 3. 1925

I regret that my objections to the draft have not been properly met in spite of the last sentence and some other minor modifications. The draft still presents what I consider to be a wholly misleading picture of the attitude of Bengal Moslems towards the British

Government in India and the British people, in connection with the Khilafat agitation. I do not know what particular opportunities Mr. Lyne had of observing the course of this movement in Bengal, but as I have been living in Bengal since my return from Madras in 1921, I can fairly claim some knowledge of the attitude of the Muhammadans of this province towards that movement. I do not in the least desire to minimise the effect which the Treaty of Sèvres and the subsequent policy of Great Britain with respect to Turkey, Palestine and Mesopotamia produced on the minds of the Muhammadans of Bengal in common with those of the rest of India, but I do say, without fear of contradiction, that most of the acknowledged Muhammadan leaders of Bengal never countenanced, and, in fact, did whatever was feasible to counteract the non-co-operation activities of the Khilafatists like Muhammad Ali, Shaukat Ali, Abul Kalam Azad, Moshin Ali and Abdur Rouf [!] none of them Bengal men - and a few Bengal Muhammadans like Akram Khan and Islamabadi and all of whom were acting under the leadership of Gandhi and C.R. Das. It seems to me that a true account of the movement should, while describing the wide-spread feelings of resentment created by what happened to Turkey, Arabia, etc., frankly and fully acknowledge the self-restraint and courage with which the leading Muhammadans of Bengal prevented the movement from affecting the Muhammadan masses of Bengal.

Abdur Rahim—23. 3. 1925

Sir Abdur Rahim's chief point seems to be that the agitators were chiefly from outside Bengal and that the real Bengal Muhammadan leaders resisted this influence to the full extent of their power. This is of course true to some extent of all provinces, but Sir Abdur Rahim contend [!] that it is truer of Bengal than elsewhere. I was connected with the Political Department during the whole time and I do not think that the future of the actual effects is overdrawn. I have added a paragraph to meet Sir Abdur Rahim's views and I think that with this paragraph conditioning the whole the account is not unfair.

It is impossible to submit the draft to detailed criticism; we shall never get it off if we do. I think Sir Abdur Rahim's main point has been met and the papers should be submitted to His Excellency for permission to issue.

H.L. Stephenson—31. 3. 1925

His Excellency handed to me this file last evening, saying that if I would put my objection in one sentence he would be pleased to embody it in his own letter. It is not at all easy to express in a sentence all that one thinks in a matter like this. But bowing to His Excellency's decision I would define my position thus:

'I am clearly of [the] opinion, without in any way minimising the effect which the Treaty of Sèvres and the subsequent policy of Great Britain with respect to Turkey, Palestine and Mesopotamia produced on the minds of the Muhammadans of Bengal in common with those of the rest of India, that the description of the Khilafat movement in this province, as presented in the draft is one-sided and does considerable.'*

History of the Non-Co-operation Movement in Bengal

A danger to be avoided in giving an account of any movement is the liability to simplify motives and tendencies. In this way attempts have already been made to portray the non-co-operation movement as part of a great popular upheaval which produced Bolshevism in Russia and labour unrest in England, or as an example of the new spirit of national self-determination which found expression in the peace treaties. While sometimes appearing to lend colour to both these theories the narrative of events in Bengal teaches us at its inception to be cautious. The movement, to begin with, was purely Muhammadan and therefore partly religious.

The reasons which induced Mr. Gandhi to champion the cause of the Khilafat are obvious. In the agitation over the terms of the

* Rest of the page missing in the original.

Turkish peace treaty coupled with the agitation over the Rowlatt Bill and events in the Punjab he must have seen an unparalleled opportunity of uniting the two leading communities in opposition to the Government. The alliance with Muhammad Ali and Shaukat Ali had been formed at the close of 1919. Its first result in Bengal was seen in the conference of the Provincial Khilafat Committee held in Calcutta in February 1920. Three of the resolutions of this Conference—that requesting Muhammadan members of His Majesty's forces to sever all connection with the British Government, moved by Mr. Fazlul Huq, that requesting Muhammadan members of Council and title holders to surrender their offices and titles, moved by Maulana Abul Kalam Azad, and that enjoining boycott of British goods, moved by Maulvi Nazimuddin Ahmad—fell within the policy of non-co-operation as afterwards defined by Mr. Gandhi. These resolutions were to be put into effect in the event of the Turkish peace terms failing to satisfy Muhammadan opinion. A 'hartal' or complete cessation of business, was also arranged for March 19th with the object of impressing that opinion upon Government

The Conference was followed by meetings at most of the important *mufassal* centres at which full advantage was taken of the anti-Turkish campaign then proceeding in Europe. It had been said that non-co-operation was introduced into Bengal from outside, and it is true that the preliminary agitation was largely conducted by up-country Muhammadans, such as Shaukat Ali, Dr. Kitchlew and Mr. Qidwai. As a result, however, of the *mufassal* campaigns influential Bengal Muhammadans like the Nawab of Dacca and Maulvi Abu Bakr of Hoogly now began to come in. Hindu extremists still contented themselves with appearances at meetings. By March 14th the boycott of British goods had begun to be put into effect in Calcutta, and the extent to which public feeling had been aroused, appeared to the Muhammadan leaders so great that, with a fear of consequence or a sense of responsibility seldom afterwards displayed in circumstances of much graver apprehension, they announced that the coolie class was not to cease work on the day fixed for the 'hartal' for more than an hour at the time of midday prayer. Before March 19th all the foreign agitators had left the Province. The 'hartal' itself, however, was practically a failure, both in Calcutta and in the rest of Bengal, except at the headquarters stations of the Chittagong, Dacca, Burdwan, Rajshahi and Pabna districts.

The month of April owing perhaps to the fact that most of the leaders were attending the abortive conferences at Delhi and Meerut, was comparatively quiet. Information however was received that orders had been issued by Shaukat Ali that the Khilafat agitation was in the meantime to be kept alive by secret agents, and on the 9th of the month a meeting was held at Gunabati, in the district of Tippera [!], at which not only boycott and 'jehad' were preached but reference was made to the Bolsheviks as possible allies. The traces of Bolshevik influence in the movement will later on require separate treatment. At present a more disquieting feature was the attempt to spread disaffection on religious grounds among the mill coolies. On April 18th a meeting at Garden Reach was attended by three thousand and during the 'National Week' subscriptions were collected throughout the mill area.

In May interest did not revive until the publication of the Turkish peace terms. These were received with general disapproval, but the provincial leaders, with the exception of the extremists Abul Kalam Azad, Akram Khan and Maniruzzaman Islamabadi still showed signs of nervousness and decided to hold no more public meetings before receiving the decision of the Central Khilafat Committee. Nothing accordingly was done before the joint conference held at Allahabad on June 1st and 2nd. The Allahabad Conference, although it revealed sharp cleavages not only between Hindus and Muhammadans but among Muhammadans themselves, resulted in the adoption of Mr. Gandhi's policy of non-co-operation by the four progressive stages of surrender of titles and honorary posts, resignation of civil employment, resignation of military employment, and lastly, civil disobedience. The Central Khilafat Committee, which met on the same days, expressed its approval.

In spite of these decisions nothing conspicuously on the lines of the new programme was as yet attempted in Bengal. Attempts were made to get Abul Kalam Azad appointed Shaikh-ul-Islam in India and to dissuade pilgrims from proceeding to Mecca. Two Swadeshi Companies were floated in Calcutta for the sale of indigenous products only. In the country the publication of the Allahabad programme was not received everywhere with the same acclamation. It was becoming increasingly apparent that there was no real enthusiasm for non-co-operation among the Muhammadans of Bengal. Steps were, therefore, taken about the middle of July to intensify propaganda. An ultimatum had previously been issued to the Viceroy that unless the Turkish peace terms were revised all co-operation with Government would cease on August 1st. Leaflets, posters and articles now appeared enjoining the observance of a 'hartal' on that date. Of this the chief perceptible result was the confiscation by Government of the securities of the *Nabajuga* and the *Mohammadi.* The 'hartal' of August 1st was even more a failure than that of March 19th. There was practically no observance outside Calcutta, and it was noticeable that except in a few districts of Eastern Bengal Hindus displayed no interest.

On the same day as the 'hartal' was received the news of the death of Tilak, and a rumour became prevalent that out of deference to his dying wishes Mr. Gandhi had agreed to postpone final ratification of the principles of non-co-operation until the special session of Congress and the Moslem League to be held in Calcutta in September. The interval before that date was variously employed by the different sections of the non-co-operation party. The Khilafat agitators who were in favour of the full policy of non-co-operation held meetings in Calcutta, Dacca and Bakarganj. There was, however, little encouragement for their efforts. The Nawab of Dacca recanted to the extent of resigning his post as Vice-President of the Reception Committee of Congress. So did Babu D.N. Dutta, Mr. Fazlul Huq, and Sir Ashutosh Chaudhuri. On the other hand the Bengal Provincial Congress Committee, whose members may have hoped to take a leading part in Provincial Government, disapproved of the boycott of the Reformed Council. When the Congress actually met the original four point of non-co-operation had been extended and modified so as to include the following seven, which were placed before the Subjects Committee:

(1) surrender of titles, honorary posts, etc.,
(2) refusal to attend Durbars, etc.,
(3) withdrawal of children from Government schools,

(4) boycott of British courts by lawyers and litigants,
(5) refusal of the military, clerical and labouring classes to serve in Mesopotamia,
(6) withdrawal from Council elections,
(7) boycott of foreign goods.

Opposition to (3), (4) and (6) on the part of Mr. C.R. Das was met by Mr. Gandhi with nothing more than an agreement to make the boycott in these cases gradual instead of immediate, and his threat to go behind the leaders of Congress and appeal direct to the masses had probably considerable effect in getting his proposals accepted in preference both to the amendment of Mr. Das and to the more definitely economic and anti-European proposals of Mr. B.C. Pal. In the full session of Congress the seven points of Mr. Gandhi were carried by more than a thousand votes, but it is to be noted that the straight issue of co-operation or non-co-operation was never put to the vote, and that three thousand delegates, more than half the total number, did not vote at all. The Khilafat Conference and the Moslem League followed the lead of Congress.

The only immediate practical result of these decisions was the withdrawal by Mr. Das and twenty-four others, many of whom had voted against Mr. Gandhi, of their candidature for the Legislative Council. At the same time the Khilafat Committee made renewed efforts to organise a determined campaign. Proposals were made for a strike of lascars and domestic servants, to be organised by Maniruzzaman Islamabadi, and for fomenting trouble in the mill area, which was to be the business of Abul Kalam Azad. Arrangements were made for opening permanent branch offices at Dacca, Chittagong, Mymensingh and other country stations. The possibility of not being able to prevent violence was openly admitted by Abul Kalam Azad, Akram Khan and others, and in Calcutta many ex-détenus registered their names as being willing to engage in propaganda among the masses. During the latter half of September a remarkable number of speeches were delivered throughout the Presidency, both by foreign and Bengali leaders, the wildest being those of Ataullah of Amritsar, who charged British soldiers with desecrating holy places and appealed to the 'danda' to save the

Khilafat, and of Abdul Gafur Peshwari, who stated that the blood of thousands of Muhammadans slain by the British could still be seen at the Cawnpore mosque. It is impossible here to give verbatim quotations, because the practice of sending reporters to take down speeches had not yet been adopted, but an analysis of the points most commonly made will later on be attempted and will tend to show that a campaign of lies was deliberately fabricated. At this period Hindu extremists like Sarala Bala Devi, Jitendra Lal Banerji and Shyam Sunder Chakravarti, first began to address meetings instead of merely attending them. Mr. B.C. Pal actually presided over a Moslem Conference at Sylhet, and an ex-détenu, Durga Das Chattarji, announced that it would be a good thing if the Maulanas could invent some story like that of the greased cartridges in 1857 to give soldiers an excuse for deserting from the army. In the midst, however, of all this forensic activity, dissension was still revealed both among Hindus and Muhammadans. An extremist branch which repudiated the methods of non-co-operation was formed by I.B. Sen after a meeting in College Square. And at the annual session of the Anjuman-i-Waizan, presided over by Abu Bakr of Hooghly, the boycott of British goods was rejected by the merchants of Chandney, Kidderpore and elsewhere.

A great deal was therefore being done to popularise the theory of non-co-operation, with very little result in practice. A scheme was formed by Abul Kalam Azad for a separate sub-committee to enforce each item of the programme but failed to find general acceptance. The only real practical developments in October were the formation of arbitration committees at Howrah and Belgachia in the 24-Parganas, and the Madrassa College strike which started on the 29th. Volunteers were being enlisted, but as yet showed little activity beyond sending threatening letters to candidates for the Council. The state of affairs was in fact such that the Secretary of the Bengal Khilafat Committee was obliged to defend himself from charges of inactivity and delay by urging pressure of work in Calcutta and bringing counter allegations against the District Sub-Committees.

The events of November and December showed in the first place that, as was to be expected, the class most likely to be seriously influenced by the non-co-operation propaganda was that of the students. Following upon a visit to Chittagong of Messrs. B.C. Pal, J.M. Sen Gupta, and others, most of the students of the Chittagong Madrassa and Moslem High English School and some from the Chittagong College and Jatra Mohan School decided to boycott these institutions form November 8th. The lead thus given was followed at Comilla, Dacca and Hooghly. At these places, however, the strike was only partial, and owing to the action taken by teachers, parents and guardians, of short duration, except in the case of one Madrassa at Comilla. Attempts to found national schools at Comilla and Faridpur were defeated by local apathy and the attitude of local zamindars. A national school was started at Dacca but obtained a very poor attendance. Another was opened in Calcutta by Mr. Gandhi on December 13th. In December, although no further strikes occurred in educational institutions, disturbances occurred in Calcutta at the Scottish Churches School and the City College, which had been selected as polling-stations for the Council elections. Many meetings of students were held to discuss the duty of students in relation to non-co-operation and to elect delegates for the All India Students' Congress which was to be held at Nagpur. Two instances of resolutions passed may be given to illustrate the weak and strong sides of student mentality of this time. At Dacca the second and fourth year students of the Jagannath College resolved to go on strike unless their examination papers were generously marked in view of the fact that devotion to politics left no time for study. At Comilla, on the other hand, the students of the Victoria College took the higher line by resolving to strike because the education imparted in Government institutions was destructive of Indian nationality. The Conference of students finally resulted in a resolution approving of non-co-operation in an 'unconditional', wholesale and immediate form, most of the delegates from Eastern Bengal voting in its favour.

In regard of classes other than students the policy of propaganda towards the end of the year showed a tendency to leave the large towns in the attempt to penetrate the interior. Village agitation was carried on by paid agents and volunteers, most notably in Eastern Bengal. Temporary excitement was often produced, but still no real effect was reported to be observable among the masses. In this direction the greatest success was achieved in the mill area. Several large Khilafat meetings were held at Howrah where a strike of 50,000 mill press men, although not definitely political in objects, reflected the condition of unrest produced by political agitation and resulted in molestation of passengers, looting of Hindu shops and some cases of assault on Europeans. It was reported that Maniruzzaman Islamabadi and other leaders hoped to take advantage of the prevailing temper to produce a general strike and resort to violence. Owing perhaps, however, to the fact that the less violent among the leaders preferred to wait for fresh directives from the Congress to be held at Nagpur, political activities showed a decline at the beginning of December which lasted till the end of the month. Interest in Bengal was chiefly focussed on the dissensions revealed in the Bengal Khilafat Committee with reference to the administration of the funds. Complaint was made by up-country members that the distribution of money was entirely in the hands of the Bengali members. Maulvi Abu Bakr, of Hooghly, had already more than once demanded a detailed account of the fund and the Ali brothers themselves had warned the Secretaries, but no accounts had been published. The dispute was marked by at least one case of physical assault and ended in the resignation of the up-country members. The other feature of the month of the election for the new Legislative Council, but it cannot be maintained that this excited any unusual interest. Evidence was received from several districts that illiterate Muhammadan voters had been taught to consider the act of voting as 'guna' (forbidden by God), and it was no doubt partly owing to the efforts of the non-co-operators, but partly also to a natural political apathy not limited to India, that the numbers of Muhammadans who voted, was in most constituencies, small. Abstentions were most noticeable in Rajshahi, Dinajpur, Bakarganj and Rangpur, but no serious attempts to prevent electors from voting were reported except from Mymensingh, where picketing was organised. Of the Nagpur Congress, little need here be said except to note the unexpected withdrawal of Mr. Das's opposition to those parts of the non-co-operation programme which did not suit his own creed. The general result of the Congress was to reaffirm the principles laid down at the special session in Calcutta in September, with the addition of provisions for the raising of a Tilak Memorial Swarajya Fund, for the organisation of village committees, and for the enlistment of volunteers. The two last are important as foreshadowing the lines upon which the movement was to develop during the year 1921. By these means swaraj was to be established within one year.

The situation at the end of 1920 may be summed up as follows: Practical response to the individual items of the non-co-operation programme had been exceedingly small. One title-holder relinquished his title. Eight gentlemen refused to attend Government functions. Ten holders of honorary offices resigned them. Six pleaders, the most prominent earning not more than Rs. 150 a month, gave up practice. Twenty-six persons withdrew their candidature for the Legislative Council. In connection with the boycott of labour for Mesopotamia no activity at all was reported. The boycott of foreign goods was practically nil. Strikes had occurred in about half a dozen educational institutions, and volunteer corps were known to have come into existence at Howrah, Kankinara in the 24-Parganas, Kharagpur, Dacca, Noakhali and Mymensingh. In spite of considerable campaigning the masses had not really been roused. The most disturbing features were the attempts to foment trouble in the mill area around Calcutta, where riots in ordinary times arise and spread with alarming rapidity, and the fact that many of the Khilafat leaders showed themselves not at all disinclined for violence. The predominantly Muhammadan character of the agitation even at the end of the year was seen in the fact that in the school and college strike of November it was chiefly Muhammadan students who were affected.

That the lesson of 1920 was not lost upon the leaders was made clear in the resolutions of the Nagpur Congress referred to above. The appeal to the educated classes had definitely failed, and it was obvious that if the administration was to be brought to a standstill systematic attempts would have to be made to stir up the common people. The aim henceforth was not only, as foretold in a circular letter of the Government of India, 'to enlist in the movement all those elements of the population which have real or imagined grievances', but to supply grievances ready made to those who possessed none of their own. It will be convenient, as far as possible, to deal with the exploitation of each class separately, and in the chronological order in which it came into prominence. In Bengal, however, before attention was finally diverted to the masses, a further more determined attempt was made to excite schoolboys and students, who alone of the literate classes had shown any specific response to the propaganda of boycott. The student movement of November had on the whole been a failure. The national schools and colleges promised by the leaders had so far failed to materialise and most of the strikers had returned to the Government institutions. Mr. C.R. Das, with the help of J.M. Sen Gupta, Durga Das Chattarji, Sirsh Chattarji of Dacca and others, now tried a different mode of address to students in Calcutta. Instead of promising to find new schools for those who consented to leave the existing ones they exhorted them to go out and engage in propaganda work so that swaraj might be obtained within one year. It was openly stated by Mr. B.C. Pal, that in the event of swaraj failing to be obtained by peaceful means and the movement turning to violence the blame would be upon the students. As a result of this preaching a strike occurred in Calcutta on January 13th, involving five colleges and three thousand students. Hindus were affected in as large a proportion as Muhammadans. By a coincidence perhaps not altogether fortuitous this outbreak came at the same time as the appointment of the first Minister for Education. Within a short time the impetus given in Calcutta spread to the country, and strikes occurred in all districts but three. Intimidation as well as genuine enthusiasm played a large part in keeping students away, and in order to free loyal students from pressure it was decided temporarily to close Government schools. Even before the end of the month, however, there were signs of uneasiness among all but the most ardent strikers at the multiplicity of counsels poured on them from all sides and the lack of provision for their employment. In February, although the situation had not to outward appearances materially altered, there was definite improvement in the Dacca Division, where the majority of institutions had reopened and were being fairly well attended. Government schools and colleges reopened on the 20th of the month and attendance was also, in the circumstances satisfactory. But the most encouraging indication of the temporary nature of these emotional demonstrations lay in the fact that fees for the public examinations of the University of Calcutta continued to be paid almost without abatement. The Matriculation Examination which was held on March 1st was not in fact attended by all the candidates who had paid the fees, but the general absence of attempts at obstruction bore testimony to the efficiency of the special arrangements made for the occasion. Some idea of the extent of the boycott may be gained from the figures published by the Education Department for the period up till the end of March. These showed that out of 103,107 attending Government and aided institutions, 11,157 were withdrawn, and 98,781 were present or absent with leave. Exact figures are not available, but of those withdrawn perhaps a third afterwards returned. Of the remainder many took up propaganda work or simply did nothing, while a smaller number joined the national schools. These institutions had at last begun to appear all over the province. By the middle of February they were to be found in nearly every district. Many collapsed from want of support within a few days of their foundation. Others at first drew away a fair proportion of boys from Government and aided schools, but as soon as it was discovered that the type of education which they had to offer was modelled almost entirely on the curriculum laid down by the Education Department, and in fact that their chief point of difference lay in absence of discipline and incompetence of the teachers, parents and guardians who had allowed their boys to join these institutions began to repent of their decision. Stagnation in the National school movement may be said to have set in April, and the action of parents in transferring their boys from the Iswar Pathsala at Comilla when the school was 'nationalised' in that month may be taken as indicative of the turn public opinion had then taken. There was, however, another side to this movement, which, not being based entirely on sentiment, was not so quick to disappear. Resignation of headmasters and teachers up till April averaged about twenty a month. That intimidation was in part responsible, is clear from the instances of violence which actually came to light. In Nadia, for example, a headmaster was stoned for not promoting a boy to a higher class, and in Faridpur another was assaulted for caning boys who had been associating with an ex-détenu. At Elliotganj, in Tippera, all the school papers were stolen, and elsewhere schools which refused to 'nationalise' were burnt down. This sort of thing had been known in Bengal before. What was new was an almost universal sense of economic grievance which, in the experience of District Officers, especially in Eastern Bengal, was to be found among even those teachers who did not go to the length of resigning. Comparisons were made between the pay of teachers and the pay of domestic servants in European service, and it was useless to point out that the real remedy was to raise the school fees. The blame for not increasing salaries was laid on Government. If, as seems probable, this grievance was deliberately fostered as an item of anti-Government propaganda, its authors certainly deserve the credit of having produced an atmosphere of discontent which still, to some extent, persists.

The first move towards capturing the sympathy of the masses on the lines of the new programme may be said to date from February. Even before the Nagpur Congress it had apparently been realised that if success was to be achieved in this direction something more concrete was required to work upon than the wrongs of the Khilafat, and accordingly in December we find proposals being made to the raiyats for the formation of national unions for the purchase and sale of all local produce without the agency of middlemen. A raiyat association had been in existence since 1913, and this was probably a move to capture the organisation. Nothing further was done, however, until the launching of the jute boycott campaign in February. The real motive behind the boycott of jute was undoubtedly nothing more than the desire to damage European trade, but other reasons had to be designed to catch the imagination of the raiyat. It was represented that the reduction of jute acreage meant more land for food grains, and in some places the raiyats were told that this was the wish of the Government. In Mymensingh the District Congress Committee went the length of issuing a pamphlet on growing cotton in place of jute said to have been drawn up in consultation with the Agriculture Department. By these and similar means cultivators in Barisal were made to vow to restrict jute cultivation to one quarter that of the previous year. At Harirampur, in the Dacca district, the area was restricted to little more than half an acre under threat of social boycott, and the price of jute seed accordingly went down from 2½ to 16 seers per rupee. Where, as in Noakhali, cultivators still proved sceptical, the crop was ploughed up by 'striker' students, who, in one instance, played football on the ground afterwards. There was a considerable increase of destruction of this sort in April, and in no case was any complaint lodged in court. In one district, Noakhali, there was found to be a belief that students were immune from legal punishment and the general respect for educated persons probably acted equally with intimidation as a deterrent factor. In spite of all this the campaign ended in failure. The jute market, partly owing to accumulation of stocks, was not affected, and in the long run it was found impossible to convince the cultivator that to grow paddy at five to seven rupees per maund was a better economic proposition than growing jute at six to twelve rupees per maund. The one result of this agitation was to make the cultivator think of other methods in which he might improve his position and to prepare the way for the no-taxes and no-rent movement which afterwards appeared in Eastern Bengal.

The other two items of the economic boycott programme were the boycott of foreign cloth and the boycott of alcoholic liquor. In March Mr. Gandhi announced that the next three months should be spent in collecting as much money as possible, in removing untouchability, in combating alcoholism and in inducing every Indian home to employ the spinning wheel. At the Bezwada Congress held in April this programme crystallised into the three main items of the acquisition before the end of June of one crore of Congress members, one crore of rupees and of twenty lakhs of *charkas* (spinning wheel). The last item had a more constructive appearance than most hitherto put forward, but since it was coupled with the boycott of British cloth, the basis of its appeal was a much the damaging of British trade as the reconstruction of indigenous industry. It was soon found in the case of the *charka* campaign as with every other part of the non-co-operation programme, that the only certain way to arouse enthusiasm greater than a passing curiosity was to appeal to the passions. Statements were accordingly circulated that the English had deliberately wrecked the Indian weaving industry by cutting off the thumbs of weavers and that the money acquired from the sale of Manchester cloth was used to make armaments for the suppression of India. In spite, however, of this type of propaganda the *charka* campaign, except in fashionable non-co-operation circles in Calcutta, made very little headway, and the boycott of foreign cloth had by August so far collapsed as to require fresh stimulus from Mr. Gandhi himself.

As with the spinning-wheel so with the anti-liquor campaign the motives of the originators may have been primarily social. At the same time there can be no doubt that this particular item commended itself to the lesser leaders simply as a means of causing loss of revenue to Government. To appeal to the people the motive had to be still further lowered by the direct introduction of racial and religious antagonism. The following passage occurs in a speech of A.P. Barman, delivered in Calcutta, in February 1921: 'Lot was a drunkard. He committed incest with his daughter after drinking wine. It is not strange that those whose preceptors drink wine and commit incest with their daughters should fill their treasury by making people drunk.' To the spirit thus engendered, and not to real temperance enthusiasm, must be attributed the picketing of liquor shops, the difficulties put in the way of finding sites for liquor shops, the garlanding of drunkards with a string of shoes, and the many incidents like that at Bogra where the sweepers threatened to throw excrement upon any one found drinking.

By a natural transition the attack on drink became involved in a movement against prostitution. At first prostitutes' quarters were picketed merely as places where drinks could be obtained. In some cases prostitutes were made to pledge twenty-five rupees to make their customers give up drink and to do so themselves. Later it was seen that prostitution itself could be made a profitable source of agitation. The perverted ingenuity by which this, of all institutions, was blamed upon a foreign Government is well illustrated in one of the later speeches, delivered by Nazimuddin Ahmed, in Calcutta in December 1921, in which the following words occur:

'The British Government openly give permission to this effect, that if some sister or mother of yours went to the Police Department and requested permission to become a prostitute and spoil the morals of her brethren, then the British Government would at once consent. They would ask her with pleasure to go and sell her chastity so that your uncles and brothers may waste their money and ruin their morals.'

Although earlier records do not exist there can be no doubt in the minds of any who came into contact with popular feeling at the time that this was the doctrine disseminated right from the beginning of the campaign.

It has been pointed out above that the attacks on jute, on foreign goods and on liquor were really attacks upon the economic resources of Government. At the same time a parallel campaign was waged, by the same methods of boycott, against the whole machinery of education and administration. The movement against Government schools and colleges has already been dealt with. The next in order of time to develop was the attempt to boycott the law courts. Mr. C.R. Das had given the lead by resigning his practice, with the exception of two cases, in January. In February nine pleaders followed suit, in March sixty-eight, and in April thirty-eight. After that resignations fell off and many in fact returned to practice. The proposed general suspension of practice was discussed and rejected at Dacca, Howrah, Mymensingh, Noakhali and Rajshahi, mainly on the grounds that it was unnecessary. Of those who did resign it was remarked that most were earning less than they could get as volunteers. On the other hand the formation of arbitration courts, which constituted the second part of this movement, proceeded with great rapidity. Only fifteen such courts were known to be in existence in February. By July the number had reached the astonishing total of four hundred and fifty, and by August another hundred had been added. In April 1922 it was computed that the total number of irregular courts of all kinds formed up to that date was no less than eight hundred and sixty-six. Of these probably not much more than half were ever functioning at the same time, but even so, when the movement was at its height, they considerably outnumbered the Government courts. They reached their greatest popularity about August 1921, and a more detailed notice of their activities will be needed later on. In the meantime agitation had commenced against other departments of Government service. Incitements to the police to resign were first reported in January. There was at this time a certain amount of discontent in the police force on the question of pay and full use was made of this economic grievance by comparisons such as that between the pay of a constable and that of a European Sergeant.

The chief appeal, however, was made on patriotic grounds, and that some impression was made, appeared from intercepted letters, from the fact that constables at Dacca and Mymensingh were heard to have joined in shouts of *Gandhi-ki-jai*, and from the information obtained by the Intelligence Branch at Kankinara, in the 24-Parganas, that the constables there would side with Gandhi when the right time came. The chief danger seems to have been among the constables from up-country with whom the reputation of Mr. Gandhi stood very high. When this method of address failed the police were subjected to abuse on every possible occasion. They were called dogs, the incarnation of dishonesty, murderers of their own countrymen, and traitors to their religion. Throughout the year they were subjected to such continual pressure from individual agitators and from public opinion, never in normal circumstances in their favour, that many officers entertained grave doubts of their being able to remain loyal in a real emergency.

In the first half of the year, however, no tangible results appeared beyond a strike of eight constables at Bhaduria, in the 24-Parganas. The Rural Police, or chaukidars, naturally attracted simultaneous attention. Their pay was possibly in some districts inadequate, but the large number of resignations which occurred from April onwards was probably as much due to intimidation as to real discontent with the standard of remuneration. Towards the end of the year and at the beginning of 1922 the position as regards the Rural Police became exceedingly serious and will need special mention. For the present it is enough to notice that the fact that chaukidars' pay is levied and distributed locally was immediately taken advantage of by attempts to bring about a general refusal to pay the chaukidari tax. This was started in Rajshahi in March, and openly proclaimed by beat of drum in Madaripur in June. Almost everywhere chaukidars' pay fell into arrears, and it was significant that chaukidars not only, as at Burdwan, ceased to attend parades, but in Madaripur were found distributing *charkas*, and in Nadia assembling villagers for non-co-operation meetings.

Some mention must be made of the agency by means of which all the items of the boycott programme were put into operation. The Nagpur Congress of December 1920 had provided for the raising of a National Service Corps for spreading propaganda in the country districts. The idea was probably a development of the old Congress volunteers, who, in the days before non-co-operation was thought of, were employed in social work or in keeping order at meetings. Enlistment under the new scheme was fairly rapid. In February eleven hundred, including many ex-students, were enrolled in the Bangiya Swaraj Sevak in Calcutta. By March there were fourteen, and by May nineteen regular corps of volunteers established in different places in the Province. The members were employed not only in enforcing the various boycotts, but as arbitration court peons, as guards over houses where meetings were being held, and in other general capacities. There was evidence that some of the corps were being given a semi-military training, and it was reported that in Madaripur the Santi Seva had been seen at revolver practice under the instruction of an ex-détenu, Purna Das, and some ex-sepoys. In almost all the corps there was a definite organisation which improved as time went on, though nowhere else did it reach the same development as at Rangpur, where by the end of the year the whole district was organised into subdivisions and thanas, with officers in charge of each, and a sufficient number of volunteers to make the working practicable. In the combination of national schools, arbitration courts and volunteer corps the activities of all of which were based on Government models, one may perhaps see a systematic attempt to set up a parallel system of administration such as had been evident in Sinn Fein methods in Ireland.

In addition to the specific propagation of individual items of the boycott the country was deluged with a flood of speeches having no other aim but the undisguised promotion of racial hatred. A certain uniformity of malevolent misrepresentation can be traced throughout the year, the commonest form being false accounts of the Jallianwallah Bagh affair, and of insults and injuries offered to the

Kaaba, the Khalif and Muhammadan religion generally. It was at first given out that the English had bombarded the holy places at Mecca, but this story was gradually improved upon until we find Abdul Rahman, Secretary of the Comilla Khilafat Conference, declaring in a speech in April that the British had not only broken down the Prophet's tomb, but eased themselves on the *Koran*, and converted the Muhammadan burial ground into a latrine. Similarly in July Abdur Razzak announced that the following words occurred in a speech of Lord Kitchener: 'If I am a true officer of the British Government, if I am really a noble Englishman, then I shall erect a wine shop in that very Mecca facing which the Moslems of the world say their prayers.'

Another common form of vilification was to slander the sexual relations of the British. The statement of Sirsh Chattarji that Indian prostitutes were chaster than English ladies does not stand alone. Accusations of the rape and other modes of defilement, of Indian women by British officers, were often conjoined with the suggestion that such was likely to happen to the mothers and sisters of those present. The depth to which unrestrained abuse of this kind could descend is illustrated in a speech of A.P. Barman, delivered in Calcutta in March 1921, in which he says: 'How were your mothers treated? Sticks were thrust into their private parts'; but the most significant thing about this highly virulent statement is that it re-occurs, in almost the same words, in other speeches of the same period.

Still further similarity is discernible in reference to historical cases of British injustice, particularly the case of Raja Ranjit Singh, and in a host of instances of malevolent accentuation of minor racial differences in clothing and social habits. On the whole, therefore, there appears reason to say that the speeches contain definite evidence of a common origin, and that the fabrications they contained were deliberate and not mere flights of oratory. It was well known that the wildest misstatements would if repeated often enough be received with implicit credulity among a population which had by this time come to believe that Gandhi was invulnerable and could be in two places at the same time.

Another type of appeal based on less familiar grounds than any of the foregoing, but revealing one definite line of influence in the movement, was the exhortation to emulate the example of Russia. Mention has already been made of the appearance of this kind of propaganda at the beginning of 1920. One or two examples may now be given from speeches and newspapers in 1921. The following passage occurs in a speech of Abdur Razzak delivered in Calcutta in April 1921: 'You all know what has happened in Russia, where all the labourers rose up, killed their Emperor and divided all his wealth and properties among themselves, so that all were there equal and everyone had to earn his own livelihood. Such a time has now come for Hindustan.' In May, J.P. Misser, also speaking in Calcutta, said: 'There are but two persons in the world to-day, one is Lenin and [the] other is Gandhi.' Later on in August 1922, the *Dhumketu* newspaper likens the Bolsheviks to the God Kalki (an incarnation of Vishnu), wielding the sharp sword on behalf of the harassed and long oppressed demons. References of this sort are not common, but they occur here and there throughout the period of agitation.

An atmosphere inflamed by the incessant preaching of racial and religious hatred and charged with credulity, ignorance and superstition is therefore the background for the events of 1921. Apart from the developments already noticed the first two months of the year were marked only by taxi and tramway strikes in Calcutta, a partial 'hartal' on the arrival of the Duke of Connaught to open the new Legislative Chamber, and the collection of large sums of money, chiefly from Marwaris, for the Tilak Memorial Fund and the general maintenance of non-co-operation activities. The sale of Khilafat notes was resumed but with no more success than in the previous year. The system of collection known as *Moosti-Bhika* (contribution of rice, etc.) was also introduced.

In March the Bengal Provincial Conference at Barisal showed the extent to which the movement had lost its predominantly Muhammadan character by omitting all reference to the Khilafat question. It also proved, what had been becoming clear for some time that the storm centre was in Eastern Bengal. Collections of money continued to be made, but in Calcutta bogus Khilafat boxes appeared, and the action of Khilafat volunteers at Narayanganj in appealing to court for an order to restrain unauthorised collections was a good instance of the ignorance and confusion of thought prevailing in the country. The publication, after long delay, of the accounts of the Bengal Khilafat Committee led to considerable dissensions among the leaders. More active campaigning was seen in the attempts to get domestic servants to leave European masters. At Dacca the matter was settled by an up-country cook informing the instigators that the servants would manage their own affairs without the help of *Babulok* or the educated classes. At Mymensingh and elsewhere a few instances occurred of Europeans and Government servants having to carry their own baggage. An order served upon Mr. C.R. Das, not to enter the town of Mymensingh in view of the proximity of the Matriculation Examination, was followed by a complete 'hartal'. 'Hartals' also occurred on the occasion of the visit of His Excellency to Dacca, and of the Divisional Commissioner to Bankura and Bogra.

The most important event of the month was the mutiny in Rajshahi Jail which broke out on the 24th. The prisoners declared a 'hartal' and said they would obey Gandhi and not the Government. At midday when the warders were being changed they rushed the gate, and escaped in a body. They attacked the Reserve Armed Police, who came up with them late in the evening, and forced the latter to fire, and it was not till some weeks afterwards that the majority were recaptured.

In April an increasing spirit of lawlessness manifested itself all over the Province. A Sub-Registrar of the Mymensingh district was assaulted for wearing a European hat and coat, and the Superintendent of a landlord's estate office was beaten with shoes for failing to attend a political meeting. A ticket collector was beaten for not allowing non-co-operating students to travel without tickets. Four or five cases occurred at Dacca of stones being thrown at Europeans, and at Comilla bricks were thrown at the wife and infant child of the Superintendent of Police. At Howrah a jute mill manager was badly injured as a result of deducting bonus from the pay of coolies who had observed 'hartal'. In the interior of Mymensingh there was a general refusal to attend police investigations and a belief that the authority of Government had gone. Prosecutions were launched against volunteers for looting and rioting in Tippera, for rescuing persons under arrest in Barisal and for preventing the unloading of Liverpool salt at Munshiganj.

In spite of the proclamation of Mr. Das that social boycott was 'strictly discarded' from the movement', this weapon came more and more into use. In one case the wife of a President Panchayat was denied the service of a midwife. Commercial boycott of shopkeepers who failed to close on 'hartal' days was also put into practice at Jagatdal, in the 24-Parganas. Rs. 1,20,000 was collected for the Tilak Swarajya Fund, but as with the Khilafat Fund dissatisfaction and suspicion were expressed at the management, especially at Dacca and Hooghly. Of the above sum all but Rs. 12,000 was contributed by Marwaris. The first instance of refusal to pay rents occurred on the estate of the Midnapore Zamindari Company at Rajshahi. This was the only European estate in the district and the only one affected. In May Congress Committees were established in all districts except Burdwan and Alipore, thus affording further proof of the hold which the movement had now obtained over Hindus. At Keraniganj boatmen refused to row Government clerks across the river, and at Akhaura in Tippera, a complete, though temporary, strike of all servants of Europeans followed upon a slap given by a jute agency assistant to an insolent *khitmatgar* [!]. An agitation against Union Boards now also first appeared and many members were forced to resign. All other events of this month, however, were dwarfed by the exodus of tea-garden coolies from Assam.

The question as to whether the Assam tea-garden coolies had any outstanding economic grievances is one which may be debated. The truth is probably that owing to the bad state of the tea trade they were rather worse off than in previous years. There is no doubt however that nothing but continuous agitation and fictitious promises made in the name of Mr. Gandhi were responsible for their sudden determination to leave the gardens and return to their own homes. By the 15th parties of destitute coolies amounting in all to about 1,500, many of whom before leaving the gardens had been induced to sell all their possessions for one or two rupees in the belief that they would be amply provided for by Mr. Gandhi when they reached their own homes, had drifted down the Assam-

Bengal Railway and accumulated at the steamer station at Chandpur. The local authorities, fearing the consequence both on public health and on the political situation of so large an influx and not knowing how many more were likely to arrive, arranged at first for transporting them westwards in the expectation that they would be repatriated to their homes. Batches of coolies all more or less without means, therefore, appeared at Goalundo, Naihati and Asansol, hence they were again moved on by train. It was decided, however, by Government that the policy of repatriation at public expense could not be maintained, and accordingly no further arrangements for shipping coolies from Chandpur were made after the 17th. The result was that by the 19th another 3,000 had accumulated at Chandpur. On that night, at the instigation of students and volunteers who had collected at the railway station, about 350 coolies succeeded in rushing the Goalundo mail steamer and had to be allowed to proceed. Others reached the receiving flat but were afterwards pushed back. A similar attempt was made on the following night but was frustrated by the District Magistrate with a cordon of armed police. On the same night Gurkha Military Police arrived from Dacca, and in order to prevent a repetition of the occurrence and to safeguard the railway premises from an attack of cholera which had already appeared, the order was given to clear the station. The coolies, encouraged by an excited crowd of Bengali youths on the station over-bridge, refused to move and two sections of the military police had therefore to be employed. They fell in with bayonets unfixed and rifles slung and used only sticks and pieces of firewood which the coolies had left lying about. A few bruised, cuts and abrasions were necessarily inflicted before the coolies started to move, but a medical inspection on the following morning and subsequent enquiry revealed the fact that no one was seriously injured. Elaborate sanitary arrangements were made by Government for the care of the coolies after they had left the station and special precautions were taken for the segregation and treatment of cholera cases. Offers were also made to provide for food and housing but the coolies were induced to prefer the hospitality of local non-co-operators. All except those too sick to be moved were eventually repatriated by private charity. On the morning after the station was cleared a complete 'hartal' was put into effect at Chandpur. The wildest and most distorted versions of the affair were circulated, largely through the agency of organised relays of volunteers, and gathered further colouring as they progressed. Hundreds of coolies were said to have been bayoneted or drowned, and by some curious psychological process, it was the Indian officers present upon whom the opprobrium was chiefly fastened. Mr. De, the Commissioner, was accused of kicking coolie women in the stomach, and Mr. Sinha, the Subdivisional Officer, of having himself thrown coolies into the river. The press at once poured forth a torrent of venomous and misinformed invective hard to parallel even in the annals of vernacular journalism. Long afterwards in villages of the Dacca district a song used to be sung how Sir Henry Wheeler, who went to Chandpur after the occurrence to make the official enquiry, conspired with the Gurkhas to bayonet pregnant women. The effect of these rumours was immediate. At Comilla the local Bar left the courts in a body, schools closed down, domestic servants almost to a man deserted their European masters, the bazaar refused to sell food to Government servants, and for a few days the European community lived almost in a state of siege. Similar conditions prevailed at Chandpur, Noakhali and Chittagong and in an incredibly short time the whole of Eastern Bengal was in a ferment. On the 24th the situation was aggravated by a strike on the Assam-Bengal Railway which rapidly became general, and on the 27th a strike occurred on the steamer service to Chandpur which in a few days spread to Goalundo, Barisal and Khulna. The mail service was maintained with difficulty by Government launches.

The purely political nature of these strikes was admitted by Mr. J.M. Sen Gupta, the organiser of the railway strike, who informed the Commissioner of the Chittagong Division that he would not order the men back to work unless Government contributed Rs. 5,000 towards the repatriation of the coolies as demanded by the Rev. C.F. Andrews. Mr. C.R. Das, who was now conducting the steamer strike from Goalundo similarly announced that he gloried in the 'National' character of the strikes. At Chittagong the strike had been easy to organise owing to the success of a strike in the Burma Oil Company's workshops which had taken place there early in May. At that time orders prohibiting meetings and processions had been successfully defied and a complete 'hartal' causing very considerable local inconvenience had only been called off on the company making a complete surrender to the strikers.

The firm action taken on the present occasion produced a very deterrent effect. At Barisal, as a result of counter-propaganda undertaken by the local officers, the steamer strike collapsed on the 25th June. All the other steamer lines resumed work in the first fortnight of July. The non-co-operators continue to attempt to produce a boycott by picketing the landing places, but local officers with the help of official and non-official workers were able to afford protection to crews and passengers. At Goalundo a system of purchase only by means of permits issued under the facsimile signature of Mr. C.R. Das, succeeded in providing a good deal of inconvenience for Government servants and loyal Indians. At Barisal trouble was again stirred up in the second week of July by the arrest of one Sarat Ghose, who had been extremely active in attempting interference with the steamer service after its resumption. A three-day 'hartal' was observed, schools were closed, volunteers lay on the roads to obstruct traffic, and public health was endangered by the prevention of municipal sweepers from going to their work. In this district a definite organisation of all Government servants and loyal Indians, with anti-non-co-operation volunteers, printed propaganda and a Government bazaar, had already been achieved by the local officers. By the means thus provided coupled with a judicious use of the armed police and a threat of the union of Government servants to impose a counter commercial boycott, the situation was gradually got in hand.

The strike on the Assam-Bengal Railway lasted longer. The men began by demanding recognition of the Railway Union with Mr. J.M. Sen Gupta, as the President. This was at once refused and the process of evicting strikers from railway quarters and taking on new men put into operation. A few trains in charge of Europeans and Anglo-Indians, were running in each section by the second half of June, and in the first half of July passenger traffic, with the help of the new staff, was resumed in full. By this time public sympathy had to a large extent been alienated by the rise in the cost of food, and the strikers themselves would willingly have returned to work had they been allowed to do so. They were still, however, though now inadequately, maintained from non-co-operation funds and, it was reasonably suspected, from money subscribed for the repatriation of the tea-garden coolies.

In the second half of July men were returning to work in large numbers, but the improvement in the situation was marred by a riot at Chittagong, where the police, while escorting a party of returning strikers, were assaulted by a mob of strikers, who still refused to return, and the armed police had to be called out to quell the disturbance. This occurrence appears to be directly due to the agency of Mr. J.M. Sen Gupta, who had exhorted the strikers to use violence, if necessary, to prevent the resumption of work. Full normal running on the Assam-Bengal Railway was resumed in August, although owing to the wrecking of two trains and attempts to wreck others, in all probability by railway strikers, night running had again to be temporarily discontinued. The strike for all practical purposes came to an end in September, when most of the remaining strikers for whom there was still room returned on the Agent's conditions. The disillusionment of the men and their disgust on discovering that they had merely been made pawns in a political game is illustrated in a letter to the *Statesman* of the 30th September in which the following words occur:

'After suffering untold misery and privations for the last three or four months, we have been obliged to come to the conclusion that our leaders are wholly incapable of controlling or managing situations created by a few shallow demagogues. They are swayed only by excitement and emotion and are wholly wanting in foresight and experience, and they are wholly careless of the lives of their countrymen when their prestige is in danger. ... All that is left to us now is to tell our brother labourers in India how we have been treated so that they may profit by our experience.'

The failure of the Assam-Bengal Railway strike was probably responsible for the failure of Mr. C.R. Das's appeals to the Eastern Bengal Railway to strike in sympathy, and possibly also for the failure to materialise of a general strike in the colliery area which was said to be under organisation.

During the period of the railway and steamer strike few other events of importance took place in Bengal. The cause of the Khilafat had naturally fallen rather into the background. In June a disclosure of large embezzlements from the sale of Khilafat notes still further diminished its popularity. That the method and doctrine of non-co-operation to some extent cut both ways was also shown in the demand of *mehtars* and *domes* in one district to be allowed the services of the general barbers and washermen, on the ground that caste equality was a principle of the movement, and by an extraordinary rumour which gained ground in Malda and Rajshahi that in order to raise money Gandhi was sending out 700 dacoits, who would ravish the women of those who refused to pay up. As a result of this rumour many women were said to have been kept concealed for days in the jungle. Another feature of this month was the formation of village unions to prevent the export of rice, corn or jute by selling to Europeans and outside traders only at exorbitant rates. The same principle was in places also put into operation against the police.

A well-thought-out conspiracy to break out of Midnapore Jail was disclosed by a convict warder and was an ominous symptom of the extent to which the spirit of unrest had penetrated. It transpired that the prisoners had been led to believe that the day of the British Raj was over and that notes and rupees were actually being coined in the name of Gandhi. In July there appeared to be a temporary improvement in the situation. Collections for the Tilak Fund were found to amount to Rs. 7 lakhs and not Rs. 25 lakhs, as previously announced by Mr. C.R. Das. An increasing number of cases were brought against volunteers for restraint, assault, looting and intimidation, and it became evident that counter-propaganda, which had been urged upon local authorities by Government, was having some effect. In the Bakarganj district a meeting of Namasudras expressed loyalty to the King-Emperor.

There was, however, disquieting evidence of unrest among the tea-garden coolies in the Duars and the Darjeeling districts. Non-co-operators had been quick to take advantage of a certain amount of genuine economic discontent to the extent of urging the coolies to take over the land and management themselves. Several strikes occurred and, in one case, where the Manager and Assistant Manager of a tea-garden had been chased to their bungalow and confined there, an attempt to arrest the ringleaders failed. A widespread rumour to the effect that on a certain date, which was put conveniently forward from time to time, a terrible storm would destroy all those who had not then declared for Gandhi, was in part responsible for temporary stoppages. The movement, however, proved to be sporadic in nature, and a great deal was done to restore confidence by concessions and propaganda undertaken by the Indian Tea Association. The only other instance of violence during July was an attempt to break out of Barisal Jail on the 27th. Convicts armed with dangerous weapons taken from the oil and weaving factories rushed into the yard with shouts of 'Bande Mataram', and the situation was only saved by the promptness of convict warders and others, who surrounded and disarmed the mutineers.

It has been stated above that the popularity of arbitration courts reached its zenith about the month of August, and it will therefore not be out of place to say something here about the working of these courts and the reason for their decline. The term 'arbitration court' naturally assumed a wide connotation. In some districts there was a fair degree of formality. In Malda model rules were issued, which laid down the fees to be charged, and the punishments to be awarded in certain cases. There were, for example, progressive punishments for drunkenness, starting with a fine and ending in social boycott. In Noakhali an appellate court was established, consisting of pleaders of the local bar, and in Bankura 50 persons were empanelled as jurors. In most districts, however, the movement gradually spread from courts constituted and recognised by the local Congress and Khilafat Committees to the ordinary village 'Salish' or 'Baithak' and to self-appointed individuals. Thus in the mill area of the 24-Parganas it was not uncommon for sirdars or foremen to set themselves up as courts and enforce their decisions by intimidation. One such was afterwards prosecuted for bad livelihood.

Although there was no appreciable set-back to the movement until August, the first signs of a loss of public confidence had manifested themselves earlier. At Howrah there was a distinct revulsion of feeling in April, due probably to the successful prosecution of persons who indulged in loot to enforce an arbitration court's order. Elsewhere the fact that some of the strongest advocates of arbitration, like B.K. Mazumdar, of Comilla, took care not to withdraw their own cases from the Government civil courts, was probably noted. By June dissatisfaction had spread to Malda, Rajshahi and Hoogly, and in and after August what were in fact appeals from arbitration courts to Government courts became common. A few instances of decisions and actions of arbitration courts will be sufficient to show the reasons for their failure. At Iswarganj, in Mymensingh, the fines were regularly pocketed by the arbitrators, and at Kodalia, Kishoreganj, in the same district, cases were decided by the *Koran* and a kind of divining rod method, which amounted to tossing up. Several cases occurred in which men were haled before the court and heavily fined for petty social offences, such as failure to attend a dinner-party. On the other hand, really serious offences, such as robbery and grievous hurt, were dismissed with a fine of a few rupees. In Rangpur a woman was hung up by the hands, whipped and starved for stealing a jack-fruit. In Malda an accused sentenced to be pulled by the ear by his younger brother went out and hanged himself. One of the most amazing decisions was that of a court which found an accused guilty of abducting a married woman, but fined the husband Rs. 12 before consenting to order the return of the woman. The husband was obliged to borrow the money, and the court then ordered the woman to be kept by the lender until the debt was paid. In all districts fines were realised by means of boycott, confinement and extortion. In addition to judicial functions several courts attempted to regulate the price of foodstuffs and of labour, the court being employers. In the face of these instances it is reasonable to suppose that the movement, even if left to itself, could not have lasted long, but its collapse was hastened by numerous prosecutions from September onwards. The movement was also largely killed because lawyers refused to give up their practice to attend to it.

The lull which had been observable in July continued through August, September and October. An impetus to the boycott of foreign cloth was given by the Bombay Congress, which Mr. Gandhi had prevailed upon not to sanction civil disobedience until this boycott was complete. But even the eloquence of Gandhi, who came to Calcutta in August, was unable to effect more than the burning of a few, chiefly unserviceable cloths, and it became necessary to organise shop to shop visitations by the volunteers. In furtherance of this campaign Mr. Gandhi visited Chittagong and Barisal, but at these places also little enthusiasm was aroused. At Barisal his appeal was particularly unsuccessful.

A list of questions had been prepared by the local officers in anticipation of his coming and his answers to these amounted to an unqualified denunciation of 'hartals', strikes and boycotts, in short, of all the methods practised by his followers in the district. In *Young India* Mr. Gandhi afterwards endeavoured to represent these answers as given in a very much modified form, but as the original speech had been taken down verbatim, the result was to furnish only another example of the inconsistency of the Mahatma. On his return to Calcutta in September, Mr. Gandhi continued the campaign with greater effect. The Marwari Chamber of Commerce decided to order no more foreign cloth until the end of the year, and forty-six picketers who, finding peaceful persuasion useless, had resorted to obstruction, had to be arrested in the streets of Calcutta. Large purchases, however, continued to be made for the forthcoming *Pujas* and *Moharrum*, and the commonsense attitude of many, who were unable to grasp the political idealism involved in the boycott, was typified in a report from Burdwan of a man being beaten by his wife for bringing her a present of 'homespun cloth' instead of a fine imported 'sari'.

The extent to which the Khilafat question had, for the time being, ceased to agitate popular imagination appeared in the little interest, outside the Muhammadan press, evinced in the arrest of the Ali brothers, in September. Muhammadan journals, while continuing to be obsessed with Turkish affairs, had for some time past devoted more attention to the situation at Smyrna than to the wrongs of the Khalifa. Britain was freely accused of having done everything possible to help the Greeks, and, in one instance at least, of having actually declared war upon Mustapha Kemal. Collections of money had been despatched to Smyrna, but well-founded rumours of their non-arrival soon damped this form of enthusiasm. News of the Moplah rebellion was received with condemnation by all sections of the press. At the same time the extremist papers displayed considerable ingenuity in laying the blame for it on official repression. The truth is that the original pretexts of the Punjab and Khilafat wrongs had now been openly dropped by many of the leaders in favour of a general agitation for swaraj, for the purposes of which any action of Government either in India or in England could, by distortion, be made equally valuable. This new attitude had been candidly admitted by Abdur Razzak, who said in July, 'So long as you do not wrest this country from them, the conceding or non-conceding of the demands in regard to Turkey and the Khilafat are all the same', and received striking corroboration in a speech of J.L. Banerji, delivered in August, in which he said,

> 'Even if the Punjab and Khilafat wrongs did not exist, if there had been no recent or immediate grievance, even then as a self-respecting people we must have refused to accord any reception to a Prince who comes to us as a reminder of our shame, our servitude and our degradation.'

In November affairs took a sudden and decided turn for the worse, and the reasons for the change are worth examining. In the first place it must be remembered, that although the calm of the previous three months had not been marked by outward disturbances comparable to those of the period of the steamer and railway strikes, there had been little, if any, diminution in the steady stream of propaganda. No less than 4,265 non-co-operation meetings were held between the beginning of June and the middle of November. It soon became evident that advantage had also been taken of the lull to perfect the organisation of volunteers. But the year within which swaraj had been promised was rapidly drawing to a close. If the leaders were to preserve their prestige, some great spectacular effect was necessary at once. A manifesto published in October, and signed by Mr. Gandhi and other prominent non-co-operators, had already laid it down that it was the duty of every Indian soldier and civilian to sever his connection with Government.

The visit of the Prince of Wales, which the August session of Congress had already decided to boycott, was now seized upon as an opportunity for a widespread demonstration of disloyalty. At the same time the All-India Congress gave its sanction to civil disobedience and Mr. Gandhi issued peremptory orders for the complete boycott of foreign cloth before the end of November. Results soon began to appear.

Settlement operations had been undertaken at the start of the cold weather in Pabna, Bogra and Birbhum. A violent campaign of opposition was at once launched by the local non-co-operators under the lead of J.L. Banerji. Cultivators were told that their rents would be increased and that a quarter of the crops would be destroyed in measuring the land. It was in vain that the Settlement Officer showed by demonstration, that the damage likely to be done was negligible, and promised to survey first the land on which crops were not yet ripe. He was himself threatened with violence, and surveyors were everywhere prevented from starting work. In some cases they were paid their fees to return home, in others they were simply driven out of the village. In Pabna the Assistant Settlement Officer was severely assaulted, and the same officer was again attacked at Bogra, although the District Magistrate had previously made a tour of the affected area, accompanied by armed police.

Simultaneously with the obstruction to settlement operations, there was a general increase of activity against the police, chaukidars or rural police, and all government servants. Volunteer organisation, as has been stated above, had reached an unusual state of development in the district of Rangpur. Here chaukidars' uniform was taken from them and burnt and an effective boycott of police and Government servants was enforced throughout the district, so that it became necessary to form a system of convoys under armed escorts to furnish supplies for outlying officers. In Midnapore the concerted agitation against the Village Self-Government Act, which came to a head in the following year and will afterwards need special mention, had already, under the direction of B.N. Sasmal, reached such a pitch, that the situation in Contai was said to be little short of civil disobedience.

On the 4th November a serious riot occurred at Howrah. A procession returning from a Khilafat meeting attacked the police on duty and forced them to retire to the police-station. Armed police were requisitioned from Sibpur, but were attacked *en route* and shots were fired before the mob was finally dispersed. One constable was killed and several wounded, and an Assistant Magistrate was slightly injured in the head. According to the papers five rioters were killed, but only one death was officially reported. Affairs came to a climax in Calcutta on November 17th, the day of the Prince of Wales' arrival in Bombay. A tramway strike was already in progress and had resulted in one riot during the previous week. On the 17th there was a complete suspension of all the public utility services, servants and clerks of Europeans were intimidated in the streets by bands of volunteers in uniform, and volunteers backed up by crowds of hooligans, openly usurped the functions of the police in stopping traffic. For one day the life of the city was paralysed, and there was general talk not of a Gandhi but a Goonda Raj. It became evident that the moral of the police was seriously impaired. A meeting on the Maidan, attended by about 200 policemen, was followed by the resignation of 30 Muhammadan constables from Bihar and the United Provinces, and, to prevent the spread of contagion, it was considered necessary to remove these men from the Presidency of Bengal. Almost in every district picketing of cloth shops was intensified to an extent which amounted to an intolerable interference with the liberty of purchasers, and a certain amount of unrest, notably in Mymensingh, was also observed among the district police.

In conformity with the policy laid down by the Government of India the policy of Government [of Bengal] in dealing with non-co-operation had originally been that of letting the movement kill itself by reason of its own inherent folly and impracticability. After the occurrences resulting from the exodus of the Assam tea-garden coolies the necessity of more active measures became apparent and district officers were instructed to resort more freely to prosecutions and propaganda. The original policy, however, was still followed to the extent of leaving the leaders of the movement at liberty while concentrating on the smaller agitators, and the general desire to avoid the appearance of repression was observable in the reluctance often displayed by district officers, perhaps not quite certain of their ground, in exercising their powers under the Criminal Procedure Code.

The alarming developments in November forced Government to give a new and very definite lead. After the 'hartal' on the 17th the National Congress volunteers and similar bodies were declared to be unlawful associations under Part II of the Criminal Law Amendment Act, 1908. The original notification was worded sufficiently widely to admit of application all over the province, but special proclamations were also made in the case of the volunteer corps at Rangpur and elsewhere. At the same time prosecutions for seditious utterances were started against some of the leaders, the most important being J.L. Banerji, Abdur Razzak and Muhammad Osman, and against several newspapers. Public meetings in Calcutta were prohibited for a period of three months. An 'anti-hartal' committee was formed for the purpose of making provisions for the running of the public utility services in the event of another 'hartal' and of instituting counter-propaganda against the campaign of intimidation. Europeans, Anglo-Indians and loyal Indians organised a Civil Guard in Calcutta, which was recognised by Government and attached to the police force. A Civil Guard was also afterwards formed in Howrah, but it was found impossible to induce Bengali bhadralok to join. In the mill area of the 24-Parganas, 'sirdars' or foremen, especially those likely to give trouble, were enrolled as special constables, and plans were made for preventing an excited mob from flowing into Calcutta when the Prince of Wales arrived in Calcutta on December 24. Action was at once taken under the terms of the proclamation. In the districts the largest number of arrests took place in Pabna, Bakarganj, Faridpur, Mymensingh, Dacca, Chittagong, Tippera, Howrah, the 24-Parganas and Rangpur, and it will be seen that, with the exception of the last three, all these districts fall within Eastern Bengal. An immediate effect was seen in the lessening of obstructions against the Settlement at Birbhum and in an easing of the situation at Rangpur. In Calcutta 50 volunteers wearing sashes and badges were arrested on the 21st and 22nd November.

On the 5th December the non-co-operators tried a change of tactics. No more uniforms appeared, but volunteers with 'khaddar' or homespun cloth and measuring rods went the round of the shopkeepers, exhorting them to observe a 'hartal' on the 24th. These youths were obviously courting arrest and were taken into custody. The policy of filling the jails had been widely preached and was now to be put into operation. Up till December 9th arrests continued in large and increasing numbers, and it was noticeable that, probably owing to the excitement caused by the unavoidable detention for a short time of Mrs. C.R. Das and other Bengali ladies on the 7th, students had now largely replaced the hooligan element. On the 8th a climax was reached in Barra Bazar, when Harrison Road was completely blocked by an excited mob. The Indian constables on duty became thoroughly demoralised, and all arrests had to be carried out by European Police Sergeants.

On the following day British Infantry was called out and posted in this quarter, and though large crowds again collected, their presence made it possible to deal with the situation. It was discovered that Forbes Mansions in Wellington Square was being used as a recruiting centre for volunteers, and the raiding of this and other headquarters on the 10th and afterwards did much to stop the supply of volunteers at the source. On the 10th also C.R. Das, S.C. Bose, B.N. Sasmal, A.P. Bajpya, and Abul Kalam Azad were arrested without causing more than local excitement. After this date, although students had now largely dropped out of the movement, the policy of challenging Government to enforce the proclamation was carried on by the enlistment of mill coolies and other low class Muhammadans, who were paid for their services. On the afternoon of 23rd December no less than 650 arrests had to be made in Bow Bazar and Barra Bazar. Jail accommodation was now taxed to the uttermost, but this proved to be the expiring effort of the opposition. On the night of the 23rd/24th the Civil Guard took over the whole of South Calcutta and also reinforced the police in the North District. The 'hartal', although successful to the extent of securing the closing of shops and markets entirely failed in its main object of causing a disturbance such as had marred the Prince's arrival in Bombay. The return of public confidence was seen in the increasing numbers who flocked to see the Prince on the succeeding days, and a successful visit culminated on the 27th, when the Prince was received with the greatest enthusiasm by immense crowds on the Maidan. In the interior, where the forces at the disposal of law and order were necessarily not so great as in Calcutta, the 'hartal' was almost everywhere successful. The opinion, however, of local officers was unanimous in favour of the new line taken by Government, and the supply of volunteers for picketing and obstructions had in many cases sunk to the level of small boys and hooligans. In Calcutta the number of arrests up to the end of December amounted to 3,230.

Nothing could be more indicative of the utter bankruptcy of 'Moderate' opinion and of its complete inability to face reality than the comments of the press, the attitude of the Legislative Council, and the many petitions submitted to His Excellency by 'Moderate' associations upon the adoption of the policy of proclaiming volunteer associations. In vain His Excellency explained the extreme gravity of the situation, the inevitability of the measures taken and the generous treatment at once accorded to any arrested volunteer who expressed sentiments of regret. The proclamation was universally denounced as an extreme instance of repression, and entirely fictitious or grossly exaggerated accounts of the ill-treatment of volunteers in jail, and of alleged outrages committed by the police and members of the Civil Guards were employed to foster belief in the aggressiveness and tyranny of Government.

The events of the first quarter of 1922 confirmed the fear that the movement had got beyond the control of the leaders. It was evident that in the interior the authority of the Bengal Congress Committee amounted to nothing, and even that of the District Committees was rapidly lost in a great wave of lawlessness, which swept over the affected area of east and west Bengal. The policy of Civil Disobedience had not been accepted by the Provincial Congress Committee, and there was no systematic inauguration of it in any definite area, but these parts of the province were clearly drifting towards it. In Calcutta picketing was resumed for a fortnight after the Prince of Wales' visit, but was then practically suspended, owing to the difficulty in finding new recruits. In its place a new campaign was started of holding meetings in defiance of the orders of the Commissioner of Police.

For the success of this movement reliance was placed, whether from design or from lack of other sources of supply, upon the activities of Bengali ladies, and their presence as organisers or speakers made the task of the police in maintaining authority immensely more difficult. The means usually adopted by the police were to disperse the audience by a baton charge and arrest any speakers other than women, and this policy, with the exception of one occasion upon which the whole of the audience was arrested, was maintained till the middle of February, when the order prohibiting meetings expired. An intercepted letter from the Secretary of the Provincial Congress Committee to the Barisal Committee stated that the Congress had decided 'that if there is no apprehension of a breach of the peace, meetings should be held by breaking the unjust law', and meetings had in fact to be dispersed by force in Dacca, Barisal and Mymensingh. In the *mufassal* [!], however, this particular form of lawlessness, which depended on organisation and a constant supply of speakers, was short-lived. The spirit of violence and contempt of all authority which now began to show its head, was not of the leaders, but of the masses.

In dealing with the various outbreaks of the next two months, it will be convenient for the most part to trace the series of events, district by district. Three occurrences of January and one of February are, however, more or less isolated and may be mentioned first. In the Serajganj subdivision of Pabna, during the course of a route march undertaken by the District Magistrate in consequence of the rescue of three arrested volunteers and the subsequent beating of the police and looting of Excise shops, the District Magistrate was himself obliged to arrest some volunteers, and was thereupon, with the armed police, attacked with clods of earth and *lathis* by a crowd of about 2,000. He was eventually, after the Deputy Superintendent of Police had been knocked down senseless, compelled to open fire, at first with blank, and then with buck-shot. It was not, however, till ball cartridges were used, that the crowd dispersed, leaving four dead and six wounded. A similar affair occurred at Tittaghar, in the 24-Parganas, where the Deputy Superintendent of Police, in effecting two arrests for assault, was hemmed in by a threatening crowd of mill coolies, and obliged to fire in self-defence, leaving one killed and forty wounded. It is remarkable, however, that no other instance of violence occurred in the mill area of the 24-Parganas, and its proximity of Calcutta, where the situation was now well in hand, may be partly responsible. The police were also attacked in the Dacca district, while making searches and arrests. Fire was opened and one death resulted. In February the hitherto quiet district of Jalpaiguri was disturbed by an attack on the police, who had just arrested four Sonthals [!] in connection with an ordinary criminal case, by a large crowd wearing Gandhi caps, and by reason of that fact proclaimed themselves to be immune from bullets. In the firing which resulted, three were killed and thirteen or fourteen wounded.

The situation in Tippera had for some time given cause for the greatest anxiety, the chief trouble being the jurisdiction of Chaudagram police-station. In this area the rural police had ceased work since November. No taxes were being paid, and no agricultural rent collected, either by Government or by private landlords. Attempts to execute distress warrants and criminal processes were met by assaults on the officers concerned, and when the armed police were sent out to make consequent arrests the villages were simply evacuated. It was remarked that the agitation was entirely Muhammadan, but not religious. The people were simply out to assert themselves, and save money. Between the 13th February and 9th March there were five determined attacks on the police. On the 24th February the police, escorting some arrested volunteers, were attacked by a mob of two hundred with *daos* and *lathis.* They were obliged to fire, but no one was injured. Trouble culminated on the 9th March, when the District Magistrate, the Superintendent of Police and 30 constables went out to conduct a house search in connection with a riot which had occurred on the 2nd March. As the police were being withdrawn, they were attacked by a frantic crowd with clods of earth and *lathis.* In the pandemonium which ensued it was impossible to hear any orders. Fire was opened, and it was afterwards ascertained that three men died of wounds, and five were injured. In this affair it was noticeable that volunteers tried to restrain the mob, but without effect. In local comment it was generally recognised that the shooting was justified, and this attitude was in marked and very instructive contrast to that displayed after the Chandpur affair, where the amount of force used was very much less. Additional police, at the cost of the inhabitants, were afterwards posted to this area, and by July, it was reported that people were again law-abiding.

Mention has already been made of the state of affairs in the Rangpur district at the end of the previous year. In addition to the organised boycott of the police, there had been a wide refusal to pay the chaukidari tax, on the grounds, which were largely true, that the chaukidars were merely servants of the police and not of the villagers, and that collecting panchayats were dishonest and assessments unfair. The refusal to pay taxes, as in Tippera, soon developed into a refusal to pay rent, and many of the local tenure-holders consequently turned against the movement. It was, however, too late to prevent conflict and bloodshed.

On the 21st December the armed police were attacked in Nilphamari bazaar, and obliged to fire, causing a few casualties. A few days afterwards the District Magistrate patrolled the area with armed forces, and chaukidari taxes were then paid. On the 20th February the Subdivisional Officer went with an armed escort to clear away a prohibited market. He was attacked, and obliged to open fire, leaving three wounded. In this instance, as in Tippera, volunteers tried to restrain the mob, but were unsuccessful. Again, on the 16th April, a Circle Officer, in execution of warrants for the realisation of chaukidari tax, went to attach property in Fulchari thana. He was obstructed, and the collecting panchayat confined by force. A few days later the police who were sent to make arrests in this case were attacked and obliged to fire. One man was killed, and two wounded. By this time, however, the situation in Rangpur had elsewhere improved.

In these two districts, and in Noakhali and elsewhere, attacks were chiefly directed against the police. The movement against chaukidars was most prominent in Midnapore. In 1921 the Village Self-Government Act had been introduced in large areas in the district. Opposition to the Union Boards established under the Act had been engineered by agitators, who took the fullest advantage of the popular prejudice against the slight increase in taxation inherent in the new system. By October refusal to pay any taxes had become general in the affected areas, and although instances doubtless occurred in which the agitation gave weak or secretly non-co-operating panchayats an excuse for defaulting, the combined nature of the movement was seen in the impossibility of realising arrears by distraint, owing to the absence of bidders at the sales. Chaukidars' pay was now in arrears since April, but intimidation and boycott, rather than discontent with the scale of pay, were responsible for the resignations which occurred. Had it been otherwise, complaints would have been heard more frequently before the start of this agitation. Not only chaukidars, but members of Union Boards resigned in considerable numbers and the general situation was such that Government considered it advisable to give Union Boards the option of deciding by [the] 16th December to revert to the Chaukidari Act. The opportunity was everywhere accepted, but a good many panchayats refused to accept office even under the Chaukidari Act. Nor was there any improvement in the collection of the chaukidari tax, although the District Congress Committee advised payment. People had been told that their subscriptions to the Swarajya Fund would exempt them from all future taxation, and the belief was literally maintained.

The authority of the Bengal Congress Committee was similarly impotent to prevent the withholding of rents. At Keshpur a dacoity was committed in the house of the one man who paid his chaukidari tax, and the only way of collecting arrears was by sending out armed police to attach the defaulting panchayats' cattle before dawn. Similar conditions prevailed in Sabong thana, and the arrest of the local leaders on March 2nd was carried out with the greatest difficulty. In this area it became necessary to post additional police; but in the Contai and Ghatal subdivisions a warning that additional police would be imposed if the tax was not paid by a fixed date was found to have sufficient effect. A route march of a detachment of the Eastern Bengal Rifles through the area where Sonthals had taken to looting and dacoity was also found beneficial. During January no less than 33 dacoities had occurred in the district, out of a total of 111 in Bengal. As a result of the measures taken the situation was in hand again by March.

The last district of which special mention need to be made is

Chittagong. The chief form which the movement here assumed was that of opposition to the Forest Department, probably because that was more productive of gain than any other, but the usual hostility to police, chaukidars and Government servants was also discernible. Additional police had eventually to be quartered in Banskhali thana in the adjoining thana of Satkania, and in the three thanas of the Cox's Bazar subdivision. In the first of these areas agitation had first become prominent in April 1921, and rapidly developed into the form of incitement to loot forest produce. Up to December losses amounting to about Rs. 4,000 had in this way been incurred by Government, but in that month this kind of activity of volunteers as a result of their proclamation as unlawful associations. Three forest houses were burnt down, meetings were held in defiance of injunctions, and twenty-four of the rural police were compelled to resign.

In Satkania thana events up to December were on the same lines. After December activity was even more pronounced. Two Forest beat-houses were burnt, the rural police were restrained and had their uniform torn off, foreign cloth was snatched from the wearers and from shops in the bazaar and burnt, foresters were beaten, constables escorting arrested volunteers were beaten, and it was impossible for police officers on tour to get boats or accommodation. In the affected thanas of Cox's Bazar looting had commenced as a result of permission given by the Forest Officer after the cyclone of May 1921 for building material to be taken free for a period of 10 days on application. It was taken without applying and thereafter, possibly with some idea of justification by reason of losses caused by the cyclone and of alleged extortions by the subordinate officials of the Forest Department, the habit of simply taking anything that was needed grew, until about May 1922 the Forest Department might have been said to have ceased to function.

Of twelve Forest Offices and beat-houses in this area eight were burnt down during the twelve months, as well as the Divisional Forest Office at Cox's Bazar. In April a conflict between armed police and a party cutting poles led to one man being shot dead. This widespread looting was not the work of volunteers, but of ordinary villagers out to help themselves, and formed another instance of the loss of control by the leaders. More organised activity was represented in the interference with the export of raw cotton from the Chittagong Hill Tracts, the stoppage of transportation of materials for the Public Works Department, and in the holding of public meetings in defiance of prohibition. As in Tippera the posting of additional police had the effect of restoring the situation by July.

The full force of the storm of mob violence which has in part been described in the preceding paragraphs was expanded by April, and the calmer political atmosphere which succeeded it may be attributed to several causes. The massacre at Chauri Chaura on [the] 4th February had been followed by the Ahmedabad Conference of Congress at which mass civil disobedience was suspended, and picketing, except of liquor shops, prohibited, a milder programme of progress by means of hand-spinning, national schools and arbitration courts being laid down instead. The effect of these resolutions was probably considerably less on the now uncontrollable masses in the affected districts than the strong measures taken by Government to put down the disorder, but the arrest of Mr. Gandhi in March and his complete failure to achieve his promise of swaraj within one year went a long way towards dispelling the clouds of superstitious credulity which had hitherto blinded the movement. Funds had also become depleted, many of the leaders were in jail and the glamour of volunteering had grown stale.

The events of the remainder of the year may be rapidly surveyed. In April there was a serious mutiny in the Presidency Jail, necessitating the calling in of the military and resulting in nine deaths before order was restored, and, as part of the same aftermath of violence, attacks on the police, which forced them to open fire, occurred in July at Chittagong and in August at Pabna and Bakarganj. Of the other practical and seditious aspects of non-co-operation there was a rapid decline. Temporary revivals of picketing became evident in September and November, but there was no disposition to court arrest, and the situation in this respect had so far improved, that at the end of the latter month Government felt able to withdraw the notifications proclaiming volunteer corps illegal.

A consequent attempt by C.R. Das to start re-enlistment met with no response, except in Eastern Bengal. The fallen repute of non-co-operation among the people was reflected in a report of the Barisal Congress Committee, previously one of the most active centres of agitation, in which lament was made of the apathy of the general public, the absence of good preachers and workers and the lack of a new sensation, 'hue and cry or hoax' [!].

Disintegration in the non-co-operation party became evident at the Bengal Provincial Conference held at Chittagong in April, and thereafter there was a gradual emergence of four groups. On the one hand were the orthodox non-co-operators and the new Swarajya party of Mr. C.R. Das. Both of these groups agreed to the principle of non-violence, but the former was pledged to attain its end by the old method of boycott, whereas the latter hoped to force the grant of immediate self-government by wrecking the reformed constitution from within. On the other hand appeared the Khilafatists, and revolutionary extremists, both inclining to more violent methods and underground working.

Of these four groups the Khilafatists were the first to drop out of the running. There had been considerable excitement among Muhammadans in September over the British attitude towards the victories of Kemal Pasha, but the news of the abolition of the temporal power of the Khalifa, although at first received with incredulity or suspended judgement and afterwards whitewashed by various authoritative pronouncements, could not in the fail to have a sobering effect. With the final conclusion of peace with Turkey in July 1923 the Khilafat party may reasonably be said to have ceased to be a separate force. Members of the old revolutionary groups had come into notice during the height of the non-co-operation campaign in connection with the drilling of volunteers and the formation of secret societies. In May 1922 there was an outbreak of dacoity in which ex-détenus were largely concerned. By June eight District Congress Committees were reported to be under the control of revolutionaries, and in November it was found that the Provincial Congress Committee now contained a large proportion of ex-détenus and ex-State prisoners. Constant interception of Bolshevik literature, the tone and tenets of which now began to affect the extremist press, revealed the new source of revolutionary inspiration, but the subsequent activities of this group form no part of the history of non-co-operation. It may be noted, however, that certain similarities between the programme put forward by Mr. C.R. Das in December 1922 and that suggested by the Communist M.N. Roy, especially with regard to the organisation of the masses for the 'final blow', did not escape comment in the press. The other distinctive part of Mr. Das's programme—that involving the destruction of the constitution from within—continued to gain acceptance during 1923. As far as local self-government was concerned the effect was not remarkable. Municipal elections continued for the most part to be fought on personal rather than on political grounds, and where, as at Midnapore and Noakhali, a majority of non-co-operators or Swarajists were returned to the District Board, their conduct of business did not conspicuously differ from that of their predecessors. But the triumph of Mr. Das and the elimination of the party of orthodox non-co-operation was seen in the Council elections of November 1923. At that point the history of non-co-operation as a united movement may be said to cease.

It is too early to attempt an estimate of the permanent effects of the movement on the temper and mind of the people. National consciousness among the upper classes and the consciousness of mass power among the lower may, to a certain extent, have been awakened. The 'pathetic contentment' of the masses has been disturbed, though perhaps only temporarily, in a manner not contemplated by the authors of the Montagu-Chelmsford report. But the ideas of nationalism and of economic revolt, which doctrinaire observers see as the prime motive factor of the agitation were clearly not to any large extent spontaneous impulses. They were imported by the leaders from abroad, and it was their failure to find responses from the people which led to the resort to the lower appeals of colour prejudice, religious fanaticism and pure love of gain. These were the main-springs of popular interest, and we may add the ordinary love of opposition to Government, and, last, but of greater potency than generally realised, the love of 'tamasha' and sensation common to simple peoples.

History of the Khilafat Movement in Bengal

In so far as tangible effects are concerned the history of the Khilafat movement in Bengal is, at any rate after 1920, so inextricably bound up with that of the general non-co-operation movement, that it is impossible to draw up a separate narrative of events which could be said to be traceable to Muhammadan influences only. Some idea of the predominantly Muhammadan character of the agitation during 1920 has been given in pages 1 to 4 of the history of the non-co-operation movement in Bengal which had already been submitted to the Government of India. The accession of Hindus to the movement has been dealt with in pages 5 to 7, and the final elimination of the Khilafat grievances as a separate line of influence has been mentioned on page 16. It will probably be enough for the present purpose if some attempt is made to illustrate the general nature of the Khilafat propaganda throughout the period, and to trace the changes in tone consequent upon the development of the situation in the Near East.

It must be borne in mind that the Khilafat movement was never indigenous in Bengal. Most of the leaders were men whose ordinary sphere of activity was outside Bengal, and though they succeeded in taking with them extremist Muhammadans in Bengal and had considerable influence on the mass of the Muhammadan population they had to contend all through against the influence of the Muhammadan moderates.

The origin of the Khilafat movement is to some extent obscure. It appears, however, to have been started by a section of advanced Muhammadan thinkers whose Pan-Islamic and pro-Turkish sympathies had been in evidence even before the war. Without entering upon a discussion of the doctrine and history of the Khilafat it is essential for a clear understanding of the issues, and particularly of the interaction of religious and political influences, to premise a few facts which, at any rate before the beginning of this agitation, were not generally recognised. The main thing to bear in mind is that in Sunni or orthodox Muhammadan opinion the office of the

Khalif, or successor of the Prophet, has always been associated not merely with spiritual leadership, but with temporal power. The Ummayad Khalifs were in fact absolute rulers, possessing unquestioned secular authority throughout the dominions of Islam. The Abbasids lost almost entirely the powers which their predecessors had won. But the theory of the office remained the same. So long as a Khalif, however shorn of power, existed and was recognised, he represented the potential headship of an ideal Muslim commonwealth. In modern times the political value of this conception was first recognised by the Sultan Abdul Hamid II of Turkey, who after his defeat by Russia in 1878, endeavoured to take advantage of the sympathy expressed by the Moslem world at the loss of his dominions by sending emissaries to Egypt, Tunis, India, Afghanistan, Java and China to impress upon the Moslems of those countries the fact that there was still a Khalif in Islam. The same insistence on the secular authority of the Khalif is visible in the doctrine of the men responsible for the introduction of the Khilafat agitation into India. To them the occupation of Constantinople by the British was an interference with the personal liberty of the Khalif, and the occupation of Palestine together with the enthronement of British nominees in Hedjaz, Iraq and Transjordania a deliberate infringement of his territorial sovereignty.

Accordingly we find that the demand put forward at the beginning of the Khilafat agitation was the restoration of the Sultan's territorial authority to the *status quo ante bellum*. At the Khilafat Conference held in Calcutta in February 1920 the resolution passed was to the effect that 'if the dominions of the Khalifa are not kept intact as they were before the war then Muslims, in obedience to the laws of Islam, will be compelled to cease all relations of loyalty with Great Britain.' It was represented that Indian Muhammadans had been induced to join in the war against Turkey only on the distinct understanding that there should be no dismemberment of the Turkish Empire upon the conclusion of peace.

In Bengal the theory of the Khilafat was not widely understood and even among Muhammadans the appeal on these grounds failed to evoke material response. To Hindus it meant nothing at all. The position was clearly admitted in a speech delivered at Barisal in

March 1922, in which it was said 'The one thing common in the composition of Indian patriotism is a deep and burning sense of wrong against the present foreign Government,' and it was to the unscrupulous inculcation of this sense of wrong that the Khilafat propaganda, having failed in its first appeal, rapidly descended.

The campaign of lies with regard to the desecration of the holy places has already been described on page 7 of the history of the non-co-operation movement. It would be easy to multiply instances of this type of propaganda throughout the whole period of the agitation, but two more must suffice. Early in 1920 and again in 1921 rumours were sedulously circulated to the effect that Government had ordered the transfer of the Muhammadan holy day from Friday to Sunday, the substitution of the name of the King-Emperor for that of the Khalif in the *Khutba* prayer, and the proscription of the Koran. This may be taken as representing the most dangerous type of misrepresentation with which Government had to deal. As an instance of the most extravagant, we may take a statement of Hakim Abu Yusuf Isfahani, made in May 1923. Speaking in Calcutta, he said:

'There is an open place surrounded by a wall in London which is called "Hedjaz", and in which there is an artificial hill resembling the sacred place "Arfat", where the "Haj" takes place every year, and people go there for target practice and amuse themselves by saying they are destroying Islam. There is also a house in London in which the picture of "Baitullah", the holy mosque of Mecca, is set up and this is similarly used as a target.[']

Enough has been said to indicate the general character of the agitation as directed towards the illiterate classes, and we may now turn to a consideration of the effects produced on the leaders of the movement by the course of events in Turkey. During the summer of 1920 Mustapha Kemal had been avoiding defeat. In 1921 he not only succeeded in stopping a further Greek advance, but drove the Greeks back to their original lines. Enthusiasm at these victories in Bengal, in the first place, took the form of a campaign initiated by the Provincial Khilafat Committee for the enrolment of 10,000 volunteers for military service in Angora. In Dacca 100 persons were said to have enlisted, but elsewhere recruiting operations were a complete failure. As a result, however, of the repeated charges brought against the British Government of giving help to Greeks and of the ensuing tendency to proclaim the war between Turkey and Greece as 'Jehad', the tone of Muhammadan speeches towards the end of the year became increasingly violent and contributed not a little to the outburst of anti-Government feeling in the weeks before the arrival of the Prince of Wales in Calcutta. The Turkish victories, although they failed to procure volunteers for Angora, were used with more success for the recruitment of volunteers for service in Bengal. Speaking in Calcutta in December, Naser [!] Ahmad said

> 'Every Moslem should become a volunteer. You will earn a greater reward than those religious warriors of Angora because you have no swords. They have strength and the sword of faith and are ready to fight the British Government. Therefore, it is the duty of all to become volunteers and liberate Islam, the Khilafat and the country;'

and appeals on these lines were common.

In the early part of 1922 the drift of the Khilafat agitation towards violence became even more marked and was aided by an intensified campaign of misrepresentation of the British. In March, Maulana Muhammad Ismail said in a speech at Noakhali that the English had outraged ten thousand Muhammadan women in Angora and Smyrna, and the infants were taken from the arms of their mothers and bayoneted. The proposals of the Allied Conference in Paris to hand over Eastern Thrace, Smyrna, Asia Minor and Constantinople to Turkey were not considered satisfactory on the essential point of Turkish supremacy over the holy places, and it was significantly declared by one speaker (Abdullahel Baki) at the Congress Committee Conference at Bogra that even if the Khilafat question were solved completely Muhammadans could not budge one inch from their purpose of gaining Swaraj.

At the same time there were indications that Muhammadan extremists were no longer prepared to follow the policy of non-violence. At the Bengal Provincial Conference held at Chittagong in April attempts were made to reverse the Bardoli decision on the subject of civil disobedience and a considerable section showed itself in favour of offensive measures; 'Abandon Mr. Gandhi's remedy of non-co-operation', said Maulvi Muhammad Kazim Ali Saheb, and 'find another path and follow it.' 'It is proper,' added another speaker, 'that there should be assaults and bloodshed and the whole Moslem world will combine to resist the British taking an inch of Khilafat land.' 'He who is your enemy,' said the President, Maulana Muhammad Shafi of Lucknow, 'should be met with the sword,' and quoted Islamic scripture in support of it. This belligerent attitude was over-ruled by a majority of the Congress, but the extent to which it represented contemporary Muhammadan feeling is emphasised in the address delivered at the same conference by Mr. J.N. Sen Gupta.

'During the last few months,' said that speaker, 'I have been moving about a good deal among my Muhammadan friends in connection with work for the Khilafat.... This hatred of the English, I must confess, as far as I have been able to observe, is more marked amongst the Muhammadans than amongst any other class of the people. I had a discussion with Muhammadan maulvis and maulanas on the subject of *Tarkem-walat*, which, I understand, means cutting off all connections with the English people as a race. If *Tarkem-walat* means that there should be no connection with the English people socially, politically, commercially, or in any other way (I hope I am wrong in this assumption), I am afraid that non-violent non-co-operation which the Congress has accepted on behalf of the nation is not the same thing as *Tarkem-walat*.'

It would be wrong to take this passage as representing the general attitude of Muhammadans, even at the height of the movement, but in laying stress upon the bitterness of feeling which had been developed among those Muhammadans who came within the influence of the agitation, it is probably correct.

The fact that in July 1922 the Allies had refused to allow Greece to occupy Constantinople was completely lost sight of in the jubilation over Mustapha Kemal's capture of Smyrna in August. This in itself was harmless, but there was a threatening undercurrent due to the suspicion that the Allies, and particularly Great Britain, would attempt to intervene. Muhammad Shafi, President of the Calcutta Khilafat Committee, announced that all Muhammadans should hold themselves in readiness to join the Kemalist Army in case of necessity. For the second time the idea of an Angora Legion was strongly taken up, and a number of names were actually sent to the Calcutta Khilafat office. The general idea, however, appeared to be that Mustapha Kemal would be successful in restoring the Khilafat without assistance, and it was decided to await orders from Bombay before taken more definite steps. That orders never came was due to the development of the situation in Europe in October.

After the signing of the Mudania [?] armistice the Angora Government took over Constantinople. The Sultan, whose position had been represented in India as endangered by the British occupation of Constantinople, was obliged to flee for his life, and the National Assembly elected in his stead his nephew Abdul Masjid Effendi, not as Sultan, but as Khalif. The plain meaning of the deposition was that the Turkish Nationalists had no intention of tolerating the presence in Turkey of any authority likely to rival their own, and the election of Abdul Majid as Khalif, but not as Sultan, probably represented not so much the limitation to spiritual dominion or 'Vaticanisation' of the Khilafat as its relegation to the position of purely nominal temporal power, which it had so often occupied in its early history at Baghdad and Cairo. To men whose hopes had been set not upon the curtailment but upon the ultimate realisation in fact of all the potentialities of the office, the change must have been humiliating. In Bengal, however, its significance was either not understood or wilfully misunderstood, and although orthodox opinion was doubtful as to the right of the National Assembly to limit the secular authority of the Khilafat, it preferred to lay stress on its undoubted right to depose an individual Khalif. The last Sultan Wahiuddin was denounced for having signed the Treaty of Sèvres with the enemies of Islam. His name was in Calcutta and elsewhere omitted from the *Khutba* prayer and that of Ghazi Mustapha Kemal substituted in its stead. An extraordinary rumour that he was to be brought to India and set up as a rival Khalif by the British found wide credence, especially amongst the extremists and general opinion appeared to crystallise into the belief that in every respect he had been merely a puppet in the hands of the British Government.

In spite, however, of the efforts of the leaders to keep it alive, popular enthusiasm for the cause of the Khilafat had suffered a decline parallel to that in the general non-co-operation movement. The announcement of the peace finally concluded with Turkey in July 1923 went far to kill any genuine feeling then left. Amongst that section of the Muhammadan leaders which had used the Khilafat agitation purely as a weapon against the British Government in India attempts were still made to retain a sense of grievance. It was announced that agitation must be continued until the control of all the holy places, including Jerusalem, was restored to Moslem authority. At a meeting in Calcutta stress was laid on the successful outcome of Hindu-Moslem unity in getting better terms for the Turks and of its potentialities as a means for the attainment of Swaraj in India. In November a day was fixed for the collection of money for the liberation of the Jazirat-ul-Arab. Attention was directed, possibly with some truth, to the oppression practised by King Hussein, the reigning Sherif of Mecca, who was declared, like the ex-Sultan Wahiuddin, to be nothing more than a puppet in the hands of the English. There was, however, a general impression that this agitation was forced and nothing practical resulted. On the question of the Khilafat the opinion of the leaders themselves was considerably disturbed by the emphatic pronouncement of Fateh Bey in December that the appointment of a Khalif was no concern of Moslems outside Turkey. It did not require much foresight so see the trend of republican Turkey's politics.

Yet the abolition in March 1924 of the office of Khalif by a decree of the Angora Assembly and the expulsion of Abdul Majid from Turkish territory came as a severe shock. Muhammadan opinion was at last united against Mustapha Kemal, and even Muhammad Ali, in a speech at the Khilafat Conference called at Calcutta to discuss the situation, was obliged, after the usual allegations of British attempts to suppress Islam, to reprove his Turkish brethren.

'When the Treaty of Lausanne was signed,' he said, 'two things remained for us to do. One was the restoration of the Jazirat-ul-Arab through the Mussalmans and the Khilafat. And the other was the re-establishment of the Khilafat itself on a firm democratic basis with a representative council of the Muhammadans of the world to assist the Khalif in his great task which had been neglected for centuries, but which we could not afford to neglect any longer. . . . It may seem that we are more Arab than the Arabs and more Turkish than the Turks, but it will be apparent that all we are is Moslems. As Moslems we cannot countenance a section of the Turkish nation disconnecting its national Government from the Khilafat.'

The truth is that all along the leaders of this type were deliberately more Turkish than the Turk and, in the words of Mr. A.K. Fazl-ul-Huq, at that time Minister for Education in Bengal, 'knew that neither Kemal Pasha nor his followers cared much for Islam, but still thought it fit to maintain the Khilafat agitation—an agitation which was unnecessary, and a dishonest propaganda against the British Government.'

The history of the Khilafat agitation as a separate force within the non-co-operation movement may be said to have ended with the treaty of Lausanne. In the subsequent political developments in Bengal the success of Muhammadan leaders in keeping the members of their community out of the anarchical conspiracy, and in large part also out of the Swarajya activities of Mr. C.R. Das, shows what little permanent impression the Khilafat movement had made.

5

Sindh C.I.D. Reports for 1921

NOTE BY J.C. CURRY, WRITTEN IN 1968

These reports are secret official documents. They must not be quoted or referred to without a consideration of the question whether, if published, they might involve an infringement of the Official Secrets Act and the customary reservation of such documents for fifty years. In any case, I must place a reservation against their being quoted or referred to during my lifetime. They might, however, be used as background information at the discretion and under the control of the Director of the South Asian Studies Centre.

I was not aware that they were in my possession when I wrote the autobiography entitled 'The Memoirs of an Indian Policeman' but I subsequently discovered them among a number of my private papers. My recollection is that I kept an extra copy for personal use to enable me to refer to them outside office hours and for this purpose they were locked away in a box containing private papers to which I have not had occasion to refer for several years.

I find it difficult to make a satisfactory assessment of these Reports as I now write in 1968. There would appear to be some inconsistency between the tenor of some of the reports and that of the chapter in the autobiography covering this period. In the autobiography I have suggested that the Mohammedans of Sind were very little affected by the Khilafatist agitation of 1921, but the weekly reports indicate that the question of the Khilafat had a considerable influence on the minds of the Mohmmedan population. In the light of hindsight it seems clear to me that these reports compiled week by week convey an impression of a greater excitement of the popular mind than was actually the case. It is quite certain that, in general, life in Sind went on in a normal way for practically all sections of the population.

As stated in the earlier reports, only a small proportion of Hindus and Mohammedans were deeply involved in the agitation created by the Congress organisation. After the trial of the Khilafatists, the excitement among the Mohammedans increased but it was of an ephemeral nature. I recall that there had been a greater disturbance in the minds of many Mohammedans in 1920 when the Khilafatist agitation had led a few hundred of them to leave British territory for the Mohammedan kingdom of Afghanistan, where they were not made welcome. Most, or all, of them returned disillusioned to India and this experience tended to minimise the effect of the renewed agitation towards the end of 1921.

The question of the Khilafat was not, in fact, germane to the agitation for the development of Swaraj or self-government in India. It was raised by politically-minded Mohammedans like Mahomed Ali and Shaukat Ali under the influence of the Hindu-dominated Congress in a vain attempt to suggest that there was a community of interest between Hindus and Mohammedans under Congress leadership. As far as my observation went, this false joinder of disparate issues did not lead to the development of Hindu-Moslem unity as was intended. On the contrary, it was, as I believe, one of the factors which helped to bring about the ultimate separation of Pakistan and India. The Mohammedans eventually realised that Gandhi and the Congress were playing on their religious feelings for political reasons. These reasons involved the ultimate aim of Congress domination whenever self-government should be achieved and Congress domination meant Hindu predominance. From this realisation sprang that of the need for a struggle for power between the two communities and therefore, logically, the need for Pakistan.

As I recall conversations with Jairamdas Daulatram and other emotional Hindu followers of Gandhi, I feel that there is something peculiarly pathetic about the story of the Hindus of Sind. They were living in the only province of British India which had a substantial Mohammedan majority, namely about three Mohammedans to one Hindu. They were descended from a very ancient race and were possibly among the first people in the world to develop the practice of trade and commerce. They were racially were different from the Sindhi and Baluchi tribesmen among whom they lived, usually in small village communities. They were pacifist by nature whereas the tribesmen had warlike traditions. They used a system of writing allied to that of Sanskrit, whereas the Sindhi and Baluchi languages were unwritten before the British introduced a modified form of the Arabic alphabet to the Sindhi language. The Baluchi rulers of Sind prior to the British occupation in the 1840s despised the art of writing and despised the Hindus whom they employed to keep accounts and records for them. Early British observers in Sind were astonished at the way in which the Hindus of Sind submitted to the utmost degradation at the hands of the Baluchis; and, as one of them put it, the fact that the Hindus remained in the country under such tyranny could only be likened to the persistence of the vegetable in remaining in its soil. Under British rule a small section of the Hindus who had been employed by the Baluchi rulers as contemptible quill drivers, rose to considerable influence because they quickly adopted English education and thus became qualified to serve as Magistrates, Collectors of Revenue, Irrigation Engineers and in other branches of the public services. It was from among this community known as Amils that Gandhi's followers, the non-co-operators, were chiefly drawn. When the magnanimous promise of early self-government was held out to India by the Montague-Chelmsford reforms of the 1920s, the Indian National Congress under Gandhi's leadership developed the policy of 'non-violent non-co-operation' instead of accepting the reforms by building up an electorate, entering the Legislatures, and accepting office as Ministers in the Councils of the Indian Provinces. It was a recognition of the lack of statesmanship in this policy which led me to remark in one of my weekly reports that Gandhi appeared to be a medical case of a peculiar psychological nature.

The pathetic nature of the non-co-operation campaign carried on by the Hindus of Sind is to be found in the fact that when India obtained self-government in 1947, a mass migration took them to Hindu India, because they were no longer willing to live under Mohammedan rule. They were no longer, like vegetables, attached to the soil of the land in which their ancestors had lived for thousands of years.

Generally speaking, no men of importance took an active part in the non-co-operation movement. The great tribal chiefs held aloof from it, as did the official classes and the Hindu and Mohammedan merchants and traders. It gradually subsided after 1921.

REPORT OF THE CHIEF CIVIL INTELLIGENCE OFFICER, SIND, FOR THE WEEK ENDING 5TH FEBRUARY 1921.
SUMMARY OF POLITICAL SITUATION IN THE PROVINCE

The political situation in Sind as in the rest of India is at present dominated by the policy of non-co-operation decided upon at the National Congress at Nagpur during the Christmas week of 1920.

The salient features of the movement, which found definite expression in the resolutions passed at the Congress and in the alterations of the Congress creed and constitution, are:

(1) the re-organisation of Committees in every Province, with subordinate Committees in Districts, Talukas and Villages, so as to provide machinery for carrying out the decisions of the Congress and 'accelerating the progress of non-co-operation'. (Note: It is also reported that the idea has been discussed of forming departments to deal separately with education, finance, &c., in the central body called the All India Congress Committee, the members of which also constitute the 'Subjects Committee' of the Congress.)
(2) The organisation of a band of national workers to be called the Indian National Service.
(3) The raising of a national fund to be called the All India Tilak Memorial Swarajya Fund to finance the movement.
(4) The movement is to be carried out by means of:
    (a) boycott of schools
    (b) boycott of law courts
    (c) boycott of foreign goods
    (d) by calling upon Indian Councillors under the Reforms Act to resign
    (e) by appealing to Government servants openly to render financial aid to the movement, pending the call of the nation to resign their service. A special reference is made to the 'growing friendliness between the police and the soldiery and the people'.

So much for the resolutions passed at the Congress the object aimed at is publicly announced to be 'the attainment of Swarajya by the people of India by all legitimate and peaceful means'. Gandhi is reported to have chided the Sindhi 'Nationalist' leaders on the backwardness of the movement in this province. Since their return from Nagpur they have displayed greatly increased activity.

The results so far have been very meagre, but constant meetings at which speeches full of racial animosity and anti-Government propaganda are indulged it, cannot but have their effect. The leaders have concentrated their attention on:

(a) the boycott of schools, as being the most favourable point of attack and that in which the maximum effect is likely to be secured. They have however met with considerable difficulty and have not yet succeeded in their attempts at securing the National College at Hyderabad owing to the fact that it is controlled by Mrs. Besant's followers who are opposed to the non-co-operation movement.

National schools are being established but so far only a few hundred boys have joined such institutions out of the thousands in Government-aided schools.

Attempts are being made to organise work under (b), (c), (d) and (e), but no very definite steps have yet been taken. Preliminary steps in connection with police and soldiery have been noticed in Press propaganda in the *Hindu* of Hyderabad. This paper is printed in Sindhi language. In this connection an extract from this office report to the Director of the Intelligence Bureau, Delhi, is appended. There is reason to believe that the leaders are giving serious attention to the problem of spreading the spirit of non-co-operation in the Indian Army.

One reason for the scanty results so far attained is to be found in the delay which has occurred in perfecting the internal organisation of the Congress Committees. This work has been taken in hand during the last week and further developments are to be awaited.[1]

[1] Pages 4 and 5 of the original are missing.

REPORT OF THE CHIEF CIVIL INTELLIGENCE OFFICER, SIND, FOR THE WEEK ENDING 12TH FEBRUARY 1921

1. During the week the activities of the non-co-operation party in Sind have been concentrated on two points, the boycott of schools and colleges and their own internal organisation, i.e., the Congress Committees. In both respects they must be bitterly disappointed, as their progress has been comparatively limited. The boycott of schools and colleges is also bringing its own reaction. Strong feelings of resentment against them have been provoked in some quarters among parents and others; and it may be expected that a number of students will return eventually as is already happening in the Punjab.

2. Agitators have however been very active and are likely to continue to be so. On Saturday, February 6th, Jairamdas Daulatram, Dr. Choithram P. Gidwani and Abdul Jabbar, pleader, come to Karachi from Hyderabad with the object (to use Jairamdas' own expression) of 'demolishing' the Sind College in Karachi. Their ultimate intention is to 'nationalise' the college if they find themselves strong enough to do so, and pending that to divert the students to the Hyderabad National College, to which course Gandhi has given his consent as a result of a detailed exchange of views, by telegram and letters between himself and Jairamdas Daulatram. It is also intended to use a number of students, who may be fitted for such employment, as 'workers' (of the 'Indian National Service' mentioned in last week's report) to spread the doctrine of non-co-operation throughout the Province.

3. At the end of the week 120 out of 350 students of the Sind College have left on account of non-co-operation. A certain number have left from various schools throughout Sind, especially in Karachi and Sukkur. It is noteworthy that no attempt has been made to 'demolish' the Sindh Madressah [!] or other similar institutions. This is doubtless the result of instructions from headquarters, and it may be taken as illustrating the leaders' appreciation of the danger of alienating the Muhammadans. The movement tends to become more and more a Hindu one.

4. V.J. Patel, a political agitator from the Bombay Presidency, arrived in Karachi on Wednesday, the 9th February, to conduct the proceedings of the Students' Convention. This institution like so

many others has been captured by the non-co-operation party, and is now used for political purposes though that was expressly prohibited by its rules. It has been in constant session for three days, the speeches being almost entirely in the nature of non-co-operation propaganda.

On his arrival at the City Station, Patel was met by the leading local agitators and an immense crowd, which threatened to become unruly. Stones were thrown at the Police, traffic seriously interfered with, and the City Police Inspector struck. These developments alarmed the agitators who hurried Patel away in a car, whereupon the crowd dispersed.

5. As regards internal organisation, a sub-committee of the Sind Provincial Congress Committee appointed to reorganise in accordance with the Constitution of the Nagpur Congress submitted majority and minority reports. The rock on which they have split is the question of a headquarter for the Provincial Committee. Long-standing jealousies exist between the Hindu Committees of Hyderabad, Upper Sind and other parts. It is for this reason that in the Constitution passed at Nagpur no capital, or headquarters, is assigned to Sind. Alternative proposals are (1) Karachi, and (2) Karachi, Hyderabad, Sukkur, Shikarpur and Larkana in rotation. In 19 of the 21 Provinces into which the Congress has divided India a headquarters was mentioned. The Congress has assigned the Native States of Khairpur and Cutch to Sind, and for reasons which are at present obscure there is also considerable difference of opinion on the treatment of these States under the constitution.

6. The net result is that there has been much discussion but little work done in the way of organising the machinery of Provincial, District and local or village Committees.

No definite steps have been taken as regards 'police and soldiery', or the boycott of foreign trade.

There are rumours but no further development as regards a railway strike. Everything in this connection waits on the Bombay Conference which has been in progress during the week. From information received it appears probable that the next move is to be in the direction of stirring up agrarian unrest in the country and labour trouble among the railway workmen and the working classes in the towns. A sinister feature of the Railway Conference in Bombay is that the Conference and the Federation of Unions are being run by political agitators contrary to the wishes of many railway employees, who wish to form genuine trade unions.

7. The results of the Conference are to be discussed with local people at a meeting at Karachi on Monday. In this connection, a telegram from Miller, the Irish agitator at Lahore to Kanti Parsad, his lieutenant in Karachi, is interesting but its meaning is partly obscure at present. It is dated [the] 12th February and reads 'Avoid misunderstanding new Union business satisfactory watch policy explained maintain prestige.'

8. Though it would be hazardous to form a definite opinion at this early stage, it is probable that this next phase (labour trouble) of the non-co-operation movement will be more dangerous than the present one, and it is possible that a situation may develop, in the event of a railway strike, in which the civil authorities will be obliged to ask for military assistance, to maintain order, in certain localities, in addition to and at the same time as the introduction of the railway strike part of the Internal Security Scheme. There is no sign of any such necessity arising in the immediate future, but the situation may develop unexpectedly rapidly.

The agitators have a great deal of ground to cover before they provoke serious agrarian unrest in Sind. It is extremely doubtful whether they are likely to have any success at all in this direction.

9. An extract from a speech by Professor Ghanshamdas at Hyderabad on the 7th February 1921 is attached[2] as a fair sample of the doctrines now being inculcated at frequent meetings all over the country and in the Press. It is clear that the term Swaraj is widely accepted as meaning complete independence.[3]

REPORT OF THE CHIEF CIVIL INTELLIGENCE OFFICER, SIND, FOR THE WEEK ENDING 19TH FEBRUARY 1921

Agitation among students has not been sustained during the week, and the non-co-operation movement among them has assumed a

[2] Not attached in the original.

[3] Page 9 of the original is missing.

much less active form in Karachi and several other places in Sind. In the D.J. Sind College, Karachi, the number of students who declared that they had non-co-operated had reached a total of 120 at the beginning of the week and there has been no material increase since. But of the 120 only about half actually sent in a notice to the Principal of the college. Seventeen have since returned and the situation at the college is nearly normal. Similarly many students have returned or been taken back by their parents to various schools in different parts of Sind. Appeals are still being made to students to non-co-operate and the agitation is not likely to be entirely dropped.

The events of the last two weeks have demonstrated the impossibility of the success of the movement in the larger sense. There are indications that it is becoming less a matter for the politicians (in the English, not the Indian sense) and more a matter for the Police. There are those among the leaders who believe in the use of violence and the failure of the campaign of non-violence is likely to lead them to engage in secret criminal conspiracies. Gandhi has published articles in his paper *Young India* which prove his fear of the consequences of appealing to the masses who, as he admits, are not capable of understanding the principles of non-violent non-co-operation. Preparations are being made in Sind, as elsewhere, to appeal to the masses and to spread new ideas such as are likely to serve the ends of the political agitators.

For purposes of propaganda, three agitators are being deputed to each of the Congress districts and two, Sheikh Abdul Aziz and Pandit Amarsen, are to tour the whole province and to formulate plans for establishing 'Agriculturists' Union'. Meanwhile about 80 students who have non-co-operated have been instructed to go to the Hyderabad Ashram to be trained in methods of political agitation under Jairamdas Daulatram and other local agitators. After a month or six weeks' instruction they are to be sent out to work under experienced agitators in the districts.

The Kasib Azadi Sabha, or Proletariat Emancipation Society of Swami Govindanand, is now being taken seriously in hand. A public meeting is being convened this evening (10th).

The Sind Provincial Congress Committee has overcome its initial difficulties in regard to its internal organisation by selecting Karachi as its headquarters and by assigning the States of Khairpur and Cutch to the Sukkur and Karachi districts respectively. It is now devoting its energies to the formation of subordinate committees and to propaganda among the masses as sketched above.

There are no further developments as regards a railway strike. Meetings have been held with official sanction to discuss the provincial proposals for the amalgamation of the two Unions as approved by the Agent, North Western Railway. A general strike in the immediate future is improbable.[4]

REPORT OF THE CHIEF CIVIL INTELLIGENCE OFFICER, SIND, FOR THE WEEK ENDING 20TH FEBRUARY 1921

The non-co-operation movement has been less actively carried on during the week as regards schools and colleges. The attention of the leaders is being devoted to creating or attempting to create mass movements among the working classes and agriculturists. At the meeting organised on the 19th February by the Kasib Azadi Sabha in Karachi (referred to in last week's report) the line taken was to appeal to the audience by dilating on the oppressiveness [!] of the Police.

Several meetings have been organised in Karachi, Hyderabad, Sukkur and other important places, at which the usual arguments and appeals to emotion have been repeated.

Importance is to be attached to a recrudescence of activity in connection with the Khilafat agitation. The occasion for this is the Near East Conference in London. A meeting of the Sind Provincial Khilafat Committee has been summoned for the 26th and 27th February at Larkana to be followed by a Khilafat Conference at Shikarpur on the 28th. Mahomed Sadik, Maulvi of the Khadda, Karachi, of Pan-Islamist tendencies, has been to Bombay to see members of the Central Khilafat Committee there. Maulvi Taj

[4] The secret report was sent by J.C. Curry to the General Staff Officer in the Sindh Rajputana District, Karachi. A copy was forwarded to the Commissioner of Sindh and the Superintendent of Police, Karachi. They were advised to either burn the report or to keep it in their personal custody.

Mahomed of Amrot, also notorious in the same connection, is to preside at Shikarpur. Jan Mahomed Junaja, the Sindhi Muhajarin leader, has been externed from the North-West Frontier Province after being refused permission to return to Afghanistan and has gone to Lucknow, presumably to meet Maulana Abdul Bari. Hindu extremists are making themselves prominent in connection with the Khilafat agitation. It is clear that the movement is being encouraged by the non-co-operation party in order to influence the Mahommedan massed by the appeal to their religious feelings as part of the general revolutionary programme. One of the most important Mahommedan agitators, Abul Kalam Azad, has recently published a long article which is frequently referred to by Sindhi agitators as a 'fatwa'. He openly declares for revolution, and explains that the fixing of the time limit of one year for the attainment of Swaraj proves that the movement is in itself essentially revolutionary. This individual has for years been connected with the most fanatical Mahommedan elements in Sind, namely Taj Mahomed of Amrot, the Jhandewalla Pirs, the Sarhandi Pirs of Tando Saindad and their circles.

A report appeared in the Press concerning the threat of a strike by Telegraph employees to secure revision of pay and the redress of other grievances. A meeting was arranged for the night of the 27th instant. The less responsible element among the employees in Karachi, who are predominantly Anglo-Indian, was in favour of precipitate action, but wiser counsels prevailed on receipt of news that Government was appointing a small committee to inquire into grievances. A plan has apparently been arranged at Allahabad for a simultaneous strike on the Railways, but there is no sign of the North Western Railway Union falling in with the proposal. The North Western Railway Union is occupied with its own internal organisation and is not likely to call a strike at present without strong outside pressure.

A small strike, affecting 300 employees, occurred at the beginning of the week in Herman's Engineering Works in Karachi. It commenced spontaneously and on economic grounds, but was immediately taken up by the Kasib Azadi Sabha. It ended in substantial concessions. It has resulted in a consolidation of the influence of the Sabha to a limited extent among a small group of workers. There is no sign of the extension of the 'strike fever' in other similar works in Karachi.[5]

REPORT OF THE CHIEF CIVIL INTELLIGENCE OFFICER, SIND, FOR THE WEEK ENDING 5TH MARCH 1921

Intensified agitation is proceeding in most parts of Sind, including meetings in the streets in Karachi, processions in Hyderabad and numerous public meetings elsewhere. A new method adopted in Karachi is for a party of singers to move round the town singing patriotic songs before sunrise.

The non-co-operation movement in schools and colleges continued to subside and attention was diverted to the Provincial Khilafat Committee meetings at Larkana on the 26th and 27th ultimo. The salient features of these were an increasing tendency to secrecy regarding the deliberations of the Committee and the participation of Hindus. The Khilafat meeting (public) at Shikarpur was remarkable for the number of Hindus who composed nearly half of the audience.

There are no developments to report concerning labour movements or the railways. According to press reports, the threatened strike of Railway and Telegraph workers which was being engineered from Allahabad has been indefinitely averted.[6]

Weekly Bulletin on the Non-co-operation Movement for the Week ending 12th March 1921

1. AGITATION

Intensified agitation is proceeding in most parts of Sind. There are signs that a body of public opinion is growing which regards the street agitators in Karachi in particular, and the movement in general as a nuisance. Nevertheless the agitators are to some extent breaking new ground in villages all over the Province, and in the towns. Attempts are being made to appeal to women to take up

[5] Addressees as in footnote 4.

[6] Addressees as in footnote 4.

Swadeshi and to organise propaganda among them.

2. ORGANISATION

Taluka and local Committees are being formed in various places. Canvassing for municipal elections by agitators continues.

3. FUNDS

No developments.

4. SCHOOLS AND COLLEGES

National schools have been started in a certain number of villages in most districts. Generally these National schools are poorly organised.

5. INDIAN NATIONAL SERVICE AND VOLUNTEERS

The position as regards the Indian National Service may now be reviewed. About 80 students, mostly from the D.J. Sind College, were instructed to go to Hyderabad to undergo training at the Ashram in order to form a nucleus for the Indian National Service in the middle of February. About 40 or 45 actually went, but a few days later the number was only 25. During the first week in March the Ashram was visited and only 5 college students and about a dozen who had left various schools were present at the time of the visit.

It was originally intended that the students, who called themselves 'Soldiers of Swaraj', should be trained for 6 weeks or 2 months, but partly because those who were to instruct them, namely Jairamdas Daulatram, Dr. Choithram P. Gidwani, Abdul Jabbar (ex-pleader) and Sheikh Abdul Majid, found it irksome to be tied to one place and preferred to be up and doing in the way of speeches and meetings, party, because the boys were impatient to take an active part and because it was considered that they should be best trained by so doing, they were sent out to preach under the guidance of more experienced agitators.

On their arrival in the Ashram, the following course of training was laid down:

(1) National songs were sung in the early morning.

(2) A course of reading the following books prescribed by Jairamdas Daulatram:

  (a) India in Parliament and Abroad. Swadeshi Movement.

  (b) Non-co-operation and Satyagraha.

(c) The United States of America by Lala Lajpat Rai.
(d) The Rowlatt Act and the Opposition meted out to it by Indians, and the result thereof.
(e) Lives of great Political Leaders and their sufferings and troubles, i.e. Mahomed Ali, Gandhi, Motilal Nehru, Tilak, /c.

(3) Courses of lectures by Jairamdas Daulatram, Dr. Choithram P. Gidwani, Abdul Jabbar and Shaikh Abdul Majid on the above books, with illustration from the history of the wars and struggles for freedom in America, Korea, Egypt, China, Poland and Russia. The part played by students in such movements was emphasised.
(4) Hand spinning.
(5) Recreation, including music.
(6) Practical work:-
(a) in the streets collecting funds
(b) preparing posters and notices
(c) distribution of posters and notices in the streets.

A play entitled the 'Punjab Tragedy' has also been written in the Ashram and is to be staged at Karachi.

This programme has given way to practical work in attendance on agitators and those students who still remain at the Ashram are employed in writing pamphlets, leaflets and posters and in doing other miscellaneous clerical work. They are also being utilised in connection with the campaign in Hyderabad to nationalise the Municipal Schools, as well as in the agitation for the boycott of sales of liquor licences. A list of existing schools in Hyderabad district has been compiled, maps have been collected and the distribution of workers to be assigned to groups of schools is being arranged, with the object of carrying the movement throughout the district and eventually securing the complete cessation of work in the schools.

The names of the students who have been sent out to the Sukkur, Karachi, and Thar Parkar Districts, have been ascertained as follows:

Sukkur

(1) Kaimdin son of Allahdino Khan, Jatoi of Madeji
(2) Gul Mahomed son of Karim Baksh, Baluch of Kot Diji, Khairpur State

Thar Parkar
(3) Nichaldas Meharsing Himatsingani of Larkana
(4) Motiram Alimchandani, Amil of Hyderabad
Karachi
(5) Alu Tekchand Gidwani, Amil of Hyderabad
(6) Nanakram Chabaldas Vaswani, Amil of Jhooramal Lane, Hyderabad
(7) Rijhumal Chandiram, Amil of Karachi
(8) Jethanand Naraindas Nagrani, near Fruit Market, Shikarpur
(9) Khuda Baksh son of Ghulam Hussain Kureishi of Arazi Larkana

Some other students have been sent to their own districts. The names of four of the five college students now at the Ashram are:

(1) Nandiram Navalrai Mahratri of Hyderabad
(2) Mulchand Mangharam Hasrajani of Hyderabad
(3) Kessumal Tekchand Jhangiani of Hyderabad
(4) Ali Ahmad son of Haji Pinial, Mohalla Memon, Hyderabad

The following have been removed by their parents:

(1) Choithram Thawardas Tahulramani of Tatta
(2) Umedali son of Haji Abdul Latif, Kureishi of Arazi, Larkana[7]

Weekly Bulletin on the Non-co-operation Movement for the Week ending 19th March 1921

1. AGITATION

Intensified agitation continues in towns and villages. Street agitation has spread to most towns.

An attempt was made to boycott the sales of liquor licenses for the year. The sales were held this month in all districts. In Karachi and Hyderabad cities where the agitation was strongest, the bidding was abnormally high. Minor non-co-operating agitators led a crowd into the Huzur Deputy Collector's office in Karachi and behaved in a disorderly manner. A few are being prosecuted. The sales were boycotted in the Thar Parkar district, apparently owing to the fact that the headquarters being a very small place the agitators were able to exert pressure against individual bidders. The failure of this

[7] Pages 19 to 21 of the original are missing.

movement exasperated the leaders, who by way of compensation and in hope of scoring a spectacular success propose to organise a hartal during the visit of His Excellency the Governor of Bombay. Extensive propaganda in favour of a temperance movement has also followed this failure.

2. ORGANISATION

Taluka and local Committees continue to be formed but the total is still very small.

Canvassing by agitators for election to the Municipality continues. Mahomed Khan Ghassi Khan, Secretary of the Sind Provincial Khilafat Committee, and Manilal J. Vyas are candidates. In this connection the lack of cohesion among the local leaders of the movement makes itself evident. A Telegram was sent to Gandhi by Swami Govindanand, Kazi Khudabux and Marriwalla which reads as follows:- 'Karachi non-co-operators wasting energy municipal elections. Instruct them withdraw candidature.' On the 19th, Gandhi wired from Nagpur to the effect that non-co-operators need not be prevented from entering Municipa-lities for the purpose of 'nationalising' school. This reply was addressed to 'Khilafat, Karachi'.

3. FUNDS

No real organisation yet.

4. SCHOOLS AND COLLEGES

The Gujerat Vidyapeth examination was organised at Hyderabad by 'Professor' Ghanshamdas J. Shivdasani. Only 23 Sindhi students appeared for the 'Matriculation' and one for the 'Inter Arts'. Of these, 8 were from Karachi, three from the 'Tilakalya' and five from 'Nawa Mahavidyala'.

The question of nationalising municipal schools is exciting interest in Hyderabad.

Reports indicate that two schools have refused to take the Government grant in Karachi during the week.

5. INDIAN NATIONAL SERVICE AND VOLUNTEERS

The 'Soldiers of Swaraj' figure prominently in street agitation and at meetings in nearly all districts.

6. LAWYERS AND COURTS

The Panchayat of Bhiria in Nawabshah District had decided two

Criminal and two Civil cases of an unimportant nature. The fines inflicted in the two Criminal cases were paid.

17. Agrarian
18. Labour including Railways
19. Strikes

} No developments

10. Boycott of British or Foreign Trade and Trading concerns

Two clerks employed by Shaw Wallace & Company were refused leave. They reminded the Manager of the present situation in India and expressed surprise at the English having failed to mend their ways yet. They declared that they would sever their connection with such a tyrannical firm, whereupon they were given notice to leave immediately. They are endeavouring to influence other clerks.

In other respects there is little sign of any movement in favour of boycott of foreign trade beyond the spread of the idea of giving up the use of foreign articles in various middle class circles. Some give up cigarettes, other socks or collars; but such ideas are put into practice in a haphazard and spasmodic manner.

The *New Times* in its issue of the 4th March 1921 gives the following account of the Karachi Piece Goods merchants:

'Karachi Piece Good Merchants'

(From a correspondent)

'Sat Narayan Piece Goods Association has sent the following telegram to the Piece Goods Association at Bombay, Madras, Calcutta, Delhi, Amritsar and Cawnpore:

'Present crisis necessitates All India Trade Conference. Wire Opinion.'

Replies of some of the Associations have been received showing complete agreement with the view of the Karachi Piece Goods Association.

The above Association has also written to the Karachi Chamber of Commerce on 28th February 1921 to fix a date and give them an interview to discuss the most difficult problem of exchange with a view to its solution. Reply of the Chamber is not yet received. The following are minutes of the General Board Meeting of the Karachi Sat Narayan Indian Piece Goods Merchants' Association held on the 2nd March 1921.

In opening the proceedings the President referred to the orders of Government regarding enhancement of duty on piece goods and other imports to have effect from 1st instant, orders in connection with which were communicated by the Chief Collector of Customs that day at about 2 p.m.

The president, Seth Motilal Goverdhandas, stated that the Government will not modify their orders but they should be requested to exempt from increased duty piece goods and other imports which had arrived at any port in British India before the 1st instant. Messrs. Harchandrai and E.L. Price may be addressed on the subject to move Government for the purpose.

Seth Chainrai said that the Government orders should be protested against vehemently. Seth Wassomal Chellaram, vice-president, supported the president's view and said that the increased taxation had been necessitated by a deficit of 10 crores and nothing would be gained by approaching the Government of India with regard to those articles of import which had been definitely sanctioned. The Government may be moved with respect to the taxation which had not yet been definitely decided upon, viz.: Income Tax, Post and Railways.

It was then unanimously resolved to send the following telegram to the Government of India, Messrs. E.L. Price and Harchandrai:-

Karachi Sat Narayan Indian Piece Goods Merchants Association requests issue of orders not to levy enhanced duty on uncleared goods lying at posts or on steamers which touched any port in British India before 1st instant.

To Messers. Price and Harchandrai only:

Karachi Sat Narayan Piece Goods Association respectfully request move legislature not accept proposed increased taxation income tax, Railway, Posts. Direct taxation retards trade demoralised and Nation already groaning under heavy taxation and please do best.[']

11. CANCELLATION OF EXISTING AND FUTURE CONTRACTS

No developments.

12. INSTANCES OF INCITEMENT TO BOYCOTT, OR OF BOYCOTT OF EUROPEANS BY THEIR DOMESTIC SERVANTS

No developments.

13. GOVERNMENT SERVICE

Swami Govindanand and other leaders have announced in various meetings that Government servants are to be induced to leave the service now. 'Munshis', 'Clerks', and 'Police' are specifically mentioned, but no results have been secured yet.

14. HOW FAR MUSSALMANS AS A SEPARATE CLASS ARE ADOPTING THE NON-CO-OPERATION MOVEMENT

A handbill has re-appeared calling for 30 lakhs required by the Central Khilafat Committee for the oppressed Mahomedans of Thrace and Smyrna, for the Khilafat and for the Muhajarin. It is strongly worded.

15. THE NANKANA AFFAIR AND ITS INFLUENCE IN SIND

The Nankana Sahib incident is still being used to further the purposes of non-co-operation movement by repeating allegations against Government and its officers.

A party of four Akalis has visited Karachi to make enquires concerning shrines here.

There are indications of resentment among Hindus over the attitude of the Akalis, especially at Sukkur, Shikarpur and Karachi.[8]

Weekly Bulletin on the Non-co-operation Movement for the Week ending 26th March 1921

1. AGITATION

Intensified agitation continues in towns and villages. Street agitators have been very active in Karachi, and parties including students who non-co-operated and were trained at the Hyderabad Ashram have visited villages in several parts of the Province. It is reported from the Sukkur District that the influential men, Zamindars and others in some of the villages have prevented agitators from addressing meetings in their villages.

Extensive propaganda in favour of the Temperance movement continues. At the Holi Festival people were urged to refrain from drinking. In Karachi, Fazal Karim, a minor agitator preached to the Dhobis and through one of their leaders named Ratna Chunilal persuaded them to take a vow of temperance and to decree a punishment of ex-communication for 12 months on any dhobi who broke it. Similar movements are reported elsewhere.

A Hartal was organised on the occasion of the visit of His Excellency the Governor to Karachi on Monday the 21st March. Unlawful assemblies collected in several parts of the city who intimidated shop-keepers to close their shops and labourers to stop their work. In at least two places rioting occurred on a small scale, stones being thrown at trams and at the police. Two men have been prosecuted under Sec. 147, I.P.C. and two men under Sec. 341, I.P.C.

[8] Copies forwarded to the Director, Intelligence Bureau, Home Department (Government of India), Delhi; the Deputy Inspector General of Police, Criminal Investigation Department, Poona.

2. ORGANISATION

Taluka and local Committees continue to be formed. The number is now becoming fairly considerable.

Canvassing by agitators for election to the Municipality continues.

3. FUNDS

No organisation.

4. SCHOOLS AND COLLEGES

No developments.

5. INDIAN NATIONAL SERVICE AND VOLUNTEERS

An officer of this department visited the Swaraj Ashram during the week and found that the course was no longer in progress [with] all students having left the Ashram. These ex-students continue to take a prominent part in agitation

There has been increased activity in connection with enlisting volunteers during the last three weeks. This activity is apparently connected with the visit of Maulvi Muhammad Sadiq of Khadda, Sind agitator No. 5, to Bombay from when he returned on the 25th February 1921. A report on his visit to Bombay has been asked for, but has not yet been received. Intercepted telegrams indicate that he went to see members of the Central Khilafat Committee. On his return he gave out that the question of volunteers had been discussed in Bombay and that it had been decided that the status of the volunteer should be improved, that they should be paid and supplied with food on days when they were called out on duty. A considerable number of the volunteers in Karachi are Muhanas of the Khadda, a notoriously criminal class who are the followers of the Maulvi. About the 15th of March a meeting was held at the Khilafat Office, Karachi to discuss the volunteer question. The Secretary Mr. Malik was replaced by Dr. Ahmad who is an active man and it expected to work with more effect. On the 21st Kazi Khuda Bakhsh mentioned at a public meeting in Karachi that a National Volunteer Corps was to be formed and it is said that the same uniform is to be worn through out India.

During the Hartal on the occasion of His Excellency's visit volunteers were much in evidence. When the armed Police appeared on the scene the Volunteers walked about telling the crowd to disperse. People however paid little or no attention to them in most cases. It has been reported on somewhat unreliable evidence that in some isolated cases volunteers excited the crowds to throw stones at trams.

6. LAWYERS AND COURTS — No developments.
7. AGRARIAN — do.
8. LABOUR INCLUDING RAILWAYS — do.
9. STRIKES — do.
10. BOYCOTT OF BRITISH OR FOREIGN TRADE AND TRADING CONCERNS — do.
11. CANCELLATION OF EXISTING AND FURTHER CONTRACTS — do.
12. INSTANCES OF INCITEMENT TO BOYCOTT OR BOYCOTT OF EUROPEANS BY THEIR DOMESTIC SERVANTS — do.
13. GOVERNMENT SERVICE

There are rumours of action by the N.C.C. party but no specific instances have been reported, except that in casual conversation agitators have said to various officers that they should resign.

14. HOW FAR MUSSALMANS AS A SEPARATE CLASS ARE ADOPTING THE NON-CO-OPERATION MOVEMENT

No developments.

15. THE NANKANA AFFAIR AND ITS INFLUENCE IN SIND

The *Hindu* in its issue of the 21st March contains an article on the Nankana affair in which it suggests that there was a plot to murder Gandhi, Muhammad Ali and other leaders at the Nankana Jalsa on [the] 5th March. This statement purports to be based on a sentence in the *Amrita Bazar Patrika* of the 3rd March to the effect that these leaders were to go to Nankana on the 5th. It also repeats allegations of officials being privy to the conspiracy.[9]

[9] Copy forwarded to the Director, Intelligence Bureau, Home Department (Government of India), Delhi.

Weekly Bulletin on the Non-co-operation Movement for the Week ending 2nd April 1921

GENERAL

In view of the decision at Bezwada not to commence 'Civil Disobedience', the situation would seem to be less threatening. It is noticeable that no members from Sind attended the Bezwada Conference.

The Sind C.I.D. is as present concentrating attention on about 16 of the leaders in Sind, and endeavouring to find out what is their general attitude in the present situation and what are their plans for the future. It is clear that the Sindhi extremists follow the lead set elsewhere. If the information contained in Sind C.I.D. No. S.B. 408 of [the] 29th March 1921 (regarding 'Civil Disobedience' and hartals) is correct, it may be inferred that a party among the extremists in Sind favours action likely to precipitate a crisis. Men like Durgdas B. Advani, President both of the Sind Provincial Congress Committee and of the Karachi District Congress Committee, Jairamdas Daulatram, Secretary of the Sind Provincial Congress Committee, and the more important extremists are keeping very much in the background at present, while Fazal Karim, the actor, and others excite the multitude.

Extracts from the *Vande Mataram* dated 28th March 1921—edited by Jairamdas Daulatram, are appended. (Not attached)

1. AGITATION

Intensified agitation continues. Propaganda in favour of the Temperance movement continues. It appears however that many people continue to drink as usual in spite of decisions to the contrary. It is reported that at Hyderabad steps are being taken to prevent liquor licensees from obtaining shops for the sale of liquor in the town.

On the 24th of March, a disturbance took place in the Market at Sukkur where a body of 40 or 50 Non-co-operationists picketed the Market to prevent people from buying fish and mutton. A complaint was filed by a man who was molested by the crowd and 7 persons were arrested the same day by the police. It is alleged that the Non-co-operators assaulted purchasers and snatched fish and mutton etc.[10]

Weekly Bulletin on the Non-co-operation Movement for the Week ending 9th April 1921

GENERAL

The intentions and plans of the leaders in Sind may perhaps be inferred to some extent from certain notes running through recent speeches. These include the formation 'as directed by Gandhi' of a large body of volunteers to preserve order when the refusal to pay taxes and resignation from the public services are commanded; it is apparently expected that these will coincide with a 'national strike'. Emphasis is laid upon the importance of hand spinning as an economic weapon which will make Swaraj possible. The religiosity of a large proportion of the population is illustrated by cases like that of an educated Hyderabadi who announced that he at first thought hand spinning madness, but that after practising it he came to regard it as a form of devotion—a prayer.

1. AGITATION

Agitation continues to grow in intensity. All districts report greater activity in connection with the national week. The hartal of the 6th April was almost complete in the large towns, viz. Karachi, Hyderabad, Sukkur, and Shikarpur, but a failure in places like Sehwun and Tatta in spite of the efforts of agitators from Karachi. Jacobabad reports a general hartal and intensified agitation for the first time.

2. ORGANISATION

No developments.

3. FUNDS

During the week agitators are concentrating on the collection of funds. No reliable information is available, but the amount probably falls short of the five lakhs expected from Sind.

[10] Pages 32 to 34 of the original are missing.

4. Schools and Colleges

There has been some talk of renewing the school boycott campaign, but the matter has been dropped.

5. Indian National Service and Volunteers

A considerable number of volunteers have been enlisted in Karachi. The local leaders ascribe the peaceful nature of the hartal of the 6th April to their presence on the streets. (Police officers attribute it to the squads of armed and unarmed police stationed at all important points, combined with constant patrolling by the Mounted Police, supported by the District Magistrates notices under the Police Act.)

6. Lawyers and Courts

No developments.

7. Agrarian

No agrarian societies exist anywhere in Sind, and the agrarian population takes no part whatever in the non-co-operation movement. (They consist almost exclusively of Sindhi Mahomedans and Baloochis.)

8. Labour including Railways

A public meeting of the artisans and labourers of Karachi was convened under the presidentship of Manilal J. Vyas at the Idgah Maidan on the 8th April 1921. The audience, which numbered about 400, was addressed by Manilal J. Vyas, Swami Govindanand, Swami Krishnanand and a couple of Cutchis of no social standing. The general tenor of the speeches was to point out the advantages of a labour movement and to refer to the treatment meted out by the rich to the poor, urging the necessity for organising an association to protect the rights of labourers. Swami Govindanand alluded to the present times as 'the Age of Labourers' who, he said, were acquiring power in Russia, Germany and England. He spoke strongly on the evils of 'Capitalism', condemning it as tyrannical. Referring to the backwardness, illiteracy and social conditions of the labouring classes, he pointed out the need for education and sanitary housing. Swami Krishnanand emphasised the strength and advantages of Labour Unions and strongly urged their formation. The meeting dissolved after the formation of a 'Sabha of Artisans and Labourers', which, it was decided, would consider the following questions:

(i) Removal of difficulties pertaining to the housing problem.
(ii) Prompt payment of wages.
(iii) Formation of a society to purchase land and build houses for labourers.
(iv) Negotiations with big contractors.
(v) Formation of a school for labourers.
(vi) Elimination of the difficulties the poorer classes have to contend with to obtain railway tickets.
(vii) Formation of a body of workers on the same basis as volunteers.
(viii) Opening of a shop and dispensary for the use of the labourers.

It was announced that about 800 members had joined the Sabha.

A public meeting of employees of the North Western Railway was held under the presidentship of Lekhraj in the Burns Gardens on the evening of the 10th instant. The meeting was convened with the object of recruiting members for the Railway Union. It is said that the Agent will not recognise it until a sufficient number of members have registered. The audience numbered about 300 persons and was addressed by Lalsingh of the Carriage and Wagons Shops, M.A. Khan (Secretary of the Railway Union, Lahore) and Kanti Parkash (Secretary of the Railway Union at Karachi). The speeches were in no way political, but were restricted to Railway Union['s] interest. The praises of Miller and M.A. Khan were sung in a Punjabi doggerel. M.A. Khan who was garlanded spoke at length of the work done by him in connection with the Union and after referring to the European Coal Crisis gave detailed descriptions of the methods employed by European strikers to obtain their demands. Kanti Parkash censured the men of the Loco Sheds for not having signed the membership forms and said that others had done so without hesitation. The meeting was then dissolved, the audience dispersing quietly. Bhai Jagatsingh of the Akali Jatha of Peshawar was noticed in the vicinity of the meeting place. He took no part.

M.A. Khan also visited Sukkur and addressed a meeting there. Nothing fresh was said.

9. Strikes — No development.
10. Boycott of British or Foreign Trade and Trading Concerns — do.
11. Cancellation of Existing and Future Contracts — do.
12. Instances of Incitement to Boycott, or of Boycott of Europeans by their domestic Servants — do.
13. Government Service — do.
14. How far Mussalmans as a Separate Class are adopting the Non-co-operation Movement

The Mahomedans of Sind as a whole, especially the cultivating classes, are almost entirely unaffected by the non-co-operation movement. All the leading Pirs (who have great influence among these classes) are against it. The Pir of Kingri, who is perhaps the most important Pir in Sind, has not only openly declared himself against it to his own murids but he advises those who consult him to remain faithful to the British Government. From information received from reliable sources it is evident that he had considered the question of publishing views based on religious writings denouncing the movement. He has decided not to take this action in view of the uncertainty of its result. There is an exception in the person of Pir Mahbubshah of the Hyderabad District, who is responsible for considerable agitation in the neighbourhood of Tando Mahomed Khan. He is influential locally but is wholly illiterate and there is some doubt as to his sanity. Other minor Rashidi Pirs (i.e. those belonging to the family of which the Pir of Kingri and the Jhandewalla Pir are representatives of the two main branches) have taken some part in agitation, e.g. Turabalishah son of Abdullashah of Kambar, Anveralishah of Larkana, Mithanshah s/o Mazhardinshah of Thulla Sharif, Ghulam Mujadid son of Abdul Halim, Sarhandi, and some of his relations are affected in the same way, but their interest is in the Khilafat movement rather than non-violent non-co-operation. The reason for men like Rashidullah Shah, the Jhando Pir, holding aloof from the non-co-operation movement, is that it is initiated and controlled by Hindus. The question of adherence to it by such men is undecided and their present attitude is to refrain from taking part in it. The only Sindhi delegate to the Meerut Conference was Pir Ghulam Mujadid Sarhandi.

15. THE NANKANA AFFAIR AND ITS INFLUENCE IN SIND

The Congress Committee, Karachi, have taken up the case of the Singh Sabha or Sikh reformers as presented (in Sind) by Jagatsingh Pardeshi, Akali of Peshawar, as a convenient weapon for calumniating Government. The Sikhs in the Railway Workshops, Karachi, asked for leave on the 5th April to enable them to mourn for the Nankana martyrs. The workmen of all classes, Hindus, Mahomedans and Christians, came out in sympathy on the 5th. They continued to absent themselves on the 6th, only about 400 men remaining at work out of 2500. Non-co-operator speakers take the line that the assistance of the Sikhs is indispensable if Swaraj is to be obtained and that they should therefore support the Sikhs in their present movement against Government. The Singh Sabha, Karachi, has ordered kirpans from the Punjab.

(A separate note on Sikh agitation in Karachi will be prepared.)[11]

Weekly Bulletin on the Non-co-operation Movement for the week ending 16th April 1921

GENERAL

I. The following is an interesting view of the present situation in Sind:

> 'Recent events have proved that the Non-co-operators in Sind have little influence. This is only what could be expected when the personality of the leaders who have been attracted by this grotesque movement is considered. There is not a single leader of any weight, position or force of character. The Mahomedans who comprise practically the whole of the zamindari and cultivating classes are practically speaking unaffected by it. The wealthy traders are, except in a few cases, absorbed too much in their business to take to it. They only wish to be left in peace and make money. There are perhaps twenty serious non-co-operators in the whole province, who make a great deal of noise and are followed by a crowd of unintelligent schoolboys and others. At

[11] Copies forwarded to the Director, Intelligence Bureau, Home Department (Government of India), Simla; the D.I.G. of Police, C.I.D., Poona.

Hyderabad, which is the chief centre of the province outside Karachi only 750 persons out of a population of 75,000 had paid four annas to join the District Congress Committee up to the end of March. (These are the figures given by Jairamdas Daulatram, Gandhi's lieutenant in Sind, in his paper *Bande Mataram*). These figures prove that apart from the noise and the violent speeches the movement is hardly worth serious consideration. The recent hartals demonstrated that the majority of the people is far from being prepared to follow the movement. They may shut their shops in response to intimidation or appeals to religious sentiment, but very few would do so if left to themselves.

On the other hand there is a widespread almost universal feeling among all thinking classes in favour of a more or less vague desire to improve the status of Indians and to secure greater control over the administration. Gandhi's movement has not captured these classes. His followers, an almost microscopic minority of the population, for the most part secretly believe in violence and revolutionary methods.'

II. The following extracts from the *Vande Mataram* edited by Jairamdas Daulatram of Hyderabad, throw interesting sidelights on local developments in Sukkur and Karachi:

(a) 'The Right Spirit'

But we may also frankly state that the Public of Sukkur do not appear to have taken the incident in the right spirit. During one of the speeches on the subject at the Sukkur meeting, there were cries of 'Shame' and at the pressing suggestion of the audience, a resolution of condemnation of the officials concerned was passed. Cries of 'Shame' and 'Condemnation' are wholly foreign to the character of the movement we are carrying on. Moreover such impotent expressions of anger do not lead us an inch nearer to the goal. If instead of indulging in such cries and resolutions, even one single boy had announced his non-co-operation with an aided institution, the cause we have all at heart would have been better served. The people of Sukkur have responded splendidly to the call of the motherland. There is hardly another town in the province which had done so well. But it is also true that the emotionalism of Sukkur needs wise guidance along proper channels. The local leaders are trusty men and we have no doubt that Sukkur will beat all its former records of national service.

(b) 'The Fatal Personal Element'

But some non-co-operators at Karachi are not doing the thing in the right spirit. Feeling there runs high between two sections of Non-co-operators who do not otherwise differ in principle. The personal element had unfortunately entered in Karachi politics so largely that organised work has to face tremendous difficulties there. Many are doing their work in their individual responsibility. Independent groups with no organic cohesion are carrying on propaganda and collecting funds. We have nothing but words of praise for all who are doing good work, but such disorganisation spells the ruin of the movement. We have no intention to repeat the recriminations and allegations mutually made in the public press by persons belonging to opposite sections, and give further publicity to statements flung at each other in no good spirit of mutual correction. We have, however, every confidence that Non-co-operators in responsible positions, stated to have appeared as litigants in a court of law, after the Non-co-operation resolution had been passed by the Calcutta Congress, will be able to give a flat contradiction to the statement and thus remove the current impression. We cannot but repeat our request to both parties to refrain from mutual recrimination, which only increases the acrimony already existing between public workers of Karachi.

1. AGITATION

The hartal of the 13th April was more widely observed than that of the 6th. In some of the smaller towns this result was directly due to the visits of leading agitators after the failure of spontaneous hartal on the 6th, e.g. Swami Govindanand visited Tatta and Pir Ghulam Mujadid visited Matiari. In the latter case a strong appeal was made about mid-day to nationalist and religious sentiment to 'confirm [!] to what was being done in the whole of India'. It succeeded in spite of the advice of the other local leaders to the contrary. Shops began to open again during the afternoon. In Karachi a greater number of shops were open than on the 6th and many of those which were shut carried on as usual by the back door. Business was otherwise almost normal. Public conveyances and carts plied very much as usual. A day of hartal was also organised in Karachi on the 14th April by certain Sikhs under the leadership of Jagatsingh Pardeshi, Akali, and a few hot-heads like Fazal Karim and Swami Krishnanand. This was done against the advice of Lalchand Jagtiani who as Secretary of the Karachi District Congress Committee declined to take any responsibility for it. Bands of persons including Sikhs, of whom a few displayed Kirpans, went round the streets and frightened people into putting up their shutters. As on the previous day, a certain number continued to sell their goods quietly. The arrest of Fazal Karim and another agitator and rumours of the arrest of several Sikhs led to the collection of crowds, who threw stones at the Police, outside the City Police Station.

2. ORGANISATION

The Non-co-operators succeeded in securing only 9 seats on the Karachi Municipality out of 45. They were much chagrined at this demonstration of the smallness of their influence.

3. FUNDS

No organised effort was made to collect funds for the National Week in Karachi. The Karachi District Congress Committee is considering means of stopping misappropriation by their collectors and there is considerable ill feeling among them in this connection.

The Hyderabad District Congress expects to collect more than its quota, but the results are not yet known.

4. SCHOOLS AND COLLEGES

A National School was opened at Hyderabad on the 11th April 1921. There are between 130 and 150 students and the District Congress Committee leaders have given out that they have sufficient funds to keep it going for a year. They have given up the idea of taking up the Besantine National College for the present.

5. INDIAN NATIONAL SERVICE AND VOLUNTEERS

So far the District Congress Committee have failed to evolve a regular volunteer corps. In Karachi mushroom organisations spring up from time to time, only to give way to another with another name a few days later.

6. LAWYERS AND COURTS
7. AGRARIAN
8. LABOUR INCLUDING RAILWAYS
9. STRIKES

} No developments.

10. BOYCOTT OF BRITISH FOREIGN TRADE AND TRADING CONCERNS

11. CANCELLATION OF EXISTING AND FUTURE CONTRACTS

Traders are not setting in accordance with the decision of the Congress Committee. The market had improved; English and American Banks and firms are making some concessions and Indian traders are in many cases taking delivery. The general opinion is that the position is gradually approaching the normal.

12. INSTANCES OF INCITEMENT TO BOYCOTT OR OF BOYCOTT OF EUROPEANS BY THEIR DOMESTIC SERVANTS — No developments.
13. GOVERNMENT SERVICE — do.
14. HOW FAR MUSSALMANS AS A SEPARATE CLASS ARE ADOPTING THE NON-CO-OPERATION MOVEMENT — do.
15. THE NANKANA AFFAIR AND ITS INFLUENCE IN SIND — do.

Weekly Bulletin on the Non-co-operation Movement for the week ending 23rd April 1921

GENERAL

Preparations are being made for Gandhi's visit next week. The members of the Congress Committee in several cases have evinced great anxiety for him to visit their towns. He is actually visiting Hyderabad, Karachi, Sukkur, Shikarpur and Larkana.

A riot occurred in Shikarpur on the night of the 20th April 1921, the opposing factions being the non-co-operators and the Pritam Dharma Sabha. The police investigation is not yet complete.

1. AGITATION

There has been a lull during the week. Swami Govindanand is awaiting trial under Section 124-A of Indian Penal Code to the great satisfaction of Professor Vaswani and others in the non-co-operation ranks who are presumably hostile to him. Three of the more irresponsible street agitators in Karachi have been convicted of rioting on the occasion of the liquor auctions in Karachi. The City Magistrate, Karachi, sentenced them to 18 months' rigorous imprisonment each.

2. ORGANISATION

The number of members in the Hyderabad District Congress Committee was mentioned as 750 in last week's report. It is now between 1000 and 1100. There are about 900 members in the affiliated Taluka Committees in that District. The Karachi District Congress Committee's registers are so carelessly kept that it is not known how many persons have joined. The number is probably about 300.

3. FUNDS

The Hyderabad Tilak Swaraj Fund receives money from Sind Workis [Workers?] abroad. On the 22nd April Nainaram Sharma received a registered letter, signed 'A servant of Bharat', written on the printed form of the firm of D. Chellaram of Casablanca (Morocco). The writer informed him that he had sent a money order for £ 7/8 i.e. about Rs. 120/- for the Tilak Swaraj Fund. A few days ago Rs. 1219/- was received by a Hundi on a firm in Hyderabad, and a few days before that Rs. 1500/- was received was draft from Samarang (Java). It is curious that in many cases the donations received from abroad are sent anonymously.

To a C.I.D. officer, Vaishnu Nainaram Sharma boasted that these donations were due to the good effect produced by the *Hindu* newspaper on Sind Workers abroad. He said that about 100 Sind Workers abroad are subscribing to his paper.

It is believed that about Rs. 25,000/- have been collected for the Tilak Swaraj Fund, Hyderabad.

4. SCHOOLS AND COLLEGES

No developments.

5. INDIAN NATIONAL SERVICE AND VOLUNTEERS

No appreciable enlistment of volunteers is taking place. It is said that 50 more names have been entered in the[12]

Weekly Bulletin on the Non-co-operation Movement for the Week ending 30th April 1921

GENERAL

Gandhi visited the following places in Sind:- Hyderabad on the 24th and 25th April, Karachi 26th, Larkana 27th, Shikarpur and Jacobabad 28th, Sukkur and Rohri 20th, Hyderabad, Kotri and Mirpurkhas on the 30th.

His visit has been fully reported in the Press and also in the weekly diaries of the Superintendents of Police. The outstanding

[12] Rest of the page missing.

features of this visit are: (1) that it was served to bring into prominence the weakness of the hold of the Non-co-operation movement over the people of Sind as a whole and the dissensions and jealousies among the local leaders, and (2) that he harped 'ad nauseam' on the need of using the spinning wheel. Gandhi has himself criticised the Sindhis for having failed to recognise any one leader, for their local jealousies, for being afraid to go to jail for the cause, and for being 'westernised'. He praised them in some cases for their generosity but in others apparently received much less than he expected. The non-co-operators proclaimed his tour through Sind as a triumphal progress. In fact it was popularly regarded as a 'tamasha', in which after once seeing him people rapidly lost interest. He was met by large crowds everywhere, but in Shikarpur and Sukkur a large proportion of the audience at the meetings made so much noise that he could not be heard, and on his second visit to Hyderabad little or no interest was taken in him, only 600 or 700 people attending the District Conference at which he presided. A fee was charged for admission and few thought it worth while to pay the small sum demanded. After he had addressed the Conference Gandhi said that it should be open to the public without charge and 200 or 300 more people then came in.

The Congress Committee of several places pressed him very hard to visit their towns.

Gandhi's own view of the means by which his movement is eventually to be successful is apparently contained in the following extract by him entitled 'The Mists', published in his paper *Young India*, dated the 20th April 1921:

'I should not be surprised if the history of the South African movement repeats itself in India. I should be surprised if it proves otherwise. The movement in South Africa started with an unanimous resolution. When the first part began, the majority weakened. Only 850 were found willing to court imprisonment. Then there was a settlement and a breach and a revival. Nobody even believed, save a few of us, that the response would come in time. Well, the last stage commenced with sixteen men and women who sought imprisonment. This was followed by a perfect storm. The whole community rose like a surging wave. Without organisation, without propaganda, all-nearly 40,000 courted imprisonment. Nearly ten thousand were actually imprisoned. The sequel is known. The community gained all it had fought for at the time. A bloodless revolution was effected after strenuous discipline in self-suffering.

I refuse to believe that India will do less. To recall Lord Canning's words, under the blue and serene Indian sky, a cloud no bigger than a man's thumb may appear on the horizon, but it may assume dimensions unexpected by any, and no man can tell when it may burst. When India as a whole will respond by action, I cannot say. But this I do say that the educated classes to whom the Congress had appealed will one day - and probably during this year - respond in a manner worthy of the nation.'

In the same paper he explains his attitude to the present movement and the anarchy which is the only possible result of its being pressed to a logical conclusion in the following words:

'As for my own attitude, whilst my faith would not permit me to invite or encourage a war of violence, I do contemplate with equanimity a state of war in preference to the present state of effeminate peace imposed by force of arms. And it is for that reason that I am taking part in this movement of non-violent non-co-operation even at the risk of anarchy being the ultimate result.'

Gandhi's conversation, his writing and his recent activities suggest that there is considerable evidence in support of the view that he is a medical case of a peculiar psychological nature.

Mahomed Ali's speech on the Afghan question had caused some alarm among Hindus in Sind. Jethmal Parsaram, editor of the *Bharatvasi* and a follower of Mrs. Besant, has been attacking Gandhi and the non-co-operation movement with renewed vigour since his recent interview with Gandhi. He also attacks the administration in connection with the case against Swami Govindanand (alias J.T. Mansukhani) under section 124-A, Indian Penal Code.

The effect of this prosecution is different in various camps. The extremists feel that it is a serious blow and that it will have a deterrent effect, but they proclaim their belief in the psychological law relating to the stimulative effect of persecution of a new faith. Moderate and loyalist opinion generally regards it with satisfaction as likely to have a deterrent effect on an agitation which had developed into a public nuisance. Other moderates regard it as a mistake on Government's part to indulge in repression as they believe the non-co-operation movement if left alone would kill itself. Among men of this view the opinion is expressed that the three non-co-operators who were convicted of rioting in the Huzur Deputy Collector's Office, Karachi, were punished too severely when they were sentenced to 18 months' rigorous imprisonment, and that the ordinary punishment for such an offence should have been inflicted in their case.

Since the conviction of these four men in Karachi, other previously almost unknown agitators have started to come forward to take their place. It is also suggested that this fact is in accordance with the laws relating to persecution mentioned above.

1. AGITATION

Street agitation had continued with rather less vigour, all interest centring round Gandhi's visit.

2. ORGANISATION

No developments.

3. FUNDS

Considerable funds are at the disposal of the Congress and Khilafat Committees both of which are giving regular salaries to a number of agitators. Allegations of misappropriation are common against certain of the more irresponsible of them and the public is inclined to be chary of giving contributions to many of them.

4. SCHOOLS AND COLLEGES

No developments.

5. INDIAN NATIONAL SERVICE AND VOLUNTEERS

Only 36 students remain on the list of active members of the Sind Students' branch of the Indian National Service. The enthusiasm of the rest has not proved great enough to carry them on.

6. LAWYERS AND COURTS
7. AGRARIAN
8. LABOUR INCLUDING RAILWAYS } No developments.

9. STRIKES

There have been small strikes among the employees of two European firms in Karachi involving about 40 men in each case which were non-political. The cause in one was that an European was alleged to have kicked an employee.

10. BOYCOTT OF BRITISH OR FOREIGN TRADE AND TRADING CONCERNS — No developments.
11. CANCELLATION OF EXISTING AND FUTURE CONTRACTS — do.
12. INSTANCES OF INCITEMENT TO BOYCOTT OR OF BOYCOTT OF EUROPEANS BY THEIR DOMESTIC SERVANTS — do.
13. GOVERNMENT SERVICE — do.
14. HOW FAR MUSSALMANS AS A SEPARATE CLASS ARE ADOPTING THE NON-CO-OPERATION MOVEMENT

There are several indications that measures to excite the Sindhi Mahommedan population are contemplated. Information has been received from a very reliable source that Pir Mahbubshah of Hyderabad, Sind, hopes to secure this object by a plan, of which the details are not known, to win over the Pirs of Sind to the Khilafat cause. Information from another source indicates that he and Pir Ghulam Mujadid Sarhandi, are collecting numbers of Maulvis talking to them quietly and urging them to preach non-co-operation and Khilafat to the rural population. From a third source comes a report that, Taj Mahomed of Amrote is working on similar lines and that he is in touch with certain Mullahs who have recently delivered inflammatory speeches in the Upper Sind Frontier District. There is evidence that the Khilafat Committee, Karachi has asked the Central Khilafat Committee for 12 propagandists preferably Sindhis. Abdul Ghani, formerly of the Larkana Madressa [!], now of the Central Khilafat Committee, Bombay, has visited Sind apparently to over-haul the working of the local Khilafat Committee.

Abdul Ghani was formerly friendly with the Deputy Superintendent of Police, Sind C.I.D. In the course of a long conversation with him last week he made remarks to the following effect which are recorded for what they are worth:

Shaukat Ali has acquired a great personal ascendancy over Gandhi and can twist him to his own purposes at will. Gandhi has convinced the two brothers that India's salvation can only be attained through non-violent non-co-operation and they fully agree with him. Nevertheless Shaukat Ali always refers to Gandhi as a Kafir.

Gandhi was strongly supported by the Central Khilafat Committee and in fact owed his position largely to them, for instance but for their support at the Nagpur Congress Session he might have been thrown over, especially in view of the opposition from the Bengal camp. The present Congress creed was inspired by the Central Khilafat Committee.

An effort was being made to relieve Mahomed Ali of the work for the National University so as to free him for a more active part in the campaign.

When he left Bombay there was a balance of Rs. 2,40,000 in the Khilafat funds and over a lac in the Smyrna Relief Fund.

Weekly Bulletin on the Non-co-operation Movement for the week ending 7th May 1921

GENERAL

There are indications that the non-co-operation movement is losing momentum in Sind. Gandhi's reference to local jealousies have accentuated rather than diminished them. It is doubtful whether the heads of National Schools in Karachi or elsewhere will consent to their being placed under the control of the District Congress Committees.

From information received it appears that currency is being given to the view that 'Swaraj within one year' means not the overthrow of the British Government, but the establishment of a separate national administration co-existing with the present one.

1. AGITATION

As a natural consequence of the loss of momentum mentioned above, certain speakers are becoming more violent in tone and more excited in their attitude, particularly Swami Krishnanand, Pir Ghulam Mujadid Sarhandi, Sheikh Abdul Aziz, and some of the minor orators. Mahomed Khan Ghassi Khan, Secretary of the Karachi Khilafat Committee, in a speech during the week expressed his belief in the ability of Indians to free themselves by force. In private conversation he repeats this opinion and emphasises his view that it is desirable to instil such a feeling of power into the Indian people.

He thus begins to depart from the attitude entailed by adherence to the non-violent programme and approaches that which recognises the use of criminal force.

2. ORGANISATION
3. FUNDS
4. SCHOOLS AND COLLEGES

} No developments.

5. INDIAN NATIONAL SERVICE AND VOLUNTEERS

A Punjabi Sewa Samiti has been started in Karachi. Extremists and non-co-operating agitators have taken part in establishing it, but have encountered difficulties owing to Punjabi Railway employees declaring that they would have nothing to do with it unless it were on purely social and non-political lines

6. LAWYERS AND COURTS — No developments.
7. AGRARIAN — do.
8. LABOUR INCLUDING RAILWAYS — do.
9. STRIKES — do.
10. BOYCOTT OR BRITISH OR FOREIGN TRADE AND TRADING CONCERNS — do.
11. CANCELLATION OF EXISTING AND FUTURE CONTRACTS — do.
12. INSTANCES OF INCITEMENT OF BOYCOTT OR OF BOYCOTT OF EUROPEANS BY THEIR DOMESTIC SERVANTS — do.
13. GOVERNMENT SERVICE — No developments.
14. HOW FAR MUSSALMANS AS A SEPARATE CLASS ARE ADOPTING THE NON-CO-OPERATION MOVEMENT

Pir Mahbub Shah's (vide last week's bulletin) plan has been partially disclosed as a result of a meeting of the Rashidi Pirs of Sind at Bangi Kelhoro, a small village near Larkana, on the 3rd May 1921. In rough outline it appears to consist of first bringing about a reconciliation among the various Rashidi Pirs, and after preliminary moves this meeting was arranged for this purpose. The following Pirs were present besides Pir Mahbubshah and his hosts Pir Shamanshah and Ghulam Mustafa Shah of Bangi Kelhoro:

(i) Pir Rashidullah Shah, son of Pir Rashiduddin Shah alias Pir Jhandewalla
(ii) Pir Turabalishah, son of Abdullashah

(iii) Pir Abdul Ghafar Shah of Relan
(iv) Pir Nurdin Shah of Relan
(v) Pir Nasirullah of a village near Kambar
(vi) Pir Imamdinshah of Thulla
(vii) Pir Hashimshah of Thulla
(viii) Pir Mithanshah, son of Mazhardin Shah of Thulla
(ix) Pir Ibrahimshah of Thulla
(x) Pir Mahomed Munirshah of village Bukhshanshah, near Naudero
(xi) Pir Baker Shah of Bukhshanshah, near Naudero

and others.

The next step was to have been for the re-united family to approach the Pir Pagaro of Kingri and through their combined influence to win over all the religious leaders in the country. In order to secure the support of their murids more easily it was proposed to abandon the practice of living on 'Piri muridi' and to organise measures for Pirs to give religious instructions to their 'murids'. The result of the meeting is not known, but it appears to have had little success as the Jhandewaro Pir and some others did not appear at a public Khilafat Conference organised on the 6th May at Dokri by the Pirs of Thulla Shariff. Only about 100 persons, mostly local rustics, were present at the Conference apart from the leaders who included Pandit Amersen of Karachi, Dwarkaprasad of Dadu and Misir Bulchand of Badah.

Pir Mithanshah is reported to have stated in private conversation that the Khilafat movement no longer appealed to the popular mind as a result of the failure of the Hijrat movement, and that people to whom he preached 'Khilafat' replied that if the leaders really believed Islam to be threatened as they stated, it was their duty to proclaim 'jehad' when the people would sacrifice all and fight to the death, but that if there was no case for 'jehad' there was no reason for them to sacrifice their interests in pursuance of non-violent non-co-operation, in which they could see no sense.

15. THE NANKANA AFFAIR AND ITS INFLUENCE IN SIND

Jagatsingh Akali is losing influence among Sikhs in Karachi. He is regarded by many as a mischief maker and impostor.

Weekly Bulletin on the Non-co-operation Movement for the week ending 14th May 1921

GENERAL

Members of Congress Committees have been giving out that in accordance with Gandhi's wishes they are devoting themselves to constructive work and in this way they account for the present lull.

Coincident with the lull in the Non-co-operation movement proper increases activity is noticeable among Khilafat workers. The Khilafat workers largely consists [!] of those who were prominent in the Pan-Islamic or Wahabi movement which came to notice in Sind during the enquiries into the Silk Letter Case.

There have been persistent rumours that Political prisoners will be released.

Gandhi has written an article in the *Bande Mataram* on Swami Govindanand; the following is the first paragraph:

'So, Swami Govindanand had got five years' transportation. He has a tough back. He had undergone previous incarcerations without trial. He had put on record his experiences of the tortures he had to put up with in the various goals in which he was placed. He has how gone through the farce of a trial and has been duly convicted. Does the transportation on that account carry any weight, or does it not rather show the hypocrisy of the whole transaction? The form is changed, the spirit remains the same.'

He concluded by the remark 'We must seek imprisonment for doing solid work.'

1. AGITATION

Speeches by minor orators and persons of no standing continue to become more and more irresponsible. The Congress workers have also taken up the plan of creating agitation against Officials particularly the Police by taking up cases of Begar, etc. The Congress office at Hyderabad had given instructions that reports of such instances should be made to them when action will be taken. Instructions have also been given to public speakers to make this known at their meetings. Such cases have been reported from the Nawabshah and Thar Parker districts.

In Karachi advantage is being taken of the shortage of water to deliver speeches attacking the Municipality, Railway, Port Trust,

Military Department and residents of Cantonment and Civil Lines to audiences of labourers. It is implied that the Europeans and the richer classes get more than their share of water.

2. ORGANISATION

Reliable figures concerning the number of persons who have joined the Congress Committee in Sind are not yet available.

The Karachi Congress Committee has divided the City of Karachi into wards for the purpose of collections for the Tilak Swaraj Fund.

3. FUNDS

Reliable figures are not yet available. It has been announced in the Press that Seth Jahi Abdullah Haroon of Karachi had given Rs. 15000/towards the Smyrna Relief Fund.

4. SCHOOLS AND COLLEGES — No developments.
5. INDIAN NATIONAL SERVICE AND VOLUNTEERS — do.
6. LAWYERS AND COURTS — do.
7. AGRARIAN — do.
8. LABOUR INCLUDING RAILWAYS — do.
9. STRIKES — do.
10. BOYCOTT OF BRITISH AND FOREIGN TRADE AND TRADING CONCERNS — do.
11. CANCELLATION OF EXISTING AND FUTURE CONTRACTS — do.
12. INSTANCES OF INCITEMENT TO BOYCOTT OR OF BOYCOTT OF EUROPEANS BY THEIR DOMESTIC SERVANTS — do.
13. GOVERNMENT SERVICE — do.
14. HOW FAR MUHAMMADANS AS A SEPARATE CLASS ARE ADOPTING THE NON-CO-OPERATION MOVEMENT

While the Muhammadans of Sind as a whole continue to hold aloof from the Non-co-operation movement increased activity is noticeable in so called Pan-Islamic circles, where the Khilafat movement has been taken up. It is proposed by the Provincial Khilafat Committee to hold an All-India Khilafat Conference at Karachi probably in July. The exact date is to be fixed by Shaukat Ali and Muhammad Ali.

Abdul Ghani (vide Bulletin for the week ending the 30th April) remained in Sind for about one month. He accompanied Gandhi during a part of his tour visiting Larkana and Sukkur. His visit appears to be connected with the increased activity noticed in the Khilafat Camp especially as regards the collection of money for the Smyrna Relief Fund. He constantly met Muhammad Khan, Secretary of the Provincial Khilafat Committee, Shams ud Din s/o Kazi Odedullah, Sh. Abdul Aziz, Pandit Amersen, and Dr. Haji s/o Ghulam Hussain Kassam. During his stay in Karachi he also visited Muhammad Sadik of the Khada and discussed the question of increasing the number of volunteers as a result of which a few more volunteers appear to have been enlisted in the Khada.

The following telegram has come to notice:

> 'From Asfahani c/o Haji Abdulla Haroon, Karachi.
> To Maulana Abul Kalam, 45 Ripon Lane, Calcutta.
> Success achieved here to certain extent money will reach you directly from donors for translation of Koran wire rupees one hundred eleven for journey expenses care Haji Abdullah Haroon returning impossible unless amount received.'

15. The Nankana Affair and its Influence in Sind

Jagatsingh Akali continues to cause dissensions among Sikhs in Karachi.[13]

Weekly Bulletin on the Non-co-operation Movement for the week ending 21 May 1921

General

An outstanding feature of the week is the growth of the feeling against Non-co-operation. This feeling is becoming vocal in the Hyderabad, Sukkur and Larkana Districts. An influential portion of the Press is writing against the movement, while only three papers of importance, the *New Times* (English, Karachi), *Hindu* (Sindhi, Hyderabad), and *Sindhi* (Sindhi, Sukkur) are to be considered organs of the Non-co-operation party. The first is run by Jeswani and

[13] Copies forwarded as footnote 11.

Vaswani, the second by Vishnu Nainaram Sharma, the third by Virumal Begraj.

Renewed efforts to stir up Mahommedan feeling in the Province continue to be made.

There are indications that men like Mahomed Khan Ghassi Khan contemplate the introduction of violence in the near future, when they expect the non-violent movement to collapse.

1. AGITATION

The volume of irresponsible and inflammatory speeches is increasing, particularly in Karachi, Thar Parkar and the Upper Sind Frontier. It is considerable elsewhere, Nawabshah being noticeable. Many of the speakers are persons of low origin, carpenters, bidi-sellers, actors, street-loafers and convicted gambling house keepers being among them. Their oratory is in most cases extremely crude.

2. ORGANISATION

Organisation continues to be very rough and ready. The number who have joined the various District Congress Committees is not large, the registers are carelessly kept and apparently include many who give their names to avoid being pestered or because they see others doing so, but have no genuine desire to take part in organising an electorate for the Congress. Announcements have appeared in the Press concerning the elections for the Provincial Committee and some of the District Committees appear to be taking up this question. Jairamdas Daulatram and R.K. Sidhva have resigned the Secretary-ship of the Sind Provincial Congress Committee. The former wishes 'to work among the masses'.

3. FUNDS

Figures are not yet available.

4. SCHOOLS AND COLLEGES

Some of the National Schools are collapsing.

5. INDIAN NATIONAL SERVICE AND VOLUNTEERS

No developments.

6. LAWYERS AND COURTS

An arbitration Court has been established at Sukkur. Mulchand Pessumal, with whom Gandhi stayed, is reported to be drawing Rs. 300/- per mensem, as president of the Court. Gandhi influenced him to resign his practice.

7. AGRARIAN	No developments.
8. LABOUR INCLUDING RAILWAYS	do.
9. STRIKES	do.
10. BOYCOTT OF BRITISH OR FOREIGN TRADE AND TRADING COMPANIES	No developments.
11. CANCELLATION OF EXISTING AND FUTURE CONTRACTS	do.
12. INSTANCES OF INCITEMENT TO BOYCOTT OR BOYCOTT OF EUROPEANS BY THEIR DOMESTIC SERVANTS	do.
13. GOVERNMENT SERVICE	do.

14. HOW FAR MUSSALMANS AS A SEPARATE CLASS ARE ADOPTING THE NON-CO-OPERATION MOVEMENT

Sheikh Abdul Majid as Secretary of the Hyderabad Khilafat Committee has published a letter in the *Hindu* of the 21st May 1921 urging the Mahomedans to join the Non-co-operation movement especially as regards Swadeshi and Boycott.

He makes a special appeal to religious sentiment in connection with Ramzan and Ramzan Id, for which he is endeavouring to persuade Mahomed Ali or Shaukat Ali to visit Hyderabad in order to lead the Id prayers.

Mahomedalishah formerly of the Pithore Madressah and now on the staff of the National College Aligarh arrived in Hyderabad on the 21st May 1921. He has come to Sind for propaganda purposes and to secure 30 or 40 more students for the National College. Seven students from the National College arrived in Sind. They were invited to see Haji Abdulla Haroon where the outlines of work and their distribution in the Province were settled in consultation with the Secretary, Mahomed Khan Ghassi Khan.

In connection with the meeting of Rashidi Pirs reported in this office bulletin for the week ending 7th May 1921 no substantial result has yet been secured, Sayad Pir Shah of Bahman who is in the confidence of the Pir of Kingri was invited to the meeting, but did not attend. He scornfully asked Pir Turabalishah what his objects were and why, if they were not directed against the British Government, but aimed solely at improving the position of the Rashidi families, the head of the Rashidi family, Pir Pagaro of Kingri, had not been consulted and the meeting had not been arranged under his directions.

Considerable resentment was caused among Pirs and Sayads by the fact that during Gandhi's visit he sat above them on a raised dais at Larkana and other places. Those who are opposed to the Non-co-operation movement are using this as an argument.

15. THE NANKANA AFFAIR AND ITS INFLUENCE IN SIND

No developments.[14]

Weekly Bulletin on the Non-co-operation Movement for the Week Ending 11th June 1921

No bulletins were issued for the weeks ending the 28th May and 4th June 1921.

Features of this period were the growth of the anti-non-co-operation movement with the heckling of Non-co-operators at their meetings in the Sukkur District (Taj Mahomed of Amrote for instance was told by the audiences at Ubauro that he was Khar-i-Dajjal); and the prominence given to cow-killing question owing to Professor Vaswani's action at Shikarpur which has brought down upon him a reproof from Gandhi. The Non-co-operators have in several cases publicly castigated them-selves for their slow progress and for the personal jealousies which they apparently consider to be responsible for this. Cuttings from the *New Times* in this connection are appended.

1. AGITATION

Irresponsible speeches continue. The tendency to work up agitation in connection with the Khilafat is noticeable.

2. ORGANISATION

Various Congress Committees have published the numbers of members which they claim to have enrolled.

For instance Karachi claims 2,500, and Hyderabad something like 3,000, but it is not clear whether these figures include Taluka Committees, and members of the Committees have recently mentioned smaller numbers in their speeches. The reports of Superintendents of Police show that accurate figures are not available.

[14] Pages 63 and 64 of the original are missing.

It is certain, however, that the figures furnish an entirely false index to the progress of the movement because many of the persons whose names are put on the roll are certainly unaware of any special meaning being attached to the fact. They have simply paid annas -/4/- and as far as they are concerned this is the end of the matter.

All the District Congress Committees have arranged to elect members of the Provincial Congress Committee by returning the requisite number of the candidates all being un-opposed. That is to say the matter had been compromised in every case so as to avoid the necessity of an election. The New Provincial Congress Committee is to meet in Karachi on the 27th June.

3. FUNDS

On the 29th of May Jairamdas Daulatram wired to Gandhi at Bombay to say that Rs. 108,000 had been collected in all Sind and that Rs. 50,000 more might be collected. Apparently these figures include the amount handed over to Gandhi on the occasion of his recent visit to Sind. The following figures for the Tilak Swaraj Fund were published in the *Sind Observer* of the 2nd June as having been sent by them by a correspondent:

Karachi	Rs. 30,000
Shikarpur	Rs. 17,245
Hyderabad	Rs. 7,433
Sukkur	Rs. 3,600
Larkana	Rs. 1,587
Jacobabad	Rs. 1,001
Rohri	Rs. 1,002
Small Sums about	Rs. 2,407
Total	Rs. 64,275

4. SCHOOLS AND COLLEGES

Most of the National Schools are now in a bad way and few are likely to survive much longer.

5. INDIAN NATIONAL SERVICE AND VOLUNTEERS

No developments.

6. LAWYERS AND COURTS

The Arbitration Court at Sukkur under the presidentship of Mulchand Pessumal continues to decide cases.[15]

[15] Pages 67 to 79 of the original are missing.

Weekly Bulletin on the Non-co-operation Movement for the week ending 18th June 1921

GENERAL

The star of the Non-co-operation movement in Sind may be said to be paling before the Khilafat movement in conjunction with the excitement over the Angora affair; and to be suffering eclipse to some extent owing to the rise of the anti non-co-operation movement. The latter is most significantly represented by the Sind Swaraj Society which is being formed at Hyderabad under the leadership of the Hon. Mr. Ghulam Mahomed Bhurgir, Member of the Council of State and Mr. Santdas Mangharam, pleader. The importance of the Khilafat movement is to a very great extent the reflex action of influence outside Sind, particularly the attitude of Abul Kalam Azad and Maulana Abdul Bari. Attention is concentrating on the All India Khilafat Conference which has been arranged for the first week in July at Karachi.

The picketing of liquor shops in most of the towns in Sind is a phase of the movement which has recently been brought into prominence.

1. AGITATION

Violent speeches have been delivered in connection with the Khilafat movement.

2. ORGANISATION

The following Press cuttings describe the state of organisation of the Sind Provincial Congress Committee:

Extract from *Sindvasi* dated the 17th June 1921.

'The report is out for 21st November, to 31st May 1921. There are 113 members. Four meetings of the general Committee and three of the Council were held. Two days were spent for framing rules. The question of the Non-co-operation movement could not be discussed. The rules were framed after the Nagpur Congress. A resolution was passed as under for the Tilak Swaraj Fund. 10% go to the Sind Provincial Committee and 25% to the All India Congress Committee. Rupees five hundred were granted to the Sukkur Congress Committee and rupees two hundred and fifty to the Nawabshah District Congress Committee to strengthen the propaganda of Non-co-operation. Some of the balance from the Sukkur Congress Fund has been given to the Sind Provincial Congress Committee.[']

Extract from the *New Times* dated the 17th June 1921.

'Sind Provincial Congress Committee'
The first meeting of the new Sind Provincial Congress Committee elected under the new constitution is to be held on the 27th instant. As mentioned in the agenda of the meeting, published elsewhere, there will be elections of the President, Vice-presidents and Secretaries for the Committee. Also nine representatives of Sind will be elected to the All India Congress Committee. It will be good if members from different parts of Sind attend this first meeting of the new Committee. In case they are unable to attend they can send votes for particular persons for particular offices by post if they so desire. The procedure this time has been a little irregular inasmuch as no regular names have been proposed and seconded before votes are invited. But we have to hurry things. But for the slackness of the Karachi Committees we could have met much earlier. We have to finish the requirements of the Bezwada programme and each one of us must do his "bit". Let the motto of each one of us till the 30th of June be: "Go ahead".'

Extract from *New Times* dated the 17th June 1921.

'Sind Provincial Congress Committee'
Meeting on 27th June
The following letter has been addressed by Mr. Durgdas to the members of Sind Provincial Congress Committee:-
Sir, Since sending the notice of meeting, I received communications form Sukkur and Larkana to the effect that the 20 will not suit Upper Sind members as they would like to attend the Khilafat Conference as well. They therefore desire a later date to be fixed. Consequently, I have altered the date and have fixed Monday the 27tn instant for the meeting.
I am sending you a copy of the rules from which you will see that you have to vote for the following:-

One President
Vice-Presidents
Two Joint Secretaries
One Treasurer
} These will be members of Council by virtue of their office.

15 Council members besides the office bearers.
9 Representatives of the Provincial Congress Committee on the All India Congress Committee
1 Auditor

If you are not able to attend the meeting you can send your vote in writing, by enclosing it in an envelope with the heading 'voting paper' on it. The envelopes will be opened and the votes counted at the meeting of the 27th.

Yours faithfully.
Durgdas B. Advani
President Sind Provincial Congress Committee

MEMBERS OF THE COMMITTEE

Karachi: Mr. Durgdas B. Advani, Seth Sunderdas Valabdas, Mr. R.K. Sidhva, Mr. Tikamdas Wadhumal, Mr. T.K. Jaswani, Mr. Lalchand A. Jagtiani, Mr. K.H. Masand, Swami Krishnanand, Seth Naraindas Anandji, Kazi Allahbachaye Kotri, and Seth Narimal-Tatta

Hyderabad: Mr. Jairamdas Daulatram; Dr. Choithram Partabrai, Mr. Abdul Majid, Mr. Abdul Jabbar, Pir Ghulam Mujadid of Matiari, Bhai Hotsing Golasing, Mahraj Vishnu Nainaram Sharma, Mahraj Hoondraj Pursuram, Mr. Kishinsing Jotsing, Bhai Khubchand Bulchand, Mr. Jhamatmal Lakhasing, and Mr. Ghanshyam Jethanand.

Larkana: Pir Turabalishah, Mr. Rijhumal, Pir Ali Anwarshah, Pir Nurdinshah, Pundit Dwarkaparshad, Mr. Ramchand, Mr. Partabrai, Mr. Tahilram, Mr. Topandas, Mr. Nanikram, Mr. Ali Ahmad, Seth Naraindas, and Mr. Pribhdas.

Sukkur: Mr. Virumal Begraj, Mr. Mulchand Bhojraj, Mr. Hiranand, Mr. Verhomal, Mr. C.T. Valecha, Mr. Hasanand Pamnani Rohri, and Mr. Bhagwandas.

Thar Parkar: Mr. Rattanmal Gidumal Pleader; Mr. Metharam Murijmal, pleader, Mirpurkhas; Mr. Dhalumal Kishinchand, Mr. Allahbux Talpur, Master Dayanand School Mirpurkhas, Dr. Vattanmal Gulabsing, Mr. N.M. Himatsingani, and Mr. Motiram Wadhumal.

Sahiti: Mr. Kessumal Tejumal, Naushehro Feroz, Mr. Manohardas Kouromal, Naushehro Feroz, Mrs. Manohardas (Ambriti Devi) Feroz, Bhai Sachanand Phernmal Feroz, and Mansing Chuhermal B. Feroz.

Nawabshah: Maulvi Abdul Khalik, Hakim, Kazi Khudabux, Hakim Mahomed Muaz, Tando Adam, and Bhai Shamdas Shahdapur.

Shikarpur: Mr. Tarachand D. Gajra, Swami Piryabharti, Mr. Ghanshamdas N. Rajpal, and Mr. Naraindas.
Jacobabad: Dr. Menghraj, Mr. T.D. Pahlajani, Mr. Kodumal, Pundit Amersen, and Seth Khushiram Daryanomal.

The Hyderabad District Congress Committee claims 3976 members and the Sukkur District Congress Committee 3181 to date.

3. FUNDS

Complaints of dishonesty and misappropriation continue. Most of the local agitators are living on the funds they collect. Collections up to date as claimed by the Congress Committee are:-

Hyderabad: 50,000

Sukkur: 9,498, including 5,000 presented to Gandhi on his visit.

Jairamdas Daulatram claims that the total collections from Sind now amount to Rs. 1,25,000.

4. to 15. No developments.[16]

Weekly Bulletin on the Non-co-operation Movement for the Week ending 25th June 1921

GENERAL

The opposition to the Non-co-operation movement is making steady progress. Several of the newspapers in the Province criticise and ridicule the agitation. The *Bharatvasi* writes alarmist articles on the dangers ahead especially in connection with Mahomedan affairs. The general feeling among the Sindhi zamindars is genuinely opposed to the movement, but in many cases demands some official support to enable it to come into the open. The formation of Aman Sabhas receives a welcome from these classes. The topsy-turviness of a situation where a convicted gambler with a very shady reputation can pose as a popular leader and endeavour to counteract the action of a big zamindar when the latter organise an Aman Sabha meeting has been illustrated at Kotri, when the zamindar's men convincingly demonstrated the relative unimportance of the local agitators.

A cutting from the *Bharatvasi* concerning the Sind Swaraj Society (vide last week's bulletin) reads as follows:

[16] Copies forwarded as footnote 11.

Sind Swaraj Society.

Name

The name of the Association shall be Sind Swaraj Society.

Creed

The object of our Association shall be attainment of Swaraj by the people of India, as early as possible, with the British Commonwealth. The object shall be attained by all legitimate and constitutional means.

Immediate Programme

The immediate programme to which this Association shall concentrate its activities is:

(a) To take the fullest advantage of the Reformed Councils and to agitate for full autonomy in the Provincial Governments and for wider powers and control in the Central Government.
(b) To press for the repeal of all repressive laws and measures and such provisions in the existing laws as are based on racial distinctions.
(c) To secure through the Reformed Councils early legislation on matters such as Village Panchayats, Trade Unions, Arbitration Courts, Liquor Prohibition, National System of Education & etc.
(d) To combat destructive part of Non-co-operation and the repressive policy of the Government.
(e) To promote the Swadeshi movement.

1. AGITATION

Agitators have concentrated on the Bezwada programme. When they do hold meetings the audiences are distinctly smaller than they were a few weeks ago.

2. ORGANISATION

The following is a copy of a cutting from the *New Times* dated the 22nd June 1921:

'Sind Provincial Congress Committee.

We understand that the following gentlemen are being proposed for the membership of the All India Congress Committee:

Seth Haji Abdulla Haroon, Professor Vaswani, Mr. Hatimbhoy A. Karimji, Mr. Mahomed Khan, Mr. Masand, Mr. Narayandas, Mr. T.K. Jeswani, Mr. Jairamdas, Mr. Abdul Jabbar, Dr. Choithram, Sheikh Abdul Majid, Professor Ghanshyam, Pir Turabalishah, Mr. R.K. Lahori, Mr. P. Tolani, Kazi Khudabux, Mr. Virumal, Mr. Mulchand Pessumal, Mr. Tarachand Gajra, and Seth Ghamshamdas.

In connection with the presidentship the name of Mr. Virumal Begraj is being proposed. The names of Mr. Jairamdas, Dr. Choithram, Pir Turabalishah, and Mr. Mulchand Pessumal are being proposed as Vice-presidents.

Messrs. R.K. Sidhva, K.H. Massand, Seth Naraindas, Mr. P.S. Tolani, and Mr. Tarachand Gajra are being proposed for the two offices of joint secretaries.

According to the Congress Constitution the name of any gentleman who is a member of any Congress Committee in the Province, and may not necessarily be a member of the Sind Provincial Congress Committee can be proposed for membership of the All India Congress Committee. Any further proposal may be sent to us for publication. The Congress Constitution has laid down that all elections should take place on the basis of single transferable vote.[']

The complete failure of the Congress organisation to represent the Province of Sind is proved when it is seen that out of 20 names proposed for the Provincial Committee there are only three Sindhi Mahomedans and no Baluchis, which communities compose about three quarters of the population.

The agitators are making strenuous efforts to complete the quota of 1,30,000 Congress members allotted to Sind. Their efforts are making them publicly ridiculous. They probably claim about 20,000 to 25,000 members, by the 25th instant. It is safe to say that not one in ten of these understands and subscribes to the Non-co-operation creed or policy.

3. FUNDS

The Sind quota is 1,30,000 rupees. This is almost certain to be exceeded. Exact figures of the present amount are not available.

4. LAWYERS AND COURTS

The Arbitration Courts of Sukkur and Kiamari are remarkably....[17]

Weekly bulletin on the Non-co-operation Movement for the Week ending 2nd July 1921

GENERAL

The idea that the new constitution of the Congress was designed to provide the machinery of government with a Ministry, and a central organisation with subordinate local organisations in each of the Provinces was spread in Sind on the return of the delegates from Nagpur. One of the local agitators talked freely about it suggesting that Gandhi was to become the President of an Indian Republic. (Vide this office No. S.B. 108 of the 27th January 1921). There

[17] Pages 78 and 79 of the original are missing.

have been several rather obscure references to this general idea in speeches from time to time, but the question has not been openly discussed in definite terms. The *New Times* of the 30th June 1921 publishes the following article which is written by Professor Vaswani of Karachi:

'The Basis of Victory

"How nice, how noble if we could establish Swaraj on the anniversary of Lokamanya Tilak's death! But my sanguine temperament cannot visualise Swaraj by the first of August next. By strenuous work it is certainly possible to establish Swaraj on the first day of October next. It must be death to the Congress if it cannot be established on or before the 31st December next." So Mahatma Gandhi in *Young India*. As we have said already Swaraj in the political sense, Swaraj interpreted as the power of the people to control the army, the civil administration, the economic and educational policies of India, is not what we for ourselves expect even in December next. The Government is still unwilling to accept our terms; the Punjab and Khilafat wrongs remain unredressed; and we do not expect the political machinery to come under popular control by December next.

But there is one thing we can do by the end of December. There are large spheres of activity which we can shape ourselves according to our ideal; we can, in several ways, organise our own life, leaving the government alone. The Congress meets in December; we can then or earlier announce it a National Legislature endowed not with legal but what is more than legal—moral—authority of the People. The crore of rupees can become the nucleus [*sic*] of a National fund; and we can open up national schools, start swadeshi shops; introduce cottage industries, establish courts of arbitration, and organise a National Service. We will thus learn self-reliance; and if we keep strictly our pledges of self-purification and non-violence, we may soon develop a moral, economic and social strength which can render impotent all the physical power of government to govern the country except on our own terms.

This self-organisation we will not call Swaraj but a preparation for the building of Swaraj. This self-organisation we can secure but not without the power of character. The important point, as we view the matter, is not a crore of rupees or several crores, but character of the members of the Congress Committees. The struggle, indeed, for Swaraj is to our mind, in the last analysis, a struggle of character between members of the bureaucracy and members of the Congress organisation. Victory will be with the party equipped with greater resources of character. The bureaucracy is strong, partly because several of its members are men of honesty, ability, industry and devotion to the sircar. Can we have in the Congress Committees a much larger number of men with greater ability and industry, with a keener appreciation of the country's needs and a deeper loyalty to the Nation? We believe we can; and we say this in the face of much that we deeply deplore in the public life of today. We have faith in the people; and they will, as the years go by, throw up, in a greater number, the right sort of men to serve the Nation. We work in this faith; should this faith not be justified by results, the hope of an early Swaraj must go. For, above the Nation stands the Law which says: Victory to the stronger in Character.'

1. AGITATION

Was concentrated on the Bezwada programme.

2. ORGANISATION

The *New Times* of the 4th July 1921 publishes the following:

'Exact figures for Congress membership and charkhas are not available, but it is roughly calculated that membership of Congress Committee amount to about 40,000.'

3. FUNDS

The same paper voices the claims of the Sind Provincial Congress Committee as follows:

Karachi	Rs.	80,000
Hyderabad	Rs.	80,000
Sukkur	Rs.	26,000
Larkana	Rs.	12,000
Shikarpur	Rs.	25,000
Jacobabad	Rs.	1,851
Sahiti	Rs.	5,600
Nawabshah	Rs.	4,625-9-1
Total	Rs.	2,35,076-9-1

The disposal of these funds is not quite clear. The total includes the money given to Gandhi as a purse when he visited Sind, the whole amount having been handed over by him to Jairamdas Daulatram before he left the Province. It is presumed that 25% of this amount is to go to the All India Congress Committee, 10% to be at the disposal of the Sind Provincial Committee, and the remaining 65% to remain at the disposal of the District Committees which collected it; but so far no action appears to have been taken to give effect to this arrangement.

Complaints of misappropriation by agitators continue to be rife.

4. to 13. No developments

14. How far Mussalmans as a separate Class are adopting the Non-co-operation Movement

(a) The attitude of the Sind Mahomedans' Association representing the views of the zamindar classes is embodied in the following resolution passed at a recent meeting of the general body held at Larkana:

'That this Association declares that they have no sympathy with the Non-co-operation movement started in the country as leading to violence and unrest; and would recommend to the Mahomedans of Sind to adopt peaceful and constitutional methods for obtaining further political rights and privileges. That while sympathising with the question of Khilafat and the custody of the sacred places of Islam the Association condemns some of the methods adopted to gain the revision of the Turkish Peace Treaty. They firmly believe that more peaceful methods without trying to tamper with the allegiance to the crown, of the people and troops would sooner accomplish the end in view.'

(b) The coming All-India Khilafat Conference in Karachi is attracting attention among Maulvis and in the usual 'Pan Islamic' circles, but not to any extent among the general body of the Mahommedan population.

(c) In Sind the Khilafat Committees generally speaking exist in name only. Most of the members belong to the Congress organisations and practically all the work is in the hands of the latter.

15. The Nankana Affair and its Influence in Sind

No developments.

Weekly Bulletin on the Non-co-operation Movement for the Week ending 9th July 1921

General

Interest during the week has centred on the All-India Khilafat Congress at Karachi on the 8th, 9th and 10th. During the Conference the Non-co-operation Sub-Committee of the Central Khilafat Committee submitted its report on Civil Disobedience, suggesting that the question should be decided by the All-India

Congress Committee (at the meeting to take place at Bombay on the 28th July).

Gandhi's new programme for the boycott of foreign cloth had caused some alarm in the trade. The general opinion among Karachi Indian merchants is reported to be that the trade will suffer for a short period—perhaps a few months. Some merchants have cancelled their orders from England by wire.

The Sind Provincial Congress Committee was asked by the *Hindu* newspaper to decide what steps should be taken in Sind, but no plans appear to have been formulated at the meeting on the 9th.

1. AGITATION

(vide paragraph above)

2. ORGANISATION

The following is a cutting from the *New Times* of the 1st July 1921.

> 'Sind Provincial Congress Committee
> Election of Office Bearers
> Single Transferable Vote
>
> The following letter has been sent by Mr. Durgdas B. Advani, President Sind Provincial Congress Committee to the members of the Sind Provincial Congress Committee:
>
> The first meeting of the newly constituted Sind Provincial Congress Committee which has had to be postponed to enable the District Congress Committees to devote their energies to the completion of the Bezwada programme by the 30th June, will be held on 9th July 1921 at 8 p.m. in the office of the Swarajya Sabha, Bunder Road, Karachi.
>
> You have to vote for:
> One President
> Two Vice-presidents
> Two Joint Secretaries
> One Treasurer
> Fifteen other members of Council
> One Auditor, and
> Nine members of the All India Congress Committee....[18]
>
> make it a point to attend. But if you are not able to do so, please send your voting paper so as to reach me before the time fixed for the meeting. The words 'Voting paper' should be put on the outside of the cover.

[18] Last line cut off.

I have sent you a copy of the rules. You will observe that under rule 8(b) at least one Vice-President, one Secretary and the Treasurer have to be from Karachi. Under rule 9(a) each district has to get some representation on the Council. Under rule 9(b) which is in keeping with the Congress constitution, the representatives of the Province on the All-India Congress Committee have to be elected from among the members of the Congress Committees in Sind.

You have to vote for nine members for the All-India Congress Committee in the order of preference, as election for these has to be by the system of single transferable vote. The gentleman whom you consider the first best should be put in as first, the second best as second and so on.

A list of names of the members of the Sind Provincial Congress Committee has already been forwarded to you.'

The following is the result of the election:

'President: Dr. Choithram P. Gidwani

Vice-Presidents: Mr. Virumal Begraj, and Seth Sunderdas Valabdas

Secretaries: Seth Narayandas Anandji, Mr. Jairamdas Daulatram

Treasurer: Mr. K.H. Masand

Auditor: Mr. M.B. Dalal (Accountant).

The following additional 15 members of the Council have been elected:- Messrs. Sheikh Abdul Majid, Lalchand A. Jagtiani, Swami Krishnanand, C.T. Valecha, Tarachand Gajra Ghanshyam Jethanand. Pir Alianwara Shah, Maharaj Dwarka Prasad, R.K. Sidhwa, Dr. Vattanmal, Kazi Khudabux, M. Mansing Chuhermal, Ram B. Motwani, Seth Ghanshamdas Rajpal, and Dr. Menghraj.'

The result of the elections of members of the All-India Congress Committee is to be announced shortly.

3. to 15. No developments.

Weekly Bulletin on the Non-co-operation Movement for the week ending the 16th July 1921

GENERAL

It is difficult to arrive at a correct appreciation of the political atmosphere resulting from the All-India Khilafat Congress at Karachi, with Mahomed Ali's talk of an Indian Republic in December, of turning the English out of India without their baggage, and of stopping enlistment and teaching Khilafat principles to the Indian Army combined with the Congress programme for the boycott of foreign cloth.

There is considerable alarm among the peacefully inclined; but little sign of their taking any active part to counter the extremists.

That is left to Government. The *Bharatvasi* fears that violence and bloodshed are coming in the near future, and considers that India is on the brink of a precipice. Even Non-co-operators like Professor Vaswani are seriously alarmed (vide 'A' attached). The *New Times* expresses this feeling.

Mahomed Ali is further reported to have said privately that he was confident that he could count on the greater part of the Indian Army taking their side when the time comes. He said the same about the railway staff.

His remarks are general topics of conversation, and they have become known in rural Sind. People are asking each other when the English are to leave the country. It is said that many people are doubtful about joining the Aman Sabhas in case they may be the victims of the vengeance of those who obtain power when the English have left.

The question of Civil Disobedience is also being discussed. One political worker (Rijhumal Kundanmal Lahori) had given out that Mahomed Ali told him that the volunteers will be called upon to undertake Civil Disobedience from the 1st of August.

1. AGITATION

Speech making is less common than it was a few weeks ago.[19]

Extract from the *New Times* dated the 13th July 1921:

> 'Recording his impressions of the Khilafat Conference Vaswani says in the course of a letter to a Muslim leader: "Violence, I know, is permitted by the Muslim shariat; but violence is against my Religious Ideals; and it should be my duty to ask my countrymen to keep clear of all counsels of passion and strife. I deeply regret the Khilafat Conference passed even an conditional Resolution about severing connection with the King. I have no quarrel with the King. Such a Resolution, if passed by the National Congress must as far as I can see, lead in due course to a physical-force conflict; and I cannot contemplate with indifference a day when India may be turned into another Ireland. I am convinced that bitterness and passion will not solve our Problem. I believe profoundly that the world's piteous need today is Brotherhood, is Love; and my daily prayer is that Allah, the Compassionate may so bless the millions of India that they may bear witness to the wisdom of non-violence in the difficult days before us."'

[19] Page 87 of the original is missing.

Weekly Bulletin on the Non-co-operation Movement for the Week ending 23rd July 1921

GENERAL

The political situation is developing more rapidly in Sind, and is approaching the point where a small minority of fanatics, with the threat of mob violence behind them, can terrorise the law-abiding population and seriously interfere with the Administration. Instances of such interference are becoming frequent and cases have occurred which suggest that the Police and other officials are losing their initiative and the power of enforcing their authority in the ordinary conduct of their official business.

When Swami Krishnanand, a leading agitator in Karachi, was arrested by the Police for assaulting a police officer who ordered him to move on, the Police Sub-Inspector to whom he was taken at the Police Station released him, because a threatening crowd collected outside, and missiles had been thrown at the Police who had affected the arrest. He was subsequently re-arrested under orders from the District Superintendent of Police and convicted.

His conviction was the signal for the crowd to hoot and throw stones at the Police, and at any European who chanced to pass by.

At Matiari in the Hyderabad district a crowd under the influence of Pir Ghulam Mujadid Sarhandi made a determined attempt to break up an Aman Sabha meeting on the 22nd July. People attending the meeting were molested, and had to be escorted by the Police. According to the evidence recorded the crowd threatened to kill the Sub-Inspector, who thereupon ordered an armed sowar to fire, which he did killing one and wounding nine men.

Similarly at Larkana on [the] 17th July 1921 and other places attempts have been made to interfere with Aman Sabha meetings.

The picketing of liquor shops in Karachi is having an insidious effect in the same direction. The public, the liquor vendors are being overawed. When a would-be purchaser insists on entering the shop in spite of the picket he is frequently subjected to threats of personal violence by rough-looking bad characters who gather round him. Actual assaults have occurred.

The failure of officials to exercise their lawful authority is also illustrated by a case in Karachi where a Municipal official and two police constables failed to execute a distress warrant. The Municipal official was intimidated by the crowd into wearing a Gandhi cap and leaving the property which he attempted to attach. Income-tax collectors are reported to be encountering difficulties as a result of this spirit of resistance to authority. Some Indian Officials are meeting such situations with timidity and vacillation, others with temper.

Wherever, as at Matiari, the official shows determination and uses force (it cannot be said before the enquiry is complete whether the Sub-Inspector used force in self-defence or not, or whether he was justified or not) agitators immediately flock to the place, interfere with the enquiry, create an atmosphere and make out a more or less plausible case to prove that 'violence' has been used by the officials without justification. They proclaim that the 'non-violent' movement will lead to bloodshed only through the 'violence' of the officials. There is evidence however that, behind this plausible argument, is the feeling and belief that their objects, the attainment of 'Swaraj' will only be secured by a resort to violence. Such ideas are gradually spreading and making their appearance in new quarters. References to this in the case of men like Mahomed Khan Ghassi Khan have been made in previous reports. Manilal Vyas in a public speech on the 25th July said:

'It is said of the Swami Ji that he beat the policeman. If the Swami had a desire to kill anybody he could have had the Magistrate, the Collector, anybody murdered in one minute. There are several men who are ready to do anything at a sign from him. But Indians are not cowards. The Government has become an owl. Its officers have become owls. When the time for using force comes, then we will show who is stronger, Government, or we, the people. They (Government) should thank Mahatma Gandhi that they have been able to take Krishnanand to jail today.'

Fazalullah son of Kazi Obaidullah one of the students of the Aligarh National University recently remarked that violence was certain to come, the Non-co-operation movement being only a foundation for a violent movement. Dr. Haji Ghulam Hussain Kasam on the 25th July told a C.I.D. Inspector quite openly that 'Non-co-operation with violence or Sinn-Feinism' will supersede

Gandhi's movement. He proceeded to display bitter racial feeling, and argued that the differences between white and coloured races could only be settled by force.

Before the Reform Schemes was undertaken it was said that with reference to political conspiracies in India that the situation was no longer a matter of police and that it required the hand of the statesman. There would seen to be reason for saying that the position is now reversed, and that it is a matter of police to deal with the political conspiracy which aims at the overthrow of the British Government under the guise of 'non-violent non-co-operation'. It is not improbably, if the developments in Sind are an index of the general situation, that the power of the police to maintain order may soon be severely strained. It is certain that the movement in Sind derives all its strength from outside, and that the agitators in Sind have little local importance. They would be immediately reduced to impotence were it not for these outside influences.

The Sind Provincial Congress men who have voted in favour of the early introduction of Civil Disobedience, and the Pan-Islamists who are behind the Khilafat agitation are the most dangerous local elements.

Weekly Bulletin on the Non-co-operation Movement for the week ending 23rd July 1921

1. AGITATION

Subsequent to the visit of the Ali Brothers to two small towns in the Nawabshah district there was a recrudescence of speech making in that district.

2. ORGANISATION

The following have been elected as members of the All-India Congress Committee to represent Sind:

Mr. Jairamdas Daulatram, Dr. Choithram, Mr. R.K. Lahori, Mr. T.K. Jeswani, Shaikh Abdul Majid, Mr. Virumal Begraj, Prof. Ghansham, Mr. Lalchand Jagtiani and Mr. Tarachand D. Gajra.

It is reported that all of them intend to proceed to Bombay for the All-India Congress Committee meeting on the 27th instant. Of seventy one members of the Sind Provincial Congress Committee sixty two voted in the election for the All-India Congress Committee.

A meeting of the Sind Provincial Congress Committee took place on the 23rd instant at Sukkur; details of which have been separately reported in this office No. S.B. 1242.

In addition to the seventy five members mentioned in last week's bulletin as constituting the Panchayat of the Karachi District Congress Committee thirty five members representing the mofussil part of the district have now been elected.

The meeting of the Panchayat of the Karachi District Congress Committee has been arranged for the 25th to elect office bearers of the Panchayat. Of the seventy five town members seventeen are Mussulmans, fifty three are Hindus, three are Hindu ladies, and two are sweepers.

Pandit Amarsen has written to the *Sind Observer* criticising the elections of the Congress Committee in Sind on the ground that as they were all carried out by means of compromise among the committee they are not in accordance with the Congress constitution and not representative of the electorate. He also points out that the Mussulmans have not been proportionately represented on the Provincial Committee or on the All-India Congress Committee and concluded by saying 'If my friends say that injustice has been done to Mussulmans the only way open to them is to set aside the elections and hold them again in strict conformity with the procedure laid down in the Congress constitution.'

The Council of the Sind Students National Service held a meeting during the week and sent an announcement on the subject to the press. They believe in a great flourish of trumpets, but there appears to be little behind it, the Students National Service consisting of a small number of swollen headed young men.

Jairamdas Daulatram and Naraindas Anandji Bechar, Joint Secretaries of the Sind Provincial Congress Committee, invite applications in the *Hindoo* dated 18/7/21 for the Provincial National Service. Applicants are required to state whether they will work with or without remuneration. This advertisement is in connection with the arrangements which are being made to improve the organisation of the Volunteers by the Congress and Khilafat Committees.

The picketing of liquor shops at Karachi has led to three or four cases of obstruction, assault etc. Swami Krishnanand was arrested by the Police on the 20/7/21. He was arrested for obstructing and striking a Police Officer. He was taken to the Police station followed by a large crowd who threw missiles at the Police. He was released by the officer in charge of the Police station at night, and his re-arrest was ordered.

At a meeting of the Sind Provincial Congress Committee at Hyderabad on the 16th instant it was resolved to recommend the name of Mr. C.R. Das for the Presidentship of the Ahmedabad Congress.

3. FUNDS

No developments. Money is still being collected.

4. SCHOOLS AND COLLEGES

No developments.

5. NATIONAL SERVICE AND VOLUNTEERS

(Vide above)

6. LAWYERS AND COURTS[20]

successful working of the arbitration courts at Sukkur and at Keamari. The cases dealt with are nearly all of a very petty nature.

It has been reported in the Press that a tailor of Dadu in the Larkana district who is being prosecuted under section 108, C.P.C. has refused to appear in court on the ground that he does not recognise the court's jurisdiction. The intention is to secure cheap advertisement by this refusal as being more effective than attending a court and refusing to plead.

7. to 9. No developments.

10. BOYCOTT OF BRITISH AND FOREIGN
TRADE AND TRADING CONCERNS

The campaign of the boycott of foreign cloth is being carried out chiefly by Congress Committees appealing privately to merchants and shop keepers. At a meeting of the Sind Provincial Congress Committee held at Hyderabad on the 16th it was resolved that the following programme should be adopted:

[20] Last line cut off.

(1) Every District Congress Committee should send out at least two workers to preach in the various towns and villages within its district.
(2) Public meetings of Consumers should be organised frequently.
(3) Arrangements should be made for having street lectures.
(4) It was resolved to print nearly one lakh of leaflets in Sindhi, Gujarati, Gurumukhi and Hindi languages for distribution all over Sind through the District Congress Committees.
(5) Letters should be written to all the Panchayats in the province in regard to the use of Khaddar and Swadeshi cloth.
(6) Each District Congress Committee should organise a big demonstration on 1st August in support of the boycott of foreign cloth.
(7) It was resolved to distribute 2,500 posters all over the province advocating the boycott of foreign cloth by 1st August.
(8) Each District Congress Committee should arrange to approach the cloth merchants and urge them not to purchase any more of foreign cloth hereafter and to endeavour to dispose of their present stocks outside India.
(9) Special meetings should be organised for ladies.
(10) The work of introducing charkhas and manufacturing Khaddar should be pushed on even more vigorously than before.
(11) District Congress Committees should be approached to send at their own expenses copied of Non.[21]

Weekly Bulletin on the Non-co-operation Movement for the Week ending 30th July 1921

GENERAL

The picketing movement with its accompaniment of terrorisation continued during the week in Karachi. Picketing is also being carried out in other parts of Sind. Volunteers who do the picketing, work for hire, and, not as a rule, on account of their members.

[21] Pages 96 and 97 of the original are missing.

The stoning of Europeans in Karachi on the occasion of Swami Krishnanand's arrest left a great deal of resentment behind it. A meeting of Europeans was organised by the European Association to call upon the authorities to take effective steps to deal with the nuisance created by the Non-co-operators.

The prospect of the early introduction of Civil Disobedience caused excitement to be worked up during the week and there was reason to apprehend disturbance in Karachi on August 1st. The news received on Saturday evening to the effect that Civil Disobedience had been postponed relieved the tension in the political atmosphere in Karachi.

The Provincial Congress Committee evinces signs of considerable lack of harmony, the Hyderabadis having secured a preponderating voice, all other communities which are represented among the Non-co-operators are jealous of them.

The Mahomedans consider that they have not been properly represented and claim a large increase in their numbers. It was noticed that the Sind members of the All-India Congress Committee when travelling to Bombay to attend the meeting there divided themselves into three separate parties, namely Hyderabadis, other Hindus and thirdly the solitary Mahomedan representative.

Similarly there is considerable feeling between two groups of the Sind Provincial Khilafat Committee. One is headed by Haji Abdulla Haroon and Mahomed Khan and the other by Sheikh Abdul Aziz, Moulvi Khudabux and Doctor Shamshuddin [!]. An attempt has been made to displace Haji Abdulla Haroon and Mahomed Khan from the Committee, but it has failed.

It is reported to be common talk of the bazaar that the British are to leave India within a few months.

The Central Khilafat Committee called upon the Provincial, District and subordinate Khilafat Committees to hold meetings on Friday the 27th to reiterate and confirm the demands of the Indian Moslems regarding Khilafat, Jazirat-ul-Arab and the holy places of Islam and to send copies of the resolutions to the Central Khilafat Committee. No action was taken in Sind except in Sukkur as the instructions were received too late. It was announced in the Press that during the Friday prayer the Khilafat and the Matiari tragedy should be mentioned in the prayers. Reports received from Karachi show that this was not done in any case. In two cases the preachers made remarks reflecting on the present form of agitation.

1. AGITATION

There have been a number of meetings especially in connection with the boycott of foreign cloth.

2. ORGANISATION

A district panchayat of 70 members has been elected under the Sukkur District Congress Committee. There is some feeling between the town and rural Congress men as it is complained that the latter are not properly represented. As in Karachi the Mahomedans are very poorly represented having only four members.

A meeting of the panchayat of the Karachi District Congress Committee was held on the 25th July. Only 40 members attended out of a total of 110. A very little of the business of the meeting was got through. At the adjourned meeting on the 30th only 11 members attended and the meeting had to be postponed for want of a quorum.

3. FUNDS

Among the items of agenda for a meeting of the Sind Provincial Congress Committee held on the 15th July at Karachi, was one for the discussion as to how 'Rs. 41,000 received from Mahatma Gandhi (out of Rs. 64,000 presented to him during his visit to Sind) should be invested.' From enquiry it appears that this question had not yet been settled, some of the money is with Naraindas Anandji Bechar, some with Lalchand Jagtiani, and some with other workers. The question of investing it in the Karachi Bank is to be discussed at the next meeting. The administration of the funds is clearly very loosely controlled.

4. SCHOOLS AND COLLEGES

The number of students attending the national schools is gradually dropping.

5. NATIONAL SERVICE AND VOLUNTEERS

The re-organisation of the National Service has been held in abeyance on account of the visit of the leaders to Bombay. A proposal was made to disband the Sind students national service and to employ the workers in the Provincial National Service, but it was negativated on the ground that several of the students are not 21 years of age.

6. LAWYERS AND COURTS

No developments.

7. to 9. No developments.

10. BOYCOTT OF BRITISH OR FOREIGN TRADE AND TRADING CONCERNS

Posters and hand bills are being distributed in large numbers in connection with the boycott of foreign cloth. They appeal to the people on religious and 'national' grounds. The movement does not however appear to be as successful as its promoters hoped.

11. and 12. No developments.

13. GOVERNMENT SERVICES

In accordance with the decisions of the All-India Khilafat Committee in Karachi arrangements are reported to have been made to approach the troops. The method adopted for the present appears to be for agitators to confine themselves to casual conversations with the individual men.

In the case of the police it is reported that agitators frequently make remarks to police officers asking when they are going to resign and so on.[22]

Weekly Bulletin on the Non-co-operation Movement for the week ending 6th August 1921

GENERAL

The picketing of liquor shops continues in Karachi and in other towns in Sind. Enquiries show that the picketers who are usually paid 8 to 12 annas a day are mostly drawn from the loafer class. The Karachi District Congress Committee is attempting to obtain more volunteers, the number having decreased during the week, in consequence of Swami Krishnanand's arrest. The attempt to obtain picketers of a better class have not fructified.

The following reports have been received concerning the attitude

[22] Copies forwarded as in footnote 11. Page 101 of the original is missing.

of District Congress Committees to the question of Civil Disobedience:

(1) The District Congress Committee, Mirpurkhas, has expressed the opinion that there is no need for introducing Civil Disobedience in that district and has recommended that it should be introduced in those parts of India where a rigorous use has been made of sections 108 and 144, C.P.C.
(2) The Jacobabad District Congress Committee unanimously decided that Civil Disobedience should be introduced but that they should await instructions from the All-India Congress Committee.
(3) The Hyderabad District Congress Committee has postponed further consideration of the matter. The leading members of this committee have voted in favour of Civil Disobedience at the Provincial Committee meeting at Sukkur. They intend that if Government resort to repressive measures a special conference should be summoned to discuss the question of the introduction of Civil Disobedience locally, in accordance with the decision of the All-India Congress Committee at Bombay.

A Deputy Superintendent of Police who is in touch with a number of agitators reports that the opinion, that the present non-co-operation movement has intended to prepared the ground for a violent revolution, is held in many quarters.

A report has been received to the effect that Jairamdas Daulatram in a course of private conversation with other Sind members of the All-India Congress Committee at Bombay remarked that they had spoiled their lives and worried their relations without doing any good to the country. He did not think that any real result could be attained by non-violent non-co-operation and that Mahatma Gandhi must fail. He regretted that they were not even able to do away with men like Nabi Baksh and Mahomed Baksh, Deputy Collectors in Sind. If they could do this they would have at least achieved some tangible result. If one community like the Bengalees brought Government to their knees by bomb throwing it was likely that the whole of India by adopting the same methods would secure immediate success. These remarks were made in the presence of Sheikh Abdul Majid, Dr. Choithram, Pandit Amarsen and one or two others. None of those present made any comment.

The *Sindvasi* dated 3rd August publishes a letter from Hakim Shamshuddin, Ex-Joint Secretary of the Sind Provincial Khilafat Committee, as under:

'I had no intention to give out the reasons of my resigning the Joint-Secretaryship but as advantage has been taken of my silence hence I want to make it clear that Mahomed Khan Secretary is so harsh and uncivilised that it is impossible for any gentleman to work with him. I feel that I could only pull on for so many days. Beside I saw that the public money was being wasted most mercilessly and in a useless way and my presence could not check it. The President drew my attention repeatedly to this, but sorry that no result came out of it hence there was only one way left for me to sever connection from it. I hope that those people who are taking illegal advantage of my silence will not oblige me to give further details about this.'

It is reported that one of the reasons for his resigning was that Shaukat Ali omitted to thank him for his exertions in connection with the All-India Khilafat Conference.

1. AGITATION

The number of meetings is on the increase.

2. to 5. Nil.

6. LAWYERS AND COURTS

Twenty two cases of a civil nature were registered at the Sukkur National court during the week ending 30th July bringing the grand total to 182 on that date.

7. to 12. No developments.

13. GOVERNMENT SERVICES

No reports have been received of the distribution of any pamphlets published by the Ulema-ul-Hind or by any other local agitators, declaring service in the military and in the police to be haram, nor has any case been reported in which any of the Aligarh students have approached any troops. A single report has been received that some unknown agitators approached a Jamadar under the A.C.R.E. Karachi, and asked him to join the Khilafat party on one third of the pay which he was drawing. It is reported that casual remarks to police officers suggesting that they should resign continue to be made.[23]

Weekly Bulletin on the Non-co-operation Movement for the week ending 13th August 1921

GENERAL

The anti-climax of the decision of the All-India Congress Committee in Bombay to postpone civil disobedience, has had the natural result causing the Non-co-operation movement to slacken in Sind. The picketing of liquor shops has been done less regularly and with less energy in Karachi and apparently elsewhere. The attempt to obtain picketers of a better class has not yet led to anything. The Temperance Committee of the Karachi District Panchayat had for this reason decided to ask the Secretaries of the Karachi District Congress Committee to appoint twenty five members of the Panchayat to do the picketing themselves. A Swadeshi Committee has also been formed in Karachi to deal with the boycott of foreign cloth, but the result of its activities are not yet apparent.

The Sind Provincial Khilafat Committee on the other hand shows signs of greater vitality; the Ulema movement is also assuming greater importance.

Reports continue to be received indicating that the idea that violence is inevitable is held by many of the agitators.

1. AGITATION

The number of meetings is less than it was two months ago, especially in Karachi.

2. to 12. Nil.

13. GOVERNMENT SERVICES

Reports have now been received that pamphlets published by the Ulema-i-Ḥind declaring, among other things, service in the military and in the police to be *Haram*, are being circulated in Karachi and in the Sind districts.[24]

[23] Pages 105 and 106 of the original are missing.

[24] Copies forwarded as in footnote 11.

Weekly Bulletin on the Non-co-operation Movement for the week ending 20th August 1921

GENERAL

The sudden rise in the price of flour has had a disquieting effect especially as regards the low-paid railway workmen and the police in Karachi. The Non-co-operators have not however made as much of the opportunity as might have been expected.

The activities of the Non-co-operators in Sind have slackened both as regards agitation and organisation. Picketing of liquor shops continues. A better class of recruits for picketing work have not yet put in an appearance. The results of the activities of the Swadeshi committee in Karachi are not yet apparent. Two or three weeks ago the demand for Khaddar in Karachi greatly exceeded the supply and all stocks were promptly sold. The supply now exceeds the demand although the supply has not increased very largely. The charm and novelty is wearing off, and those classes of persons who are likely to adopt such clothing have to a great extend obtained as much as they want for the time being.

The Sind Provincial Congress Committee is reported in the press to have framed a budget for the current year with an estimated income of Rs. 23,000. This is confirmed by information from inside sources, from which it is also apparent that the work of the committee is being handicapped by personal jealousies. The Hyderabadi party have succeeded in getting control of the Provincial Committee into their hands, and the other people do not work willingly with them. The following account of a meeting of the Council of the Sind Provincial Congress Committee held at Hyderabad on the 13th instant, which appeared in the press, substantially agrees with our information:

'A meeting of the Council of the Sind Provincial Congress Committee was held at Hyderabad on the 13th instant. Dr. Choithram presiding. Twelve members were present.

(1) It was resolved that the President and Secretaries should dispose of the applications for Sind National Service and make appointments and intimate to the Council.

(2) It was decided to appoint a travelling Inspector of Accounts to examine the accounts of all Congress Committees and give them guidance as to keeping of accounts. The post should be advertised for and the pay should be according to qualifications.

(3) It was further resolved that every District Congress Committee should prepare a monthly balance sheet of the accounts of its district and send a copy of it to the Council of the Provincial Congress Committee before the 15th of the following month. The first monthly balance sheet should contain the balance sheet from January 1921.

(4) The general body be recommended to make a rule that if the District Committee does not submit the balance sheet in time, its representatives on the Provincial Committee shall not have the right to vote till the balance sheet is received.

(5) The President and Secretaries are also authorised to go through the accounts of the Congress Committees.

(6) The letters of Mr. A.S. Motwani and Mr. Lalchand A. Jagtiani were read and it was unanimously resolved following the example of the settlement of the question of Bengal and Madras elections by the Working Committee, that the elections of the Karachi District Congress Committee should not be disturbed in view of the need for intensive Congress work and shortness of the time available for it.

(7) Rules for the Sind National Service were passed.

(8) Mr. Parsaram Tahilramani who has had complete theoretical and practical training in spinning and weaving at Mahatma Gandhi's Ashram was appointed Weaving Officer for Sind and enrolled in the Sind National Service.

(9) The Secretaries were authorised to send press telegrams about proceedings of Provincial Committees and important Sind news.

(10) The budgets of seven districts were discussed, Karachi and Shikarpur budgets not having been yet received. Six of the districts were requested to redraft the budget so as to cut down unnecessary expenditure.

(11) In view of the fact that Mahiti District Committee has only Rs. 500 in hand distributed in eight committees and Jacobabad District Committee had only Rs. 180 in hand it was resolved, pending the passing of the final budget, to sanction Rs. 1000 for Mahiti and Rs. 500 for Jacobabad Committee with a view to prevent stoppage of work in those districts.[']

There has been considerable discussion in the Committee concerning the legality of the elections. It has been decided to postpone the matter for the present and it is expected that a new election will be held shortly.

The Sind Provincial Khilafat Committee's activities are chiefly evident in the circulation of large numbers of the pamphlet containing the Ulemas fatwa describing police and military service as Haram. The Sind Provincial Khilafat Committee also issued instructions in accordance with the instructions of the Central Khilafat Committee concerning 'cow sacrifice' at the Bakri Id. This had little effect in Karachi where Ghau-kushi [!] was performed in several places on the Id day. In Hyderabad and elsewhere beef is not commonly eaten by Mahomedans and no action was therefore taken by the local Khilafat committee.

A scare has been started in Karachi on the ground that theft and house-breaking have become very common in the city and a deputation of moderate leaders approached the District Magistrate in this connection. The English and vernacular press has also been full of it. It appears however to have little foundation in fact and no abnormal amount of crime has been reported to the police. After this scare had been worked up for a few days the Non-co-operators took part in meetings to organise Volunteers to watch the streets at night in certain parts of the city, and their speeches are full of arguments to the effect that Government has now lost the power to protect the people against criminals and that the people, under their leaders, must protect themselves.

1. AGITATION

The number of meetings has increased slightly in Karachi and is considerable in the Nawabshah district. In the latter district several objectionable speeches have recently been delivered.

2. to 5. Nil.

6. LAWYERS AND COURTS

The arbitration court at Keamari is held every Sunday. The following is a report by a police officer who attended the 'court' on Sunday:

'Court sat from 4 to 6.30 p.m. Dr. Tarachand J. Lalwani presided. There were six 'jurymen' including a Port Trust clerk, a shop keeper and a serang of Brigstocke Jeewanji and Co., Stevedores and Contractors. The first case concerned a mortgage of some ornaments three years previously for Rs. 300/- and the claim now amounted to Rs. 600/- including interest. The matter was compromised by the bania agreeing to forego a part of the interest and the debtor agreeing to pay the debt in instalments through the President of the 'court'. The second complaint concerned a barber's instruments left in a shop which he had vacated, the claim being against the owner of the shop. It was decided that the owner of the shop should pay half the value of the instruments, the value to be assessed on the following Sunday. These are typical instances of the cases decided by this 'court'.

7. AGRARIAN

Nil.

8. LABOUR INCLUDING RAILWAYS

There have been several rumours that railway employees in the Carriage and Loco shops were likely to go on strike in consequence of the dearness of wheat. One Ganpat, an electrician, is reported to have left Lahore for Karachi at the end of the week and to have informed the Karachi people that a meeting was to be held in Lahore on Saturday evening to decide what action should be taken. After his arrival talk of the possibility of a strike was current. Subsequent reports are to the effect that Kanti Parkash, the local Union Secretary, had said in private conversation that a general strike on the railways was impending, from which Government would learn a lesson they were not likely to forget. The report from another source is to the effect that Kanti Parkash, Ahmed Din Mistri of the Loco Shop, Ali Mahomed Fitter of the Engine Shed, Mathradas a clerk and Gurdayal a fitter were influencing the illiterate work people to make trouble over petty matters, to be united among themselves and generally to inculcate a spirit of bad discipline. Mistri Chuharsingh Labhsing, Tahilsing, Suleiman and Brooke were said to be working in the same way in the Carriage shops.

These reports at present lack confirmation.[25]

Weekly Bulletin on the Non-co-operation Movement for the week ending 27th August 1921

GENERAL

The leaders of the Non-co-operation movement in Sind have been comparatively quiet, though many of the lesser lights among them have been indulging in objectionable speeches. The principal leaders say that they are devoting themselves to the organisation of committees and to the Swadeshi campaign. There are various signs

[25] Copies forwarded as in footnote 11.

that the movement is at present undergoing a disintegrating process in the absence of any special cause of excitement or of any special call from Gandhi such as would arouse more enthusiasm than the Swadeshi movement does. Local jealousies are more than even apparent.

1. AGITATION

The number of meetings in small towns and villages shows some signs of increasing.

2. ORGANISATION

District Congress Committees have occupied themselves in forming Swadeshi Committees to deal with the Swadeshi movement and they have drawn up budgets. Vide 'Funds'.

3. FUNDS

The total contribution of Sind to the Swaraj fund at the end of June was two lakhs thirty five thousands. This amount had not all been collected, a certain proportion, probably 25 per cent, was only promised. Full details are not yet available. The district committees are apparently budgeting on the strength of promises many of which they have not collected. In the case of the Karachi District Congress Committee, this has led to ill-feeling among the members of the Committee, some of whom have challenged the correctness of such a policy. It is worth noticing that payment of propagandists is one of the largest items in more than one of the budgets, of which particulars have been published.

4. SCHOOLS AND COLLEGES

The Tilakalya School at Karachi which was one of the most successful of the National Schools established in Sind is now broken up for lack of funds. Lalchand Jagtiani (under the advice of Gandhi) has turned the school into a spinning and weaving school. A number of the students and masters have in consequence left.

5. NATIONAL SERVICE AND VOLUNTEERS

Disintegration is most marked in this connection, almost all the corps in Karachi being practically non-existent. Very few volunteers were enlisted in other parts of the province and they also appear to exist chiefly on paper. The same remark applies to Sewa Samitis. The only volunteers now in existence are those who picket liquor shops for daily hire. Many of these are men who are unable to obtain other employment and have no sympathy with them in the non-co-operation movement.

6. LAWYERS AND COURTS

No new courts have been formed. The failure to do so in Hyderabad is worth noting. The arbitration 'court' at Kiamari continues to work on the lines indicated in previous reports.

7. AGRARIAN

Nil.

8. LABOUR INCLUDING RAILWAYS

Rumours of an impending strike on the railway have now died down, and there does not appear to be any reason to anticipate trouble in the immediate future.

9. to 12. Nil.

13. GOVERNMENT SERVICE

Pamphlets concerning the police and the army continue to be put into circulation. No reports have been received of any case in which Aligarh students have attempted to approach military or police sepoys. A clerk named Valiram Gulrazani employed in the office of the Assistant Director Military Works, Sind Rajputana District, has published a letter in the papers to the effect that he was discharged for wearing Gandhi clothes, and another appealing to the 'better feelings of clerks' and calling them to be men, and not to fail their country in its dire need and not to be dictated to in the question of national dress.[26]

Weekly Bulletin on the Non-co-operation Movement for the week ending 8th October 1921

GENERAL

No weekly bulletin was prepared in this office for the week ending 24th September and 1st October. The small staff employed in this C.I.D. was overwhelmed with the clerical labour connected with

[26] Copies forwarded as in footnote 11. Pages 116 to 118 of the original are missing. No reports for September 1921.

the preparation of the cases against the Ali Brothers and other and by other incidental enquires in Sind and in other provinces which were conducted under instructions received from the Commissioner in Sind with a view to connecting the accused in the conspiracy case with the distribution of the fatwas in the army.

During the three weeks ending the 8th October there has been little change as far as the internal organisation of the Congress and Khilafat Committees in Sind is concerned. The arrests and trail of the accused was followed by a combined meeting of the Provincial Congress and Khilafat Committees, at which it was decided that Civil Disobedience should be introduced with effect from the 1st November. The question as to which laws should be broken is understood to have been referred to the Working Committee of the All-India Congress Committee and the result of this reference is not yet known. Otherwise there has been little outward manifestation of excitement in connection with the case. There is not a strong body of well-informed moderate opinion in Sind. Many of those who condemn the Non-co-operation movement also condemn the Government, especially in connection with any action against agitators. On the whole public opinion has been considerably influenced by the speeches made by the accused in their defence. They are widely regarded as having made a strong case in support of their claim that the actions for which they are charged were based on religious grounds.

The necessarily rough and incomplete analysis indicates that from 60 to 70 per cent of the Khilafat agitators in Sind are impelled by religious motives, and that among the remaining 30 to 40 per cent motives of personal vanity and the necessity of making a living are the predominating influences. Outside the towns of Karachi and Hyderabad it is probable that about 10 per cent of the educated Mahomedans are definitely and strongly affected by the Khilafat agitation and ten per cent definitely loyal and that the remaining 80 per cent are neutral or uncertain. Those who have joined the Khilafat movement for the most part belong to the class locally known as Nimazees [!], i.e. those of a deeply religious turn of mind. The uneducated classes of Mahomedans who form the great mass of the rural population have been very little affected by the agitation. The Baluchis as a rule follow the Sayads, and Sayads are not inclined to take a very favourable view of Turkish rule in Arabia.

Reports continue to be received to the effect that there is a certain amount of talk in extremist circles about the inevitableness [!] of violence superseding the present non-violent movement, and also to the effect that a certain number of people in sympathy with the Khilafat agitation expect an outbreak of violence to follow the conviction of the Ali Brothers.

The Congress and Khilafat Committees have shown indecision in connection with the question of distributing fatwas to the troops in Sind and also with that of confirming the 6 resolution of the All-India Khilafat Congress of July. From information received it appears that they entertain hopes of persuading some police officers to resign in connection with the Ali Brothers' case. Discontent among various grades of police officers in connection with the high cost of living, pay and conditions of service therefore constitutes a danger which should not be overlooked. Police officers, especially those connected with the case, have been to some extent disturbed by talk of the social boycott of those concerned in cases against agitators. But so far nothing definite in this connection has eventuated.

1. to 14. No developments.[27]

Weekly Bulletin on the Non-co-operation Movement for the week ending 15th October 1921

GENERAL

It is now expected that Civil Disobedience will be introduced from the 1st November in Sind. The passing of resolutions on the lines of the 6 resolutions of the All-India Khilafat Conference which has been done at numerous meetings has been described in the Press as virtual civil disobedience. Nearly all districts report an increase of agitation and speeches tend to become more objectionable. Lies concerning the Holy places continue to be repeated. The Karachi

[27] Copies forwarded as in footnote 21.

District Congress Committee has indulged in 'intensive agitation', meetings being held daily. Special attempts have been made to excite the religious feelings of the Pathans and Mekranees in Karachi and it is beyond question that the present form of agitation is calculated to create conditions of 'preparedness for violence'. Hayat and Ishfauk, both described at secretaries of Mahomed Ali, Akhtar Ali reported to be the attendant of Shaukat Ali and their relation Moazzim Ali have all taken part in this intensive agitation in Karachi. It is noteworthy that men of this type should continuously harp on the question of wearing Khadi. (It is not clear whether Hayat is the same person as Mahomed Hassan Hayat mentioned in the Director's weekly report of the 5th instant). It is reported that European firms in Karachi have in some instances dismissed or removed clerks for wearing Gandhi caps and that they have been induced to reinstate them through a move on the part of the agitators to supply Gandhi caps to all of the staff of offices where such action was taken. It has also been suggested that these firms were apprehensive, that they would in some cases lose trade if they maintained this attitude.

One Mahomed Baksh was arrested on the 4th instant in Hyderabad and sent up for trial under section 131 I.P.C. for distributing copies of the Ulemas fatwa, as printed at the Shauk Press in Lahore, to military sepoys. Interviewed in jail by the Superintendent of Police, Sind C.I.D, he asked to be pardoned, but at the same time stated that he would rather die than give evidence against anyone else in court. He stated that he had received the copies for distribution from one of the Secretaries of the Hyderabad Khilafat Committee. He had formerly served in the Police as a constable. He believed that the pronouncement of the Ulemas that it was Haram to serve in the Police and the army, and the orders of distributing it were binding on the Mussalmans, and he regarded this as an article of religious faith.

It is to be feared that the obstinate spirit of this man is being all too widely spread by agitators who are playing on the religious feelings of Mahomedans. No resignations in the Police in Sind have so far been reported as a result of this agitation. Failure in this respect has perhaps led the agitators to announce falsely that certain policemen had resigned. At the same time, as reported last week, discontent among Sub-Inspectors and Inspectors and also in the Police clerical establishment in consequence of their pay not having been increased in proportion to the rise in the cost of living is a serious factor in the general situation. There is also some discontent among the Constabulary owing to the recent reduction in the rates of travelling allowance.

The District Superintendent of Police, Karachi, reports that from information received it appears that fatwas are being distributed secretly among the troops in Karachi and that a military sepoy in Karachi is concerned in a plan to forward the fatwas to Basra where his father is said to be regimental mulla. Fatwas have also been posted in public places. No other case in which any person has been concerned in distributing these fatwas has been reported to the police in Sind so far as reports received in this office go.

The following rumours in Karachi may have some significance:

(1) It is stated that the British Agent who had been deputed to discuss peace terms with the Amir of Kabul, was compelled to return to India as the Amir had finally decided not to be on friendly terms with the British.

(2) It is said that the Amir of Kabul has informed his Military to keep themselves in readiness to fight with the British in case they did not give freedom to India. It is also stated that the Afghans will declare war with the British by the end of November, 1921.

1. AGITATION

See above.

2. ORGANISATION

No further steps have come to notice as being taken in connection with the organisation of Congress and Khilafat Committees in Sind but Jairamdas Daulatram is in correspondence with Gandhi concerning the constitution of the Provincial Committee and the election of members of the All-India Congress Committee, as can be seen from the following telegram:

Mahatma Gandhi, Sabarmati

Under our provincial committees rules all Sind delegates numbering 71 elected by members of Congress Committees will form next years Provincial Committee and under Congress constitution 9 all India Committee members from Sind are to be elected by Provincial Committee. Please wire how resolution 6 of Calcutta working committee is to be carried out by us is it meant that 62 delegates are to be elected by general electorates and 9 more by provincial committee latter delegates also constituting all India Committee members.

Jairamdas.[28]

Weekly Bulletin on Non-co-operation Movement for the week ending 22nd October 1921

GENERAL

In the first sentence of this office weekly bulletin for the week ending the 15th October, 1921, the words 'It is now expected that Civil Disobedience will be introduced from the 1st November ...' should have read 'It is not now expected that Civil Disobedience will be introduced....' During the current week intensive agitation continued in Karachi and elsewhere. In Karachi there were some signs of an attempt to stir up excitement among Mekranees, Pathans and other ignorant tribesmen. The effect of this does not however appear to have been very great. Reports continue to be received of the passing of resolutions on the lines of the [sixth] resolution of the All-India Khilafat Congress, and of the distribution of fatwas declaring it to be *haram* to serve in the army and the police. So far not a single instance has come to notice, during the last three months, in which any police officer has resigned as a result of this propaganda. No further case has been reported in which any evidence is forthcoming against any person for taking part in distributing fatwas or otherwise behaving in a manner actionable under Section 131, I.P.C.

The Karachi District Congress Committee proposed to hold.[29]

[28] Rest of the page is missing.

[29] Pages 125 to 127 of the original are missing.

Weekly Bulletin on the Non-co-operation Movement for the week ending 29th October 1921

GENERAL

This, the week of the trial in the Sessions Court, Karachi, of the case Crown versus the Ali Brothers and others, opened with a severe set back to the Khilafat movement in Sind, in the shape of the apology and pardon of Pir Turabali Shah, a member of the leading family of the Rashidi Pirs. The Khilafat agitators showed obvious signs of regarding it as a very serious blow to their cause.

The atmosphere surrounding the proceedings was, from the police officers' point of view, uncomfortable in view of the fact that a certain Pir had given information to a Police Inspector of the District Police to the effect that he had seen a number of revolvers in the possession of Pir Imamshah son of the Jhandewalla Pir of the Hyderabad District, and that he had learned that this Pir was collecting arms and that it was intended that these arms should be used against police officers or other officials or against the witnesses in this case. This information appeared somewhat suspicious for certain reasons but was efficiently circumstantial to receive serious attention. It was also alleged that Pir Mahbubshah, whose apology was accepted by Government last year, was implicated in this plot. Steps were taken which resulted in various members of the Jhandewalla Pir's family, who had come to Karachi in connection with the trial, returning to their village. Enquires which have been made up to the date of writing indicate that it is extremely improbably that any of the Jhandewalla family should be concerned in any such plot. The same cannot be said with any certainty as regards Mahbubshah who is an eccentric man and probably not quite sane. If he is concerned in any such plot it is almost certainly limited to persons under his immediate influence. The proceedings themselves passed off without any incident which need be mentioned here except possibly Shaukat Ali's remarks, to which the Judge when summing up referred as a threat of assassination.

On the whole comparatively little excitement was aroused in connection with the case so far as the collection of crowds was concerned. A number of plain clothes police officers were detailed to mingle with the crowd surrounding the court, and there were times when there was hardly anyone there at all so that the officers were compelled to leave the immediate neighbourhood to avoid making themselves conspicuous.

The week was also marked by the Conference organised by the Sind Provincial Congress Committee, Mirpurkhas, under the presidentship of Mrs. Sarojini Naidu. This Conference, especially in the Subjects Committee, brought into a strong light the hollowness of Hindu-Muslim unity in Sind. Mrs. Naidu and Jamnalal Bajaj, who accompanied her, regarded this matter in a serious light and on their arrival in Karachi arranged a special meeting on the 28th October at which the principal provincial workers, then in Karachi, were present, to discuss the question of Hindu-Muslim unity in Sind. The chief result of this meeting was to demonstrate the absolute lack of unity both among the Hindu and among the Muslim workers and their mutual jealousies. The principal bone of contention at the Subjects Committee meeting at Mirpurkhas had been the subject of the wording of the resolution dealing with the Moplah rebellion in Malabar. The Hindus wished to insert a paragraph condemning the excesses of the Moplahs. This the Mahomedans refused to admit. Kazi Khuda Bakhsh of More and Abdul Jabbar ex-pleader of Hyderabad led the Mahomedans, urging that some of the Moplahs [...?] had taken refuge in a mosque others had refused to surrender them and Government had besieged the mosque and that the Moplahs had become infuriated because they considered that by this act Government had interfered in their religion. Mrs. Naidu, Jairamdas Daulatram, and Dr. Choithram of Hyderabad tried to placate the Muslims and effect a compromise but without success. At the Karachi meeting Jamnalal Bajaj advised the Muslims to accept the condemnation of the Moplah excesses as a matter of policy in order to maintain Hindu-Muslim Unity rather than to maintain their attitude on religious grounds. No settlement however was effected at this meeting nor has any news been received of any success in this direction before these leaders left Sind.

Generally speaking there are various signs of slackness in the non-co-operation movement in Sind at present. Activity in any given direction is not sustained. Just as the movement for the boycott of schools completely ceased soon after its inception, so the movement to register members of the various committees has been almost entirely dropped, the collection of funds proceeds but is badly organised and a large part may reasonably be supposed to find its way into the pockets of the collectors instead of being contributed to the general funds. In this connection it is worth noting that from information received here it appears that Mrs. Mahomed Ali appropriates all or nearly all the funds which she collects to her own use. The Swadeshi movement had made not real progress. Uptil about the middle of September the demand for Khadar exceeded the supply. Since then the supply has exceeded the demand and progress in organising production has been negligible.

Talk about the declaration of a republic in Ahmedabad about December is now fairly general in extremist circles but the debate on a draft resolution in the Subjects Committee at the Mirpurkhas Conference throws an interesting light on this. Maulvi Mukham Din of Jamesabad proposed a draft resolution in the following terms: 'If the Khilafat and Punjab wrongs are not redressed and Swaraj is not attained by the end of December a republic should be declared at the Ahmedabad Congress.' He spoke at some length in favour of this resolution but Pandit Amarsen remarked that a declaration of a republic and non-violent non-co-operation were incompatible. A kingdom within a Kingdom would mean war. When the flag of Swaraj was hoisted, who, he asked, would protect it. He suggested that aeroplanes would destroy Congress building and its inmates without any difficulty. Mukham Din replied that if they did not declare a republic the whole movement would fail and the people would desert them. To this the Pandit replied that if they could [not] protect the Swaraj flag the people would desert them. Thereupon Mrs. Naidu asked whether she should put the matter to the vote or whether Mukham Din would withdraw his resolution and he withdrew it.

During this week no reports have been received of the resignation of any police officers in response to the Ulema Fatwas.

While Jamnalal Bajaj was in Karachi he was present at a meeting of the Merchants Association called for the purpose of hearing his advice on the subject of boycott. The meeting was arranged for 12.30

on the 29th October, by 1 p.m. no merchant had appeared. Jamnalal and Mrs. Naidu were noticed in the precincts of the Sessions Court where the trial of the Ali Brothers was proceeding wearing a worried air. Jamnalal suggested that motors should be sent to the leading merchants to bring them to the place of the meeting. By about 2 p.m. about 200 cloth merchants assembled. The result of the meeting appears to have been that about sixty Marwari and Shikarpuri merchants pledged themselves to place no further orders until December and then to examine the result of the movement.

1. AGITATION

While speech making was dropped in Karachi during the trial reports from other districts show that virulent and objectionable speeches continued to be made.

2. ORGANISATION

Vide para General above.

3. FUNDS

Vide para General above.

4. SCHOOLS AND COLLEGES

No developments.

5. INDIAN NATIONAL SERVICE AND VOLUNTEERS

No developments.

6. LAWYERS AND COURTS

The number of cases dealt with by the Arbitration Court at Sukkur is 296. It is reported that the court is likely to be discontinued.

Dr. Tarachand Shahani continues to conduct the arbitration court at Keamari (Karachi Harbour) where he is consolidating his influence by this means among the dock labourers. According to one report he is in close touch with Kanti Parkash, Secretary of the North Western Railway Union.

7. AGRARIAN

No developments.

8. LABOUR INCLUDING RAILWAYS.

Vide para 6 as mentioned above. Dr. Tarachand Shahani and Kanti Parkash Secretary of the North Western Railway Union are reported to be acting together. It is suggested that they may attempt concerted action in effecting a simultaneous strike of dock labourers and on the railway, but there is nothing to show that they have secured any definite results and there is a long way between intention and execution in such a matter.

9. to 13. No developments.

14. HOW FAR MUSSALMANS AS A SEPARATE CLASS ARE ADOPTING THE NON-CO-OPERATION MOVEMENT

Khilafat Affairs. A meeting of the Working Committee of the Sind Provincial Khilafat Committee was held in the Khilafat office on the 30th October and the following persons were present: 1. Mahomedkhan Ghassikhan 2. Maulvi Mukham Din Allahbux 3. Haji Abdullah Haroon 4. Sayed Abdullah Shah of Tikhar 5. Abdul Jabbar Mahomed Yakub 6. Maulvi Abdul Khalik Morai 7. Pir Mahomed Umar of Matiar [!] 8. Fazal Muhammad Naushahrai 9. Kazi Khudabaksh 10. Shahbudin Aminuddin and a few others. It was decided that:

(1) A Khilafat paper should be started; Kazi Abdul Rahman, Editor of the *Al Wahid* who was convicted for articles which appeared in that paper last year is expected to be released in December and it was decided to appoint him Editor of the new paper.

(2) Maintenance allowance should be regularly paid to the dependants of workers who go to jail: Rs. 40/- was sanctioned in the case of the daughter of Sheikh Abdul Majid (Aminuddin N. Munshi was censured for troubling Sheikh Abdul Majid's family and for not paying them regularly). Rs. 50/- was sanctioned for the family of Maulvi Fatehali of Sujawal; similarly various amounts were sanctioned for other cases and the secretary and treasurer were authorised to disburse these amounts monthly without further sanction.

(3) Maulvis should be appointed for propaganda (Haji Abdullah Haroon however pointed out that the Khilafat Committee could not pay more to Maulvis than they paid to the Aligarh students and that no Maulvi would work for such meagre pay. The question was accordingly postponed apparently because the Committee was not prepared to sanction expenditure on a large scale.)

[30] Rest of the page illegible, page 133 of the original is missing.

(4) A separate Khilafat Committee for Karachi town should be appointed with Subject Committees for each ward and a Panchayat of 50 members. The Khilafat Committee is also to the organised for the Karachi district.

The same day a meeting was held to establish a separate Khilafat Committee for Karachi the following persons were present.[30]

Weekly Bulletin the Non-co-operation Movement for the week ending 5th November 1921

GENERAL

The conviction of the Ali Brothers and the other co-accused was received very quietly in Sind, particularly in Karachi. Since the day of conviction there has been a considerable amount of talk in Khilafat circles in Karachi to the effect that Government is likely to effect a compromise over the Khilafat question and that there will be a cessation of agitation in India within two months.

Further enquiries have been made regarding the information concerning Pir Imamshah son of Pir Jhandewalla and Pir Mahbubshah without any definite result. Pir Imamshah has however made it his business to approach an Inspector in the Sind C.I.D., apparently in order to give certain information concerning the Khilafat movement and his own and Pir Mahbubshah's connection with it. His information is of a vague nature and it is therefore probable that his real object is to endeavour to find out what information the C.I.D. possess concerning them. He has referred to a conspiracy to murder Europeans and says that it is not intended to attack Indian Police Officers. It seems probable that he has some information of events connected with the 'Court Kazi Bomb Case' in the Punjab, and that emissaries connected with that conspiracy have been in touch with certain people in Sind.

Slackness in the Non-co-operation movement continues in Karachi but agitation continues to be general and virulent. It is reported that respectable Mahomedans are being to some extent terrorised and are afraid to appear in public through fear of insult in Sukkur. The conditions also appear to be similar in Hyderabad where respectable Mahomedans are somewhat diffident about assisting the Police especially in any matter connected with 'politics'.

One Head Constable of the Karachi City Police is reported to have resigned in connection with the Fatwa of the Ulema but he did not give that as a reason when submitting his resignation. It is reported that he is being financed by Haji Abdulla Haroon to the extent of Rs. 40/- per month and it is reported this individual proposes to pay other policemen who resign on a similar scale.[31]

Only about three or four Mahomedans of the village attended the funeral, all the others kept away although they were told of the death and funeral.

14. HOW FAR MUSSALMANS AS A SEPARATE CLASS ARE ADOPTING THE NON-CO-OPERATION MOVEMENT

Khilafat Affairs. A reprint of the Sharai [!] Fatwa of the Ulema has been circulated in Karachi which bears the name of no press but purports to be circulated by the members of the Khilafat Working Committee, Delhi, and other copies are reported to be in circulation in Karachi, Hyderabad and Sukkur.[32]

Weekly Bulletin on the Non-co-operation Movement for the week ending 12th November 1921

GENERAL

There have been no further developments in connection with the aftermath of the Ali Brothers case except that it is reported in Karachi that a family of Sayads of only local importance and of no real standing are inciting Mekranees of the lowest classes to proceed to the Karachi Jail on Friday the 18th November 'to release the Ali Brothers or to enter the jail themselves.' This report gained currency after Friday prayers on the 11th. Further enquiries concerning the

[31] Page 135 of the original is missing.

[32] Copies forwarded to the Director, Intelligence Bureau, Delhi; the Commissioner in Sindh; the Deputy Inspector General of Police, C.I.D., Poona; the General Staff Officer, Sindh Rajputana District; all the Superintendents of Police in Sindh.

alleged conspiracy of Pir Imamshah and Pir Mahbubshah have not led to any definite result.

The Non-co-operation movement continues to loose momentum, and in spite of Gandhi's intention to start Civil Disobedience at an early date, which became known in Sind at the end of the week, no excitement is evident. On the contrary Congress Committee meetings are very dull affairs and in one case the Provincial Committee failed to meet for lack of a quorum. In Hyderabad it is particularly noticeable that Mahomedans take little or no part in Congress meetings.

On the other hand the Khilafat movement is becoming more intense and more general. While the trial of the Ali Brothers among other things caused the idea to crystallise that the Ali Brothers were endeavouring to give a political agitation a cloak of religion, general feeling in sympathy with the religious view of the Khilafat question is very widespread. It is not confined to those who have joined the ranks of agitators but is growing in intensity among all classes of educated Mahomedans in Sind. Moderate opinion among the educated classes in Sind is chiefly centred in Hyderabad and Karachi. In these circles 'repressive' action taken against the minor agitators in cases where there has been no incitement to violence is viewed with great dislike; the results of Gandhi's Civil Disobedience and of the possible reply of Government are viewed with serious apprehension; and the danger of the spread of fanaticism among Mahomedans is also regarded as real. The general feeling among Mahomedans is reflected in increased activity to collect money for the Angora Relief Fund.

1. AGITATION

Agitation continues to be virulent.

2. ORGANISATION

The elections of delegates to attend the All-India National Congress has been held in Hyderabad, Sukkur and other places. Generally speaking results are to [...][33] places. Generally speaking results are to send a very disproportionate number of Hindus. In Hyderabad the eldest son of the Pir Jhandewalla and Pir

[33] Rest of the line illegible.

Mahbubshah are among the candidates. On the whole the proportion is one Mahomedan to about 8 Hindus.

3. FUNDS

The Karachi District Congress Committee has published the following statement of accounts for the period ending the 8th September:

Receipts

To Mahatma Gandhi Fund Account		
Donations announced	Rs. 25183- 4- 0	
Less Arrears	Rs. 1726- 0- 0	
Net received in cash	Rs. 23457- 4- 0	
Collections during the visit of Mahatma	Rs. 6716-14- 4	Rs. 30174- 2- 4
To Tilak Swaraj Fund		
Donations	Rs. 6877-13-16	
General Collections	Rs. 3255-12-18	
Collections by ladies	Rs 2228-13-10	
Sale of tickets	Rs. 7575-13-10	Rs. 19938- 5- 0
To Membership subscriptions		Rs. 1667- 9- 0
To interest earned		Rs. 154- 9- 0
	Total	Rs. 51934- 8- 4

Payments

By	Deficiency Old Account (Mr. Lalchand Jagtiani)	Rs. 255-19-0
"	Remittances to Mahatmaji	Rs. 25500-10-0
"	Reception to Mahatmaji Expenses	Rs. 155-18-3
"	Temperance Account	Rs. 1250-10-0
"	Swadeshi Account	Rs. 2622-10-8
"	Tilak Swaraj Fund Account Expenses	Rs. 292-19-0
"	Postage and Telegrams	Rs. 34-18-0
"	Stationary and Printing	Rs. 799-19-0
"	Establishment	Rs. 244-19-9
"	General Garri Hire	Rs. 35-14-0
"	Travelling Expenses	Rs. 20-10-0
"	Lights, Hire of Hall, Tarpaulins etc.	Rs. 77-10-0

[By] Miscellaneous Expenses	Rs.	19-15-3
	Rs.	31306-13-2
Balance Cash (With New Treasurer)	Rs.	20620-12-2
Balance Cash (Naraindas Anandji Bechar)	Rs.	5-15-0
Total	Rs.	51935- 8- 4

Certified Correct
Sgd M.B. Dalal. Hon. Auditor

Note: It is not clear what is meant by saying that Rs. 25500 have been remitted to Gandhi instead of the percentage laid down to be remitted to the All-India Congress Committee and the Provincial Committee. This is being enquired into further.

4. SCHOOLS AND COLLEGE

No developments.

5. NATIONAL SERVICE AND VOLUNTEERS

It is reported that the organisation of the Sind Students National Service is being amalgamated with that of the Aligarh students.

6. to 15. No developments.

Weekly Bulletin on the Non-co-operation Movement for the week ending 19th November 1921

GENERAL

(a) *Congress Affairs.* The Non-co-operation movement continued to show signs of slackness. It was remarkable how little excitement was aroused by Gandhi's announced intention to start Civil Disobedience. A C.I.D. officer who visited the Hyderabad Congress Committee Office on the 4th November noticed that no Mahomedans appeared to take any part in the work in the office, but that about a dozen Hindu Amils were busy sorting the votes for the delegates to the Ahmedabad Congress. Dr. Choithram, President of the Provincial Congress Committee remarked that 'it was necessary to include the names of five clod-hoppers (Sindhi, Jats) among the twelve delegates from Hyderabad so that the Mahomedans should at least nominally take part in the proceedings.'

Reports indicate that it was the intention of the Provincial and Congress Committees in Sind that Civil Disobedience should not be adopted in Sind until the issue of Gandhi's experiment in Gujerat had made the position clear. On the receipt of the news of the rioting in Bombay and of Gandhi's postponement of Civil Disobedience the general opinion among agitators was that the whole of the Congress programme has been spoiled. This opinion was voiced at a private and informal meeting of workers in Karachi on the 19th evening. The only dissenting voice was that of Mahomed Khan Ghassi Khan whose remarks left the impression that he considers mob violence an essential part of the programme, and that he thinks that Gandhi ought to be persuaded to adopt the same view.

After the return of the Sind members from the All-India Congress Committee meeting at Delhi information was received from various sources to the effect that there was considerable opposition in the Congress Camp to Gandhi's programme. It is said that the Madras and Maharashtra and the Bengal parties are almost solidly in favour of reverting to constitutional methods as the best means of attacking Government, and that many leaders from other parts of India also agreed in this view. It is said that Gandhi's programme would be watched by all these politicians till the end of the current year and that after that they would adopt an entirely different method of working. No one in Sind however appears to have any definite idea of what the future programme is to be. There is considerable talk of the probability of an outbreak of mob violence or of acts of fanaticism, but there is nothing to indicate that any one of the Sind Congress workers is definitely in favour of violence as part of the programme unless it be Mahomed Khan Ghassi Khan who strictly speaking belongs to the Khilafat party.

(b) *Khilafat Affairs.* The feeling concerning the Khilafat question continues to be very strong. As reported last week this feeling is reflected in increased activity to collect subscriptions for the Angora Relief Fund. The most noticeable incident in this connection occurred on the night of the 9th November in Karachi where the Marwari (Mahomedan) Silawat community collected Rs. 8,000/-, an Honorary Magistrate being one of the largest donors. It is also reported that a decision was at the same time made to send Zakat to Angora instead of distributing it in charity in India. It is also reported that many Mahomedan Government servants sympathise strongly with the objects of the Angora and Smyrna Relief Funds.

Reference was made last week to a report that a certain family of Sayeds was inciting Mekranees in Karachi to proceed to the Karachi Jail on the 18th November and 'release the Ali Brothers or to enter jail themselves.' Enquiries indicate that a young member of the family took part in inciting the people for this purpose. He is habitually under the influence of intoxicating drugs. On the 15th November, one of his followers, a Pathan, took part in assaulting another Pathan. It is alleged by the prosecution that he was assaulted for refusing to join the Khilafat volunteers, and that the assault was abetted by another member of the Sayed's family. Counter allegations have been made to the effect that the quarrel was due to a long standing dispute and that the reference to the Khilafat was an invention. The case is sub judice. The effect of this case and other enquiries by the Karachi Police concerning the Sayeds was to prevent any further action being taken and Friday passed off without incident.

On his return from the Delhi meeting of the Khilafat Conference, Mahomed Khan Ghassi Khan, Secretary of the Provincial Khilafat Committee, initiated three new moves, (1) to form a Khilafat Panchayat of fifty members, (2) to form a working committee of twenty members, and (3) to appoint a Sub-Committee for the purpose of raising Volunteers. This Sub-Committee includes the name of Anwarshah, the person referred to above as having incited Mekranees to proceed to the Jail. Mahomed Khan was also present at a meeting held in the Mekranee Quarter for the purpose of enlisting volunteers.

2. AGITATION

(a) and (b) Agitation continues to be virulent, Khilafat questions and Swadeshi being the principal themes.

3. ORGANISATION

(a) The election of delegates to the Ahmedabad Congress has taken place but the results have not yet been announced. There is a great preponderance of Hindu candidates in spite of the fact that the population of the province consists of three Mahomedans to every Hindu.

(b) As mentioned in para GENERAL above the organisation of the Provincial Committee is being revised. Organisation of district and other local committees is generally speaking poor and many are reported to be inactive. Full details have not yet been received in this office.

4. FUNDS

(a) With reference to the amount of Rs. 25,000 mentioned under this heading last week, as having been given to Gandhi, the explanation is that a purse of this amount was given to Gandhi when he visited Sind, by the Karachi District Committee. This amount with similar purses received from other districts in Sind amounting to Rs. 41,000 in all was returned by Gandhi to the Sind Provincial Congress Committee. The Provincial Committee has retained the amount pending the settlement of the dispute with the district Committees as to whether the Provincial Committee should deduct the ten per cent allotted to it. The District Committee urges that this should not be done on the ground that its financial position is weak.

(b) No further details are available concerning the funds of the Provincial Khilafat Committee since this office report of the 16th August, published in the Bombay Secret Abstract, para 764 (1) of 1921. According to accounts then obtained Rs. 30,000 had been remitted to the Central Khilafat Committee, Rs. 20,000 to the Smyrna Relief Fund, Rs. 16,000 had been spent locally and there was a balance of Rs. 24,000 in hand on the 31st July 1921. Information from a reliable source is to the effect that these accounts were 'cooked' for the benefit of the auditor from the Central Khilafat Committee and that subsequently the accounts have not been properly or accurately kept.

5. SCHOOLS AND COLLEGES

No developments.

6. NATIONAL SERVICE AND VOLUNTEERS

(a) No developments.

(b) An attempt is being made in Karachi to enlist Mekranees and others in the Khilafat Volunteer Corps. Mahomed Khan, the secretary who is the moving spirit in the matter, is said to be urging the enlistment of at least a thousand men, but so far apparently only fifty names have been registered.

7. LAWYERS AND COURTS

(a) The Sukkur Court has now taken up 304 cases of which 184 are said to have been decided and the remaining 120 to be pending as the parties evade attendance.

8. to 11. No developments.

12. LABOUR INCLUDING RAILWAYS

There have been strong rumours during the week that a strike was to be anticipated on the North Western Railway at an early date, and at a meeting called by the Union on Sunday the 20th instant, where the attendance was five or six hundred out of nearly 2,500 employees in Karachi, a vote in favour of a strike was passed. Information received by this department is to the effect that this move is largely bluff as far as the Union officials are concerned and that provided that some of their many demands are met not strike is likely to take place.

13. to 15. No developments.[34]

Weekly Bulletin on the Non-co-operation Movement for the week ending 26th November 1921

GENERAL

(a) *Congress Affairs.* The absence of any great interest in Congress Affairs continues in spite of the elections of members of the Sind Provincial Congress Committee who are also delegates to the Ahmedabad Congress. The final results is to return 45 Hindus and 24 Mahomedans. (The members of the Sind Provincial Congress Committee are, according to a resolution passed at the last Mirpurkhas. Conference, also delegates to Ahmedabad.) The use of Khadi is steadily diminishing in Karachi and Hyderabad.

[34] Note [by Curry]: (a) refers to Congress, (b) to Khilafat matters under each subhead. Copies forwarded as in footnote 32.

(b) *Khilafat Affairs*. The Non-co-operation movement is compounded of three separate movements, viz. the movement among the educated classes in favour of a change in the present system of Government, the Mahomedan movement to restore and maintain the position of Islam and an underlying current of racial hatred, present to some extent in many communities and in many individuals. All three are reflected very strongly in the present agitation in Sind which is becoming more intense and more virulent especially in its presentment [!] of the religious and racial issues. The Non-co-operation leaders have labelled these three movements with convenient tickets, Swaraj, the Khilafat and the Punjab wrongs. The first or political demand admits of compromise, the second admits of none. The racial under current generally remains below the surface. To this cause of disorder there are many palliatives in everyday life.

These introductory remarks are made to explain the conclusion to which observation of the progress of the Non-co-operation movement in Sind forces us. It is that the driving force behind the whole movement is Mahomedan religious feeling. This religious feeling has recently found an outlet in subscribing to the Angora Fund, a fund the objects of which more than any others seem to meet the common feelings. Rs. 20,000/- were collected in Karachi alone within a month, as compared with Rs. 20,000 for Smyrna Relief and Rs. 30,000 for Khilafat Agitation from the whole of Sind during a year or more. The idea of helping the Angora Government which is regarded as the champion of Islam appeals to many people of various communities who have taken no part in the agitation for Swaraj and have previously evinced no sign of anti-Government or anti-British feeling. The Khilafat propagandists, Pirs, Mouvlies [!] and others are spreading the infection of religious enthusiasm among many classes of the inhabitants of Sind who have hitherto taken their religion comparatively quietly. In the hands of many of these propagandists the underlying ideas which appeal to the more thoughtful are distorted by falsehoods concerning the Holy Places so as to make them more strikingly anti-British. Among the more thoughtful people the British Government are regarded as being responsible for the humiliation of Islam and as having broken their promise concerning the Holy Places. Such are the professed views of many who wish to remain loyal to the present Government.

Similar views were expressed this week by Haji Abdullah Haroon one of the chief Khilafat leaders in Sind and a member of the Central Khilafat Committee, Bombay. He also said that he had no real belief in the Non-co-operation movement. It had been useful as an expedient and had helped to prevent outbreaks of violent fanaticism which would have occurred but for the leaders' insistence on the non-violent programme. He stated that many people in Karachi had urged him to break away from that programme, but that he had always advised patience. Whether Gandhi's Non-co-operation movement succeeded (which he did not consider possible) or failed it would be equally useless in the long run. If it succeeded it would mean disaster similar to the Russian catastrophe. Personally, as a merchant, he desired peace and facilities for trade, but everything else gave way to religious con-siderations. Many were ready for martyrdom.

Information received by this department from other sources confirms his view that a desperate state of mind is developing among Mahomedans and that there is increased talk of becoming martyrs (shahid).

On the other hand the news of the Afghan Treaty which has come as a great surprise to the Pan-Islamists in Sind is likely to prove a strong deterrent to their movement. The Shia community which is a comparatively small one among the Mahomedans of Sind is also showing signs in some cases of sympathising with the sentiment concerning the Angora Government in spite of their different religious standpoint as regards the Khilafat.

2. AGITATION

(a) and (b) Agitation continues to be virulent. Khilafat questions and Swadeshi being the principal themes. There have also been several very objectionable passages of a racial nature in recent speeches.

3. ORGANISATION

(a) Results of the elections of delegates to the All-India National Congress (and of members of the Sind Provincial Congress Committee for the year 1922) are as follows:-

Karachi District: (1) Mahomedkhan Ghassikhan (2) Manilal Y. Vyas (3) Lalchand A. Jagtiani (4) Naraindas A. Bechar (5) Saraswati Devi w/o Motiram (6) Dr. A.H. Ahmad (7) Seth Haji Abdulla Haroon (8) Seth Sunderdas Valabdas (9) Narsinglal Dhamanlal (10) Kazi Abdul Rahman wd Mahomed Sidik (now in jail) (11) Dr. Haji Ghulam Hussain Kassim.

Hyderabad District: (1) Jairamdas Daulatram (2) Choithram Partabrai Gidwani (3) Ghanshamdas J. Shivdasani (4) Dr. Chimanlal Isardas (5) Jhamatmal Lakhasing (Jagtiani) (6) Fateh Chand Bijasing (7) Ziauddin Shah wd Rashidullah Shah of Pir Jhandewalla (8) Pir Mahbubshah of Bakar Nizamani (9) Kazi Asadullah Shah of Tikhar (10) Aminuddin N. Munshi (11) Abdul Jabbar Mahomed Yakub (12) Lokram Nainaram Sharma.

Larkana District: (1) Rijhumal Kundansing (2) Ramchand B. Motwani (3) Sukhramdas Towermalani (4) Partabrai Visomal (5) Metharam Isardas (6) Pribhdas Sakhawatrai (7) Mr. Shankarlal (8) Pandit Udhebhan (9) Mrs. Sarsoti Devi Tahil Ramani (10) Pir Ali-Anwarshah (11) Pir Mithal Shah of Thula Sharif (12) Pir Illahibux of Aligarh National University (Student) (13) Pir Nudinshah.

Nawabshah District: (1) Hakeem Mahomed Maaz (2) Kazi Khuda Bakhsh (3) Moulvi Abdul Khalik (4) Seth Bhojraj s/o Sachanand.

Sahaiti District: (1) Kessumal Tejumal (2) Manohardas Kauromal (3) Parsram Naraindas (4) Mansing Chooharmal (5) Moulvi Fazal Mahomed.

Shikarpur District: (1) Seth Naraindas Thakurdas Utradi (2) Pherwani (Lilaram) (3) Maulvi Abdul Karim (Chisti) (4) Sobhraj Valecha.

Sukkur District: (1) Virumal Begraj (2) Mulchand Pessumal (3) Bhojraj Motomal (4) Vehromal Vaparimal (5) Jashanmal Ramchand (6) Mahbubalishah wd Sardaralishah.

Jacobabad District: (1) Dr. Menghraj Chainrai (2) Ramchand Bansiram (3) Kodumal Hiromal (4) Newandram Tirathmal (5) Pandit Amarsen (now dead).

Thar Parkar District: (1) Pir Mahomedali Jan Sarhandi (2) Kanwar Vinjhraj (3) Mir Allah Bux Talpur (4) Maulvi Fateh Mahomed (5) Maulvi Mokhamdin (6) Dhalumal Kishenchand (7) Motiram Wadhumal (8) Nichaldas Mehrsing (9) Vatanmal Gulabsing.

Note: There are apparently three vacancies in the Upper Sind Frontier District. Two of the elected candidates are Hindu Ladies.

(b) The Khilafat Organisation had recently been improved in the Hyderabad District. There is a City Khilafat Committee with the following office bearers:

President	Abdul Jabbar
Vice-President	Aminuddin N. Munshi
Secretary	Sheikh Abdullah
Treasurer	Shahab ud Din
Muhasib (Examiner)	Haji Ahmed Patoli

There are fifty members of the Managing Committee.

There are twelve members of the Karobari Committee (Working Committee) as under:

(1) Sheikh Abdullah (2) Abdul Jabbar (3) Aminuddin N. Munshi (4) Asadullah Shah (5) Abdul Latif Memon. Names of others are not yet available.

The membership is about 2,384.

There is also a District Khilafat Committee of which the President is Asadullah Shah and the Vice-President Agha Umar Jan Sarhandi. Village Khilafat Committees are reported to exist in twenty five villages and small towns in the Hyderabad District.

14. FUNDS

(a) The Sind Provincial Congress Committee has sent Rs. 2250 to the Kerala Provincial Congress Committee as a first instalment of Sind's contribution to relief in Malabar.

(b) Haji Abdulla Haroon states that Rs. 20,000 has been collected in Karachi for the Angora Fund. It is reported that the Hyderabad Khilafat Committee has forwarded Rs. 1000/- to the Bombay Central Committee for the Angora Fund.

The Sind Provincial Khilafat Committee publishes its accounts for October in the *New Times* of the 26th November. Total receipts are given as Rs. 1347/-, total expenditure as Rs. 1678/-.

15. SCHOOLS AND COLLEGES

Lalchand A. Jagtiani is experiencing great difficulty in keeping the Tilakalya in existence for lack of sufficient funds. He is endeavouring to get money from the Congress Funds apparently without success.

16. INDIAN NATIONAL SERVICE AND VOLUNTEERS

(a) and (b) There is no body of volunteers organised for military purposes in Sind and neither the Congress nor the Khilafat volunteers have received any drill or any other form of military training.

17. LAWYERS AND COURTS

Nil.

18. SWADESHI MOVEMENT

The Swadeshi movement is generally speaking losing ground in Karachi and Hyderabad but it is reported to be more successful in Upper Sind.

19. BOYCOTT OF EUROPEANS BY THEIR SERVANTS

Nil.

10. GOVERNMENT SERVICES

There have been a few isolated cases of lower subordinates such as tapedars and police constables resigning and giving religious grounds as the reason.

11 to 14. No developments.

15. MISCELLANEOUS

The Ulema Movement. A meeting of the Sind Ulema was held at Matiari on the 14th November. The attendance which was very small included the following:- (1) Maulvi Taj Mahomed of Nasarpur (2) Pir Nur Shah s/o Pir Jhandewalla (3) Pir Imam Din Shah, s/o Pir Jhandewalla (4) Asad Ullah Shah of Takhur (5) Pir Umar Jan Sarhandi (6) Khalifa Mahomed of Hala (7) Abdul Jabbar. We have not been able to obtain details of what was done at this meeting. The chief subjects of discussion was the collection of money for the Angora Fund. No important decision was arrived at. Pir Umar Jan was elected Secretary of the Jamiat-ul-Ulema in Sind in place of Pir Ghulam Mujadid Sarhandi.[35]

[35] Copies forwarded as in footnote 32.

Weekly Bulletin on the Non-co-operation Movement for the week ending 3rd December 1921

GENERAL

(a) *Congress Affairs.* The absence of activity among the Congress Committees in Sind continues. There is general expectation that a new programme will be evolved at Ahmedabad at Christmas. It is understood that the question of Civil Disobedience has been postponed until after the Ahmedabad Congress and there is little or no talk about it in Congress circles in Sind.

The following extracts from the *Sind Observer* dated the 30th November 1921, are of interest. In connection with the Ali Brothers case the paper says

> 'by the withdrawal of the two undefended cases against the two Maulanas Government have showed clearly that they were animated by no spirit of repression or persecution even towards men who had abused them right roundly, but were content with the barest vindication of the laws in accordance with the findings of the jury in the first case.'

In connection with the general question of the Non-co-operation programme it says

> 'India is going to get Swaraj and get it soon, unless the activities of the Mahatma and his colleagues put the hands of the clock back by many years. These activities are rushing India to the edge of a precipice from the bottom of which it will take her many years to climb up again. Every sane Indian begs of the Mahatma and asks of himself "Whither are you going?" and with all the emphasis at his command he appeals to him and to every one in India of whatever race or creed to practice and preach the doctrine of courtesy and good will in the place of that of hate, to throw his influence into steadying the country and into restoring peace and plenty and to reopen the markets at least for foreign goods already in the country and by constitutional agitation to work for the due realisation of Swaraj.
>
> I appeal to Government servants of every class to avoid even a suspicion of repression in any of their acts and to the Government itself to do its utmost to meet at an early date the wishes of its Mahomedan subjects regarding the Khilafat question and sympathetically support the aspirations of all its subjects towards Swaraj.[']

(b) *Khilafat Affairs.* Apart from collections for the Angora Fund which are being vigorously pushed, there has been little activity in Khilafat circles during the week.

2. AGITATION

(a) and (b) Agitation continues to be virulent but there has been some decrease this week.

3. ORGANISATION

(a) An ordinary general meeting of the Sind Provincial Congress Committee was held at Larkana on the 2nd of December. The following office bearers were elected:

Dr. Choithram—President

Mr. Veeromal Begraj and Mai Saraswati Devi—Vice-Presidents

Mr. Jeramdas and Kazi Abdul Rahman—Secretaries

Mr. Naraindas A. Bechar—Treasurer

Mr. Dalal—Auditor.

In addition to the above the following were elected members of the Council: Messrs. Ram B. Motwani, Kazi Khuda Bakhsh, Lilaram, Watanmal Ramchand, Ellahi Bakhsh Shah, Moulvi Abdul Karim, Abdul Jabbar, Lalchand A. Jagtiani, Hasanand Pamnani, Bhejsing Ajwani, Gansham Jethanand, Chimandas and Nichaldas.

The following were elected as representatives of Sind on the All-India Congress Committee: Messrs. Choithram, Jeramdas, Abdul Jabbar, Mahomed Khan, Naraindas Bechar, Lalchand, Kazi Abdur Rahman, Kazi Khuda Bakhsh, and Professor Ghanshyam.

It will be notified that the Hyderabadi Amils have secured more than their share of influence in the Council and the Provincial Committee where they have seven representatives including the President and one of the secretaries, while there are only five Mahomedans. Similarly among the representatives of the All-India Congress Committee there are four Amils of Hyderabad, four Mahomedans and no Hindu from any other part of Sind.

Complaints about the elections of members to the Provincial Committee and to the District Committees are general and there is a great deal of internal jealousy. A letter has been received recently in the Congress office at Karachi, where jealousies and rivalries are particularly acute, in which the writer states that the Congress Committees compose a more satanic bureaucracy then the bureaucracy of the Government. This phrase has passed round among Non-co-operators in Karachi and is said to be recognised as having hit the nail on the head. The work of the Committee in Karachi has got into the hands of Manilal Vyas and Mahomed Khan Ghassi Khan, a fact which is very displeasing to the Hyderabad element.

(b) Reports indicate that fresh Khilafat Committees are being formed in a number of places especially in the Hyderabad district.

4. FUNDS

(a) Nil.

(b) The figures concerning the Angora Fund are not available but collections are being made in many places. The butcher community of Karachi collected Rs. 4,000 for the Angora Fund since last week. Abdul Jabbar has visited Dadu where he has distributed Angora Fund receipts among the Moulvies for sale. He is reported to have disposed of Rs. 1,000 worth of receipts in Dadu and other considerable amounts in other places which he has visited.

5. SCHOOLS AND COLLEGES

Lalchand Jagtiani has obtained the sanction of the Provincial Committee to a loan of Rs. 2,000 for the support of the Tilakalya in Karachi and the Karachi District Congress Committee has been instructed to find the funds.

6. and 7. Nil.

8. SWADESHI MOVEMENT

The Swadeshi movement is recognised by the Karachi Chamber of Commerce to be one of the causes, with exchange difficulties and general trade depression, of the decrease in the import of foreign cloth. The *Sind Observer* writing on this subject says:

> 'We have only to look around to see that the boycott of foreign goods has practically ruined the commercial community. There is hardly a merchant in this city who has not suffered heavily from it. Many have been ruined by the boycott, coming as it did on top of the heavy fall in exchange. If protection is needed for our Indian industries, the Indian members of the Fiscal Commission new amongst us will doubtless recommend it, so that, by a protective tariff, we may make foreign goods pay us to enter the country and not ruin those who imported these goods long before the boycott was thought of and are now deprived by it of any market for their goods, in which they have in many cases invested all their capital.'

While the paper appears to exaggerate the effect of the Swadeshi movement as apart from the other larger causes, it is correct that the Indian mercantile community appear to regard the Swadeshi movement as largely responsible for the present state of affairs.

19. Nil.

10. GOVERNMENT SERVICES

Cases of resignation continue but are very limited in number. No case of resignation among the police has been reported during the week.

Reference has been made in this bulletin from time to time to discontent among the police concerning their pay. The difficulties arising out of the high cost of living and the insufficiency of the pay of the constabulary and of the clerical establishment under the circumstances are particularly acute in Karachi where the cost of living is exceptionally high. The unrest here has come to a head during this week and both the clerical establishment and the constabulary threaten to strike unless their difficulties are met by some increase immediately. The constabulary and clerks appear to believe that they have no chance of obtaining any redress unless they take drastic action of this nature. Enquiries made by both the C.I.D. and by the officers of the Karachi District Police both indicate that the discontent is essentially economic and is not directly due to political unrest. Political agitation outside the Police Force has however affected the men in various ways and they command much less respect than formerly and are even subject to public insult on occasions. The agitators in Karachi are not unaware of this movement among the police and have been reported to have evinced some disposition in a few individual cases to encourage the idea of striking for more pay, their object being to increase the embarrassment of Government by helping to increase the cost of the police establishment. The fact that the organisations of the Congress and the Khilafat are not in a position to take advantage of the very general and deep feeling of discontent among the police which is partly to be attributed to the fact that they would not be able to finance any large movement among members of the force, is an indication of the real weakness of these organisations. They are not in a position to act when a very great opportunity to embarrass the local authorities had occurred.

11. Nil.

12. LABOUR INCLUDING RAILWAYS

Vide Weekly Bulletin for the week ending 19th of November. The meeting reported as having taken place on the 20th of November appears to have been organised by the officials of the Union without the consent of the Central Delegates Committee. In this connection it is learnt that a meeting of the Central Delegates Committee is to be held at Lahore on the 9th, 10th and 11th December. On the agenda are:-

1. Unconstitutional attitude of four servants of the Union, namely: Mr. Miller, Mr. M.A. Khan, Mr. Mehraj-ud-Din and Mr. Siraj-ud-Din.
2. To get the opinion of the members of the C.D.C. over the question of direct action, if the Agent fails to redress our grievances specified by the Executive Committee and circulated to the District and Sub-Committees.
3. To consider the question of period of the services of the staff employed in the Association to be treated as continuous as regards privileges of leave etc.
4. To decide the question of Union Workers' rights if they can attend public meetings and take active part in it, while off duty and off from Union platform. To treat Union employees as the workers and elements of the Union and their right to vote in the Executive and District Committees.
5. Miscellaneous.

There are no signs of any direct connection between the officials of the N.W. Railway Union and the N.C.O. party, but it appears that men like Kanti Parkash, the local secretary, are anxious to be allowed to take part in political movements outside their sphere of activities as Union servants.

13. and 14. Nil.

15. THE ULEMA MOVEMENT

Maulana Murtaza Hussain of Deoband has written to Maulvi

Mahomed Siddik of the Khada to say that it was incumbent on the Sind Ulema to attend the meeting of the Jamiat-ul Ulema Hind to be held at Budaun on the 10th and 11th December at which the most important subject of discussion was the appointment of an Amir ul Shariat for India. The Subject Committee of Ulema appointed at the last Ulema Conference at Lahore will submit its report on the question of the appointment of an Amir ul Shariat for India at this meeting.

The meeting of the Sind Jamiat-ul-Ulema took place at Dadu on the 4th December. It is reported that the meeting has decided to publish a fatwa describing all members of the Aman Sabhas as Kaffirs and their children as 'walad-uz-zana' (illegitimate).

It was also decided to establish a Jamiat-ul-Ulema for the Larkana District with its headquarters at Dadu. The following are the office bearers:

Sadar (President): Moulvi Mahomed Amin Shah of Aminani Taluka Dadu

Secretary: Moulvi Mahomed Salch of Dadu[36]

Weekly Bulletin on the Non-co-operation movement for the week ending 10th December 1921

GENERAL

A rumour has been reported in Karachi to the effect that an outbreak of violence or general open rebellion is to be expected in Christmas week.

2. AGITATION

(a) *Congress,* and (b) *Khilafat.* Agitation continues to be virulent but on the whole the number of meetings is decreasing in nearly all districts. Mahomedan religious feelings continue to prove themselves the chief motive underlying the non-co-operation movement in Sind. Anxiety concerning the Khilafat questions is undoubtedly on the increase. Religious and racial questions predominate in the speeches of most of the local agitators. Mahomedans are reported to be taking

[36] Page 153 of the original is missing.

a greater interest in agitation in Sukkur and the same holds good in other places.

3. ORGANISATION

(a) *Congress.* The recent elections continue to cause a great deal of jealousy and ill-feeling among the Congress members particularly as between Hyderabadis and non-Hyderabadis. There are also personal quarrels and disputes on several committees. It is reported that Virumal Begraj will resign the Vice-Presidentship of the Sind Provincial Congress Committee on account of the preponderating influence of the Hyderabadis among the office bearers. Other concrete instances are (1) One Dharamdas has wired from Larkana to Mahatma Gandhi to the effect that Larkana delegates are self-elected and not representatives of Larkana and that the facts will be clear from the record. He asks Gandhi to take necessary steps. (2) In Nawabshah the Secretary of the Nasrat Congress Committee has written to the *Bharatvasi* complaining that the election for the All-India Congress Committee and the Sind Provincial Congress Committee have been held in a high-handed and irregular way. His protests to the Sind Provincial Congress Committee have not been heeded and he considers that the elections should be cancelled. (3) In Mirpurkhas similar dissensions have occurred and have been mentioned in the Press. (4) In Karachi (Vide last week's reference to the letter to the District Congress Committee complaining of the 'satanic Congress bureaucracy' and the feeling against Manilal and Mahomed Khan[).] (5) In Jacobabad candidates are apparently not forthcoming for the Congress Committees as there are three vacancies and not a single Mahomedan from that district has been elected as a delegate or as a member of the Sind Provincial Congress Committee.

From information received it appears that many persons who have habitually attended the Congress in the past and have dissociated themselves from the Congress during the non-co-operation phase will not go to Ahmedabad this year. In some cases this may be due to the fact that the politicians of the old school have drifted away from the Congress, in others it is said that apprehension of trouble resulting from the rowdy attitude of the young extremists is a reason for no going there.

(b) *Khilafat*. Reports continue to be received of the formation of new Khilafat Committees in small villages.

A meeting of the Hyderabad District Khilafat Committee is to be held on the 12th of December, the following are on the agenda:

(1) the promotion of the non-co-operation movement

(2) the Angora Fund

(3) starting a newspaper

(4) National education

(5) to consider the present situation

(6) to increase the vigour with which propaganda work is conducted.

7. FUNDS

(a) Jairamdas Daulatram wired from Hyderabad, Sind to Congress, Allahabad on the 10th December to say that the total for the Tilak Swaraj Fund in Sind amounted to Rs. 207539/3/0.

(b) Haji Abdulla Haroon wired to the Secretary, Khilafat, Bombay as follows: 'Total income 82275 amount sent 28607 sending today 2500 Reserve 15825. Kindly despatch immediately ten rupees Smyrna receipts worth 25000 five rupees worth 12500 one rupee 20000.'

Collections for the Angora Fund continue vigorously, the following committee has been appointed to make collections for this fund on behalf of the Provincial Khilafat Committee in the Hyderabad district. (1) Kazi Asadullahshah of Tikhar (2) Abdul Jabbar wd. Mahomed Yakub pleader (3) Sheikh Abdullah Secretary Khilafat Committee Hyderabad (4) Pir Mahbubshah of Bakar Nizamani (5) Pir Abdulla Jan Sarhandi.

The Arab community in Karachi, mostly Arab merchants from Koweit, have contributed over Rs. 6000/- to the Angora Fund.

5. SCHOOLS AND COLLEGES

The Karachi District Congress Committee has sanctioned Rs. 5000/- for the upkeep of national schools. Lalchand Jagtiani had apparently not yet obtained the Rs. 2000/- sanctioned by the provincial committee as he wired to Dr. Choithram on the 7th asking him to intimate the Secretary of the District Congress Committee to pay that amount for the Tilakalya.

(b) It is reported that a school has been started in a small village in the Larkana district which is to be maintained from Khilafat funds. The present attendance is 32.

6. INDIAN NATIONAL SERVICE AND VOLUNTEERS

(a) Nil.

(b) During the week under report a letter was received in the Khilafat office, Hyderabad, Sind, from Mahomed Amir Ali, Captain of the Muslim Volunteer Corps, Madras, remarking that apparently no such volunteer Jamait [!] had been organised in Sind and urging that this should be done. As a result of this letter Mian Mahomed Shafi has started to enlist Mahomedan Volunteers in Hyderabad. It is reported that Hyderabadi Mahomedan leaders displayed such lack of initiative in the matter as to postpone action pending the return of Jairamdas Daulatram who had gone out of Hyderabad.

7. LAWYERS AND COURTS

Two arbitration courts are reported to have been established in two small villages in the Kotri taluka of the Karachi district.

8. SWADESHI MOVEMENT

Nil.

9. BOYCOTT OF EUROPEANS BY THEIR SERVANTS

Nil.

10. GOVERNMENT SERVICES

The Deputy Conservator of Forests, Sind Circle reports the resignation of a Forester on Rs. 50/- per mensem, who was in charge of the Hyderabad range in the Hyderabad Forest Division, in connection with the Khilafat movement.

11. AGRARIAN TROUBLES

Nil.

12. LABOUR INCLUDING RAILWAYS

Non-co-operator agitators in Karachi especially Saraswati Devi, Dr. Haji and Mahomed Khan are conducting agitation among the Municipal sweepers and extending their influence over these classes. They apparently propose to arrange for a strike at the time of the Prince of Wales' visit.

A lengthy leaflet is being distributed among European and Anglo-Indian employees of the North Railway in Karachi. It is issued from Calcutta under a forwarding letter by T.H.W. Dowman and contains the prospectus of the 'Society of European Railwaymen of India and Burma to be brought into existence from the 1st of January 1922.'

Mr. Dowman in his foreword writes as follows:

> 'Fellow-workers, - Practical experience has conclusively proved that it would be to the advantage of European and Anglo-Indian Railwaymen to organise separately from the Indians for the protection of their own particular rights.
>
> While always maintaining amicable relations with our Indian fellow-workmen, and treating kindred organisations with friendliness and sympathy, it is our bounden duty to adopt the best expedient to ensure the prosperity and general welfare of the European and Anglo-Indian Community serving on the railway systems of India and Burma. The following scheme has been drawn up by me which if brought into operation will quickly attain the desired end.
>
> All that is necessary is to wake up from lethargy and indifference, and to take the deepest interest in the efforts to build up and perfect an organisation which would be the only barrier between ourselves and injustice.
>
> All who agree with my sentiments and opinions are requested to communicate with me, enclosing stamps for replies if any are asked for.'

There are 41 draft rules of which No. 14 says that Mrs. Ethel E. Dowman shall be admitted to be the proprietor and Editor of *The Advocate of Railwaymen*.

It is reported that the Central Delegates Committee of the North Western Railway Union, Lahore, has divided into two parties of which the Constitutionalists are led by Hall and the Extremists by Miller and M.A. Khan. The latter are said to be agitating for direct action but it is not yet clear what they mean by direct action.[37]

Weekly Bulletin on the Non-co-operation Movement for the week ending 17th December 1921

GENERAL

The rumour that an outbreak of violence is to be expected in Christmas week is now general [*sic*] in Karachi. People of the lowest classes are talking of Gandhi hoisting the flag at Ahmedabad. Other

[37] Copies forwarded to the Commissioner in Sindh; the Director, Intelligence Bureau, Delhi; the D.I.G. of Police, C.I.D., Poona; the General Staff Officer, Sindh Rajputana District; all Superintendents of Police in Sindh; all District Magistrates in Sindh.

alarmist rumours are also current, for instance it is reported that talk is to be heard at all railway stations to the effect that a general strike on the railway is to take place on the 2nd of January, that a general strike among prisoners in jails is to be organised on the 1st of January, that European firms in Karachi are failing in consequence of the Non-co-operation and are going to discharge their clerks on the 1st of January. The fact that the tendency to strike has spread to the Police in the Hyderabad and Larkana Districts is also noticed. All these alarmist rumours appear to be without serious foundation. There is no sign of anything unusual in the Provincial Congress Office, and Congressmen are preparing to proceed to Ahmedabad without any sign of serious disturbance being expected by them. There is no immediate likelihood of a railway strike if the attitude of the Union officials is a reliable indication (Vide para 12 below). The behaviour of the Police leaves no room for doubt that their action is due to economic difficulties.

Moderate politicians in Sind and the moderate and anti-Non-co-operation Press in Sind are strongly opposed to the action taken in Bengal and other provinces to suppress the volunteer corps and to arrest the leaders of the Congress and Khilafat movements. The extremists generally expect that the moderates will resign form the Councils and adopt an attitude of opposition to Government and thus strengthen the Congress cause.

None of the Congress leaders in Sind appear to have any information of the future programme of the Congress. It is probable that Jairamdas Daulatram who is in the confidence of Gandhi and of other leaders may have this information, but if so he appears to have kept it very discreetly to himself. None of the other Congress politicians in Sind are men of any standing. Information from a well informed source is to the effect that the question of starting the non-payment of taxes is being seriously proposed as a step to be initiated after Ahmedabad.

2. AGITATION

(a) and (b). The number of meetings has decreased throughout Sind. The religious and racial questions continue to predominate in most of the speeches.

3. ORGANISATION

(a) *Congress.* Recriminations over the recent elections continue. The *Bharatvasi* points out that if as the Non-co-operators urge last years Council elections were not representative as very few people votes, the same argument applies with even greater force to the recent Congress elections. The paper says that only 10 per cent of the Congress members voted at Hyderabad and even less at Sukkur and other places where as in the Council elections in some places 50, 60 or 70 % of the electorate voted. Virumal Begraj has resigned the Vice-Presidentship of the Provincial Congress Committee to show his dislike of the Hyderabadi intrigues and Rijhumal Kundanmal Lahori has resigned the Presidentship of the Larkana District Congress Committee on account of similar feelings of partnership.

(b) *Khilafat.* Nil.

4. FUNDS

(a) *Congress.* Nil.

(b) *Khilafat.* Collections for the Angora Fund continue to be organised with energy. Attached marked (a) is a rough translation of a poster which has been circulated. Vide last week's telegram by Haji Abdulla Haroon, according to a report in the *New Times* the Sind Provincial Khilafat Committee remitted Rs. 25,000 to the Central Khilafat Committee on the 11th December and expected to send Rs. 60,000 more including Rs. 50,000 from Seth Haji Abdulla Haroon.

5. SCHOOLS AND COLLEGES

Nil.

6. INDIAN NATIONAL SERVICE AND VOLUNTEERS

(a) At the Provincial Congress Committee meeting at Larkana on the 2nd December the following Board was appointed to deal with the question of volunteers in Sind:- Jairamdas Daulatram, Abdul Jabbar, Lilaram Pherwani, Hassanand Pamnani, Shankarlal Ratansing. Hyderabad is declared to be the Volunteer Headquarters. A meeting was held at Hyderabad on the 9th December at which a large number of members of the Hyderabad District Congress Committee enrolled themselves as volunteers. Again at a meeting on the 11th at Hyderabad Dr. Choithram and Messrs. Ladharam, Aminuddin and Jairamdas appealed to the people to rise to the occasion and take up the challenge by Government in other provinces and to enlist in the volunteers. According to Jairamdas who telegraphed the above facts to the leading papers throughout India, fifty persons came forward at this meeting. It was decided according to the same telegram, to postpone considering all these applications until the rules of the Central Volunteer Board were published. (This telegram was stopped as objectionable under the Indian Telegraph Act.)

Since then enrolments of Volunteers is reported in Karachi and other places but so far no further developments are apparent. The Congress Committees and the persons who have enrolled themselves declare that they are prepared to challenge Government. They appear to hope that the Criminal Law Amendment Act will be applied to Sind to give them an opportunity to do so. So far they did not appear to have given Government any excuse for applying this enactment as their organisation is merely nominal and they have not taken part in any systematic intimidation or in interfering with the rights of others.

It is reported that a detachment of 25 women volunteers is being enrolled in Karachi.

7. LAWYERS AND COURTS

The Arbitration Court in Unerpur in Kotri taluka disposed of a number of petty cases. The most noticeable case is that of a driver who was prosecuted by the local police and fined Rs. 8/-, and thereupon complained to the Arbitration court against a fellow villager who had informed the police against him.

8. and 9. Nil.

10. GOVERNMENT SERVICES

It is reported that a clerk of the Educational Inspector named Khushaldas Kiaram has resigned in pursuance of the orders of the Congress.

11. AGRARIAN TROUBLES

Nil.

12. LABOUR INCLUDING RAILWAYS

(a) A copy of the proceedings of the 6th meeting of the District Committee of the N.W. Railway Union held at Karachi on the 5th December is attached, marked (B).[38] An Associated Press message dated Lahore 12th December stated that the Central Delegates Committee representing a majority of all classes of the N.W. Railways employees on the 11th idem passed a resolution empowering the executive to declare a strike immediately if the authorities fail to meet the union's legitimate demands which had been communicated to the authorities a month previously. To avoid a catastrophe and irrespective of the hostile attitude of the agent of the railway who was misinterpreting the situation His Excellency [the Viceroy?] was prayed to appoint a conciliation board.

From information received by this department it appears that it is proposed to ask for the appointment of a conciliation board consisting of three representatives each of the Union, of Government and of the public respectively in order to obtain the Union's demands, and that talk of a strike is largely bluff. Information from a well-informed source is to the effect that there is no likelihood of the Union officials advocating a strike in the immediate future.

Miller, M.A. Khan and Kanti Parkash are proceeding to the Ahmedabad Congress as delegates. It appears that the Punjab Provincial Committee have reserved ten delegates' seats in the Congress for Labour members and these and other railway union officials are obtaining some of them. According to a recent resolution of the N.W. Railway Union, members of the Union are permitted to take part in political movements as individuals, but union officials and members are not as such permitted to involve the union in any purely political movement.

13 and 14. Nil.

15. THE ULEMA MOVEMENT

In consequence of the arrest of Abul Kalam Azad the Ulema Movement appears to have come to a temporary stand-still. Moulvi Mahomed Sadik of the Khadda was to have gone to a meeting at Baduan [!] on the 11th December, but this meeting was not held. It is said that a meeting of the All-India Ulemas may be held at Ahmedabad during Congress week.

[38] Not printed.

APPENDIX 'A'

Message for Indian Muslims from Hazrat Ghazi Mustafa Kamal Pasha and the Representatives of the Islamic Kingdom of Angora through the Khilafat Deputation

'Pecuniary help is the greatest help which the Mussalmans of India can render us'.

This is the message of those who are the last protecting body of the Khilafat Islam on the face of the Earth and those who are the only body which has been performing the defensive duty.

Will the Mussalmans of India respond to this call of brotherhood? Will not they sacrifice their property even for those who are sacrificing their lives and everything for the sake of Islam? Uptil now we have been making promises, announcements, and have shown our intentions, but will not the world see some scene of our action?

The first action for Khilafat and Islam is that every Muslim should be ready to respond to this message and should do the greatest pecuniary sacrifice in his life.

The Central Khilafat Committee has opened Angora Fund.

At least Rs. 50,00,000/- within two months.

Signatories.

Mian Muhammad Haji Jan Muhammad Chhotani—President

Masih ul Mulk Muhammad Ajmal Khan

Maulana Abdul Bari

Dr. Mukhtar Ahmad Ansari

Maulana Abul Kalam Azad

Ahmad Haji Siddiq Khatri

Honorary Secretaries, All India Central Khilafat Committee, Sultan mansion, Dongri, Bombay

Printed in Mustafai Press, Kumbharwara Gali No. 2, Bombay 4.[39]

Weekly Bulletin on the Non-co-operation Movement for the week ending 24th December 1921

General

A meeting of the Swaraj Society of Hyderabad was held on the 11th December 1921 in the office of Mr. Santdas Mangharam, Pleader. The question of the 'repressive' policy was considered. There was

[39] Copies forwarded as in footnote 37.

considerable difference of opinion among those present concerning the wording of the resolution on the agenda. Some expressed the view that the Government was in a difficult position and that repressive measures were inevitable or unavoidable. They unanimously agreed on one point viz.: that they protested against the action of the Government in bringing the Congress Committee's meetings under the scope of the Seditious Meetings Act. This was with special reference to the arrest of Lala Lajpatrai. The majority of those present were not willing to condemn the policy of the Government in other respects. The meeting was postponed to the 16th December. On the 16th, Mr. Bhurgri was in Karachi. Mr. Gopaldas Jhamatmal was away. Mr. Santdas could not attend. The meeting was postponed indefinitely. This party's difficulty seems to be that they cannot frame a resolution which will satisfy their own apprehensions concerning peace and order, and at the same time avoid too obvious antagonism to the extremists.

Rumours about probably disturbances in Ahmedabad caused some Congressmen to hesitate to leave for Ahmedabad under pressure from their relations. The communiqué issued by the District Magistrate, Ahmedabad, reassured them. Lalchand A. Jagtiani at a public meeting addressed the ladies of Hyderabad and called upon them to allow their husbands, brothers and sons to go to Ahmedabad, citing the example of the Indian ladies of ancient days who used to send their relations to the battlefield with exhortations not to retreat.

The Sind Provincial Congress Committee held a meeting in Hyderabad on the 20th and passed resolutions, after Gandhi's example, giving authority to the President and the Working Committee to appoint successors in the event of arrest. (Details given below—ORGANISATION.)

A report has been received to the effect that Dr. Nur Mahomed has written to Pir Abdul Satar Jan to say that he may return to Sind under arrangements to be made by the Kabul Government. He refers to the treaty and remarks that it will shortly be known whether it is to be a lasting one or not.

In the absence of any well organised volunteer corps, and consequently of any action to suppress them, there is little or no disturbance in the political atmosphere, except for a mild repercussion resulting from events in other Provinces.

The arrest and conviction of Jairamdas Daulatram for a mischievous article concerning the Bombay riots in the *Hindu* of Hyderabad, leaves the Sind Congress party without its most able organiser and its most determined disciple of Gandhi in the 'non-violent' programme.

2. AGITATION

(a) *Congress.* There is a general decrease in the number of meetings. The Non-co-operators explain the present lull in the movement by saying that the decision of the coming Congress is awaited and that they are preparing to go to Ahmedabad.

The arrest of Jairamdas Daulatram led to a crowded meeting held in Hyderabad where a few volunteers were enlisted for the National Corps and a member of the Aman Sabha resigned his membership.

As a result of the exertions of Saraswati Devi, the ladies of Karachi have held several meetings in Karachi, where the resolutions passed by the Karachi Municipality to give an address to H.R.H. the Prince of Wales had been condemned.

(b) *Khilafat.* A meeting was held in Badin, where it was decided to increase the number of propagandists, and to start a paper.

3. ORGANISATION

(a) *Congress.* A meeting of the Council of the Sind Provincial Congress Committee was held on the 19th December 1921 when the accounts sent in by the various Congress Committees with explanations from their Secretaries were considered. The following questions were decided:

1. Protest against Larkana delegates' election. It was decided that no interference was necessary.
2. A grant of Rs. 400/- was sanctioned for the Thar Parkar District Congress Committee.
3. Application from Hassanand [Pamnani?] of Sukkur for a grant of Rs. 400/- to publish a dictionary written by him was considered and it was decided that no grant should be given.

On the same day a meeting of the general body was held under the Presidentship of Dr. Choithram when the following resolutions were passed:

1. In case delegates from any district are arrested their places both as delegates and members of the Provincial Congress Committee shall, pending their release, be filled by those who stood next in order at the last election.
2. Where voting did not take place, or where the list of unsuccessful candidates is exhausted, the executive committee of the district or the remaining members are empowered to elect substituted pending the release of those arrested.
3. If a situation arises preventing the holding of meetings of the Provincial Congress Committee all its powers can be exercised by the Provincial Council till the general body can meet.
4. If a critical situation arises the President or the acting President can exercise all the powers of the Council and is empowered to appoint his successor till the next meeting of the Council and nominate the members of the general body in the places of those arrested till their places are filled by the Executive Committees of the respective district.
5. In case any member of the All India Congress Committee is arrested, his place, pending release, will be filled by the candidate standing highest among the unsuccessful candidates.
6. The letter sent by Virumal Begraj, Vice President, sending his resignation on account of no member having been elected on the All India Congress Committee from Upper Sind and the reply of the President and further reply from Virumal was read. It was proposed that his resignation be accepted with regret. An amendment was proposed that his resignation should be accepted and regret should be expressed for his writing such a letter. Votes were taken and by the casting vote of the President it was resolved that the resignation of the Vice-President was accepted with regret.
7. The members of the Provincial Congress Committee with two ladies were enrolled as volunteers of the 'National Volunteer Corps'. The rules and regulations will be according to those passed by the All India Congress Committee's Working Committee on the 24th November 1921 at Bombay. The vow to be taken will be the same. Mr. Jairamdas proposed that the volunteers should not be authorised to carry sticks as sanctioned by the Working Committee of the All India Congress Committee, but Kazi Abdul Rahman protested against this and the resolution as drafted by the Working Committee was passed.
8. Rules regarding the powers of supervision and control of district and other committees by the Provincial Congress Committee were also passed.

The following attended the meeting of the General Body:
Karachi: Mahomed Khan 2. Haji Abdulla Haroon 3. Lalchand

Amardinomal 4. Kazi Abdul Rahman 5. Naraindas Anandji.

Hyderabad: Choithram P. Gidwani 2. Jairamdas Daulatram 3. Abdul Jabbar, Pleader 4. Ghanshamdas Jethanand Shivadasani 5. Dr. Chimandas Isardas 6. Jhamatmal Lakhasing 7. Aminuddin N. 8. Lokram Nainaram Sharma 9. Fatehchand Bijasing.

Sukkur: Hassanand Pamnani.

Shikarpur: Maulvi Abdul Karim Chisti.

Larkana: Pir Ali Anwarshah 2. Pir Mithalshah.

Nasrat: Kazi Khudabux 2. Maulvi Abdul Khalak.

Only half a dozen out of more than thirty members from Upper Sind were present. The Hindu members of Upper Sind have taken offence at the conduct of the elections to the All India Congress Committee. Dr. Choithram has tried to placate Virumal Begraj, the backbone of the Congress workers of Upper Sind, by wiring to him that he is elected on the All-India Congress Committee, vice Jairamdas in jail.

(b) *Khilafat*. A meeting of the Sind Provincial Khilafat Committee was held on the 20th at Hyderabad, when elections of the office-bearers were held. Haji Abdulla Haroon was re-elected as President. Mahomedkhan, Secretary, has been replaced by Kazi Khudabux and Kazi Shamshdin. The following were elected as representatives of Sind on the Central Khilafat Committee, Bombay: 1. Haji Abdulla Haroon of Karachi 2. Kazi Asadullahshah 3. Kazi Khudabux 4. Kazi Abdul Rahman 5. Mahomed Khan Ghazikhan 6. Mir Allahbux Talpur 7. Mahomed Sadik of Khadda, Karachi 8. Mirza Ghulam Dastgir 9. Abdul Jabbar, Pleader 10. Abdul Khalik Morai.

Information about the elections of members on the Sind Provincial Congress Committee from Hyderabad has been received to the effect that the majority of members are either Sarhandi or Rashidi Pirs and their adherents. The following is a list of these from the Hyderabad District:- 1. Pir Abdul Sattar Jan 2. Mir Mahbubshah 3. Qazi Asadullah Shah 4. Sayad Kamar Ali Shah 5. Abdul Jabbar, Pleader 6. Sheikh Abdullah 7. Maulvi Ghulam Muhammad 8. Maulvi Ahmed Salah, Badin 9. Pir Muhammad Umer Khan 10. Khilafa Muhammad Hasham 11. Sayyad Allah Bachayo Shah of Matiari and 12. Maulvi Taj Muhammad of Nasarpur.

It is to be noticed in the first place that the Rashidi and Sarhandi Pirs with two or three exceptions did not attend this meeting. Apparently these Pirs are taking more keenly to the collections of funds for Angora, which appeals to the religious feelings, and also no doubt to their self-interest. It is unlikely that all or even a large part of the money will pass through their hands and reach Angora.

The most significant and perhaps the most important development in Sind during the recent months follows as a result of the Pirs' defection whereby the 'young Khilafatists' have secured all the seats on the Central Khilafat Committee. These men are likely to support Abul Kalam Azad and Hazrat Mohani in the Central Khilafat Committee, and they now control the whole organisation of the Khilafat party in Sind. The results are likely to be far-reaching. The 'young Khilafat' party have come to the conclusion that the Pirs are unreliable, especially in view of Turabalishah's and Mahbubalishah's apologies. At the same time they cannot entirely cast them adrift on account of their very great influence over the Sindi [!] and Baluchi tribes. A list of the Sind representatives on the outgoing Central Khilafat Committee is attached, marked (A).

4. FUNDS

(a) *Congress*. Nil.

(b) *Khilafat*. A rough translation of an article contributed by the President of the Sind Provincial Khilafat Committee (Haji Abdulla Haroon) to the *Hindu* dated 9th December 1921 is attached, marked B.

The Angora Fund is still being collected vigorously. A local paper announces subscriptions as under:

Ganchi Hallai Community Rs. 1200/- through the efforts of Haji Abdulla Haroon.

Pir Sahib of Jhando is said to have collected Rs. 2600/-.

Seth Osman Saleh Mahomed who has contributed donations to several funds has also given Rs. 251/- to Angora Fund.

A letter from Haji Abdulla Haroon to the address of the Central Khilafat Committee explains the reposition as regards the Khilafat and Angora Funds in Sind.—Copy attached marked C.

5. SCHOOLS AND COLLEGES

Nil.

6. Indian National Service and Volunteers

No definite development in connection with volunteers has so far taken place in Sind. Speakers are urging people to enlist as volunteers. Kazi Abdul Rahman made a few speeches in Naushahro Feroze Division and emphasised this question.

The Karachi Congress Committee are understood to intend organising Volunteers after the Ahmedabad Congress. 450 names are said to have been obtained.

The Naushahro Feroze Congress Committee formed a volunteer corps and enlisted about 16 volunteers.

Bhojraj Motumal and Dr. Mahomed Yamin from Sukkur have invited applications for enlistment as Volunteers.

In a public meeting at Hyderabad a few Volunteers were enlisted.

According to an informant Pir Abdul Sattar was asked by the Khilafatists to secure volunteers and he replied that if his father took the matter up many of his followers would be ready to join.

On the 23rd December 1921 a volunteer was noticed in Karachi picketing a liquor shop. He was arrested as he was obstructing the road and using objectionable language. He was sent up before the City Magistrate, Karachi, who sentenced him to 14 days' imprisonment on the 23rd December 1921. Otherwise no picketing of liquor shops has occurred.

7. Lawyers and Courts

Ratanmal Walad Gidamal has suspended practice in Court. He had a poor practice in Mirpurkhas district and is likely to make as much out of agitation.

Court of Arbitration at Sukkur

About 340 cases have been taken up of which about 250 have been decided. An extremist paper of Sukkur states that in only 2 or 3 cases the parties are displeased with the decision and are making preparations for filing appeals.

The paper further states that Mulchand Pessumal has worked for the last 8 months instead of 7 according to the orders of Gandhi. After the Congress it will be decided whether Mulchand is to suspend his practice any further or not. If not Lakhasing Karamchand, Pleader, Rohri will replace him.

It is rumoured that he is tired of his present occupation and that he will soon re-start practising in Court, unless Gandhi persuades him to stay on.

18. SWADESHI MOVEMENT

Nil.

19. BOYCOTT OF EUROPEANS BY THEIR SERVANTS

Nil.

10. GOVERNMENT SERVICE

Haji Khan Walad Yacub Khan, Supervising Tapedar of Sukkur District resigned his appointment 'owing to the repressive policy of Government and religious feelings.'

11. AGRARIAN TROUBLES

Nil.

12. LABOUR INCLUDING RAILWAYS

The *Railway Union* dated the 16th December states that if no reply is received within 2 weeks to the telegram sent to H.E. the Viceroy, Miller, M.A. Khan and Shamsuddin Hassan (Editor of the *Railway Union*) will tour the North Western Railway and will ask the District Secretaries to organise a general strike as an effective measure.

On the other hand information has been received from a reliable source that the Agent has issued orders that no deductions on account of subscriptions should be made officially by the Railway authorities on behalf of the Union. This is likely to lead to a decrease of 50% in the number of members of the Union. (The Subscription has been officially deducted from pay and credited to the Union funds. Several employees were not otherwise willing to remain in the Union.) This may lead the Extremist heads of the Union to advocate a strike. The majority of the Railway employees and members of the Union are not in favour of a strike.

13. THE TEMPERANCE MOVEMENT

Nil.

14. PROSECUTIONS OR PREVENTIVE ACTION

Nil.

15. MISCELLANEOUS

A Khilafat Volunteer named Mahomedbux was prosecuted for disseminating a proscribed leaflet among military sepoys in

Hyderabad. He subsequently apologised but was convicted by the Sessions Court, Hyderabad and sentenced to undergo six months' Rigorous Imprisonment. He is an ex-constable of police. No other case has occurred in Sind.[40]

APPENDIX A

List of Sind Representatives on the outgoing Central Khilafat Committee of India.

1. Seth Abdulla Haroon	Napier Road, Karachi
2. Mr. Mahomed Khan, Secretary Khilafat Committee	McLeod Road, Karachi
3. Pir Syed Turab Ali Shah Saheb	Kambar (Distt. Larkana)
4. Maulvi Din Mahomed Saheb Wafai	Al Haq Office, Sukkur
5. Maulana Taj Mahomed Saheb	Amrote, Sind (via Ruk)
6. Moulvi Abdul Khalique Saheb	Naro (Distt. Nawabshah)
7. Pir Mahomed Imam Shah Saheb	v. Pir Saheb, Jhanda
8. Mr. Jairamdas	c/o 'Bharatvasi, Hyderabad
9. Moulvi Mahomed Siddiq Saheb	c/o Sind Khilafat Committee, Karachi[41]

APPENDIX B

Extract from the *Hindu* of Hyderabad, dated the 9th December 1921:

> Protection of Islam Angora Fund Protection of Islam
>
> On the questioning of a member in the Parliament whether the Greeks were helped by the Europeans against Turkey, Mr. Lloyd George, the Prime Minister, has said: 'The Greeks have purchased their ammunition from the Europeans. We have no objection if any body gives the similar help of ammunition to the Turks also.'
>
> Oh! Relatives, these Turks have been defending our religious sacred places these last four hundred years at the cost of their lives and which they are still

[40] Copies forwarded as in footnote 37.

[41] Line missing.

doing. Is it then the duty of other Muhammadans also to do so? If we cannot join them in fight on account of certain reasons we should at least help the Ghazi Mustafa Kamal Pasha with money. The present question does not related to co-operation or to Non-co-operation. It is hoped that our Pirs, Zamindars and Jagirdars in special would collect subscriptions from their friends as well, and send them to us; for by the end of December we have to collect fifty lakhs of rupees.

SD/- Abdullah Haroon
President, Khilafat Suba, Sind, Karachi

APPENDIX C

Letter, intercepted on 17th December 1921, from Haji Abdoola Haroon, President, Sindh Provincial Khilafat Committee, Karachi, dated 12th December 1921, to the Honorary Secretary, Central Khilafat Committee, Bombay.

Dear brother—The expenses incurred during the Trial days amount to Rs. 7046-9-0 out of this amount Rs. 3041-1-3 being the expense of meals of the guests and the leaders in the Jail, have been contributed by the citizens of Karachi. The rest of the expenses Rs. 4005-7-9 have been debited to the Central Khilafat Committee accounts and the Vouchers of those expenses are sent to-day per registered parcel. Further a Hundi of Rs. 20994-8-3 is sent herewith to complete (Rs. 4005-7-9 plus 20994-8-3) rupees 25000/-. You will please credit Rs. 23000/- for Angora fund and Rs. 2000/- for Smyrna Fund and send duplicate receipts for the sums noted below as one is to be kept in the office and the other to be given to the heads of the communities and other individuals, who have contributed big sums. Besides strenuous efforts for collections are going on both in the city and the Province. The Arab community have promised Rs. 5000/- and the Butcher Community Rs. 4000/-.

Angora

1.	Through Mir Mohd. Sahib Baloch collected from Musalman community, Ranchore Lines	Rs. 10303/-
2.	Syed Abdul Rahim Shah of Sijwal	Rs. 5000/-
3.	Through Maulana Mohd. Sidiq Sahib, collected from Khadda people	Rs. 2264/12/-
4.	Through Pir Jhandewalla	Rs. 1524/2/-
5.	Through Osman Hamid collected by Memon Volunteer Corps	Rs. 931/-
6.	Haji Khajoo Sahib	Rs. 450/-
7.	Mufti Saadulla Sahib of Khairpur State	Rs. 100/-

Smyrna

8. Syed Abdul Rahim Shah Sahib	Rs.	2000/-
9. Balance	Rs.	2426/13/-
	Rs.	25000/-/-

Yours fraternally
SD/- H.A. Haroon
P.S. A bill for Rs. 666/- (Taxis) in connection with the Trial expenses is still pending.

Weekly Bulletin on the Non-co-operation Movement for the Week ending 31st December 1921

1. General

The following note has appeared in the *New Times*:

'Mr. Ramchand Alimchand, Pleader writes to the *Bharatvasi* that we will move in the next general meeting of the Hyderabad Municipality that the Government should be thanked for the adoption of repressive policy because it will bring Swaraj nearer and consequently the Municipality request the Government to put the repressive policy in full swing in Sind.'

The *Sind Observer*, a moderate newspaper of Karachi, commenting on the Presidential address at the All India Congress, writes:-

'...But we join issues with him when he claims that the Non-co-operation movement is a positive success, has had a large response from the country, and appealed to one and all. There is no doubt that Mr. Gandhi on the eve of and after the Bombay riots, was getting extremely disappointed at the feeble response to the sound that had emanated from his trumpet. The schools and colleges and the law courts have, contrary to the boasting of the extremists remained what they were. The councils have been filled. It is not true to say these councils are a failure....'

A special correspondent of the same newspaper writing from Ahmedabad about the Congress as under:-

'On the whole it was a nice family arrangement, the [?]* dominating it all.'

The Hon'ble Mr. G.M. Bhurgri has contributed a [?] to the *Sind Observer* under the heading 'A call for [?], suggesting a Round Table Conference to be preceded by a Conference between Extremists and Moderates.

* Original partly illegible.

According to a reliable report all the Mussalman members from Sind and Virumal Begraj supported the resolution of Hasrat Mohani in the Subjects Committee at Ahmedabad. The Sind Muhammadans on the All India Congress Delegation are, Mahomed Khan Ghassi Khan, Abdul Jabbar, Pleader, Hyderabad, Kazi Khudabux Morai, and Kazi Abdul Rahman, ex-editor of the defunct *Al Wahid*.

2. AGITATION

During the absence of the leading agitators there has been practically no agitation in the Province except for a number of political addresses by Maulvi Abdul Karim Dars in the form of 'Mawluds' in Karachi.

3. ORGANISATION

(a) *Congress.* The latest press messages state that Dr. Choithram Partabrai Gidwani has been elected a member of the All India Congress Working Committee in place of a member in jail.

[?] President of the Sahaiti [?] District Congress Committee, has elected; [?] Editor of the *Shakti* to act as President owing to the former having gone to jail for 12 months in default of giving security for good behaviour.

(b) *Khilafat.* Nil.

4. FUNDS

(a) *Congress.* Complaints about the administration of funds continue to be common. The following is a brief not on various funds in Sind:

Karachi Congress Committee. Tattacharry, a Madrasi boy, who was working in the Karachi Congress Office left Karachi suddenly and it is learnt that he has drawn about Rs. 1818/- by forging the signatures of the Secretary and the President of the Congress Committee.

A member of the Panchayat has put several questions to the Secretaries of the Karachi District Congress Committee about the ornaments and money collected for the Tilak Swaraj Fund but has not been able to obtain satisfactory replies for the last six months. It is generally believed that the money and ornaments have been embezzled.

Hyderabad District Congress Committee. The President of the Sind Provincial Congress Committee has announced that a cash box containing over Rs. 300/- was stolen from the Congress Office and that the amount had been written off.

Nawabshah District Congress Committee. The Secretary of the District Congress Committee invites the attention of the people to the fact that the President appointed a man named Habib Ullah on Rs. 50/- to do his household work, and that he was not doing any propaganda work though he was shown as a propagandist on the District Congress Committee records.

Thar Parkar Congress Committee. A local newspaper recently criticised the use of funds by Dr. Vatanmal who had enlisted some of his relations as propagandists and as teachers in the National School. A dismissed Tapedar was given Rs. 50/- p.m. to work as a propagandist.

Jacobabad District Congress Committee. The Ex-Secretary of Congress Committee has published several questions regarding the misuse of funds.

(b) *Khilafat.* The following statements of accounts of the Sind Provincial Khilafat Committee from November 1919 to 17th December 1921 has been published in the *New Times* of the 27th December 1921:

Income				
Khilafat Fund	Rs.	68,284	8	9
Smyrna Fund	Rs.	28,293	0	7
Sale of Books	Rs.	29	6	0
Sale of Khilafat Receipts	Rs.	5,178	0	0
Angora Fund	Rs.	29,187	5	2
	Rs.	1,30,972	4	6
Expenditure				
Office Expenditure	Rs.	2,187	1	10
Post and Telegrams	Rs.	2,348	7	0
Printing	Rs.	6,226	2	0
Propaganda	Rs.	9,240	12	0
Local Meetings	Rs.	216	4	9
Travelling expenses	Rs.	396	6	6
Guests a/c	Rs.	212	8	9

Help to Khilafat Sufferers	Rs.	1,356 11 3
Sent to Sub-committees	Rs.	1,325 7 0
Miscellaneous	Rs.	1,558 0 2
Sent to Central Khilafat Committee,		
Bombay as Khilafat Fund	Rs.	31,607 0 0
—do— Smyrna Fund	Rs.	25,000 0 0
—do— Angora Fund	Rs.	23,010 0 0
Khilafat Receipts	Rs.	4,000 0 0
Angora literature etc.	Rs.	569 15 0
Total	Rs.	1,09,254 12 4
Balance	Rs.	21,717 8 2

A letter from Din Mahomed of the Sind Provincial Khilafat Committee to the Secretaries, Central Khilafat Committee, Bombay, given the recent income and expenditure of the Sind Provincial Khilafat Committee:

Dear Brother,

With reference to the figure of income, expenditure and the reserve, wired to you yesterday, I give below their details:

Amounts sent

Heads	*Date*	*Amount*
Smyrna	3. 5. 1921	Rs. 20,000/-
Sale of receipts	26. 8. 1921	Rs. 4,000/-
Smyrna	- do -	Rs. 3,000/-
Khilafat	5. 8. 1921	Rs. 107/-
Khilafat	15. 11. 1921	Rs. 1,500/-*
Angora	12. 12. 1921	Rs. 23,000/-
Smyrna	- do -	Rs. 2,000/-
	Total	Rs. 53,607/-*

*N.B. This amount was given to the *New Times* for purchasing 2000 copies of the Historic Trial at a concession rate of 12 annas each settled by Seth Sahib. It has been debited to your accounts. Kindly credit Rs. 1500/- for Khilafat and pass a receipt.

Total amount sent to Central Khilafat Committee	Rs. 53,607 - 0- 0

Total expenses till 12-12-1921	Rs. 11,831 - 5- 8
Total	Rs. 65,438 - 5- 8
Total income of 1921 on 12-12-1921	Rs. 82,275 -15- 5
Reserve	Rs. 16,837 -9- 11

Details of the Reserve according to Heads

Khilafat	Rs. 11,920 - 2 - 8
Smyrna	Rs. 3,293 - 0 - 7
Angora	Rs. 417 - 0 - 8
Receipts	Rs. 1,178 - 0 - 0
Khilafat literature	Rs. 29 - 6 - 0
	Rs. 16,837 - 9 - 9

The Angora Fund is being collected by volunteers and by the Khilafat Committees. During the week an appeal for the Angora Fund was made in a mosque in Karachi after Friday prayers and about Rs. 50/- were collected.

5. SCHOOLS AND COLLEGES

Nil.

6. INDIAN NATIONAL SERVICE AND VOLUNTEERS

Nil.

7. LAWYERS AND COURTS

The *Sindhi* dated the 24th December 1921 states that Mr. Harjandas, Pleader, has resigned his honorary appointment of Assistant Public Prosecutor in the Sukkur District owing to the repressive policy of Government.

A meeting was held in Rohri where Mr. Lakhasing, Pleader, and others exhorted the audience to start a National court in Rohri.

8. SWADESHI MOVEMENT

Nil.

9. BOYCOTT OF EUROPEANS BY THEIR DOMESTIC SERVANTS

Nil.

10. GOVERNMENT SERVICE

Nil.

11. AGRARIAN TROUBLES

Nil.[42]

[42] Rest of the report missing.

6

History of the Non-Co-operation and Khilafat Movements in the North-West Frontier Province

The Khilafat Movement in the North-West Frontier Province

To appreciate fully the initial force of this movement it is necessary to recall some of the events which shortly preceded it.

These were:

(a) The Rowlatt Bill Agitation.
(b) M. Gandhi's Satyagraha, or Passive Resistance Movement.
(c) The Punjab Disorders of 1919.
(d) The Third Afghan War of 1919.

Of these four, the first and last reacted noticeably in Peshawar.

Another important movement which, coming at the same time as the Khilafat agitation, influenced the latter in no small measure was Mr. Gandhi's non-co-operation campaign.

Shortly after the Armistice there had appeared in India a movement directed towards the obviation of any harshness in the terms to be offered to Turkey. Indian Mussulmans felt that they had contributed greatly to the defeat of the Ottoman Empire, and they naturally desired that the post-war settlement should accord with their own predilections. Little by little an enthusiastic section of advanced Muhammadan opinion, aided first by the delay in the conclusion of the settlement, and secondly by the Indian reaction to a wave of anti-Muslim feeling which swept Europe and America, succeeded in arousing the bulk of their community to a lively apprehension that the Christian powers of the world were about to destroy the last remaining bulwark of Islam. Gradually the whole of Indian Muslim opinion, Shia as well as Sunni, became consolidated into a untied [united] front for the support of Turkey's cause.

On the Armistice in November 1918, the All-India Muslim League specially invited the foremost 'Ulemas' of the country to their 1918 Session in Delhi, in order to record a definite decree regarding the Khilafat.

The speech of Dr. Ansari, Chairman of the Reception Committee, was the first official statement of Muslim demands, which were detailed in Resolution Nos. 7 and 8 passed at this session.

Dr. Ansari's speech contained incitement to acts of violence and disloyalty, and its publication was therefore prohibited by the Punjab Government (Notification No. 2615-J. of 29th Jan. 1919).

As no copies of this speech appeared in the North-West Frontier Province, no action was taken here.

Later in the year, on September 21st, 1919, the All-India Muslim League held a special session at Lucknow, where the following resolutions were passed:

(i) That October 17th, 1919, be observed by all Mussulmans in India as a special day for meetings, and for prayers for the safety of the Khilafat.

(ii) That a Central Khilafat Committee be established in Bombay with branch sub-committees all over India.

Mr. Gandhi, in his paper *Young India* called upon all Hindus to show their sympathy by observing October 17th as a day of national humiliation.

The effect of this session was to launch an active campaign of Khilafat agitation.

Special efforts were made to make the First Khilafat Day, October 17th, 1919, a striking success throughout the country, but in the North-West Frontier, as elsewhere, the response was poor. Only in Kohat did any meeting take place, and even there no persons of note attended.

Later enquiries showed that it was only the special efforts of men down country, which had convened this half-hearted meeting in Kohat.

The practical failure of the First Khilafat Day necessitated some further action, and the Mussulman leaders therefore summoned a special conference—the First All-India Conference at Delhi.

This conference met on 22nd November 1919, 23rd November 1919 and passed the following resolutions:

(i) Boycott of all Peace Celebrations.

(ii) Despatch of a deputation to England.

(iii) Non-co-operation with Government.

A committee was formed to give practical effect to their edict of non-co-operation and various leading Hindus, invited to a special session of this conference, confirmed the resolution to boycott the Peace Celebrations.

In only a few places in India was there any real response to these directions, and in the North-West Frontier Province the Peace Celebrations passed off successfully at all Head Quarters.

Dissatisfied with this result the leaders held a special conference (Second All-India Khilafat Conference) at Amritsar during the Christmas week of 1919, and a resolution was passed expressing extreme regret and sorrow that, not only had the demands of Muhammadans not been conceded regarding the Khilafat, Jazirat-ul-Arab, the Holy Places, and the integrity of the Ottoman Empire, but that, on the contrary, the speeches of British Cabinet Ministers gave rise to strong suspicion that the British Government did not support these demands. The resolution to despatch a deputation to England was reaffirmed.

Later these resolutions were practically repeated by the Ulemas Conference, the Muslim League, and the Congress.

Early in 1920 the Khilafat Deputation sailed for England to lay its case before the Ministers of the Crown.

In February 1920, yet another Khilafat Conference was held in Bengal, in which a resolution was passed declaring that Muhammadans would be forced to sever their loyal connection with the British Throne unless the peace terms did actually conform with Muslim demands.

At this session the 19th March 1920 was fixed as the second Khilafat day.

It appears probable that this date would witness some excitement in the North-West Frontier Province, and, in order to forestall any hostile demonstrations, Sir Abdul Qayum Khan, K.C.I.E., convened a meeting in Peshawar on March 5th, 1920, and passed a nominal resolution expressing general sympathy with the agitation down country.

Meanwhile Mahatma Gandhi had busied himself with his efforts to make March 19th a really successful day of national mourning, and, on March 10th, he issued his manifesto (Annexure III).

In support of this a meeting was held in Peshawar on March 17th and directions were issued for the 19th to be observed as the Second Khilafat Day.

The resolutions of this meeting are filed as Exhibit A.

A proposal was carried, which asked the Chief Commissioner to disregard the orders of the Government of India's telegram of March 14th and to allow all officials to attend the meeting on the 19th March.

March 19th saw a complete *hartal* in Peshawar, where a meeting of protest was held in the Idgah.

Resolutions passed are marked as Exhibit B, and copies of telegrams despatched are filed as Exhibits C-I, C-II, and C-III.

Exhibit C-I is noticeable as having emanated from the Islamia College.

The first Provincial Khilafat Committee was formed on this occasion, and it included a Sikh as Assistant Secretary.

Outside Peshawar there was only one demonstration, and that a serious one, in the Hazara District. This was the work of certain fanatical anti-British Mullahs, headed by Muhammad Ishaq, Imam of the Juma Mosque in Manshera, who managed to acquire a commanding influence over the northern portion of the Hazara District. By the end of April 1920, Muhammad Ishaq had become the leading figure in the district.

Every Friday crowds assembled at his mosque to hear his speeches which revealed a strong anti-British feeling.

In May he turned his attention to other parts of the district where he was also received with considerable enthusiasm.

By the end of June his influence was nearing its height and he was by this time deep in transborder intrigue.

By July he had become blatantly disloyal and openly abusive of Government and all Government servants. He held open *darbar* and started settling cases, both civil and criminal, reports to the Police rapidly declined and they were subjected to every kind of abuse and insult.

He had appointed his own local agents all over the District and it was firmly believed that Government dared not cross swords with him.

August saw the zenith of his power: the Pakhli plain was openly hostile and the Police Station at Shinkari was isolated in the midst of a hostile community. Day after day large crowds, many of them carrying arms, assembled to hear Muhammad Ishaq's inflammatory harangues, and, on August 22nd before a crowd of over 20,000 he announced that the time for *jehad* had arrived. This was the signal for a rising of the Black Mountain Tribes and for serious trouble among the residents of Agror.

The time for action had now arrived and it was taken.

A moveable column left for Oghi on the 24th August and Muhammad Ishaq, his chief lieutenant, Muhammad Irfan, and a large number of his so-called officers were promptly arrested.

The effect was instantaneous: the trouble subsided and the authority of Government was restored.

Meanwhile Mahatma Gandhi, to commemorate the Punjab oppression of 1919, had fixed April 6th-13th, 1920, as his so-called National Week.

His programme was followed in Peshawar, where the opening meeting was held on 6th, a Khilafat meeting on the 9th, and a final meeting on the 13th.

The special resolutions prescribed for this week were adopted without much discussion: these demanded the settlement of the Turkish question in conformity with Muslim wishes, and the redress of the Punjab wrongs.

Except in Peshawar, the week passed almost unnoticed in the Province.

The next step in the general campaign was the special conference at Delhi on the 19th and 20th April 1920, and it was at this meeting that the *hijrat* decision was first reached.

Abdul Ghaffar of Utmanzai in the Peshawar District attended this conference.

Shortly afterwards the news of the San Remo decision reached India and created considerable alarm.

Mr. Gandhi's speech in this connection is shown as Annexure D. Non-co-operation, he declared, was the only remedy.

In view of the suppressed excitement the Chief Commissioner, on the 6th May 1920, summoned a meeting of the more influential Frontier leaders to Government House, where speeches were made, and discussion held, with a view to the prevention of the more regrettable incidents of the previous year: an account of this meeting is given as Exhibit D-I.

On the 15th May, Ghulam Muhammad Aziz, Amritsari, Secretary of the Anjuman Muhajirin of Delhi, arrived in Peshawar, and a local Hijrat Committee was then formed.

About the same time various resignations, due to Khilafat grievances, were reported from Peshawar: four were from the Primary Schools and two from the Canal Department, and it is generally believed that a young School Master in Peshawar was responsible for them.

Later came the resignation of a Probationary Sub-Inspector of the Dera Ismail Khan Police.

On the 20th May 1920, the first batch of Muhajirin started for Afghanistan, a small part of 21 in all.

The three succeeding months, however, witnessed an alarming increase in this movement, more especially in the Peshawar District.

While it is certain that the movement was largely exploited, for political reasons only, by leaders from down country, and that every questionable method was employed, and every possible excuse used, to stimulate the religious zeal of the ignorant villagers, yet it must be admitted that a certain number of educated men went with their eyes open, and in the firm belief that the religious oppression of the British and Indian Governments left them no course but to emigrate.

Over 95 per cent of the emigrants, however, can safely be regarded as ignorant dupes who had been deliberately misled not only by the malicious distortion of actual facts, but also by the impure invention of the wildest stories, many of which were so grotesque as to be incapable of belief in any ordinary times. The time, however, was not ordinary, and the most fantastic tale was readily accepted by the ignorant villager, whose religious enthusiasm was stirred to a pitch closely resembling frenzy. In the Swabi and Charsadda Tahsils of the Peshawar District the exodus at one time threatened to become a stampede, and although the great majority of emigrants came from the Peshawar District, the movement gained some support also in Hazara, Bannu and Dera Ismail Khan.

In Peshawar two special incidents served to give stimulus to the movement.

These were the death of a frenzied Muhajir, at the hands of a British soldier, on Kacha Garhi Railway Station, and the arrival in Peshawar of the special train of religious emigrants from Sind.

It is estimated that some 24,000 persons, animated in a high degree by religious enthusiasm, moved from this Province to Afghanistan during the months of May to Aug. 1920, and the movement still showed no noticeable signs of collapse when the Afghan Government suddenly became alarmed and forbade the Muhajirin entry into Afghanistan.

Of the unhappy experiences of these Muhajirin, of their treatment in Afghanistan, and of the sad awakening from their dreams of religious glory, much could be written: it will suffice to mention here that special arrangements were made by Government to mitigate their hardship and to re-settle them in this province on the lands which they had so rashly abandoned.

A separate note is submitted (Exhibit E) on the Khilafat Volunteer movement, which came into prominence during the *hijrat* movement of 1920.

The Third Khilafat Day passed, during the *hijrat* period, with a *hartal* in Peshawar City; elsewhere it went by almost unnoticed.

It was in September 1920, that the Indian National Congress, in a special session at Calcutta, gave its sanction to the non-co-operation movement, and in the next month the movement began to show signs of life in this Province.

Bannu reported the resignations of 12 Lambardars and, in November, some 15 students of the Islamia College, following the lead given by Aligarh College, went on strike and left to join Muhammad Ali's National University.

Next came the confirmation of the programme from the Jamiat-ul-Ulema at their Delhi Conference, and, early in December 1920, a movement was started in Peshawar to open an Azad High School.

This idea, however, got no further than the mere opening ceremony on December 9th, 1920; this was not surprising in view of the differences of opinion among the promoters of the movement (see Exhibit F).

At the end of December the formation of Khilafat tribunals, for the settlement of civil cases, was reported from the Bannu District, and in Jan. 1921, Mazullah Khan, a retired Inspector of Police, and President of the Bannu Khilafat Committee, resigned his post of Honorary Magistrate and Assessor.

Provincial interest now centred in the Bannu District and three Pleaders, who were leading the non-co-operation movement, were refused licenses to practice. They came out into the open, and placed themselves at the head of all agitation, with the result that, by the end of January 1921, village committees had been started in most of the Bannu villages, which were regularly visited by the leaders of the agitation.

Early in February came the expulsion of Sayad Habib Shah of the *Siyasat*, and this was made an excuse for further agitation.

By March 1921, it had become clear that some sedative was necessary for the district, and orders were therefore served on the leaders to refrain from holding political meetings. This action had the desired effect, and *ex*-Inspector Mazullah Khan thought it advisable to slip across the border into Afghan territory.

By May the situation in Bannu had improved, and the Lambardars then asked to be allowed to withdraw their resignation.

Meanwhile, in Dera Ismail Khan some 30 students of the Biradari High School had attempted to boycott the school, and had engineered a strike in February 1921. This whole affair was childish, and the strike quickly collapsed.

In March 1921, the Kohat Khilafat Committee declared itself to be an Arbitration Court; this court, however, does not appear to have been called upon to perform any duties during its short life, and a similar proposal in Peshawar also died a natural death.

The result of the Divisional Khilafat Conference in Rawalpindi, in March 1921, was to infuse new life into the Peshawar Khilafat Committee, which had remained inactive after the *hijrat* fiasco.

Certain Hindus of the Congress Committee secured election in the Peshawar Khilafat Committee and in this way an alliance was established between the two bodies.

National Primary Schools were opened in Nowshera and Utmanzai under the aegis of the Anjuman-i-Talim-ul Quran of Nowshera; these schools still exist.

Hartal was observed in all District Head Quarters and, although only partially successful in other districts, was complete in Peshawar, where the week was marked by continuous political agitation ending with an extensive *hartal* on the 13th.

Four meetings were held in Peshawar during the week under the joint auspices of the Congress and Khilafat Committees, and the use of intemperate language created some bitterness of feeling.

Three leading agitators were, therefore, placed on security, others were served with notices under Section 144, Criminal Procedure Code, and 'agitation meetings' were prohibited in Cities and Cantonments.

On May 11th, 16 students from Aligarh University arrived in Peshawar for propaganda work. These were all ex-students of the Islamia College, Peshawar, who had previously left in pursuance of non-co-operation. Their enthusiasm and hope were somewhat damped by finding the Peshawar Khilafat Committee in a chastened mood owing to the recent arrest of its leaders. A note of their activities is given as Exhibit G.

The veto on political meetings in Peshawar prevented local agitators from protesting against the arrest of the Ali Brothers as vehemently as they desired; they endeavoured, however, to evade the orders, and to hold a monster meeting of protest in the mosque of Mahabat Khan, but their plans failed to mature.

Persistent meetings were, nevertheless, held in Kohat and Dera Ismail Khan, where feelings ran high and language exceeded the bounds of propriety. In Kohat three men were sentenced for refusing to furnish security, and in Dera Ismail Khan it was found necessary to place 8 persons in confinement.

The Ulemas' Conference in Lahore attracted a number of agitators from the Province; among these were several Khilafat Volunteers and the Lahore member of the North-West Frontier student propagandists. The effect of this visit to Lahore was disquieting, and there were indications of a dangerous revival of 'volunteer' interference.

Their activities, however, were somewhat cramped by the news of the action taken in other provinces against volunteer corps and non-co-operation agitators. Their misbehaviour and truculence, nevertheless, necessitated action in Peshawar also, and 8 of the most vehement agitators were placed under arrest.

This was made the excuse for violent meetings of protest, and many inflammatory speeches were delivered, in which the repetition of the proscribed *fatwa*, and the determination to cause a *hartal* during His Royal Highness the Prince's visit, were loudly emphasised.

This particular agitation mostly confined itself to the lower strata of the city population, but the increasing participation of raw youths of immature age provided a feature of ugly significance.

Careful inquiries, made with a view to ascertaining the details of the organisations, and the depth of the general support and feeling behind the various Khilafat movements in this Province, revealed the fact that only in two districts was there anything worthy of the name of organisation, and even in these two districts - *viz.* Peshawar and Kohat - the entire absence of any regular financial support - from Muhammadans of position was striking evidence of the extremely artificial nature of the whole movement so loudly voiced by Khilafat Committees, Volunteer Corps, and the like.

The Utmanzai National School, which was doing useful education work was the sole example of any genuine or spontaneous public support.

While all patriotic Muhammadans naturally rejoiced at the Turkish victories over the Greeks, it was only the newspaper-reading community which was roused to any pitch of enthusiasm.

Meetings of congratulations were held in Peshawar City, Ziarat Kaka Sahib, Utmanzai, Tangi and Nowshera, and in these the popular catch phrase was Great Britain's perfidy with the Turks.

Responsible Muhammadan opinion underwent little change in consequence of this *coup d'etat*, thus proving how little they had really sympathised with the previous artificial agitation. The agitators themselves were somewhat non-plussed to find that the Turkish Government had itself knocked the bottom out of the spurious agitation, and, after looking unsuccessfully for a clever lead from down country, they very conveniently arranged to forget, or disregard, the incident.

The Lauzanne [*sic*] Conference attracted more attention, but, curiously enough, the breakdown of the negotiations was marked by no outburst of vehemence. It is possible that the eloquence of the local leaders was somewhat cramped by feat of yet another *volte face* on the part of the Turkish Government, whose previous, and totally unexpected, deposition of the Khalifa had placed them in a wholly ridiculous position.

The final conclusion of peace between Turkey and the Allies was welcomed by all responsible Muhammadans, whose feelings were marked more by relief at the removal of a cause for agitation than by any great enthusiasm.

In November 1923, the news of the final abolition of the Khilafat in Turkey removed all remaining force from the Khilafat agitation. An article from the *Muslim Outlook* is given at Appendix R. [Not reproduced]

The death-knell having thus sounded the leaders of all anti-Government agitation, in spite of laborious efforts, failed to attract any popular attention towards their Jazirat-ul-Arab Day.

This question, after the death of the Khilafat movement, remained the only possible excuse for agitation, but the population in general refused to be moved to any feeling of enthusiasm, or, indeed, to display any real personal interest.

Even this last remaining grievance was removed in the following year, 1924, by the expulsion from the Hedjaz of King Hussain, who was commonly believed to be under the influence of Great

Britain. The advent of the Wahabis is not objected to by Sunnis or Shias, and their régime will naturally be judged on its merits.

The total amount of money contributed to the various funds connected with the Khilafat movement is believed to be as follows:-

Statement showing amounts of Funds contributed towards Khilafat movement under different heads as follows (up to 30th June 1922)

Khilafat Fund	Rs. 55,784 - 0 - 0
Angora Fund	Rs. 28,919 - 4 - 3
Smyrna Fund	Rs. 5,008 - 0 - 0
Moplah Fund	Rs. 209 - 0 - 0

The following are the outstanding events in the North-West Frontier Province:

(1) The Khilafat Day, 19th March 1920; *hartal* and meetings in Peshawar; formation of Peshawar Khilafat Committee.

(2) First National Week, April 6th-13th, 1920; various meetings held in Peshawar.

(3) The Hijrat movement of 1920.

(4) First local results of non-co-operation movement, 1920; strike in Islamia College, Peshawar, and resignation of Lambardars in Bannu.

(5) Second National Week, April 6th-13th, 1921. Meetings and dangerous speeches in Peshawar; prohibition of meetings and restrictions on leaders.

(6) Arrival of Islamia College strikers, in the rôle of student propagandists from Aligarh, and their activities in this Province, May 1921.

(7) The Lauzanne [*sic*] settlement, July 1923; general satisfaction and subsequent decline of agitation.

(8) The separation, by the Angora Assembly, of the temporal and religious powers of the Khalifa, this unexpectedly removed the corner-stone of the agitation platform, and completely stultified all previous eloquence of the agitators. November 1923.

(9) The Turkish abolition of the Khilafat, resulting in the final collapse of the agitation in India. March 1924.

(10) Abdication of King Hussain, and the end of the Jazirat-ul-Arab grievance.

With the ground well-prepared by the agitation over the Rowlatt Bill the seeds of the Khilafat movement flourished early. The First Khilafat Day was fully observed in Peshawar, and the First National Week, supported by the Central Khilafat Committee and hallowed by Mahatma Gandhi's personal edicts, also proved a success in Peshawar City.

The *hijrat* calamity had ended, and general agitation was on the decline, when the non-co-operation movement commenced and affected the Islamia College and the Bannu District.

On each occasion the situation was kept in hand by timely action, the restriction of firebrand leaders, and the prohibition of agitation meetings were always effective as remedies, and it was only during the frenzy of the *hijrat* fever that Fabian tactics were at all successful.

The Amir's desire to make the *hijrat* movement an Afghan success was frustrated by the country's lack of organisation and resources, while the force of the movement at its height created genuine alarm in Kabul and Jalalabad.

The Angora Assembly struck a heavy blow at the Khilafat movement when it forced the Khalifa from his throne, and finally killed it outright by abolishing the office itself.

Moslems are of the opinion that the general agitation was successful in that it influenced the Home Government, and thereby secured more favourable terms for Turkey.

There is nothing to prove that the movement in this Province was in any way connected with the more dangerous Pan-Islamic movement in India; the object was to secure the full restoration of the Khilafat, and the overthrow of the existing Government was never contemplated.

Hindus joined the movement in the hope of enlisting Muhammadan support in their own grievance—*i.e.* the Punjab wrongs of 1919.

The history of the movement indicates that eloquent, and

unscrupulous, leaders can raise the masses to a high pitch of religious enthusiasm, without the latter fully understanding the actual grievances, or the cause and remedies for them.

Of this the *hijrat* fiasco is a striking example and it is safe to say that, of the Peshawar emigrants, not one-tenth fully understood the reasons for their own actions.

On the other hand it is not, perhaps, too much to hope that the more responsible leaders have learnt the danger of playing with fire, and have now realised that, by enlisting the support of ignorant villagers, they can achieve the reforms necessary for the community at large, but that by goading the masses into a state of religious frenzy they render them useless for any sane purpose.

ANNEXURE I

Dr. Ansari, as Chairman of the Reception Committee, delivered a lengthy speech. Dealing with the Moslem world situation, he said that the time has come when the Mussalmans demand that the Ministers of the Crown, who are in charge of the destinies of the British Empire, shall do their duty by the Mussalmans of India.

We all know how Islam has suffered in its temporal power since the latter half of the nineteenth century. Each succeeding generation has witnessed the gradual disruption of the House of Islam. Diverse reasons have been brought forth and plausible explanations have not been wanting; lofty political doctrines have been invented to screen aggressive designs and humanitarian principles have been advanced to justify the acts of robbery done to Islamic Kingdoms. The 'white man's burden' too has been paraded before an innocent and all-believing world. But bereft of all the verbiage of innocent-looking doctrines and high-sounding principles, this tragedy can be traced to the common dislike of the Moslem or the avarice and greed of the chancelleries of Europe.

He next gave a history of the Khilafat asserting that the Sultan is the only lawful Khilafa [*sic*] and that Sharif Hussain who, actuated by personal ambitions and self-interests, raised the standard of revolt against the Sultan, not only disregarded political morality but according [to] Moslem belief and religious teaching broke the explicit and clear commandment of God and His Prophet; the revolt of the Sharif is totally *haram*.

As regards the Holy Places the most important duty of the Khalifa is to keep them under Moslem protection. This protection means nothing less than the complete and unquestioned sovereignty of the Sultan over them and their immunity from interference on the part of non-Moslems. It is the firm conviction of the Moslem world that the house of Osman has discharged its duties in respect of the Holy Places to its entire satisfaction.

He next proceeded to answer the question: what are the Holy Places of Islam? and cited various traditions regarding the boundaries of 'the island of Arabia'. The Holy Places are Mecca and Medina and Jerusalem which ranks next to the Ka'aba, Najaf and Karbala and Baghdad. The achievements of Salah-ud-Din and the blood of millions of *mujahidins* did not flow in the days of the crusades to lose Palestine to a people who cannot put forward any recognisable claim to it. Pain and resentment have been created among the Mussalmans of India to see that the attitude of their Government in connection with this matter has been diametrically opposed to their wishes and sentiments.

He next said that Moslems are deeply interested in the future of four hundred millions of their co-religionists and demand that not only the integrity and independence of the present Moslem States be maintained intact but the wrong done to the Arabs of North Africa and the Tartars and Turks of Central Asia be redressed and all these people be given a free chance of determining their own form of Government.

He reviewed the position of Mussalmans in India, saying that the period of war, as far as the relations of the officials and the Mussalmans are concerned, has been one varying from bias against them to one of antipathy, suspicion, mistrust and even dislike. As if the anxieties and agonies of the war were not sufficient in India, Moslems were being subjected to a treatment which by no self-respecting people would be tolerated. He then spoke in the usual manner on Moslem interments, the Moslem Press and Moslem meetings with special reference to the stoppage of the Calcutta meeting of September. He argued that the two avenues of the [*sic*] ventilating grievances—a free press and the right of association—had been closed to them.

He next mentioned that there was a growing feeling among Mussalmans that attempts have been made to interfere with their religious liberty. He instanced the indirect influence brought to bear upon the managers of mosques to remove the name of the Khalifa from the Friday prayers, and the peregrinations of certain persons in search of signature on the *fatwa* purporting to declare the rebel Sharif of Mecca to be the future Khalifa of Muhammadans.

Arguing on behalf of Hindu-Moslem unity, he appealed to the Hindus to take effective measures to prevent any recurrence of deplorable incidents such as that of Kartarpur, and he concluded his speed by demanding the application to India of the doctrine of self-determination.

ANNEXURE II

Resolution No. 7 (Holy Places). The All India Moslem League enters its strong protest against the occupation of Jerusalem and Najaf-i-Ashraf by His Majesty's forces and having regard to the solemn promises given to the Mussalmans regarding those places, hopes that all such places will be immediately restored.

The League further requests His Majesty's Government that in view of the wishes of the Mussalmans of India it will use its good offices to dissuade other allied powers from taking any step which might affect the position and status of their Holy Places.

Proposed by Nawab Zulqader Jang of Lucknow.

The speech of the proposer was but a brief introduction to Maulana Abdul Bari's which followed. The Maulana opened by asserting that the Mussalmans should not have allowed Union Jacks to be put up in the hall in which they were deliberating upon national subjects; although it was the flag of their rulers it contained the cross which they could never respect. He then commenced to read its [*sic*] written speech but had to desist owing to his voice being feeble. Muhammad Shoa'ib then tried to read it but the Maulana's writing was too much for him and the speech was eventually read by his attendant. He said that Dr. M.A. Ansari had already dealt with the question of the Holy Places, the Sharif and the Caliphate and that he had very little more to say. He discussed the terms Dar-ul-Aman, Dar-ul-Islam and Dar-ul-Harb and said they were not concerned with the latter at present. In Dar-ul-Aman there should be a Shaikh-ul-Islam and in Dar-ul-Islam there should be a complete religious freedom. In the event of an attack on any Moslem country it is incumbent on the inhabitants of a Dar-ul-Islam to defend their Moslem brethren.

As regards the exclusion of *mushrikin* (non-believers) from the Jazirat-ul-Arab (the island of Arabia), referred to by Dr. Ansari, the Maulana said that he could quote a clearer *hadis* to the effect that Christians and Jews should at all costs be driven out of this land. The Holy Places should be evacuated by non-Moslems. He deprecated the idea of the Caliphate being conferred on any one but the Sultan of Turkey, and added that it was the duty of every Mussalman to help the Sultan. He concluded with the remark that a rebel could not be chosen to be Caliph, hence the Sharif was not eligible.

Maulvi Kifayat-ullah, supporting the resolution, thanked the League for the warm welcome extended to the Ulema. He read from the proceedings of a meeting of Ulama held at the Fatehpuri mosque on December 31st a resolution regarding the Holy Places passed by that body, and said that Government had made a clear promise and should abide by it and evacuate Jerusalem, Najaf-i-Ashraf and other Holy Places. If they failed to do so he could not say to what extent the Moslems would remain loyal. He added that they were apprehensive from the accounts of the returned Hajis and from the news that British warships were in Jeddah harbour, that the British Government was not going to keep its promise to maintain the sanctity of the Holy Places. Khawaja [*sic*] Abdul Majid proposed an amendment asking for the evacuation of the Holy Places. He was supported by Haji Musa Khan of Aligarh. The president asked him to withdraw it but he refused. Maulana Abdul Qadir Azad Subhani then opposed the amendment and appealed to the Khwaja to withdraw. The Khwaja said he would do so at Maulana Abdul Bari's bidding. The Maulana then got up greatly exited and said that any one who considered the action of the English right was dishonest and a single movement of his pen and tongue would shake the world. He would do more than the Khwaja wanted but would do it in his own time. The Khwaja then withdrew his amendment and the resolution was declared carried.

Resolution No. 8 (Khilafat). The All-India League deem it necessary to remind the Government of the decalration of the policy made by His Majesty's Government that the question of the Khilafat is one for Moslem opinion alone to decide and begs to point out that any departure from that policy will cause great resentment and ill-feeling among the Mussalmans. The League further requests His Majesty's Government to dissuade all allied power that might contemplate any interference with this question from taking any action in this matter.

Proposed by Mr. Muhammad Asghar, Barrister-at-Law (Hyderabad).

Seconded by Mr. Ghulam Mohi-ud-din (Punjab).

The proposer's speech was not remarkable. Maulana Ahmad Said said that Maulana Abdul Bari had told him that he had seen in Al-Qibla the Sharif styled as Amir-ul-Mominin; the Mussalmans would not have the Sharif as custodian of the Holy Places as Sheikh Faisal in reply to an address in England said that the Holy soil of the *haram* and the Holy land of the Hedjaz which had been forbidden grounds for non-Moslems, was now open to the white men.

Ghulam Mohi-ud-Din of the Punjab said that Salah-ud-Din had defended the Holy Places at the sacrifice of thousand Moslem lives against

Christian hordes and the Holy Places should remain under the Caliphate of the Sultan of Turkey. Maulvi Sana-ullah, Ahl-i-Hadis, said that a non-Moslem cannot select an Imam for an ordinary Muhalla mosque, not to speak of selecting the Caliph for the Mussalmans of the universe.

ANNEXURE III

Now a word as to what may be done if the demands are not granted. The barbarous method is warfare, open or secret. This must be ruled out if only because it is impracticable. If I could but persuade every one that it is always bad, we should gain all lawful ends much quicker. The power that is irresistible. But my argument to-day against violence is based upon pure expediency, *i.e.* its utter futility. Non-co-operation is therefore the only remedy left open to us. It is the cleanest remedy as it is the most effective when it is absolutely free from all violence. It becomes a duty when co-operation means degradation or humiliation or an injury to one's cherished religious sentiment. England cannot accept a meek submission by us to an unjust usurpation of rights which to Mussalmans means a matter of life and death. We may therefore begin at the top as also the bottom. Those who are holding offices of honour or emolument ought to give them up. Those who belong to the menial services under Government should do likewise. Non-co-operation does not apply to services under private individuals. I cannot approve of the threat of ostracism against those who do not adopt the remedy of non-co-operation. It is only a voluntary withdrawal which is effective. For voluntary withdrawal alone is a test of popular feeling and dissatisfaction. Advice to the soldiers to refuse to serve is premature. It is the last, not the first step. We should be entitled to take that step when the Viceroy, the Secretary of State and the Premier leave us.

Moreover every step withdrawing co-operation has to be taken with the greatest deliberation. We must proceed slowly so as to ensure retention of self-control under the fiercest heat.

EXHIBIT A

(1) This meeting agrees with the resolution proposed on the 5th March, that a petition should be submitted to the Secretary of State, through the Chief Commissioner and His Excellency the Viceroy, that our Holy Places should not be taken from the Turkish Government, and the Sultan should not be removed from Constantinople.

(2) All political prisoners should be released.

(3) The persons who were put under security during the last trouble should be released.
(4) The strike should be made quietly on the 19th March. No processions will be taken out, and no black mark will be worn. Nothing would be done against law.
(5) After the Juma prayer all Hindus and Muhammadans will attend a meeting at the Idgah. If it rains the meeting will be held in the Mohabat Khan's Mosque.
(6) One Ali Gul, son of Abdullah of Mohallah Shahghasi Nazim, stood up and up a resolution that the Chief Commissioner would attend the meeting of the 19th March. This proposal was seconded by Hasan Jan, son of Agha Dilawar Jan of Peshawar, and was carried.

EXHIBIT B

(1) Expression of sympathy with the Sultan of Turkey over his troubles.
(2) Association of the Sultan's name as the 'Khalifa' with every Juma prayer; any 'imam' omitting this to be ousted.
(3) Restoration of the Holy Places.
(4) Indignation at the attitude adopted by the Archbishop of Canterbury and his Colleagues.
(5) Occupation of Constantinople to be disallowed.
(6) Expression of thanks to Enver Pasha, and Mustapha Kemal Pasha, for their exertions in the Islamic cause.
(7) Preference being given to Swadeshi goods over those of the foreign manufacture.
(8) General agreement with the proceedings of the Central Khilafat Committee.

EXHIBIT C-I

To the Secretary of State, London

Students, Islamia College, Peshawar, strongly protest against proposed dismantlement of Turkish Empire. Condemn agitation for expulsion of Sultan from Constantinople.

Earnestly urge Holy Places should continue under direct control of Khalifa.

(Sd.) Abdul Qaiyum (for students)

EXHIBIT C-II

To the Private Secretary, Viceroy's Camp

Respectfully request Your Excellency to convey to His Majesty the King-Emperor that if peace terms with His Majesty the Sultan of Turkey are not in accordance with the dictates of 'Shariat' then commandments of Islam will force Muhammadans to sever loyal connections with British throne.

(Sd.) Sayed Maqbul Shah, President Khilafat Meeting.

EXHIBIT C-III

To His Excellency the Turkish Premier, Constantinople

A representative meeting of Muhammadans of Frontier Province professes profoundest love, obedience and loyalty to His Majesty the Sultan and humbly pray God to make the Khalifat-ul-Mominin victorious.

(Sd.) Maqbul Shah, Chairman

ANNEXURE D

The decision is bound greatly to disturb the Muhammadan mind ... The issues involved are tremendous. Greatest self-restraint is, therefore, absolutely necessary. Non-co-operation is, I remain convinced, the only remedy enabling India to give disciplined expression to the deep wound that is being made into her very wound.... To these who distrust non-co-operation I can only say, in all humility, you will accelerate eruption of violence if you succeed in defeating the scheme of non-co-operation, and cannot replace it by some definite course of strong action which must be more than a mere protest; so much more that resort to it must bring about the desired result.

EXHIBIT D-I

A meeting was held in the grounds of Government House, Peshawar, on the 6th May 1920, at 11-30 A.M.

In addressing those present (in Urdu), the Chief Commissioner said he wished to speak about three main points:

(1) The Khilafat.
(2) Political agitation.
(3) The Amir of Afghanistan.

1. In answer to the Chief Commissioner's question as to who would be Khalifa, Sharif Ullah Khan said 'no body can say who will be the Khalifa'. Arbab Dost Muhammad Khan, who rose after him, said that it was a matter for the Ulemas to decide.

2. The principal points under this head were last year's incidents and Hindu-Muslim unity. The Hon'ble the Chief Commissioner said that the regrettable incidents of last year had now been closed and that if there was any genuineness in the Hindu-Muslim unity - which would be for the good of the administration - it was welcome, otherwise not.

3. The object of the Mussorie Conference was to dispel mal-impressions which had come about through garbled and distorted accounts being conveyed to Afghanistan from time to time. It was not known whether the recent activities on the part of Afghans in Kurram, Chitral, and Chman had taken place with the Amir's concurrence. Other matters dealt with under this head were the abduction of women across the border etc.

In concluding his address the Hon'ble the Chief Commissioner expressed the hope that, if necessity arose, help such as had been rendered hitherto would be forthcoming. With one accord the audience replied in the affirmative.

I. Captain Ahmad Nawaz Khan of Dera Ismail Khan. He was the first speaker after the Chief Commissioner; he delivered his address and said that just as Hon'ble the Chief Commissioner had spoken of them as being like children whose welfare was at heart, in the same manner were they prepared to sacrifice their all. Peace was desired by the people of his district; the people of Punjab were more enlightened on account of their advance in education, hence more agitation.

The question of Khilafat should be settled by the people of Arabia, for that was the birthplace of Islam and the Koran.

That, if necessity arose, more help than was given last year would be forthcoming.

II. Captain Muhammad Akbar Khan of Hoti then said that anybody could be Khalifa (? *i.e.* Arabian) and that just as they (he and his forefathers) had fought against Turkey in the Great War, they would fight against any other foe (of Great Britain) in the future.

III. Muhammad Azam Khan said he could not say if the present Khalifa could be Khalifa for all time, but as they (he and his forefathers) had been loyal to Government in the past, they were ready to help in every way in the future.

IV. Arbab Dost Muhammad Khan said that the question of the Khilafat could best be settled by the Ulemas, and that he was ready to serve Government when required to do so.

V. L. Dewan Chand, Public Prosecutor, Peshawar, said that Hindus say they are in full agreement with Mussalmans regarding the Khilafat but that he did not know how it affected them. He had never been affected by it.

In connection with political agitation he said that Vakils in the Punjab, to become popular, assumed leadership and presidentship, but that the people (the Bar) in Peshawar were satisfied with their lot; that neither he nor any member of the Bar ever participated in political meetings - only meetings which were to the interests of Government. He continued to say that there were few Hindus in Peshawar and that political agitation had no meaning for them, that they were ready to help heart and soul, and that the loyalty of Hindus would never be shaken.

VI. Abdul Aziz, Bar-at-Law (Indistinct)

VII. Maulvi Abdul Ghafur started by addressing Captain Ahmad Nawaz Khan, who, he thought, was not quite right in what he said about the Khilafat. The Khilafat was a matter to be decided by the Ulemas.

Turning to the Chief Commissioner he said that it was his intention to correct or interpret rightly that which was wrong. 'You are bound to sympathise with those who are grieved; you are powerful (?) to do so'. These words were said in connection with the disposition of the Khilafat and of Wahabis, Qadianis and Qoraishis being candidates therefor. The Hon'ble the Chief Commissioner said that he was not concerned with this matter as he did not understand anything of it.

The Maulvi then alluded to Ghulam Naqashband as having said (to the Chief Commissioner) that the Khalifa should be the Amir of Kabul, and that it was an error to place faith in the saying of a few when the majority was overwhelming. He was told that the source of information could not err.

'You are bound to side with the majority' said the Maulvi, 'and it is not my intention to quarrel; I simply wish that you (C.C.) should not err, or be led astray, and there may come a time when you would wish to recall your decision (?).'

He advocated the preaching (by way of explanation) of Khilafat to the masses.

VIII. Sardar Jan Gul Khan said that a Qoraishi should be the Khalifa.

IX. Amir Chand Bamwal averred that his *jirgas* were not anti-British, nor was there any anti-British resolution passed when he was present. He was at once told that evidence disproving this statement could be produced.

The Chief Commissioner spoke of the exaggerated accounts which had been published by him (Amir Chand).

However, both Sardar Jan Gul Khan and Nawab Saifulla Khan said that it was due to his meetings that mischief had been caused.

Amir Chand then spoke of the Frontier Crime Regulation being too drastic, and said that he had never spoken against Government.

The Deputy Commissioner, Peshawar (Colonel Keen), then addressed the audience in Urud and Pushto. He said that he had nothing to do with the Khilafat and that whoever was to be the Khalifa it would be known. There had been agitation last year, but that whatever had happened was finished and done with. His door was not closed to anybody who wished to represent anything to him, but they should desist from holding meetings in the Shahi Bagh without the Chief Commissioner's permission. He then spoke of the Municipal elections.

The next man was Abdul Ghaffar of Utmanzai. He was called to the Hon'ble the Chief Commissioner, and his allegation regarding the unjust treatment of the Principal of the Islamia College and the expulsion of Muhammad Akbar Qoraishi from the College, was read out to him.

The Chief Commissioner said it was known what interest he took in the Islamia College and therefore enquired into the matter saying if it was true, it was bad. The Registrar, Punjab University had struck the student's name off the rolls for non-attendance at lectures. And that in the face of such doings, if true, could anyone continue to send his son to such a College (All replied 'No').

Abdul Ghaffar said it should be ascertained as to how many students there were on the College rolls this year and how many last year to find out the truth. It was not his intention to vilify Government.

The Chief Commissioner then told him that he was prepared to mete out justice, if matters were represented to him in the proper way, but did not wish everything to find a place in the newspapers.

Amir Chand Bamwal then said that his meetings were not anti-Govt, but that they were held in order to ventilate the grievances of the people; than when one was hungry, one must ask for food.

Sardar Kanshi Nand then spoke on the three points of the Chief Commisioner's speech, namely the Khilafat, Political agitation and Afghanistan. He said that the Hon'ble the Chief Commissioner had made his meaning clear, and that, if there was a difference of opinion, it should be made known now and now only.

He said that if there was such a thing as Hindu-Muslim unity, it should be turned towards giving one College a firm foundation instead of thinking of setting up other Colleges; by writing to the papers people think they are becoming popular but this is not so. It is no good saying that the Chief Commissioner had a meeting in his house at which so many people were present, and add a little more, and, when questioned, to say that 'this was not my meaning, but became so or was interpreted as such by the reader.' Thereby your good intentions are turned into harm.

He then turned to the Chief Commissioner and, like others, assured of his ready help.

Mr. Bolton, Revenue Commissioner, Peshawar, then addressed the gathering. He said that they knew well that his years had been passed in this Province, and that he was sure that help would be readily given as on previous occasions of necessity.

With regard to meetings he said that it was a new departure which had come into being during the last three years; that one does not ride a horse one is not acquainted with: the same with a meeting. That it was dangerous to conduct meetings when one was ignorant of the way in which it ought to be conducted; the result was much harm and that his advice was 'a little knowledge is a dangerous thing.'

The Hon'ble the Chief Commissioner thanked those present for their attendance, and was glad to see that everything was discussed in a manner which would leave no place for doubt.

EXHIBIT E

Note on the 'Volunteer' Movement, 1920

Prior to the Khilafat agitation the 'Volunteer' movement found expression in the local Sewa Samiti, but this organisation retained a more or less non-political character and its object was primarily social service. With the advent of *hijrat,* however, the movement underwent considerable expansion and the bodies formed by the various Khilafat Committees were, both by their size and their later activities, a source of growing concern and anxiety. Whilst drawing into their ranks a certain number of the student class they also found room for the large element of rakish youths and loafers who abound in all centres of population. It was these latter who were the most vociferous and who, on more occasion then one, came within measurable distance of a collision with the forces of law and order. Originally recruited for the purpose of lending assistance to the Muhajirin, by arranging accommodation and providing for their comfort in other ways, they eventually developed into a medium for political propaganda, for the spreading for wild and alarming rumours, and for enforcing *hartals* when these were not spontaneously performed by shopkeepers. With the extension of their activities and their sphere of influence these volunteer corps began to ape the military. Uniforms, which distinctive badges in red and green, were adopted; formations were regularised, and officers carrying the usual military ranks appointed; drill was resorted to as means of inculcating discipline.

In the later stages of the *hijrat* fever an amalgamation was effected between the newly-raised Khilafat volunteers and those of the Sewa Samiti. Their political character was evidenced by the mere fact of coalition, and was more clearly demonstrated by the attempts to foster Hindu-Muhammadan unity. With the collapse of *hijrat*, and the temporary lull in agitation, the volunteer corps have withdrawn into the background; but their continued existence is undoubted. Any sign of a recrudescence of the agitation which prevailed this year will witness their reappearance on the stage. Besides the potentialities for evil which they possess in the direction of uniformed and dangerous political propaganda it is very doubtful whether a protracted continuance of their activities is possible without a transgression of the bounds of law and order.

EXHIBIT F

Opening Ceremony of the Azad Muslim High School

I. The ceremony was performed at Mufti Ibrahim's house, a portion of which has been dedicated to this school.

II. Maulvi Abdul Ghafur explained the object which, he described, was to provide for religious education side by side with secular education.

III. Master Autar Singh extolled the opening of the school and read an exciting poem on martial law incidents from the *Akali* and further recited some similar verses, finishing with inviting jail for himself, as he usually does.

IV. Dr. Ghosh spoke on the benefits of technical education suggesting arrangements being made here for spinning, weaving, carpentry and masonry in this new school.

V. Maulvi Abdul Ghafur flouted the Doctor's ideas and suggested agriculture as a subject fit for adoption here.

VI. Abdul Rahim, Head Master of the Nowshera Islamia High School, mentioned the following defects in the present system of education:-

(a) Multiplicity of subjects.

(b) Repetition of the same subjects from class to class.

(c) Text of books in a foreign language, *i.e.* English.

He suggested a special curriculum of instruction in arts after primary education in reading, writing and arithmetic. His arguments were so fallacious that it is a pity that no one was allowed to speak against them.

VII. Muqarrab Hussain, a student of Bannu, who got his education down country, delivered an exciting speech particularly advocating non-co-operation and suggesting formation of associations by all working bodies, volunteers, non-co-operators, and others. He referred to services done by the country and said that injustice was done instead. Describing non-co-operation as a religious duty he talked of Gladstone dishonouring the Qoran, and Kitchener speaking lightly of it - as he said, they regarded it as an impediment in obtaining superiority over Musulmans.

Describing Khilafat work in Bannu, he mentioned that 200 Lambardars had resigned their posts, while a Khan Bahadur had renounced his title, an Honorary Magistrate had left his office, and a District and a Provincial Darbari had vacated their seats.

He advised Mullah being particularly associated with the movement.

He talked much of the services of Gandhi, Shaukat Ali and Mohammed Ali.

As to the curriculum of education in the new school he suggested following the lead from down country where, he said, experts were sitting for the purpose.

He called for sacrifices again and again.

He cursed the reporters particularly.

His speech all along showed the danger of allowing young men to indulge in politics.

VIII. Resenting certain remarks about the backwardness of Peshawar in non-co-operation as compared with Bannu, Maulvi Abdul Ghafur ridiculed some of Muqarrab Khan's arguments; the latter tried to speak again in reply, but, when arguments developed, he embraced the Maulvi in token of a compromise and thus avoided a collision.

IX. The meeting dispersed with a long prayer for the success of Islam over its enemies.

X. It was announced that admission to the school would begin tomorrow morning.

The attendance, it was noticed, was poor, and no men of any importance attended.

EXHIBIT G

In accordance with Mohammed Ali's instructions issued verbally to Abdul Qayum, Secretary Khilafat Committee, Peshawar, the Aligarh student-propagandists placed themselves under the orders of the latter on their arrival in this Province. It soon became obvious to them, however, that the field of their activities was restricted, that the action taken here in April to suppress agitation had narrowed their prospects of Swaraj propaganda, and that Mohammed Ali's calculations of success in this direction had not been unerring. Thus disappointed they scattered to their respective homes with vague instructions to get in touch with Khilafat and other political bodies in their Districts, and to carry on their propaganda clandestinely. Their distribution was -

A.	Hazara	6
B.	Peshawar	4
C.	Bannu	3
D.	Dera Ismail Khan	2

The 16th student, Allah Bux, returned to his home in Dera Ghazi Khan, from where he has occasionally visited Dera Ismail Khan.

A. The prompt arrest of the Hazara students on arrival in their District, and their production before the Deputy Commissioner who warned them against participation in agitation served as an effective curb to any activities they may have contemplated. One of their member, Sultan Abdur Rashid, evaded arrest for a day or two, and openly boasted that he had written to Mohammed Ali describing the high-handed manner in which they had been treated, and asking that 10 more students should be sent to the District. But beyond this display of truculence none of the 6 students figured in any way. They dispersed to their homes and Mohammed Alam informed Aligarh that it was impossible under the circumstances to carry out the work which had been allotted to him. Of the 6 Hazara students 4 have gone to Lahore, Mohammed Alam himself to Aligarh, and one, Gauhar Rahman, is at his village, Kira. This latter is viewed as a renegade who has been evicted from the fold because of the undertaking he gave to abstain from politics.

B. Shortly after their arrival the Peshawar students, with their parents, were summoned by the Deputy Commissioner and warnings were administered in each case. Although none of them has figured conspicuously or displayed any unusual activity, yet a short note on each seems necessary in view of the fact that they have not remained entirely inactive.

(a) Mohammed Asim of Badrashi was appointed Captain of the student party from Aligarh. On the 13th May 1921, he addressed a meeting in the Mohabat Khan Mosque in Peshawar when he advocated *jehad* as being incumbent on all true Muslims. Swadeshi and boycott of law courts were also urged by him upon the audience. Since then he has remained in constant and close touch with the Khilafat Committee at Peshawar, and during his visits he availed himself of the opportunity of visiting the Islamia College. This latter fact was significant in view of the instructions he had from Abdul Majid Khwaja of the National Muslim University, who in one of his letters said: 'Your first and foremost duty is to send students here so that men may be trained and prepared for your assistance.' Mohammad Asim, however, was unsuccessful in his attempts to seduce students away from the College.

(b) Abdul Maruf of Rajjar, Charsadda, attended the meeting at Mohabat Khan's Mosque in the City on the 13th May 1921, and has since maintained a close touch with the Peshawar Khilafat Committee. Shortly after his arrival he contributed an article to the Vernacular Press in which he gave a distorted and exaggerated account of the action taken against the student-propagandists in Peshawar and Hazara. Has interested himself in the Utmanzai National School, of which he has been made Superintendent by Abdul Ghaffar Khan. Has endeavoured to promote Swadeshi, but his success in the sale of country cloth in the Peshawar City has been meagre.

(c) Litaf Gul of Ziarat Kaka Sahib attended the meeting at Mohabat Khan's Mosque in Peshawar City on the 13th May 1921. His visits to Peshawar have been infrequent. On 4th June 1921, he presided over a meeting at Ziarat, where he spoke on non-co-operation and advocated the boycott of foreign goods.

(d) Nasrulla Jan of Ismaila on return to his village he interested himself in the proposal to establish a National School there. In a letter, dated the 24th May 1921, to the Secretary, Khilafat Committee, Peshawar, Nasrulla mentioned his success on starting this unaided school as also his intention to establish a Shariat tribunal in the village. Neither the school not [*sic*] the tribunal have yet materialised.

All four students have busied themselves in the collection of funds. In a recent communication from the Central Khilafat Committee they were asked by Mohammed Ali to make special efforts for the Tilak Swaraj Fund.

C. The Bannu students arrived in their District on the 15th May 1921.

Two of them, who belonged to Mira Khel, were reported to have established a Khilafat Office in the village. During their visits to Bannu they were engaged in the collection of funds but beyond this have not come to notice.

D. On the 2 Dera Ismail Khan students there is practically nothing to report. One of them, Ramzam, made a speech at a mosque at Kulachi on the 3rd of June 1921, in which he expatiated on the brutal treatment meted out to the Turks, and made the usual implication that responsibility for this rested with the English.

Viewed as a whole it may be safely said that the student-propagandists have failed in their mission. The reason for this is no doubt to be found in the change of Government policy in this Province towards agitation, and the consequent restrictions which were placed on them at the very outset. It is not difficult to imagine what mischief they would have done had their potentialities for evil not received an initial check.

EXHIBIT H

Extract from the *Muslim Outlook* of Lahore, dated 11th November 1923.

THE KHALIFA

It was some time ago that the National Assembly of Angora took the momentous decision of separating the Khilafat from the Government of Turkey and locating it in Constantinople. Since then important changes have been introduced in the Turkish constitution, and a full-fledged Turkish Republic which had perhaps been the object in view of the Assembly ever since that body came into being, is now an accomplished fact. As we pointed out the other day, the ultimate political power, which in every politically organised society must rest somewhere, has been vested, in the case of Turkey, in her people, the functionaries and agents of Government having been made subject and fully responsible to the popular will. This last development in the Turkish constitution does not, of course, exercise any new effect on the position and status of the Khalifa who was already separated from all temporal powers. But it does call to one's mind the fact that the exact status of the Khalifa and the precise nature of his constitutional relations to the Turkish Government, as they are to be in future, are as yet undefined and unexplained. Questions regarding these points arose in people's minds at the first announcement of the separation; but owing to the rapid course of Turkish transition they have, to a great extent, remained unexpressed, and therefore unanswered. Now that a more or less stable and definitely written constitution of Turkey has come into being, the omission therein of any definite statement on this subject has naturally attracted the attention of Mussulmans in this country.

From what some Turkish politicians have said in the recent past regarding the Khilafat question it would appear that although they recognise their duties as a self-governing Muslim nation, of defending and serving the Khilafat they have yet no desire to make this institution and questions relating to it their exclusive concern. 'The future position of the Khalifa is' one of them said some months ago addressing the Muslim world, 'what the Muslims outside Turkey choose to make it. We have re-established the Khilafat at Constantinople and will defend it. The rest concerns you others.' In the light of recent developments the significance of these words is that the Turks regard the Khilafat as an institution for the upkeep and maintenance of which the whole Muslim world is equally responsible. They think that this responsibility devolved upon Turkey only as much as it devolves on the rest of the Mussalmans; and that they alone should not be made to suffer from the effects of temporal despotism simply because the Muslim world must have a Khalifa endowed with temporal powers. The argument is at once lucid and convincing although the problem to which it gives rise is an immense and an embarrassing one. The Turkish people are perfectly within their right in demanding for themselves a democratic Government, such as is the pride or ambition of the entire world to-day. They cannot reasonable be asked to pay for the upkeep of the Khilafat with their political liberties, since the Khilafat is to function not in the interest of the Turks alone, but in that of the whole Muslim world. But should the Khilafat therefore be deprived of all temporal power, and should the Khalifa become something like a Pope exercising his spiritual overlordship over the Muslim world?

The problem is an extremely difficult one, and will have to be considered seriously by Muslims all the world over. The institution of the Khilafat has to be maintained in accordance with the traditions of Islam, and as an indispensable safeguard for the religious interests of Muslims considered as a world-wide fraternity. These interests, however, cannot be safeguarded unless the Khalifa is made powerful enough to defend them, if need be, with his sword. It is, of course, absolutely unnecessary from the view-point of the Khilafatists that the Khalifa should have the final say in matters of Turkish internal administration, or that he should possess a particular pedigree or belong to a particular nationality. All that is necessary is that besides having at his command the physical force to resist all encroachments on the religious rights and interests of the Muslim world, he should also have the power to decide whether a particular event did or did not amount to such an encroachment. The second item of the Khalifa's powers, it will be clear to all students of constitutional law, is as important as the first. But has the Khalifa, under the present circumstances, these powers?

The opinion to which a majority of Muslims in the country seems to subscribe, and to which colour had been given by the utterances of some Turkish politicians, is that he possesses both these power even now. It is believed that although he has been separated from the Government of Turkey, that Government is still pledged to place all its physical resources at his disposal, whenever he has need to wage war upon an enemy of Islam. If this is so, then the essential requirements of a real and effective Khilafat would seem to be fulfilled. It goes, of course, without saying that Turkey will have to be compensated for her sacrifices in that case by the entire Muslim world to the latter's utmost capacity. But in order that all doubts of Mussalmans on this subject may be allayed, a provision to this effect ought to be embodied in the Turkish constitution. If, on the other hand, the opinion is not well founded, then means will have to be devised by the Mussulmans of the world for restoring the Khilafat to its former status, if need be, by transferring it to some other person or to some other part of the Muslim world. In any case it appears necessary now to hold a conference of the representatives of all Muslim countries at some central place, to arrive at a complete understanding on these points. The Khilafat Committee of India will do a most valúable service to the cause for which it stands, if it sends a deputation to the Near East in the near future in order to make a move in this matter.

The Non-Cooperation Movement in the North-West Frontier Province

The programme of the Non-co-operation movement was the withdrawal from Government, of all co-operation by the following progressive stages:-

(i) The renunciation of titles, and all honorary ranks and offices.

(ii) The boycott of -
- (a) The Councils
- (b) Courts
- (c) Schools and Colleges
- (d) Foreign goods

(iii) Resignation from all civil and military services under Government

(iv) Refusal to pay taxes.

The idea was first mooted at a joint conference of Hindus and Muhammadans at Delhi in November 1920.

It was later adopted, in the form of a resolution, by a special meeting of the Central Khilafat Committee in June 1921.

This resolution is filed as Annexure I.

It was formally inaugurated by Mahatma Gandhi on Aug. 1st, 1921, on his First Non-co-operation Day.

He preceded his action by a message to His Excellency the Viceroy, which was issued at the same time as a similar message from Mussulman leaders.

These messages are marked as Annexures II and III.

Non-co-operation day was supported in Peshawar by a general *hartal.*

In September 1921, the general programme of the movement was sanctioned by the Congress at a Special Conference in Calcutta.

This resulted in an increase in the general agitation in the North-West Frontier Province; resignation of Lambardars in the Bannu District followed, and a strike occurred in the Islamia College in Peshawar.

In November 1921, the Ulemas Conference at Delhi hallowed the movement with their *fatwa*, and the result was a further increase in agitation in Peshawar.

The Khilafat Committee in Kohat declared itself to be an Arbitration Court, and the Peshawar Congress Committee also formed a local Arbitration Tribunal consisting of 3 Hindus and 2 Muhammadans.

No particular notice was taken of this movement, which later wilted away in its own futility.

In Bannu, however, the idea reached the villages, and Panchayat Courts were established in various groups of villages.

Shortly afterwards the Islamia College strikers, after some training at Aligarh, returned as student-propagandists; a note on their activities is attached.

The general *hartal*, ordered for the day of the Prince's arrival in Bombay, was duly observed in Peshawar, Abbottabad and Dera Ismail Khan. Considerable propaganda had been employed, and the success of the agitators was very marked in these three places. There is little doubt, however, that the almost universal response was due to fear of the agitators and the Khilafat Volunteers, for the action of shopkeepers was by no means spontaneous or voluntary.

For this result, government is, among the responsible and loyal citizens of Peshawar City, held partly responsible: it was argued that Government had treated the volunteer movement with altogether too much toleration and had, by its attitude of amused contempt, allowed a movement, which was originally confined to comic bands of cheeky youths in fancy dress, to become an actual menace to authority by developing into organised gangs of city roughs and hooligans.

On the occasion of the Prince's visit to Peshawar City there was a complete *hartal* throughout the City. Picketting by volunteers was conducted on an extensive scale, and every effort was made to ridicule and annoy prospective spectators, while aggressive insults were hurled at Civil and Military pensioners.

The culminating point was the insulting cries of two parties in close proximity to the Hastings Memorial, while the Provincial Address was being presented to His Royal Highness. Various acts of hooliganism occurred later in the day, and the afternoon was marked by a state of acute tension in the City.

Not content with this disgraceful effort, the volunteers next turned their attention to the picketting of the City brothels; their example was quickly followed in Kohat, where a regular and rigid system of pickets was rapidly instituted.

The news of Mahatma Gandhi's arrest and conviction, and the special measures taken in Peshawar City, did much to remove the menace of the Non-co-operation movement in this Province.

Reinforcements were drafted into the City, and a system of intensive patrolling was brought into force; meetings of agitators were forbidden and, where necessary, broken up, while a few of the worst offenders were placed under arrest.

These obvious signs of Government's intention to crush the menace of hooliganism in the garb of Non-co-operation, coupled with the judicial conviction of the author of the movement, had a marked effect upon the Province. The loyal population, which had previously remained quiet in the background, alarmed and puzzled at Government's extraordinary patience and toleration, now came into the open and threw its weight into the scales. The Non-co-operation movement declined rapidly and soon faced out of the picture. In the Punjab it probably emerged again in the form of Akali agitation, but in the North-West Frontier Province it remained moribund until the recent acute Hindu-Muslim tension finally extinguished its last remaining spark of life.

ANNEXURE I

This meeting re-affirms the movement of Non-co-operation in accordance with the four stages already approved by the Central Khilafat Committee, and appoints a committee, consisting of the following gentlemen with powers to add to their number, to give practical effect to the movement without further delay:-

Mahatma Gandhi, Maulana Shaukat Ali, Maulana Abul Kalam Azad, Moulvi Mohammad Ali (Bombay), Mr. Ahmad Haji Siddick Khetri, Dr. Kitchlew, and Maulana Hasrat Mohani.

ANNEXURE II

Mr. Gandhi Again
Impertinent letter to the Viceroy
Claims He prevented Violence

His Excellency invited to join Extremists

A message from Bombay states that Mr. Gandhi has forwarded a most impudent letter to the Viceroy explaining his conduct in the Khilafat question. Mr. Gandhi claims to have succeeded in weaning Mussulman extremists from violence by placing before the alternative of non-co-operation. He asserts that the British constitution does not support the weak but only those who show themselves strong. He hopes, therefore, that justice may somehow be done if Mussulmans and Hindus show the necessary capacity for suffering. They must run some risks to avoid greater risks. These risks, however, may be avoided if His Excellence will place himself at the head of the agitation for revision of the Turkish treaty as his distinguished predecessor did at the time of the South African trouble.

The following is the full text of Mr. Gandhi's letter:

Your Excellency,—As one who has enjoyed a certain measure of Your Excellency's confidence and as one who claims to be a devoted well-wisher of the British Empire, I owe it to Your Excellency and through Your Excellency to His Majesty's Ministers to explain my connection with and my conduct in the Khilafat question. At the very earliest stage of the war, even whilst I was in London organising the Indian Volunteer Ambulance Corps, I began to interest myself in the Khilafat question. I perceived how deeply moved the little Mussulman world in London was when Turkey decided to throw in her lot with Germany. On my arrival in India in Jan. 1915 I found the same anxiousness and earnestness among Mussulmans with whom I came in contact. Their anxiety became intense when the information about secret treaties leaked out. Distrust of British intentions filled their minds and despair took possession of them. Even at that moment I advised my Mussulman friends not to give way to despair but to express their fears and their hopes in a disciplined manner. It will be admitted that the whole of Mussulman India has behaved in a singularly restrained manner during the past five years and that the leaders have been able to keep the turbulent sections of their community, under complete control. The peace terms and Your Excellency's defence of them have given the Mussulmans of India a shock from which it will be difficult for them to recover. The terms violate the Ministerial pledges and utterly disregard Mussulman sentiment. I consider that as a staunch Hindu, wishing to live on terms of closest friendship with my Mussulman countrymen, I should be an unworthy son of India if I did not stand by them in their hour of trial. In my humble opinion their cause is just. They claim that Turkey must not be punished if their sentiment is to be respected. Muslim soldiers did not fight to inflict punishment on their own Khalifa or to deprive him of his territories. The Mussulman attitude had been consistent throughout these five years. My duty to the Empire to which

I owe my loyalty requires me to resist the cruel violence that has been done to Mussulman sentiment. So far as I am aware Mussulmans and Hindus have as a whole lost faith in British justice and honour. The report of the majority of the Hunter Committee, Your Excellency's despatch thereon, and Mr. Montagu's reply have only aggravated the distrust. In these circumstances the only course open to one like me is either in despair to sever all connection with British rule or, if I still retained faith in the inherent superiority of the British constitution to all others at present in vogue, to adopt such means as will rectify the wrong done and thus restore confidence. I have not lost faith in such superiority and I am not without hope that somehow or other justice will yet be rendered if we show the requisite capacity for suffering. Indeed, my conception of that constitution is it helps only those who are ready to help themselves. I don't believe it protects the weak. It gives free scope to the strong to maintain their strength and develop it. The weak under it go to the wall. It is then because I believed in the British constitution that I have advised my Mussulman friends to withdraw their support from Your Excellency's Government and the Hindus to join them should the peace terms not be revised in accordance with the solemn pledges of Ministers and Muslim sentiment. Three courses were open to Muhammadans in order to mark their emphatic disapproval of the utter injustice to which His Majesty's Ministers have become a party, if they have not actually been the prime perpetrators of it. They are (1) to resort to violence, (2) to advise emigration on a wholesale scale, (3) not to be a party to the injustice by ceasing to co-operate with the Government. Your Excellency must be aware that there was a time when the boldest, though also the most thoughtless among Mussulmans favoured violence and that *jikrat* [*sic*] (emigration has not yet ceased to be the battle-cry). I venture to claim I have succeeded by patient reasoning in weaning the party of violence from its ways. I confess that I did not attempt to succeed in weaning it from violence on moral grounds but purely on utilitarian grounds. The result for the time being at any rate, has, however, been to stop violence. The school of *hijrat* has received a check if it has not stopped its activity entirely. I hold no repression could have prevented a violent eruption if people have not had presented to them a form of direct action involving considerable sacrifice and ensuring success, if such direct action was largely taken up by the public. Non-co-operation was the only dignified and constitutional form of such direct action, for it is the right recognised from times immemorial of the subject to refuse to assist the ruler who misrules. At the same time I admit that non-co-operation practised by a mass of people is attended with grave risks. But in a crisis such as has overtaken the Mussulmans of India no step that is unattended with large risks can possibly bring about the desired change. Not to run some risks will be to court much greater risks, if not virtual destruction of law and order but there is yet an escape from non-co-operation. Mussulman representation has requested Your Excellency to lead the agitation yourself as did your distinguished predecessor at the time of the South African trouble. But if you cannot see your way to do so and non-co-operation becomes a dire necessity, I hope Your Excellency will give those who have accepted my advice and myself credit for being actuated by nothing less than a stern sense of duty.

ANNEXURE III

Mussulman's Message
Non-co-operation to begin 1st August.

In pursuance of the decision arrived at by the special meeting of the Central Khilafat Committee held at Allahabad in regard to the non-co-operation movement the following letter signed by about 90 Sunni Mussulmans from various parts of India, including Yakoob Hassan, Mazhar-ul-Haq, Maulana Abdul Bari, Maulana Hasrat Mohini, Kitchlew, Mian Mahomad Chotani and Shaukat Ali was sent to the Viceroy from Bombay on Tuesday:

> Your Excellency,—We the undersigned claim to represent the largest body of Sunni Muslim opinion. We have most carefully read the Turkish Peace Terms and we consider them to be in direct violation of the religious sentiments of the Mussulmans. They violate obligations imposed upon the Sunnis and wound the susceptibilities of all Mussulmans. They are contrary to the pledges of British Ministers on the strength of which it has been admitted it was possible to draw upon India for Muslim recruits during the war. We hold the British Empire, which is the greatest Muhammadan power in the world, cannot treat the Turkish Empire which represents the Khilafat, in the same manner that it may treat a defeated enemy. Indeed, we contend in certain respects Turkey has been treated worse than other powers. We respectfully submit in the treatment of Turkey the British Government are bound to respect Indian Muslim sentiment in so far as it is neither unjust nor unreasonable. In our opinion the position taken up by the Indian

Mussulmans is simple. They cannot bear the thought of the temporal power of the Sultan being adversely affected by way of punishment for his having joined Germany under circumstances which need not be examined here. But we have no desire to ask for anything that would interfere with the principle of self-determination. We have no desire to uphold any misrule such as has been attributed to Turkey. Our delegates in Europe have asked for an independent commission of inquiry to investigate the charge of wanted cruelty said to have been practised by Turkish soldiers in Armenia. We cannot look with indifference upon the partition of Turkey and her empire for the sake of punishment for humiliating her. We would therefore request Your Excellency and your Government to ask His Majesty's Ministers to secure a revision of the peace terms and tell them that on the failure to do so Your Excellency will make common cause with the people of India. We make this suggestion as Your Excellency has repeatedly declared your Government has consistently and often pressed upon the attention of His Majesty's Ministers the case of Indian Mussulmans in this matter of vital concern to the vast majority of them. We feel therefore we have a right to ask Your Excellency to reassure Mussalmans of India they still retain your active co-operation and powerful advocacy in the prosecution of their claims, even to the point of resignation of your high office should His Majesty's Ministers fail to secure a revision of the terms consistently with pledges and sentiment mentioned above. We venture respectfully to suggest had India been a Dominion enjoying full self-government her responsible Ministers would have as a matter of course resigned as a protest against such a serious breach of pledges and flouting of religious opinion as are involved in the peace terms. If unfortunately Your Excellency will not adopt our humble suggestion we shall be obliged as from 1st August next to withdraw co-operation from Government and ask our co-religionists and Hindu brethren to do likewise. We ask Your Excellency not to regard our statement as a threat or in any way as a mark of disrespect. We claim to be as loyal subjects of the Crown as any in India but we consider our loyalty to an earthly sovereign to be subservient to our loyalty to Islam. The latter enjoins upon every Mussulman to consider those who wantonly injure the status of the Khalifa to be enemies of Islam and to resist them with arms if necessary. We recognise that even if we had power we must not resort to arms so long as any other means are at our disposal. We feel the last a Mussulman can do in these circumstances if not to assist those who are guilty of trying to reduce the Khilafat practically to nothingness. It would therefore become our painful duty to refuse to co-operate with Government which accepts the peace terms and advises the acceptance thereof by us. We shall hope that such a serious step as Non-co-operation will not become necessary but should it unfortunately happen to be otherwise we assure Your Excellency we shall strive our utmost to avoid violence. We fully recognise our responsibility. We know any eruption of violence must check and injure the peaceful demonstration contemplated by us and what is more sacred the cause which is dear to us as life. We shall therefore take up Non-co-operation in progressive stages so as to cause the least necessary dislocation or embarrassment to Government and so as to enable us to control and discipline popular feeling.

[Exhibit G, The Non-co-operation movement in the North-West Frontier Province corresponds to Exhibit G, Khilafat Movement in the North-West Frontier Province.]

Biographical Notes

'Abd al-Ahad

Belonged to the Nanotawi family of Deoband; a graduate of Allahabad University; Secretary of the Anjuman-e Muid ul-Islam in Delhi; President, Delhi Haj Committee; Secretary, Anglo Arabic School, Delhi; Trustee of the MAO College; refrained from taking part in the Khilafat movement, funeral obstructed by Khilafatists.

'Abd al-'Aziz

Delhi based lawyer; active in the Home Rule movement; loyalist.

'Abd al-'Aziz, Shaykh

1881-1971

Politician and social reformer; educated at Lahore; taught in Islamia College, Lahore; participated in the national movement; member, Sindh Provincial Khilafat Committee; attended the RTC in London.

'Abd al-Bari, Mawlana

1876-1926

Alim of Firangi Mahal, Lucknow and Pir of the Ali brothers; travelled extensively in the Ottoman Empire; President, Majlis-e Muid ul-Islam, Lucknow, 1910; one of the founders and President of the Anjuman-e Khuddam-e Kaaba; took a leading part in the Kanpur mosque agitation and the Khilafat movement; President, Jamiat ul Ulama-e Hind, December 1919; opposed Hijrat to Afghanistan, 1920; after 1923 estranged from the Congress; opposed Ibn Saud during the Hijaz crisis, 1924-26.

'Abd ul-Ghaffar

From Utmanzai; active in Hijrat movement.

'Abd ul Ghaffar, Mawlawi

Took part in loyalist meetings in Peshawar.

'Abd-al Ghaffar, Qadi

1888-1956

Studied at the MAO College; a leading Urdu journalist; resigned Government service to join Muhammad Ali's *Hamdard*; founded *Jamhur*, and after its suppression *Subah* (Delhi) and later *Payam* (Hyderabad); externed from Bengal 1918; General Secretary of the All India Muslim League, 1918; Secretary to Chotani during his visit to Britain with the non-official Khilafat Delegation, 1921; special representative of Central Khilafat Committee to Ismet Pasha in Switzerland to plead for restoration of the Khalifa's temporary power, 1922; biographer of Hakim Ajmal Khan.

'Abd ul-Ghafur Peshawari

Pan-Islamist 'Alim and Khilafat worker from Peshawar; Secretary, Khilafat Committee, Peshawar City.

'Abd al-Ghani

Khilafatist of Hindi Districts of Central Provinces.

'Abd al-Ghani

Teacher at the Larkana Madrasa; member, Central Khilafat Committee, Bombay.

'Abd ul-Halim, Mawlawi

Head of the Anjuman Qasim ul Ma'rif, Mainpuri; follower of Ahmad Reza Khan of Bareilly; arrested for breach of the Prevention of Seditious Meetings Act.

'Abd al-Halim Sarhandi

Religious leader from Larkana, who signed the fatwa-i Khilafat, published in the form of a pamphlet 'Tahqiq ul Khilafat' in favour of British Government and against the Turkish Empire in 1919.

'Abd al-Hamid

Sweetmeat seller from Delhi; member Legislative Assembly, 1920.

'Abd al-Harun, Shaykh Hajji

Member, Working Committee of the Central Khilafat Committee.

'Abd al-Jabbar

Pleader from Hyderabad; member, Sindh Provincial Congress Committee for Hyderabad, 1921-22; member, Working Committee of the Sindh Provincial Khilafat Committee, 1921-22; President, City Khilafat Committee of Hyderabad.

'Abd al-Karim, Mawlawi

Chishti Pir; member, Sindh Provincial Congress Committee for Shikarpur District, 1922.

'Abd al-Khaliq Morai, Hakim Mawlawi

Sindh representative of the Central Khilafat Committee of India; member, Working Committee of the Sindh Provincial Khilafat Committee; member, Sindh Provincial Congress Committee for Nawabshah District, 1921-22.

'Abd-allah, Shaykh

Elected member, Sindh Provincial Congress Committee 1921; Secretary, Hyderabad City Khilafat Committee; member, Hyderabad City Khilafat Working Committee; member, Committee for the collections for the Angora Fund, Hyderabad District.

'Abd al-Majid, Khwaja

1885-1962

Educated at Aligarh and Cambridge; practised law at Aligarh and Patna; elected Trustee Aligarh, 1912; succeeded Shaukat Ali as Secretary of the Aligarh Old Boys' Association, 1915; organised the Home Rule League at Aligarh; gave up practice during the Non-Co-operation movement; Principal, Jamia Millia Islamia, 1922; Secretary, Congress Working Committee, 1923; member, Muslim Nationalist Party.

'Abd al-Majid, Shaykh

1888-1978

Belonged to the Narayani caste Hindu family of Thalka, embraced Islam in 1908 at the hands of Shah Abdur Rahim and was named Abdul Majid; settled in Hyderabad where he edited Sindhi daily *Al Amin*; detained for three years for collaborating with Maulana Ubaidullah Sindhi in the 'Silk Letter Plot'; participated in Khilafat movement; associated with Ali brothers and attended All Parties Conference in Allahabad, 1929; strongly pleaded Sindh's separation from Bombay; elected to the Provincial Assembly Sindh, 1937; joined Muslim League in 1938; later left Muslim

League and joined All Pakistan Awami Party in 1949; later he joined National Awami Party.

'Abd al-Majid Bada'uni

1887-1931

A close follower of Maulana Abdul Bari of the Farangi Mahal in Lucknow; taught at the Madrasa Qadaria in Badaun; involved in the Kanpur Mosque agitation in 1913; associated with the Anjuman-e Khuddam-e Kaaba, the Khilafat Conferences and the Jamiat-ul Ulama-e Hind.

'Abd al-Maruf

Student agitator from Rajjar, Charsadda; Superintendent, Utmanzai National School.

'Abd al-Qadir

1874-1950

Lawyer and politician of Kasur; editor of *The Observer* and *Makhzan*; practised in Delhi for two years; Khilafat leader; rejected Bardoli programme; member, Panjab Legislative Council, 1923; President of Council, 1925.

'Abd ar-Rahim, Sir

1867-1952

Called to the Bar (Middle Temple), 1890; practised law at the Calcutta Magistracy, 1900-03; member, Royal Commission in Public Service, 1913-15; officiated as Chief Justice, Madras High Court, 1916 and 1919; member, Executive Council of the Governor of Bengal, 1920-25; elected to Central Legislative Assembly in 1931 and was its President, 1935-45.

'Abd ar-Rahman

Pleader; member of the Reception Committee of the second All India Social Service Conference and treasurer of the Central Bureau for the Relief of Muslim Internees; member of the Satyagraha Sabha.

'Abd ar-Rahman

Secretary of Comilla Khilafat Conference.

'Abd ar-Rahman, Khan Bahadur Sayyid

Elected to the Central Provinces Legislative Council for the Liberal Party.

'Abd ar-Rahman, Qadi

Editor of *al Wahid*; member, Sindh Provincial Congress Committee for Karachi District, 1922; Secretary, Sindh Provincial Congress Committee; representative for Sindh to All India National Congress, 1922; representative for Sindh to Central Khilafat Committee, Bombay.

'Abd ar-Rahman Sindhi, Dr.

Accompanied Dr. Ansari on the Red Crescent Medical Mission; General Secretary of the Central Bureau for the Relief of Muslim Internees.

'Abd ar-Rashid, Sultan

Student agitator from Hazara District.

'Abd ar-Ra'uf, Sayyid

Muslim League leader from Allahabad; took part in the agitation against Nagri resolution, 1900; Vice-President, U.P. Muslim League in 1909 and later President; Trustee, Aligarh Muslim University; member, U.P. Legislative Council, 1913-16; took part in Khilafat movement.

'Abd as-Salam, Mawlawi

Educated at Deoband; prominent Alim at Jabbalpur; opposed to the Non-Co-operation movement and organised Muslims against it.

'Abd as-Samad

Maulvi of Badaun.

'Abd as-Subhani

Khilafat leader from Bombay.

Abhyankar, M. V.

1886-1935

Barrister-at-law; close associate of Lokamanya Tilak in Nagpur; participated in the Home Rule movement; attended Amritsar Congress, 1919; leader of the Central Provinces (Marathi) pro-Council party; joined the Hindu Mahasabha in 1922; member, Swaraj Party; led anti-Simon Commission agitation; participated in Civil Disobedience movement; member, Indian Legislative Assembly, 1934.

Abu Bakr, Mawlawi

Resident of Hoogly; presided over 1920 session of Anjuman-i Waizan.

Abu Yusuf Isfahani, Hakim

Khilafatist orator.

Advani, Durgadas Bhojraj

1880-1965

Educated at D.J. Sindh College, Karachi; joined Tilak's Home Rule League; editor, *Home Ruler*, 1918-19; convicted and sent to two years' rigorous imprisonment for printing a pamphlet; President, Sindh Provincial Congress Committee, 1920; member, Karachi District Congress Committee, 1920; member, Bombay Legislative Council, 1923-29; Municipal Commissioner of Karachi for several years; Mayor of Karachi; Chairman, Jai Hind Cooperative Bank.

Aga Khan (H.H. Aga Sultan Muhammad Shah)

1875-1957

Head of Ismaili sect, who are represented in Bombay by the Khoja community; headed Simla Deputation in 1906; leading in movement for Muslim University; financed Muhammadan delegation to Europe, 1919.

Agvani, Bhai Singh

Member, Sindh Provincial Congress Committee, 1921.

Ahmad, 'Ali

Son of Haji Pinial; left college during Non-Co-operation; studied at Congress Ashram in Hyderabad, Sindh; member, Sindh Provincial Congress Committee for Larkana, 1921.

Ahmad, Dr. A.H.

Educated at Karachi; took part in the freedom struggle; Secretary, Sindh Khilafat Working Committee; member, Sindh Provincial Congress Committee for 1922.

Ahmad, Hamid

Member of the Allahabad District Conference and of the Khilafat Committee; was sentenced in May 1921 to three years' rigorous imprisonment.

Ahmad, Mawlawi Bashir

Took part in Khilafat Workers' Conference, Delhi 1920.

Ahmad, Mawlawi Nazim ad-Din

Member, Bengal Provincial Khilafat Committee, 1920; led the boycott of British goods.

Ahmad, Nasir

Recruitment of Khilafat volunteers in Bengal.

Ahmad, Nur

Barrister from Delhi; boycotted for standing for the Council elections, 1920.

Ahmad, Sayyid Zuhur

1882-1952

Educated at Aligarh and England; Bar-at-Law; practised at Allahabad High Court; Joint Secretary, London Muslim League, 1908; member, Council of All India Muslim League, 1910; elected to Allahabad Municipal Board, 1916, became Secretary in 1920; took part in Khilafat and Non-Co-operation movements; member, U.P. Legislative Assembly, 1937-51; General Secretary, Reception Committee of All India Muslim League, Allahabad.

Ahmad Madani, Mawlawi Husayn

1879-1957

Educated at Deoband, 1892-99; joined its teaching staff on graduation and was Principal of the Dar-ul Ulum from 1926-57; joined Mahmud Hasan in his pan-Islamic schemes, 1915-16; arrested along with his leader and three other associates, 1916; interned at Malta by the British, 1917-20; joined the Khilafat movement; interned for supporting the Karachi resolutions, 1921-23.

Ahmad Shirwani, Nithar

1887-1956

Educated at Aligarh and Lucknow; younger brother of T.A.K. Sherwani; joined Government service as Superintendent of Post Offices, 1910; resigned in 1921 and took part in Non-Co-operation movement; imprisoned for two and a half years; member, U.P. Legislative Assembly, 1946-51; Minister for Agriculture, U.P. Government, 1946-51.

Ahmad Uthmani, Mawlana Shabbir

1885-1949

Educated at Deoband; taught at Dar-ul Ulum, Deoband, 1910-

28; head teacher, Madrasa Fatehpuri, Delhi for two years; head teacher, Dar-ul Ulum, Dabhel, Surat for fifteen years; superintendent, Dar-ul Ulum, Deoband, for six years; participated in the Khilafat movement; member, Working Committee Jamiat-ul Ulama-e Hind, 1922-43; Founder-President, Jamiat-ul Ulama-i Islam, 1945; member, Pakistan Constituent Assembly, 1947-49.

'Alam, Dr. Shaykh Muhammad

1892-1947

Educated at Oxford and Dublin; Bar-at-Law; gave up practice to join Non-Co-operation movement; member, Central Khilafat Committee; member, Punjab Legislative Council, 1927-30; represented Central Khilafat Committee at All Parties National Convention, Calcutta 1928; participated in Civil Disobedience movement; member, Congress Working Committee, 1931-34; member, Muslim League, 1938-44; member, Punjab Legislative Assembly, 1937-45; Director, Panjab Communal Harmony Board, 1946.

'Alam, Muhammad

Studied at Aligarh Muslim College; student-propagandist at Hazara District during Khilafat agitation.

Alekar

Member of the extremist faction of Congress in Nagpur; stood for boycott of elections in 1920.

'Ali, Amjadi (Mrs. Muhammad 'Ali)

1878-1931

Active in the campaign to secure the release of the Ali brothers; associated with Women's Khilafat Committee.

'Ali, Asaf

1883-1953

Prominent lawyer; founder member of the Home Rule League; rose to prominence during the Rowlatt satyagraha in Delhi; arrested in 1921; associated with Dr. Ansari; Ambassador to the United States in 1947; appointed Governor of Orissa in 1948.

'Ali Brothers

(see Ali, Muhammad and Ali, Shaukat)

'Ali, Akhtar

Attendant of Shaukat Ali; political agitator in Karachi, 1921.

'Ali, Mas'ud

Selected by Central Khilafat Committee to serve on deputation with the Civil Disobedience Enquiry Committee.

'Ali, Mawlawi Hamid

Originated from Bilaspur; established branch of Jamiat-ul Ulama in Jabbalpur in 1921; prosecuted for sedition in 1922 for inciting the police to resign.

'Ali, Mawlawi Muhammad Qasim

Member, Bengal Provincial Conference, 1922; pleaded for abandonment of Non-Co-operation.

'Ali, Mu'azzam

1880-1941

Barrister and politician from Rampur; brother-in-law of the Ali brothers; educated at Rampur, Aligarh and London (Oxford?); practised law in Patna and Moradabad; took leading part in the Khilafat movement and left practice, 1920; succeeded Shaukat Ali as Secretary Central Khilafat Committee, after the latter's arrest, 1921; member, AICC; member, Khilafat Civil Disobedience Enquiry Committee, 1922; Legal Advisor to the Maharaja of Indore; Chief Justice and Home Minister of Rampur State.

'Ali, Muhammad

1878-1931

Educated at MAO College, Aligarh, Allahabad and Oxford; Chief Education Officer, Rampur State, 1902-03; served in Baroda State, 1904-10; attended Muslim League Session, 1906; founded *Comrade*, 1911, and *Hamdard*, 1913; participated in Kanpur mosque agitation and Pan-Islamic movement; interned 1915-19; attended Congress sessions at Amritsar, 1919; member, Khilafat delegation to London, 1920; President, Khilafat Conference, Karachi, 1921 and Calcutta 1928; tried for sedition and imprisoned, 1921-23; President, Congress session at Cocananda, 1924; attended All Parties National Convention at Calcutta, 1928; opposed Nehru Report and left Congress; attended First Session of RTC, 1930.

'Ali, Muhammad Amir

Captain of the Muslim Volunteer Corps, Madras.

'Ali, Muhsin

Khilafat leader; favoured Non-Co-operation.

'Ali, Salamat

From Lucknow; held Non-Violent Non-Co-operation to be insufficient to help the Turks.

'Ali, Sayyid Hifazat

Elected in 1923 as an independent candidate for the Nerbudda constituency to the C.P. Legislative Council.

'Ali, Sayyid Rida

1882-1949

Educated at Moradabad and Aligarh; at first Congressman, later joined Muslim League; member, U.P. Legislative Council, 1912-25; led the Khilafat agitation in Allahabad, 1919-20; sat on the Council of State, 1921-26; President, All India Muslim League, 1927; appointed Agent of the Government of India in South Africa, 1935.

'Ali, Shawkat

1873-1938

Educated at the Aligarh College in 1888; Sub-Deputy Agent till 1912; founded the Anjuman-e Khuddam-e Kaaba with Maulana Abdul Bari in Lucknow in May 1913; interned with Muhammad Ali from May 1915 to December 1919, and again in 1923; President of the Khilafat Conference in Kakinanda in 1923; attended Second Session of RTC in 1930-31; member, Indian Legislative Assembly, 1934-38.

Alimcand, Ramcand

Pleader.

Alimcandani, Motiram

Amil of Hyderabad; student agitator in Thar Parkar District, Sindh.

Allah Bakhsh

Student agitator from Dera Ghazi Khan.

Amar Sen, Pandit

Congressman from Karachi; took active part in Non-Co-operation and Civil Disobedience movements; was against declaration of republic in 1921; was imprisoned several times.

Amardinomal, Lalcand

Attended Sindh Provincial Congress 1921 as delegate from Karachi.

Ambriti Devi (Manohardas, Mrs.)

Member, Sindh Provincial Congress Committee for Sahiti District, 1921.

Amin ad-Din, Shahab ad-Din

Member, Working Committee of the Sindh Provincial Khilafat Committee, 1921.

Amin ad-Din N. Munshi

Vice-President, Hyderabad City Khilafat Committee, 1921; Member of Sindh Provincial Congress Committee for Hyderabad, 1921.

Anandji, Seth Narayan Das

1892-1960

Labour leader from Sindh; educated at Karachi; joined Home Rule League in 1919; participated in Non-Co-operation, Civil Disobedience and Quit India movements; member, Sindh Provincial Congress Committee for Karachi, 1921 and 1922; Secretary, Sindh Provincial Congress Committee; member, Karachi Municipal Corporation, 1923, 1931-47; member, Bombay Legislative Council, 1926-29 and Sindh Legislative Assembly, 1937-46.

Aney, M.S.

1880-1968

Prominent Congressman of Berar; member, AICC, 1920-34; President, Berar Provincial Congress Committee, 1921-30; member, Central Legislative Assembly, 1924-35; member, Congress Working Committee, 1924-25 and 1931-34; Secretary, Nationalist Party, 1926-30; Acting President, Indian National Congress, 1933, member, Governor-General's Executive Council, 1941-43; representative of Government of India in Sri Lanka, 1943-47; member, Constituent Assembly, 1947-48; Governor of Bihar, 1948-52; member, Lok Sabha, 1959-67; awarded Padma Vibhushan, 1968.

Ansari, 'Abd-al Aziz

Arrested in September 1921.

Ansari, Dr. Mukhtar Ahmad

1880-1939

Studied medicine in Allahabad and Edinburgh; led the Indian Medical Mission to Constantinople (July - September 1912); one of the architects of the Home Rule League; President All India Muslim League, Nagpur 1920; President, Khilafat Conference, Gaya 1922; President, Congress Session Madras 1927; founded the Nationalist Muslim Party in 1929; he was a close associate of Gandhi and deeply involved in the nationalist movement.

'Aqil ar-Rahman

Speech against CID reporters.

Asghar, Muhammad

Barrister-at-Law, Hyderabad; member, All-India Muslim League.

Asim, Muhammad

Student agitator from Badrashi.

'Ata'-allah Banarasi

Member, Subjects Committee of the Khilafat Workers' Conference, 1920; favoured policy of jihad.

Avari, Manchersha

b. 1898

Congressman from C.P. and Berar; educated in Bombay University; joined freedom movement in 1918; took part in Non-Co-operation and Civil Disobedience movements and was imprisoned several times; member, AICC and President, Nagpur Congress Committee for several years; elected to the M.P. Legislative Assembly in 1952 as independent candidate.

Ayengar, Srinivas

1874-1941

Educated from Madura and Presidency College, Madras; member, Madras Bar Council; member, Madras Senate, 1912-16; President, Madras Social Reforms Association, 1916-20; actively participated Congress sessions from 1921-29; member, Madras Legislative Council, 1920; elected from Madras to the Central Assembly; organised Independence League.

Azad, Abul Kalam

1888-1958

Traditional education; joined group of revolutionaries in Bengal;

edited *al Nadwa* (Lucknow), *Vakil* (Amritsar), *al Hilal* (Calcutta), *al Balagh* (Calcutta); joined Gandhi's Non-Co-operation movement, 1920; President, All India Khilafat Congress, Calcutta, 1920; President, Jamiat-ul Ulama, Bareilly, 1921; imprisoned, 1921-23; President, Special Congress Session, Delhi, 1923; participated in Civil Disobedience campaign; President, Indian National Congress, 1940; participated in Quit India movement; represented Congress in Simla Conference, 1945; Education Minister, 1947-58; member, Constituent Assembly; Member of Parliament, 1950-52; member, Lok Sabha, 1952-58.

'Aziz ad-Din, Khan Sahib

Affluent trader and man of considerable influence in Delhi; closely connected with various educational and religious associations, including the Anjuman-e Muhafiz-e Auqaf.

'Aziz Amritsari, Ghulam Muhammad

1896-1971

Secretary of the Anjuman-e Muhajirin of Delhi; organised Khilafat Workers' Conference, Delhi, 1920.

'Aziz, Ghulam Muhammad

Originally from Amritsar, established hijrat office in Delhi.

Bajaj, Seth Jamnalal

1889-1942

Jain of Wardha; industrialist and financier; close associate of Gandhi; no-changer; member of the Congress Working Committee and Treasurer of the Indian National Congress for many years.

Bakhsh, Muhammad

Ex-constable; Khilafat volunteer in Hyderabad; active in propagating Non-Co-operation among sepoys.

Bal, Suraj

Prosecuted for seditious speech in Najafgarh.

Ballab, Radha (alias Som Dutt Sarma)

Brahman of Mathura District; political agitator; arrested during Non-Co-operation.

Baluch, Mir Muhammad Sahib

b. 1872

Belonged to the Salavala Jamat family of labourers; landlord and general merchant; studied Gujarati at Mission School, Karachi; left school at the age of 12 to work in a stone quarry near Karachi; connected with prominent firms in England, America and Germany; Honorary Magistrate; Municipal Councillor of Karachi, 1916; gave up all Government work to participate in national movement and joined the Congress; took active part in Khilafat movement; member, Bombay Legislative Council, 1927-31.

Bamsiram, Ramcand

Member, Sindh Provincial Congress Committee for Jacobabad district for 1922.

Bamwal, Amir Cand

Wavered between loyalty to and criticism of the Government.

Banarji, Jitendra Lal

Congressman; took active part in the Rowlatt agitation and Non-Co-operation movement; organised hartal in Bengal on the day of the Prince of Wales' arrival.

Baptista, Joseph

1864-1930

Took an active part in the Indian Home Rule and Labour movements; President, Bombay Provincial Conference, 1915 and Indian Home Rule League, 1916-26; member, Legislative Assembly, 1926-27; President, All-India Trade Union Congress, 1922-23; Labour delegate to the Labour Conference, Geneva, 1924; President, Bombay Municipal Corporation, 1925.

al-Baqi, 'Abd-allah

Speaker at the Congress Committee Conference at Bogra.

Barman, A.P.

Active in Temperance movement; non-co-operator.

Batla, Muhammad Ahmad

Wrote leaflet enjoining government servants to resign.

Besant, Annie

1847-1933

Came to India in 1893 to work for the Theosophical Society; founded the Home Rule League in 1916; arrested in June 1917; her arrest sparked off widespread protest; elected Congress President in December 1917.

Bhagvan Das

Member, Sindh Provincial Congress Committee for Sukkur District, 1921.

Bhagwandin

Jain from Aligarh; ex-railway employee; disciple of Gandhi who conferred on him the title of Mahatma; imprisoned during Non-Co-operation campaign, 1921.

Bhojraj, Mulcand

Member, Sindh Provincial Congress Committee for Sukkur District, 1921.

Bhojraj, Seth

Member, Sindh Provincial Congress Committee for Nawabshah District, 1922.

Bhurgri, Ghulam Muhammad

1878-1924

Educated at Karachi, Aligarh and London; practised law in Hyderabad, Sindh; member, Bombay Legislative Council, 1910-1919; member, Council of State, 1921; presided over All India Khilafat Conference, Bombay, 1920; President, Lucknow Session of the Muslim League, 1923; member, Indian Legislative Assembly, 1923-24; started Sindhi weekly *Illa Meen*.

Bijasingh, Fatih Cand

Member, Sindh Provincial Congress Committee for Karachi, 1922.

Bijraj, Virumal

1874-1955

Social and political worker; started the weekly *Sindhi*; established a branch of Tilak's Home Rule League at Sukkur; member, Sukkur Municipality for 16 years; President, Sukkur District Congress Committee; Vice-President, Sindh Provincial Congress Committee; President, Sindh Branch of the Hindu Mahasabha.

Bobde

Congressman; led the extremist faction of Nagpur; stood for boycott of elections in 1920.

Bolcand, Bhai Khubsabd

Member, Sindh Provincial Congress Committee for Hyderabad, 1921.

Bolcand, Misir
Khilafat leader of Badah.

Bose, Khudi Ram
Bengali anarchist.

Bose, Sarat Candra
1889-1950
Elder brother of Subhas Chandra Bose; Bar-at-Law; joined Non-Co-operation movement, 1921; member, Bengal Legislative Council, 1927-29; took part in Civil Disobedience movement and was arrested in 1932; elected to Indian Legislative Assembly, 1934, Bengal Legislative Assembly, 1937; arrested, 1941-45; elected to Constituent Assembly, 1946; member, Congress Working Committee, July 1946-January 1947; joined Interim Government, 1946; resigned November 1946; formed Socialist Republican Party after resigning from Congress, 1947; elected to Bengal Legislative Assembly, 1949.

Bose, Sir Vipin Krsna
b. 1851
Educated from Presidency College, Calcutta; began practice in Jabbalpur; Government Advocate, Nagpur; Member, Supreme Legislative Council, 1902-05; leader of the moderates in Nagpur.

Brooke
Labour leader in the railway union of Sindh.

Bukhari, Mawlawi 'Ata'-allah Shah (Amritsari)
1891-1967
Started as a religious preacher in a small mosque in Amritsar; Ahl-e Hadith; took leading part in the Khilafat agitation in the city; first President of Majlis-i Ahrar-e Islam-e Hind; took part in the Civil Disobedience movement and was imprisoned; member, Jamiat-ul Ulama-e Hind; opposed to Partition, but went to Pakistan after 1947.

Cainraj, Dr. Menghraj
Member, Sindh Provincial Congress Committee for Jacobabad District, 1922.

Cainraj, Seth
Member, Karachi Piece Good Merchants' Association.

Cakravarti, Syam Sundar
Congressman from Bengal; linked with Aurobindo Ghose and

the *Bande Mataram* group; leader of educational boycott, 1905; organised Railwaymen's Union, 1906; Editor, *Servant*; imprisoned in 1922.

Cand, V.L. Diwan

Public Prosecutor, Peshawar.

Candiram, Rijhumal

Amil of Karachi; student agitator during Non-Co-operation.

Caturvedi, Makkhan Lal

1889-1968

Hindi Poet and writer; member, Hindi Provincial Conference; sub-editor of *Karmavir*; imprisoned during Non-Co-operation movement; no-changer; President, All India Hindi Sevak Sangh, 1943; received Sahitya Academy Award, 1955; surrendered Padma Bhushan in protest against the Official Language (Amendment) Bill, 1958.

Celaram, D.

Merchant from Casablanca in Morocco; contributed to Tilak Swaraj Fund.

Celaram, Seth Vasumal

Vice-president, Karachi Piece Good Merchants' Association.

Chattarji, Durga Das

Associate of C.R. Das; imprisoned during Non-Co-operation.

Chattarji, Siris Candra

1873-1966

Educated at Dhaka; associated with Anushilan Samiti; acted as Defence Counsel in Dhaka conspiracy case, 1910, Barisal conspiracy case, 1913, Gauhati shooting case, 1917; took part in Non-Co-operation movement and gave up practice; Secretary, Khilafat Committee, Dhaka; joined Swaraj Party; opposed Gandhi's resolution on Dominion status, 1928; took part in civil Disobedience and Quit India movements.; opposed Partition and stayed in Pakistan after 1947; elected to Constituent Assembly of Pakistan; leader of the Opposition, 1948-55; came to India in 1962.

Chaudhuri, Sir Asutos

1860-1924

Eminent lawyer and jurist; educated at Calcutta and Cambridge; called to the Bar from Middle Temple, 1886; practised law in

Calcutta High Court; Judge Calcutta High Court, 1912-20; Knighted in 1917; member, Bengal Legislative Council.

Cholkar, Dr. M.L.

1882-1962

Educated at Nagpur, Bombay, Berlin and London; Maratha Brahman; medical practitioner of Nagpur; a follower of Tilak; member, Nagpur Municipal Committee, 1912-25 and its President, 1921-25; member, AICC, 1916-24; Secretary, C.P. and Berar PCC, 1918-20; Deputy Leader, Congress Medical Mission to China, 1938; Director, Medical Mission to Malaya, 1946.

Chotani, Mian Muhammad Haji Jan Muhammad

1883-1932

Belonged to the Memon community; a wealthy timber merchant and government contractor from Bombay; large contributions towards the war effort, First World War; closely associated with Abdul Bari; President, Central Khilafat Committee, 1919-23; associated with the scheme for the initiation of the Non-Co-operation movement; member of AICC, 1920-21; member, second Khilafat delegation to Europe, 1921; signatory to a manifesto regarding Turkish management of Angora Fund.

Chuharmal, Mansingh

Member, Sindh Provincial Congress Committee for Sahaiti District, 1921-22.

Ciyaram, Kusaldas

Clerk of the Educational Inspector; resigned during Non-Co-operation.

Cunnilal, Ratna

Leader of the Dhobi Temperance movement in Karachi.

Curiwala, 'Abd-allah

Shoe-merchant of Delhi and active pan-Islamist; member of Delhi Khilafat committee; leader, Khilafat volunteers of the Khudam-i Watan; imprisoned during Non-Co-operation.

Dalal, M.B.

Congressman from Sindh; member and auditor of Sindh Provincial Congress Committee, 1919-26; imprisoned during the Khilafat movement.

Das, Chiman

Member, Sindh Provincial Congress Committee, 1922.

Das, Cittaranjan

1870-1925

Joined legal profession after his return to India in 1894; came into prominence as counsel for the defence in the trail of Aurobindo Ghose; member of non-official Jallianwala Bagh enquiry committee; allied with Gandhi, 1920, and became leader of Non-Co-operation movement in Bengal; President, Indian National Congress, 1922; organised Swaraj Party with Motilal Nehru; elected to the Bengal Legislative Council, 1923; Mayor, Calcutta Corporation, 1924-5; chief architect of the 'Bengal Pact'.

Das, Devi Basanti (Mrs. C.R. Das)

1880-1974

Joined politics in 1917; participated in the Non-Co-operation movement, 1921; withdrew from politics after the death of C.R. Das in 1925.

Das, Purna

1889-1959

Involved in training of volunteer corps in Bengal; leader of revolutionary group in Madaripur, Bengal; joined Swaraj Party; joined Forward Block.

Dastgir, Mirza Ghulam

Representative of Sindh on the Central Khilafat Committee, Bombay, 1922.

Datta, Babu D.N.

Resigned as Vice-President for the Reception Committee for the Calcutta session of the Congress.

Daulatram, Jairam Das

1892-1979

Eminent lawyer from Sindh; took active part in the freedom movement and was imprisoned several times; editor of *Bharatvasi*, 1916, *Hindu* (Sindhi), 1920, *Hindustan Times*, 1925-26, *Young India*, 1930; member, Bombay Legislative Council, 1927-29 and Congress Working Committee, 1929-41; General Secretary, Indian National Congress, 1931-34; member, Constituent

Assembly, 1946-47 and 1948-50; Governor, Bihar, 1947-48; Minister for Food and Agriculture, Government of India, 1948-50; Governor, Assam, 1950-56; member, Rajya Sabha, 1959-76.

Da'ud Ghaznavi, Mawlawi Muhammad

1895-1963

Imam of the Ghaznavi Mosque, Amritsar; Ahl-e Hadith leader; member of the All India Muslim League; supporter of the declaration for complete independence in 1921.

Dayanomal, Seth Khushiram

Member, Sindh Provincial Congress Committee for Jacobabad District, 1921.

De

Commissioner of Chandpur, Bengal.

Devi, Sarala Bala

1872-1945

Social worker and educationist; niece of Rabindranath Tagore; advocated Hindu-Muslim unity through her journal *Bharati*; worked for popularising swadeshi goods; joined Congress in 1919.

Devi, Saraswati

Member, Sindh Provincial Congress for Karachi, 1922; Vice-President, Sindh Provincial Congress Committee.

Dhaka, Nawab of (Sir Khwaja Salim-allah)

1884-1915

Prominent landowner and politician of East Bengal; took prominent part in organising the Simla Deputation of Muslims to the Viceroy, 1906; Vice-President, AIML, 1910, President, 1912; withdrew from active politics after the annulment of the partition of Bengal.

Din, Mawlawi Mukham

Of Jamesabad; proposed resolution for republic at Mirpurkhas Conference; member, Working Committee of the Sindh Provincial Khilafat Committee, member, Sindh Provincial Congress for Thar Parkar District, 1922.

Dowman, Ethel E.

Editor and proprietor of *The Advocate of Railwaymen*.

Dowman, T.H.W.

Leader of European and Anglo-Indian railway-workers in Karachi.

Fakhr, Muhammad

Muslim Leader from Allahabad; close associate of Abdul Bari of Firangi Mahal; took part in Non-Co-operation and Khilafat movements; member, All India Central Khilafat Committee.

Fatih 'Ali, Mawlawi

Of Sujawal; imprisoned during Non-Co-operation movement.

Fazl al-Haqq, A.K.

1873-1962

Eminent lawyer of Calcutta; member, Bengal Legislative Council, 1913-34; member, Central Legislative Assembly, 1934-36; Premier of Bengal, 1937-41; headed a Coalition Ministry in Bengal, December 1941-March 1943; headed the United Front Ministry in East Pakistan in 1954; Central Minister in Pakistan, 1955-56; Governor of East Pakistan, 1956-8.

Fazl-Allah

Student agitator from Aligarh National University; son of Qazi Obeidullah.

Fitr, 'Ali Muhammad

Railway leader from Karachi.

Gajra, Taracand D.

Member, Sindh Provincial Congress Committee for Shikarpur District, 1921; representative for Sindh at All India Congress, 1921.

Gandhi, Devidas

1900-57

Son of Mahatma Gandhi; journalist; joined *Independent*, 1920, *Young India* and *Navjeevan*, 1923-24; editor, *Hindustan Times*.

Gandhi, Mohandas Karamchand

1869-1948

Barrister from Gujarat; educated from Rajkot, Bhavnagar, London; editor, *Young India*; practised in South Africa for 17 years; gave up practice to lead 'Passive resistance' on behalf of Indian settlers, 1908; returned to India, 1915; leading figure of Indian National Congress till his assassination in 1948.

Ganpath

Leader, Railway Union Karachi.

Ghansam Das, Professor

Activist of national education; member, Sindh Provincial Congress Committee for Hyderabad District, 1922.

Ghose, Surat Candra

1883-1958

Religious leader; studied scripture at Brindaban; developed Samanvaya Dharma and preached his new ideas; took part in Non-Co-operation, Civil Disobedience and Quit India movements and was imprisoned several times.

Ghosh, Dr.

Active in the establishment of the Azad Muslim School, Peshawar.

Ghulam Muhammad, Mawlawi

Member, Sindh Provincial Congress Committee for Hyderabad, 1922.

Gidamal, Ratanmal Walad

Lawyer from Mirpurkhas District, gave up practice during Non-Co-operation; member, Sindh Provincial Congress Committee for Thar Parkar District, 1921.

Gidvani

1891-1935

Educationist from Gujarat; Principal of Ramjas High School in Delhi, resigned during Non-Co-operation, Principal of Gujarat Vidhyapith for many years; was arrested along with Jawaharlal Nehru at Nabha in 1923.

Gidvani, Alu Tekcand

Amil of Hyderabad; student agitator in Karachi.

Gidvani, Dr. Caitram Partabrai

Active in promotion of national schools and colleges in Sindh; member for Hyderabad and President, Sindh Provincial Congress Committee, 1921-22; representative for Sindh to Indian National Congress, 1921.

Gmeiner, Leonora

Of Australian origin; principal of the Indraprastha School, Delhi; founded the Delhi branch of the Home Rule League in 1916, after which the Government grant to the school was discontinued.

Gokhale, Gopal Krisna

1866-1915

Education from Deccan College, Poona and Elphinstone College,

Bombay; joined Deccan Education Society, Poona; Lecturer at Fergusson College, 1885-1902; member, Indian National Congress; elected member, Bombay Legislative Council, 1899 and Imperial Legislative Council, 1902; founded Servants of India Society in 1905.

Gokulji, Radha Mohan

President, first Maratha Central Provinces Volunteers' Conference.

Golasingh, Bhai Hothsingh

Member, Sindh Provincial Congress Committee for Hyderabad, 1921.

Govardhana Das, Seth Motilal

President, Karachi Piece Good Merchants' Association.

Govindanand, Svami (alias J.T. Mansukhani)

Labour leader and non-co-operator; President, Kasib Azadi Sabha; imprisoned for seditious speeches.

Gul, Ali

Khilafat leader from Peshawar.

Gul, Litaf

Of Ziarat Kaka Sahib; advocated Non-Co-operation and the boycott of foreign goods.

Gulab Singh, Dr. Vatanmal

Member, Sindh Provincial Congress Committee for Thar Parkar district, 1921-22.

Gulrazani, Valiram

Clerk in the office of the Assistant Directory Military Works, Sindh Rajputana District, discharged for wearing Gandhi clothes.

Gurudayal

Leader, Railway Union Karachi.

Habib-Allah

Worked as President, Nawabshah District Congress Committee.

Hajji, Dr. Ghulam Husain Qasim

Khilafat leader from Sindh; member, Sindh Khilafat Working Committee; representative of Sindh to Indian National Congress, 1922; member, Sindh Provincial Congress for Karachi District, 1922.

Haksar, Siv Narayan

b. 1878

Editor of *Hindi Samachar*; captain of Home Rule League

Volunteer corps, Delhi; delegate to the Congress Session in 1917, 1918, 1919; took part in the Non-Co-operation and Civil Disobedience movements.

Hanswi, 'Arif

1888-1936

A leading Delhi based journalist; active in the Congress movement; leader of Volunteer movement; arrested during Khilafat movement; took part in the Civil Disobedience movement in 1930.

Harcand Rai

Member Karachi Piece Good Merchants' Association.

Harjan Das

Lawyer of Sukkur District; resigned honorary appointment of Assistant Public Prosecutor during Non-Co-operation.

Harun, Seth Hajji 'Abd-allah

1872-1942

Leading businessman and politician from Karachi; organised the Khilafat movement in Sindh, made huge contributions to the Khilafat funds; President, All India Muslims' Conference; member, AIML Council; elected member at Bombay Legislative Council, 1924-26; member, Central Assembly; President, Central Khilafat Committee, 1927.

Hasan, 'Aziz

Delhi Naqshbandi; leading member, Anjuman-e muhafiz-e masjid.

al-Hasan, Mahmud

1851-1920

Graduated from Deoband in 1873 and joined the staff there; Principal of the Dar-ul Ulum, 1890; launched an anti-British campaign in favour of Turkey, 1911; moved to the Hejaz with his associates to avoid arrest, 1915; arrested by the British in 1916 and interned at Malta, 1917-20; returned to India in June 1920 and joined the Khilafat movement.

Hasan, Mawlawi Sultan

Religious leader of Ajmer; speaker at Khilafat Workers' Conference.

Hasan, Ya'qub

1875-1940

Khilafat leader from Madras; editor, *Qaumi Halchal* and *Muslim*

Patriot; member, Muslim League; resigned Madras Legislative Council, 1920; supported Gandhi Calcutta Special Congress.

Hasham, Khalifa Muhammad

Member, Sindh Provincial Congress Committee for Hyderabad District.

Hasrajan, Mulcand Mamgharm

Student agitator form Hyderabad.

Hayat

Brought up in Lahore, settled in Aligarh; left study in 1920 to join Non-Co-operation movement; secretary of Muhammad Ali; member, Red Crescent Mission; went to England as Secretary to Muhammad Ali in the Khilafat Deputation of 1920.

Himmat Singhani, Nichaldas Meharsingh

Student agitator from Larkana District; member, Sindh Provincial Congress Committee for Thar Parkar.

Hiranand

Member, Sindh Provincial Congress Committee for Sukkur District, 1921.

Horniman, Benjamin Guy

1873-1948

Came to India in 1906; founded the *Bombay Chronicle* with Pherozshah Mehta in 1913 and the *Indian National Herold* in 1926; associated with the Home Rule League and the Satyagraha Sabha; deported to England in 1919; during 1943-44 editor-in-chief of *Bombay Sentinel.*

Husayn, Muhammad

Barrister; selected by Central Khilafat Committee to serve on deputation with the Civil Disobedience Enquiry Committee.

Husayn, Muqarrab

Student agitator from Bannu District.

Husayn, Mawlana Murtada

Religious leader from Deoband, active in the Jamiat ul Ulama-e Hind.

Husayn, Mawlana Sa'adat

Active in the Hijrat movement in Delhi.

Husayn, Nadhir

Of Muzaffarnagar; speaker at Khilafat Workers' Conference at Delhi.

Husayn, Sayyid
1886-1949
Moved a resolution demanding responsible government in the provinces in 1918; a well known journalist; worked with the *Bombay Chronicle*, 1917-19 and the Allahabad paper *Independent*; spread the cause of Indian independence in America through nation-wide lecture tours; president, National Committee for India's Independence in America in 1939; India's first Ambassador to Egypt; died and buried in Egypt; closely connected with the Nehru family.

Husayn, Sayyid Mubarik
Secretary of the Congress Volunteer Corps, Delhi.

Husayn, Sayyid Muzaffar
Swarajist member, Central Provinces Legislative Assembly, 1923.

Ibrahim, Mufti
Active in the opening of the Azad Muslim High School in Peshawar.

Indarjit (Indira Vidyavacaspati)
b. 1891
Son of Swami Shraddhananda; edited the newspapers *Vijay* and *Arjun*; scholar of Sanskrit; taught at Gurukul Kangri.

Iqbal
Member of the Delhi Khilafat Volunteer Corps.

Irfan, Muhammad
1888-1939
Close collaborator of Muhammad Ishaq, Imam of the Jama Masjid of Manshera and leading Khilafatist of Hazara District.

Isvar Das, Dr. Cimanlal
Member, Sindh Provincial Congress Committee for Hyderabad District, 1922.

Isvar Das, Metharam
Member, Sindh Provincial Congress Committee for Larkana District, 1922.

Ishaq, Muhammad
Leader of the Askar-e Islamia Volunteer Corps of Delhi.

Ishaq, Muhammad
1888-1962
Imam of the Jama Masjid of Manshera; leading Khilafatist of Hazara District.

Ishfaq
Secretary of Muhammad Ali; took part in Khilafat agitation in Karachi.

Isma'il, Mawlana Muhammad
Religious leader and Khilafat orator.

Jagatsingh
Akali of Peshawar; member of the Singh Sabha of Sindh.

Jagtiani, Lalcand A.
Secretary, Karachi District Congress Committee; member, Sindh Provincial Congress Committee for Karachi, 1921-22; representative for Sindh to All India National Congress, 1921; co-founder of the Tilakalya National School in Karachi.

Jalib, Basharat 'Ali
d. 1930
Sub-editor of Muhammad Ali's paper *Hamdard*; edited the *Hamdam* from Lucknow; closely associated with the politics of the Ali brothers.

Jan, Hasan
Khilafat leader from Peshawar.

Jan, Nasr-allah
Student agitator of Ismailia College, Peshawar.

Jang, Nawab Zulqadar
From Lucknow; member, All India Muslim League.

Jesvani, T.K.
Editor of *New Times*, Karachi; member, Sindh Provincial Congress Committee, 1921; representative for Sindh to Indian National Congress, 1921.

Jethanand, Ghansyam
Educationist, journalist and politician from Sindh; eminent Congressman; took active part in Non-Co-operation, Civil Disobedience and Quit India movements and was imprisoned several times; member, Sindh Provincial Congress Committee;

leader of the Congress party in the Sindh Legislative Assembly.

Jhamatmal, Gopaldas

Member, Swaraj Society of Hyderabad.

Jhangiani, Kessumal Tekcand

Student agitator from Hyderabad.

Jinaya, Jan Muhammad

Sindhi Muhajirin leader.

Jinnah, Muhammad 'Ali

1876-1948

Barrister and politician from Bombay; educated at Karachi and London; joined Muslim League in 1913; principal negotiator of Lucknow Pact with the Congress, 1916; President, Muslim League, 1916, 1920, 1934-48; President, Home Rule League, Bombay, 1917-20; first Governor-General of Pakistan, 1947-48.

Josi, Vasudev Ganes

1854-1944

From Amraoti; educated at Poona; actively supported the revolutionaries for the independence of India; took part in Home Rule movement, Non-Co-operation and Civil Disobedience; imprisoned several times.

Jotsingh, Kisinsingh

Member, Sindh Provincial Congress Committee for Hyderabad, 1921.

Karamcand, Lakhasingh

Pleader from Rohri; involved with Court of Arbitration at Sukkur.

Karim, Fadl

Leader of the Temperance movement among the Dhobis of Karachi; arrested during Non-Co-operation.

Karimji, Hatimbhay A.

Member, Sindh Provincial Congress Committee, 1921.

Kauromal, Manohardas

Member, Sindh Provincial Congress Committee for Sahaiti District, 1922.

Kaynath, Sundarlal

From Mirzapur, United Provinces; educated from Dayanand Arya

Vedic College at Lahore; studied law; suspected in Delhi conspiracy case; in-charge of National School in Nagpur; imprisoned during Non-Co-operation; President of Provincial Congress Committee.

Kelkar, Narsimha Chitanmani

1872-1947

Tilak's most prominent colleague; editor of *The Mahratta*, 1897-1919, and *Kesari*, 1897-99, 1901-1931; member, Maharashtra Home Rule League; President, Bombay Provincial Conference, 1910; member, Congress Working Committee for several years; advocated entry into the Councils.

Kelkar, Rao Bahadur

Minister of Education, Central Provinces; defeated by Swaraj Party in the elections of 1923.

Khajoo, Hajji

Donated to the Angora Fund.

Khan, 'Abd ar-Razzaq

1900-1984

Educated at Collins Institute, Calcutta; associated for some time with *Rozana Hind* of Calcutta; took part in Khilafat, Non-Co-operation, Civil Disobedience and Quit India movements; imprisoned several times; member, Indian National Congress, 1920-46; member Bengal Provincial Congress, 1938-40 and AICC, 1938-40; one of the founder members of the CPI in Bengal; Vice-President, Provincial Kisan Sabha, 1939-53, its President 1954; member, Rajya Sabha, 1954-60; CPI member of Legislative Assembly, 1969-70; Minister for Relief, W.B. Government, 1969-70.

Khan, Arbab Dost Muhammad

Loyalist Muslim leader from Peshawar.

Khan, Arbab Muhammad Azam

Loyalist Muslim leader of Peshawar.

Khan, Captain Ahmad Nawaz

Loyalist Muslim leader of Dera Ismail Khan.

Khan, Captain Muhammad Akbar

Loyalist Muslim leader of Hoti.

Khan, Hajji Khan Walad Ya'qub

Supervising Tapedar of Sukkur District; resigned during Non-Co-operation.

Khan, Hakim Ajmal

1863-1927

Belonged to a leading Hakim family of Delhi; physician to the Nawab of Rampur; founded Tibbia College; received the title of *Haziq ul Mulk* in 1907 from the Government of India; took a leading part in the Rowlatt satyagraha and the Khilafat movement; one of the founders of Jamia Millia Islamia; Congress President in September 1921.

Khan, Khatim

Assistant Secretary to the Provincial Khilafat Committee; resigned in 1921.

Khan, M.A.

Secretary of the Railway Union, Lahore; delegate to Ahmedabad Congress as labour member.

Khan, Mawlana Ahmad Razzaq

Religious leader from Baus Bareilly; held that the King of Hedjaz was rightful claimant to Khilafat.

Khan, Mawlana Akram

1868-1968

Educated in Madrasa, Calcutta; editor, *Mohammadi* (monthly), 1903; founded Anjuman-e Ulama-e Bangla, 1913; President, Bengali Muslim Literary Conference, Chittagong, 1918; published *Zamana* (Urdu) and *Sheblok* (?) (Bengali), 1920; participated in Khilafat movement; imprisoned, 1921-23; President, Shirajganj Provincial Congress, 1924, Bengal Provincial Congress, 1926, and Surma Valley Muslim Conference, 1930; joined Muslim League, 1936; member, Bengal Legislative Council, 1937-44; President, Bengal Muslim League, 1941-47; member, East Bengal Provincial Muslim League, 1947-51; President, Anjuman Taraqqi-e Urdu, 1948; left Muslim League in 1954.

Khan, Mazullah

Inspector of Police; President of Bannu Khilafat Committee; resigned post of Honorary Magistrate during Non-Co-operation.

Khan, Muhammad 'Ali
Elected to Central Provinces Legislative Assembly for the Liberal Party.

Khan, Muhammad Khan Ghazi
Secretary of the Sindh Provincial Khilafat Committee; Secretary, Karachi Khilafat Committee; representative for Sindh to All India Congress Committee, 1921.

Khan, Muhammad Mas'ud
Elected to Central Provinces Legislative Council in 1923 for the Swaraj Party.

Khan, Nawab Saifullah
Loyalist Muslim leader.

Khan, Pir Muhammad 'Umar
Pir of Matiar; member, Sindh Provincial Congress Committee, 1922; member, Working Committee of the Sindh Provincial Khilafat Committee.

Khan, Sami'-allah
Leading pleader of Nagpur; Secretary of the Nagpur Congress Committee; member, Central Khilafat Committee; elected to Central Provinces Legislative Council for the Swaraj Party in 1923.

Khan, Sardar Jan Gul
Loyalist Muslim leader.

Khan, Sharif Ullah
Loyalist Muslim leader.

Khan, Sir Abdul Qayum
K.C.I.E.; sympathy with the Khilafat agitation.

Khan, Zafar 'Ali
1873-1956
Educated at MAO College, Aligarh, from where he graduated in 1895; joined the service of the Nizam of Hyderabad; took over as editor of the *Zamindar*; visited Turkey in 1912 to deliver the purse collected by the Indian Muslims through the Indian Crescent Mission; one of the leading figures of the Khilafat movement; went to England, Paris and the Middle East as member of the Khilafat delegation, 1925; joined the Ahrar Party in 1929; member, Panjab Legislative Council, 1937-46.

Khaparde, G.S.
1854-1938
Pleader from Amraoti in the Central Provinces; follower of Tilak; opposed Gandhi's Non-Co-operation movement.

Khatri, Ahmad Hajji Siddiq
1888-1943
Educated at Bombay; cloth merchant; participated in the Swadeshi and Non-Co-operation movements; Secretary, All India Central Khilafat Committee, 1922-29; member, Greater Bombay Municipal Corporation, 1922-26.

Khatri, Narayan Svami
Hindu religious leader from Amritsar; prosecuted for seditious speeches during Non-Co-operation.

Khuda Bakhsh
Student agitator from Arazi Larkana.

Khuda Bakhsh, Mawlawi Qazi
Participated in the freedom movement and was imprisoned during the Khilafat movement; member and Secretary, Sindh Khilafat Working Committee; member, Central Khilafat Committee; member for Nawabshah District, Sindh Provincial Congress Committee, 1922; Sindh member on All India Congress delegation, 1922.

Kichlu, Dr. Sayf ad-Din
1884-1963
A contemporary of Jawaharlal Nehru at Cambridge; prominent leader in Panjab during and after the Rowlatt satyagraha; gave up his practice in 1920; organised the Tanzim campaign, 1925; Chairman, Reception Committee of the Lahore Congress, 1929; President, All India Peace Council, 1950; awarded Lenin Peace Price, 1952.

Kifayat-allah, Mufti Mawlawi Muhammad
1875-1952
Teacher, political leader and writer; graduate of Deoband; taught at the Madrasa Aminiya in Delhi where he stayed from 1903 till his death; founding member of the Jamiat-ul Ulama-e Hind.

Kisancand, Dhalumal
Member, Sindh Provincial Congress Committee for Thar Parkar District, 1921-22.

Kodumal, Hiromal

Member, Sindh Provincial Congress Committee for Jacobabad District, 1921-22.

Kotri, Qadi Allah Bachhaye

Pan-Islamist activist from Hyderabad, Sindh; member, Sindh Provincial Congress Committee for Karachi; imprisoned during Khilafat movement for one year.

Kouromal, Manohardas

Member, Sindh Provincial Congress Committee for Sahiti District, 1921.

Krsnanand, Svami

Labour leader in Karachi; member, Sindh Provincial Congress Committee for Karachi, 1921; arrestted during Non-Co-operation movement; his arrest sparked off violence in Karachi.

Labhsingh, Mistri Chuharsingh

Leader, Railway Union of Karachi.

Laddharam

Leader of the Congress Volunteer movement in Hyderabad District.

Lajpat Rai, Lala

1865-1928

Congress leader from Panjab; author and journalist; edited *Punjabee* and *Bande Mataram*; was actively associated with the Arya Samaj; deported in 1907; President, Indian National Congress, Calcutta Session, 1920; assaulted by the police during anti-Simon Commission demonstrations, Lahore 1928; died soon afterwards.

Lakhasingh, Jhamatmal

Pleader from Hyderabad; member, Sindh Provincial Congress Committee for Hyderabad District, 1921-22.

Laksman

Arya Samaj leader from Delhi; member of Sew Samiti Volunteer Corps.

Lal, Pandit Sundar

1886-1981

Educated at Saharanpur, Lahore and Allahabad; founder-editor of *Karmayogi*, 1909-10; Secretary, Tilak's Home Rule League, U.P., 1917; Member, AICC, 1920-36; took part in Non-Co-operation movement and was imprisoned, 1921; President, C.P. Hindustani Congress Committee, 1922-25; jailed for organising Flag satyagraha in Jabbalpur, 1923; participated in Civil Disobedience and Quit India movements; Vice-President, U.P. Provincial Congress Committee, 1931-36; edited and published *Naya Hind*, 1946-58; Vice-President, later President, Indian Peace Council, 1952-63.

Lal, Sankar

b. 1885

Secretary, Delhi Home Rule League; leader of the Home Rule League Volunteer Corps; manager of the Swadeshi Co-operative Store; treasurer of the Satyagraha Sabha; sentenced to three years' imprisonment during Non-Co-operation movement; took part in Civil Disobedience movement, 1930.

Lal Dhamanlal, Narasingha

Member, Sindh Provincial Congress for Karachi, 1922.

Lalsingh

Leader, Railway Union of Karachi.

Lalvani, Dr. Taracand J.

Presided arbitration court at Keamari.

Lekhraj

Leader of North Western Railway Union.

Lotan

Ex-Chaprasi of the Chief Commissioner of Delhi; organised and led parades by Bhojla Pahari Volunteers, Delhi (affiliated to the Askar-e Islamia).

Ma'adh, Hakim Muhammad

Member, Sindh Provincial Congress Committee for Nawabshah District, 1922.

Malik

Secretary, Khilafat Committee, Karachi.

Malik, Khan Bahadur

President, Nagpur Khilafat Committee; resigned after adoption of Non-Co-operation.

Malaviya, Pandit Madan Mohan

1861-1946

Leading figure in Allahabad; founded the Hindu University in

Benares; President of the Congress, 1909 and 1918; President of the All India Hindu Mahasabha and closely connected with the Sangathan movement.

Mangharam, Santdas

Pleader from Hyderabad; leader of the Sindh Swaraj Society.

Marathi, Namdiram Navalraj

Student agitator from Hyderabad.

Marriwalla, H.D.

1892-1982

Joined Indian National Congress in 1913; President, Indian Home Rule League, 1916-20; took active part in Non-Co-operation, Civil Disobedience and Quit India movements and was imprisoned several times; Captain, Sindhi Volunteers for Dharsana Salt Deport Raid, 1930; editor, *The Congress*; translated several books of Tagore into Sindhi.

Masamd, K.H.

Member, Sindh Provincial Congress Committee for Karachi; Treasurer, Sindh Provincial Congress Committee.

Matharadas

Leader, Railway Union, Karachi.

Mazhar ad-Din

Khilafat leader; issued *fatwa* that co-operation with British was unlawful.

Mazhar al-Haqq

1866-1930

Prominent lawyer from Bihar, who came into contact with Gandhi during the Champaran satyagraha; liberal politician who promoted Congress-Muslim League rapprochement that led to the Lucknow Pact in 1916; the same year he presided over the Home Rule League in Bihar; gave up his practice during the Non-Co-operation movement.

Mazumdar, B.K.

1876-1944

Noted revolutionary and freedom fighter from Bengal; took part in anti-Partition agitation, 1905 and was imprisoned; organised Jugantar Party in Comilla and Chittagong; participated in Non-Co-operation, Civil Disobedience and Quit India movements;

imprisoned several times; member, Bengal Congress and All India Congress Committee.

Memon, 'Abd al-Latif

Member, Working Committee, Hyderabad City Khilafat Committee.

Menghraj, Dr.

Member, Sindh Provincial Congress Committee for Jacobabad District, 1921-22.

Miller

Irish labour leader at Lahore; labour delegate to the Ahmedabad Congress for the Punjab Provincial Congress Committee.

Mi'raj ad-Din

Leader of the N.W. Railway Union, Karachi.

Misra, Gauri Sankar

1885-1955

One of the founders of the U.P. Kisan Sabha; member of the Indian National Congress.

Misra, Gokaran Nath

Congressman.

Misser, J.P.

Congressman.

Mistri, Ahmed ad-Din

Leader, Railway Union, Karachi.

Mohani, Hasrat

1878-1951

Leading journalist, poet and politician; founded the *Urdu-e Moalla* in 1903; attended the Surat Congress in 1907 and joined the 'extremist' group of Tilak; was in the forefront of the Kanpur mosque affair and the Khilafat Conference at Delhi, November 1919; President, Khilafat Workers' Conference, Delhi 1920; demanded complete independence for India at the Congress at Ahmedabad, December 1921; President, All India Muslim League at Ahmedabad, December 1921; imprisoned in 1922; participated in Civil Disobedience movement; member, U.P. Muslim League Parliamentary Board, 1937; elected to the U.P. Legislative Assembly in 1946, Constituent Assembly; resigned from Muslim League, 1947.

Motvani, A.S.
Congressman from Sindh.

Motvani, Ramcand B.
Congressman from Larkana; Chairman, Municipality of Larkana; took active part in separation of Sindh from Bombay.

Muhammad, Dr. Shaykh Nur
Medical practitioner and pan-Islamic leader from Fakir-jo-Pir, Hyderabad, Sindh.

Muhammad, Khalifa
From Hala; member, Sindh Ulama Conference.

Muhammad, Mawlawi Fadl
From Naushahr; member of the Working Committee of the Sindh Provincial Khilafat Committee; member, Sindh Provincial Congress Committee for Sahaiti District, 1922.

Muhammad, Mawlawi Fatih
Member, Sindh Provincial Congress Committee for Thar Parkar District, 1922.

Muhammad, Mawlawi Sayyid
Elected to Central Provinces Legislative Assembly for the Liberal Party, 1923.

Muhammad, Nur
Drawing master; member, Khuddam-e Watan.

Muhammad, Seth 'Uthman Salih
Contributed to Angora Fund.

Muhammad, Shaykh ad-Din
b. 1886
Educated at Lahore; practised law, 1910-33; member, Sindh Provincial Khilafat Committee; Additional Judge, Lahore High Court, 1934-36; Puisne Judge, 1937-46; Chief Justice Bahawalpur; member, Punjab Boundary Commission, 1947; Governor of Sindh, 1948-52; Advisor on Kashmir Affairs, Government of Pakistan, December 1955.

Muhammad Bakhsh
Khilafat Volunteer; ex-Constable of Police.

Muhammad Bakhsh
Deputy Collector of Sindh.

Muhyi d-Din

Khilafat leader from Allahabad; imprisoned during Non-Co-operation.

Muhyi d-Din, Ghulam

Representative for Punjab to the All India Muslim League.

Mu'izz, Hakim Muhammad

Member, Sindh Provincial Congress Committee for Nawabshah District, 1921.

Mukhtar, Ahmad

Delivered speech in Meerut as first act of Civil Disobedience in United Provinces.

Munir az-Zaman Islamabadi

Organised strike of lascars and domestic servants.

Munji, Dr. B.S.

1872-1948

Physician of Nagpur; attended Congress Session, 1904; joined the extremists during the Surat split in 1907; joined Home Rule League organised by Tilak, 1916; member, Swaraj Party; member, Central Legislative Assembly, 1926-30; President, Hindu Mahasabha, 1927; founder of the Sangathan movement and associated with the Shuddhi movement.

Munshi, Amin ad-Din

Member, Sindh Provincial Congress Committee for Hyderabad District, 1922; Vice-President, Hyderabad City Khilafat Committee.

Nabi Bakhsh

Deputy Collector of Sindh.

Nadwi, 'Abd ar-Razzaq

Delivered speech in Lucknow.

Nadwi, Sayyid Sulayman

1884-1953

Religious leader from Azamgarh; disciple of Shibli; signed Khilafat fatwa, member, Working Committee of the Central Khilafat Committee; edited *al-Nadwa*; member, Khilafat delegation to Europe, 1920; and of delegation of the Hijaz, 1924-25.

Nagrani, Jethanand Narayandas

Student agitator from Shikarpur.

Naidu, Sarojini
1899-1949
Educated at London and Cambridge University; member Congress Working Committee in 1925; President, Congress same year; arrested during Civil Disobedience movement; delegate to the 2nd Round Table Conference, 1931; distinguished poet; Governor of Uttar Pradesh from 15 August 1947 until her death.

Nand, Sardar Kanshi
Loyalist from Peshawar.

Nanikram
Member, Sindh Provincial Congress Committee for Larkana, 1921.

Naqshband, Ghulam
Allegedly supporting claim of Amir of Kabul to Khilafat.

Narayan, Babu Prag
Delivered speech against the British at Agra.

Narayan, Laksmi
Convicted in Benares conspiracy case.

Narayan, Raj
Lawyer, stood for Council elections in Delhi during Non-Co-operation.

Narayandas, Parasram
Member, Sindh Provincial Congress Committee for Sahaiti District, 1922.

Narimal Tatta, Seth
Member, Sindh Provincial Congress Committee for Karachi, 1921.

Nasr-Allah, Pir
Religious leader from Kambar.

Nath, Bisamber
Leader of the Indraprastha Sewak Mandli, Delhi.

Natik, 'Abd al-Hasan
Nagpur maulvi, advocated Non-Co-operation; Assistant Secretary to the Provincial Khilafat Committee.

Nehru, Jawaharlal
1889-1964
Educated at Harrow and Cambridge; involved in all the nationalist

agitations since Non-Co-operation, 1920; General Secretary, Congress 1928; President of the Congress, 1929, 1936, 1946; member, External Affairs of Interim Government, 1946-47; Prime Minister and Minister for External Affairs, 1947-64; delivered anti-British speech at Kheri.

Nehru, Motilal

1861-1931

Lawyer and politician from Allahabad; educated at Muir College, Allahabad; practised as vakil, 1883-95; enrolled as advocate, Allahabad high court, 1895; President, Indian National Congress, 1919 and 1928; suspended legal practice in pursuance of Non-Co-operation, 1920; former with C.R. Das the Swaraj Party, 1923; MLA, 1923; resumed legal practice, 1925.

Ogale

Editor of the *Maharashtra*.

Pagaro, Pir (Sibghat-allah Shah)

1858-1943

Influential religious leader of Sindh; became Pir in 1922; chief of the Hurs, a tribe in Sindh; sentenced to death by a Martial Law Court for conspiracy to wage war against the King in March 1943.

Pahlajani, T.D.

Member, Sindh Provincial Congress Committee for Jacobabad District, 1921.

Pal, Bipin Candra

1858-1932

A leading Bengali journalist and politician; one of the chief architects of the Swadeshi movement in Bengal.

Pamnani, V. Hasanand

1899-1940

Educated in Bombay, joined Government service and was the head of the Teachers' College, Hyderabad (Sindh); resigned in 1921 in response to call for Non-Co-operation; member, Sindh Provincial Congress Committee for Sukkur District, 1921; took part in Civil Disobedience and Quit India movements; elected to the Sindh Legislative Assembly.

Pande, Pandit Dev Narayan

Leader, Home Rule League.

Paranjpe, Dr. N.S.
Khilafat leader from Yeotmal; Tilakite; prosecuted for sedition during Non-Co-operation.

Parsaram, Jethmal
Editor of *Bharatvasi*; follower of Annie Besant.

Pasumal, Mulcand
President, arbitration court at Sukkur; member, Sindh Provincial Congress Committee.

Patel, Vallabhbhai
1875-1950
Patidar Gujarati lawyer; educated at Nadiad and Bardwar; called to Bar, Middle Temple, 1913; Gandhi's confidant in Gujarat; first Home Minister after Independence.

Patel, V.J.
1873-1938 (or 33)
Elder brother of Vallabhbhai Patel and eminent barrister at Bombay; member, Bombay Legislative Council, 1912; President, Indian Legislative Assembly, 1925-29 (or 30); joined the national movement soon after the Lahore Congress and was arrested but released because of ill-health.

Patoli, Hajji Ahmad
Accountant of the Hyderabad City Khilafat Committee.

Piyari (?) Lal, Rai Sahib
Prominent Delhi lawyer, who took part in the Home Rule League; senior Vice-President of the Municipal Committee; President of the Delhi Bar Association; represented Delhi in 1923 to the Imperial Legislative Assembly.

Pheranmal, Sacanand
Member, Sindh Provincial Congress Committee for Sahaiti District, 1921.

Phirvani, Lilaram
Member, Sindh Provincial Congress Committee for Shikarpur District, 1922.

Piryabharti, Svami
Member, Sindh Provincial Congress Committee for Shikarpur District, 1921.

Prakas, Kanthi
Collaborator of Miller in the Labour movement of Karachi;

Secretary, Railway Union of Karachi; labour delegate to the Ahmedabad Session of the Indian National Congress.

Prasad, Pandit Maharaj Dvarika

Congress leader from Dadu, Sindh; member, Provincial Congress Committee, Sindh; participated in the Non-Co-operation, Civil Disobedience and Quit India movements; took active part in organising agitation against the Simon Commission; member, Sindh Legislative Council, 1921-26.

Prasad, Rai Bahadur Siv

Honorary magistrate and banker of Delhi; received the title of *Rai Sahib* in 1908 as a leading citizen who was noted for his 'generosity and loyalty'; received a CIE in 1911 for his wealth and position in Delhi; appointed provincial Darbari.

Prasad, Rajendra

1884-1963

Advocate, Calcutta High Court, 1911-16, Patna High Court, 1916-20; suspended practice and joined Non-Co-operation movement in 1920; member, Congress Working Committee; President, Indian National Congress, 1932, 1934, 1939 and 1947; member, Interim Government, 1946-47; Chairman, Constituent Assembly; first President of the Indian Republic, 1952-62.

Price, E.L.

Member Legislative Council [?].

Pursuram, Hundraj

Member, Sindh Provincial Congress Committee for Hyderabad, 1921.

Qa'im ad-Din

Student agitator from Madeji.

Qamr ad-Din, Seth

Central Provinces' delegate to All Indian Muslim League, 1919, resigned as Secretary of Khandwa Khilafat Committee, 1920 as protest against Non-Co-operation.

Qidwa'i, Mushir Husayn

1878-1937

Belonged to a petty zamindar family of Gadia in Barabanki District; one of the founders of the Anjuman-e Khuddam-e Kaaba; President, Awadh Khilafat Conference, 1929; joined the Swarajists in 1923; President of the Socialist group of Legislative Assembly members formed in 1924.

Qurayshi, Shu'ib 'Ali

1891-1962

Educated at the MAO College, Aligarh and Oxford; joined Dr. Ansari's medical mission; son-in-law of Muhammad Ali and connected with his political activities; worked for the Sultania College Scheme in Bhopal; migrated to Pakistan after Independence.

Qutb ad-Din

Nephew of Maulana Abdul Bari of Firangi Mahal; active in cow slaughter prohibition; edited *Congress* newspaper.

Rahman, Gauhar

Student agitator from Hazara.

Rajagopalacarya, Cakravarti

1879-1972

Educated at Central College, Bangalore, Presidency College and Law College, Madras; joined Rowlatt Act satyagraha and Non-Co-operation movement; General Secretary of Indian National Congress in 1921-22; member, AIWC of the Indian National Congress; President, Tamil Nadu Provincial Congress Committee till 1935; elected to Madras Legislative Assembly; leader Congress party in the Madras Legislative Council.

Rajpal, Ghamsam Das N.

Member, Sindh Provincial Congress Committee for Shikarpur District, 1921.

Ramani, Parasaram Tahal

Weaving Officer for Sindh.

Ramani, Sarasvati Devi Tahal

Member, Sindh Provincial Congress Committee for Larkana District, 1922.

Ramcand, Jasanmal

Member, Sindh Provincial Congress Committee for Sukkur District, 1922.

Ramcand, Watanmal

Member, Sindh Provincial Congress Committee, 1922.

Ramzam

Student agitator from Dera Ismail Khan.

Rao, Raghavendra

1889-1942

Bar-at-Law; President, C.P. Provincial Congress Committee, 1921; member, C.P. and Berar Legislative Council, 1923-30; Minister, C.P. and Berar, 1927-28; Home Minister, 1930; Acting Governor, C.P. and Berar, 1936; elected to the C.P. and Berar Legislative Assembly, 1937; Premier, C.P. and Berar, April-July 1937; advisor to the Secretary of State for India, 1939; member, Viceroy's Executive Council, 1941.

Ratansingh, Sankarlal

Member, Sindh Provincial Congress Committee.

Ridwi, Wakil Ahmed

President, Central Provinces Khilafat Committee.

Rijhumal Kundansingh Lahori

Member, Sindh Provincial Congress Committee for Larkana District, 1921-22; President, Larkana District Congress Committee; representative of Sindh to All India National Congress, 1921.

Roy, M.N.

1887-1954

Revolutionary from Bengal; became member of the Jygantar Party; accused in Howrah Conspiracy Case, 1910; founded the Communist Party in Mexico, 1919; presented the decolonisation thesis at the second Congress of the Communist International, 1920; accused in the Kanpur and Meerut conspiracy cases in 1927 and 1929; expelled from the Communist International, 1929; contested election to Indian National Congress Presidentship, 1940; organised the Radical Democratic Party and Indian Federation of Labour to support the war effort; established the Indian Renaissance Institute in Dehra Dun, 1946.

Sa'ad-allah, Mufti

Of Khairpur State; donated to Angora Fund.

Sadiq, Mawlawi Muhammad

Of Khadda; leader of Volunteer movement; representative for Sindh on the Central Khilafat Committee, Bombay.

Sahani, Dr. Taracand
President of arbitration court at Karachi harbour; leader of dock labourers.

Sahay, Hanvant
Joined the Revolutionary Party of Rash Behari Bose; involved in the Hardinge Bomb Case of 1912 and the Delhi Conspiracy Case, 1914; joined the Congress in 1920.

Sa'id, Mawlawi Ahmad
1888-1959
Educated Madrasa Husainia Bazaar, Matia Mahal, Delhi; Leading theologian, associated with the Madrasa Aminiya; active during the Rowlatt satyagraha with Maulawi Kifayat Ullah; Secretary, Jamiat-ul Ulama and a prominent Khilafat leader; opposed Communal Award, Separate Electorates and demand for Pakistan; attended All Parties' Conference in 1928; President, Bihar Muslim Independent Party Conference, 1936, Azad Muslim Conference at Delhi, 1940.

Sakhawatrai, Prabhudas
Member, Sindh Provincial Congress Committee for Larkana District, 1921-22.

Salah, Mawlawi Ahmad
Member, Sindh Provincial Congress Committee for Hyderabad.

Salamat-Allah, Mawlana
Religious leader from Firangi Mahal; closely associated with Abdul Bari; member, Anjuman-e Muid-al Islam; Member, Jamiat-ul Ulama.

Salih, Mawlawi Muhammad
Of Dadu; Secretary, Jamiat-ul Ulama for Larkana District.

Sankarlal
Member, Sindh Provincial Congress Committee for Larkana District, 1922.

Sarma, Lokram Nayanaram
1890-1933
Freedom fighter and journalist from Sindh; took an active part in the first Sindhi Provincial Congress in 1907; organised first Swadeshi exhibition in Sindh, 1908; started a nationalist Sindhi monthly, *Sindh Bhasker* in 1911; converted it into a weekly in

1916 and changed its name into *Hindu*, since 1917 daily newspaper; took part in Home Rule movement, Non-Co-operation, Civil Disobedience movements and was imprisoned several times.

Sarma, Neki Ram

Agitator from Rohtak District; tried and acquitted in Delhi for public speech in spite of prohibition.

Sarma, Ram Candra

Editor of the local *Congress* newspaper.

Sarma, Visnu Nayanaram

b. 1895

Younger brother of Lokram Nayanram Sarma; received training in journalism from his brother; editor of the *Hindu*, a Sindhi newspaper from Hyderabad; came into close contact with Choitram P. Gidwani; member, Sindh Provincial Congress Committee for Hyderabad District, 1922.

Sarup, Santi

Of Farrukhabad; member, Khilafat Workers' Conference;

Sasmal, B.N.

1881-1934

Educated at Calcutta and London; Bar-at-Law; participated in Swadeshi movement; suspended practice to join Non-Co-operation movement, 1921; Chairman, Midnapore District Board, 1923-26; Secretary, Bengal Provincial Congress Committee and Bengal Provincial Swaraj Party; elected to Bengal Legislative Council as independent candidate; President, Bengal Provincial Conference, Krishnagar, 1926; defended the accused in Chittagong Armoury Raid case, 1930 and Doughlas (?) shooting case, 1932; member, Calcutta Corporation, 1933-34 and Indian Legislative Assembly, 1934.

Sastri, Srinivasa

1869-1946

Social worker and freedom fighter from Madras; joined Servants of India Society, 1907 and later became its President; member, Legislative Council, Madras, 1913-16; member, Imperial Legislative Council, 1916-20; opposed Non-Co-operation programme of the Congress.

Sen, I.B.

Extremist; repudiated Non-Co-operation.

Sen Gupta, Jitendra Mohan

1885-1933

Bar-at-law; joined the Non-Co-operation movement, 1921; led railway and labour strikes, 1921, was arrested; member, Congress, Working Committee, 1922-23; Bengal Legislative Council, 1923-30; after the death of C.R. Das in 1925 became President of Bengal Provincial Congress Committee and leader of the Swaraj Party in the Council; Chairman, Reception Committee, Calcutta Congress Session, 1928.

Sethi, Arjunlal

1880-1941

Congressman from Ajmer; suspected of terrorist activities and imprisoned 1914-20.

Shafi', Mawlawi Muhammad

Originated from Lucknow; educated in Firangi Mahal; President, Calcutta Khilafat Committee.

Shafi', Muhammad

Of Hyderabad; leader of Muhammadan Volunteer movement.

Shah, 'Abd ar-Ra'uf

Khilafat leader from Akola, Berar; opposed removal of boycott of the Councils; attended Gay Conference of the Congress.

Shah, Ghulam Mustafa

Rashidi Pir from Bangi Kelhoro.

Shah, Mawlawi Muhammad Amin

Religious leader from Aminani Taluka Dadu; President of the Jamiat-ul Ulama for the Larkana District.

Shah, Mazhar ad-Din

Pir of Thulla Sharif; father of Pir Mithan Shah.

Shah, Mithan

Rashidi Pir of Thulla Sharif; Khilafat leader.

Shah, Muhammad Anwar

Issued Non-Co-operation fatwa.

Shah, Pir 'Abd al-Ghaffar

Chief Pir of Relan, Sindh; avoided direct involvement in political activities but encouraged the Muslims to take active part in the Khilafat and Non-Co-operation movements.

Shah, Pir 'Ali Anwar

Sufi Pir from Larkana; took part in the Non-Co-operation and Khilafat movements; member, Sindh Khilafat Working Committee; member, Sindh Provincial Congress Committee for Larkana, 1921-22; imprisoned for one year.

Shah, Pir Bakr

Religious leader of Bukhshan Shah, near Naudero.

Shah, Pir Hashim

Belonged to the Rashidi Pirs of Thulla Sharif.

Shah, Pir Ibrahim

Belonged to the Rashidi Pirs of Thulla Sharif; encouraged his Murids to fight the British to save the Khilafat.

Shah, Pir Illahi Bakhsh

1897-1975

Prominent religious leader from Larkana, who took active part in politics; educated at Aligarh; participated in Non-Co-operation movement; member, Central Khilafat Committee and Sindh Khilafat Working Committee; Member, Sindh Provincial Congress Committee; President, Sindh Azad Conference, Larkana District; elected to the Sindh Legislative Assembly in 1939 and 1946; Minister in the Minsitry of Sir Ghulam Husain and Khan Bahadur Allabaksh; Chief Minister of Sindh, April 1948-January 1949.

Shah, Pir Imam ad-Din

Son of Jhandewalla Pir of Hyderabad District; one of the prominent pro-Khilafat Pirs; gathered about 200 Pirs and Maulawis in March 1919 to sign the fatwa issued by Maulana Abdul Bari; accused of arms traffic during Khilafat movement.

Shah, Pir Mahbub

Khilafat leader from Hyderabad District; Pir from Tando Muhammad Khan; supported the Hijrat movement.

Shah, Pir Mahbub 'Ali

Member, Sindh Provincial Congress Committee for Sukkur District, 1922.

Shah, Pir Mithal
Pir from Thula Sharif; member, Sindh Provincial Congress Committee for Larkana District, 1922.

Shah, Pir Muhammad Munir
Religious leader from Bukhanshan Shah, near Naudero.

Shah, Pir Nur
Son of Pir of Jhandewalla; leader of Sindh Ulama movement.

Shah, Pir Nur ad-Din
Pir of Relan; Member, Sindh Provincial Congress Committee for Larkana, 1921-22.

Shah, Pir Rashid-allah
Pir of Jhando, Sindh; exponent of Jihad and forceful believer in *tauhid*; opposed to the Non-Co-operation movement.

Shah, Pir Thaman
Religious leader of Bangi Kelhoro; active in the reconciliation of the different branches of the Rashidi Pirs.

Shah, Pir Turab 'Ali
Son of Abdullah Shah, Pir of Kambar; member, Jamiat-ul Ulama; participated in Sindh Provincial Khilafat Conference; representative of Sindh to Central Khilafat Committee; member, Sindh Provincial Congress Committee for Larkana, 1921; later apologised to British Government.

Shah, Qadi Asad-allah
Pir from Tikhar; member, Sindh Provincial Congress Committee for Hyderabad, 1922; member, Sindh Provincial Khilafat Committee; representative for Sindh to Central Khilafat Committee, Bombay.

Shah, Sayyid 'Abd ar-Rahim
From Sijwal, donated to the Angora Fund and Smyrna Fund.

Shah, Sayyid Allah Bachhaye
Member, Sindh Provincial Congress Committee for Hyderabad, 1921; Pir of the Shrine of Matiari.

Shah, Sayyid 'Abd-allah
From Tikhar; member, Working Committee of the Sindh Provincial Khilafat Committee.

Shah, Sayyid Habib
Editor of the *Siyasat*, Peshawar (?).

Shah, Sayyid Maqbul
President, Khilafat meeting in Peshawar.

Shah, Sayyid Qamar 'Ali
Member, Sindh Provincial Congress Committee for Hyderabad.

Shah, Sayyid Pir
Rashidi Pir of Bahman; confidant of Pir Pagaro of Kingri; against Non-Co-operation.

Shah, Zia ud-din
Member, Sindh Provincial Congress Committee for Hyderabad District, 1922.

Shahab ad-Din
Treasurer, Hyderabad City Khilafat Committee.

Shadapur, Bhai Samdas
Member, Sindh Provincial Congress Committee for Nawabshah District, 1921.

Shams ad-Din
Joint Secretary, Sindh Provincial Khilafat Committee; resigned in 1922.

Shams ad-Din, Qadi
Secretary, Sindh Provincial Khilafat committee.

Shirwani, T.A.K.
1884-1935
Leading barrister and politician from Aligarh; contemporary of Jawaharlal Nehru at Cambridge; took part in Aligarh College and Home Rule League movements; member, U.P. Congress and AICC, 1919; Councillor, Muslim League; selected by the Central Khilafat Committee to serve on deputation with the Civil Disobedience Enquiry Committee; founder member, Swaraj Party, 1923.

Siddiq, Mawlana Muhammad
Collected donations for Angora Fund in Ranchore Lines.

Siddiq, Mawlawi Muhammad
Religious leader from Kheda; representative for Sindh to the Central Khilafat Committee.

Siddiqi, A.K.
Circulated Non-Co-operation fatwa; established branch of Jamiat-ul Ulama at Jabbalpur; attended special All-India Congress Session

at Delhi as delegate for Jabbalpur; attended Gaya Congress, declared in favour of Council-entry.

Siddiqi, M.K.

Elected as member to the Central Provinces Legislative Assembly for Swarajist Party.

Sidhva, R.K.

Secretary, Sindh Provincial Congress Committee; member, Sindh Provincial Congress Committee for Karachi, 1921.

Singh, Balvant

Prosecuted for inflammatory speaking; fled Delhi Province.

Singh, Gurbakhsh

Leader of extremist Sikh group in Delhi; founded Sikh Female Society.

Singh, Jagannath

Leader, Indraprastha Sewak Mandli Volunteer Corps, Delhi.

Singh, Master Autar

Speaker at the opening of the Azad Muslim High School, Peshawar.

Singh, Nanak

Imprisoned during Non-Co-operation for violent speeches.

Singh, Ser

From Muzaffarnagar; violent speaker.

Singh, Sundar

Tailor employed in the police lines; leader of the Sikh volunteers of Delhi.

Siraj ad-Din

Labour leader.

Sirhindi, Agha 'Umar Jan

Vice-President of Hyderabad District Khilafat Committee.

Sirhindi, Pir 'Abd-allah Jan

Brother of Pir Abdul Sattar Jan of Thando Saindad; took part in Khilafat movement and was imprisoned but was released when promised to refrain from agitation in future.

Sirhindi, Pir 'Abd as-Sattar Jan

Belonged to the influential Pir family of Thando Saindad; commanded the respect of a large body of murids; member of the committee formed to co-ordinate the League's propaganda campaign; instigated pro-Khilafat enthusiasm; Member, Sindh Provincial Congress Committee.

Sirhindi, Pir Ghulam Mujaddid

1881-1958

Belonged to Matiari, Sindh; Alim, follower of Maulana Abdul Bari in Lucknow; took part in the Non-Co-operation movement; im-prisoned along with the Ali brothers for supporting the resolution adopted at the All India Khilafat Conference, Karachi, 1921, which forbade Muslims to serve in the Army; member, Sindh Provincial Congress Committee.

Sirhindi, Pir Muhammad 'Ali Jan

Prominent Qandahari Pir of Thando Saindad; supported Khilafat movement; member, Sindh Provincial Congress Committee for Thar Parkar District, 1922.

Sirhindi, Pir Muhammad 'Umar Jan

Played important role in popularising the Khilafat cause; member, Sindh Khilafat Committee; Secretary of Jamiat-ul Ulama in Sindh.

Sraddhanand, Svami

1856-1926

Educated at Queen's College, Benaras and University College, Lahore; started legal practice in 1885; took an active interest in the Arya Samaj and emerged leader of its Gurukul section in 1893; founded the Gurukul at Hardwar in 1902; organised the Rowlatt satyagraha in Delhi; Chairman, Reception Committee of Congress, Amritsar, 1919; launched Shuddhi movement, 1922; killed by a Muslim fanatic.

Subhani, Azad

b. 1873

Prominent during the pan-Islamic agitations for 1913-14; leading agitator during the Kanpur mosque agitation; joined the Anjuman-e Khuddam-e Kaaba; President, All India Khilafat Conference, September 1920; introduced resolution demanding complete independence at the Muslim League Session in January 1922; associated with the Labour movement in Kanpur.

Sulayman

Leader of Railway Trade Union in Karachi.

Sultan Singh, Rai Bahadur

Prominent banker and industrialist; Director of the Delhi Cloth and General Mills; member of the Delhi Municipal Committee; Chairman of Delhi Co-operative Stores; supported the Home Rule movement; joined the Provincial Congress Committee and Indian Association in 1917.

Sundarlal

Editor of *Bhavishya* (Allahabad).

Tahalram

Member, Sindh Provincial Congress Committee for Larkana District, 1921.

Tahalsingh

Labour leader, Railway Union of Karachi.

Tahulramani, Caitram Thavardas

Student agitator from Tatta.

Taj ad-Din, Mawlawi

Attended the All India Khilafat Conference in 1921; member of the Boycott of British Goods Committee; edited the *Taj* (Jabbalpur) and *Khilafat* (Delhi); President, DCC Jabbalpur; temporary Superintendent of the Central Bureau for the Relief of Muslim Internees; closely associated with Dr. Ansari and Shaukat Ali.

Taj Muhammad, Mawlawi

From Amrot; preached Non-Co-operation and Khilafat to rural population of Sindh; representative for Sindh to the Central Khilafat Committee.

Talpur, Mir Allah Bakhsh

Member, Sindh Provincial Congress Committee for Thar Parkar District, 1921-22; representative for Sindh to Central Khilafat Committee, Bombay.

Taqi, Muhammad

b. 1887

Lawyer; gave up practice during Non-Co-operation; Secretary of the Delhi Congress for several years.

Tattacarya

From Madras, worked at Karachi Congress Office; accused of forging signatures of the Secretary and President.

Tejumal, Kesumal
Member, Sindh Provincial Congress Committee for Sahaiti District, 1921-22.

Thana'-allah, Mawlawi
1868-1948
Punjab leader, first of the Deoband school, later of the Ahl-e Hadith; founder and editor of *Ahl-e Hadis*, Amritsar; leader of the Khilafat movement; member of the Khilafat Conference; founder member of Jamiat-ul Ulama-e Hind; member of the Boycott of British Goods Committee; migrated to Pakistan, 1947.

Tilak, Bal Gangadhar
1856-1920
One of the founders of the Deccan Education Society and the Ferguson College in 1885; imprisoned for sedition on 14 September 1897 and in July 1908; released on 17 January 1914; launched the Home Rule Agitation in 1916.

Tirathmal, Nivandharm
Member, Sindh Provincial Congress Committee for Jacobabad District, 1922.

Tolani, P.
Member, Sindh Provincial Congress Committee.

Topandas
Member, Sindh Provincial Congress Committee for Larkana District, 1921.

Towermalani, Sukharamdas
Member, Sindh Provincial Congress Committee for Larkana District, 1922.

Udhebhan, Pandit
Member, Sindh Provincial Congress Committee for Larkana, 1922.

'Umid Ali
Son of Hajji Abd al-Latif Qureyshi; student agitator from Larkana.

'Uthman, Muhammad
Prosecuted for seditious speeches during Non-Co-operation.

Uttardi, Seth Narayandas Thakurdas
Member, Sindh Provincial Congress Committee for Shikarpur District, 1921-22.

Vadhumal, Motiram
Member, Sindh Provincial Congress Committee for Thar Parkar District, 1921-22.

Vadhumal, Tikamdas
Educated in Karachi and Bombay; practised law in Bombay High Court; Municipal Counsellor, Bombay; one of the signatories of the petition for the separation of Sindh; member, Sindh Provincial Congress Committee for Karachi, 1921.

Vajpeyi, A.P.
Arrested in 1921 during Non-Co-operation movement.

Valecha, C.T.
Member, Sindh Provincial Congress Committee for Sukkur District, 1921.

Valecha, Sobhraj
Member, Sindh Provincial Congress Committee for Shikarpur District, 1922.

Vallabhdas, Seth Sundardas
Member, Sindh Provincial Congress Committee for Karachi, 1921-22; Vice-President, Sindh Provincial Congress Committee.

Vaparimal, Virumal
Member, Sindh Provincial Congress Committee for Sukkur District, 1921-22.

Vardhacarya
Delegate from Madras to the Delhi Congress Conference; opposed Council entry.

Vasvani, Nanakram Chabaldas
Amil of Jhuramal Lane, Hyderabad; editor of *New Times*, Karachi; member, Sindh Provincial Congress Committee.

Vinjhraj, Kanvar
Member, Sindh Provincial Congress Committee for Thar Parkar District, 1922.

Visomal, Partabrai
Member, Sindh Provincial Congress Committee for Larkana District, 1922.

Visomal, Pratabrai
Member, Sindh Provincial Congress Committee for Larkana District, 1921-22.

Vyas, Manilal J.

Candidate to Municipal Elections, 1921; labour and artisan leader of Karachi; member, Sindh Provincial Congress Committee for Karachi District, 1922.

Vyas, Ramalal

Tilakite; Khilafat leader from Berar.

Wafa'i, Mawlawi Din Muhammad Sahib

Religious leader from Sukkur District; representative for Sindh to Central Khilafat Committee.

Yamin, Dr. Muhammad

Leader, Sindh Volunteer movement.

Yasin, Mawlawi Muhammad

Religious leader from Raipur; co-founder of Jamiat-ul Ulama in Jabbalpur.

Zafar al-Mulk

d. 1947

Editor, *an Nazar* (Lucknow) and *Haqiqat*; took part in the Khilafat movement and supported Non-Co-operation; convicted for sedition, 1920; member, Khilafat Workers' Association.

Chronology

Delhi	United Provinces	Central Provinces	Bengal	Sindh	NW Frontier Provinces
1911	Turkish-Italian War				
	Foundation of Red Crescent Society in Kolkata				
(Dec.)	Revocation of the partition of Bengal				
1912 (Dec.)	Dr. Ansari leads Medical Mission to Turkey				
1913	Kanpur agitation				
(May)	Foundation of Anjuman-e Khuddam-e Ka'ba				
1914 (1.11)	Turkey joined war against the Allies				
(Dec.)	Sultan declares Jihad				
1915 (Jan.)	Gandhi returns to India				
(May)	Internment of the Ali Brothers				
1916 (June)	Revolt of Sharif Husain against Ottoman Empire				
(Aug.)	Silk Letter Conspiracy				

Delhi	United Provinces	Central Provinces	Bengal	Sindh	NW Frontier Provinces
(Dec.)	Maulana Mahmud Hasan interned at Malta				
(Dec.)	Lucknow Pact between the Muslim League and the Congress				
1917	Foundation of the Central Bureau for the Help of the Muslim Internees				
	Bihar Satyagraha				
(19.2) Establishment of a branch of the Home Rule League		Foundation of several Seva Samitis			
(March)	Fall of Baghdad				
(May) Foundation Indraprastha Sewak Mandli					
(11.9) Foundation Home Rule League Volunteer Corps					
(Oct.) Tension due to synchronised Ram Lila and Moharram celebrations					
1918	Passive resistance movement in Khaira District				
(1.5)	Lloyd George: pledge to maintain Turkish sovereignty after the war				
(April)	Delhi Imperial War Conference; Gandhi presents Muslim viewpoint				
(18.4) Gandhi inaugurates Swadeshi stall					

(May) Foundation of Hindu volunteer corps by Swami Shraddhanand	
(July) Beginning of Muslim activity through Central Bureau for the Relief of Muslim Internees	
(30.10)	Turkey signed armistice at Mudros
(Nov.) Foundation Muslim League Volunteer Corps	
11.11	German capitulation
(Dec.)	Delhi Session of the Muslim League and the Congress; participation of ulama
1919 (Jan.)	Beginning of peace conference at Paris
(Feb.)	Introduction of the Rowlatt Bills
	(Feb.) protest meetings, but not satyagraha; little Muslim agitation
(Feb.)	Gandhi Satyagraha in Ahmedabad; foundation Satyagraha Sabha
(Feb.)	Assassination of Habib Ullah Khan, Amir of Afghanistan
(3.2.) Beginning of the Rowlatt satyagraha	
(March)	Rapprochement Gandhi–Abdul Bari
(March)	Foundation Khilafat Committee at Bombay
(19.3)	General hartal

Delhi	United Provinces	Central Provinces	Bengal	Sindh	NW Frontier Provinces
(30.3) Hartal; Swami Shraddhanand invited to speak from pulpit of Jama Masjid; heavy clashes between demonstrators and police					
(6.4)	General hartal				
(13.4)	Jallianwala Bagh Massacre				
(17.4) Seditious Meetings Act applied; Satyagraha Sabha dissolves itself					
(May)	Afghan attack on British India				
(15.5)	Greek landing in Izmir				
(21.9)	All India Muslim Conference at Lucknow				
(Oct.)	Appointment of Hunter Committee				
(Oct.)	Foundation All India Trade Union Congress				
(17.10)	Khilafat Day				
	(17.10) observed mainly in Allahabad, Gorakhpur, Agra and Kanpur (Oct.) formation of local Khilafat committees				(17.10) Practical failure to observe Khilafat Day

(Nov.) Martyrs' Week			
(11.11.)	Bombay Khilafat Committee changed name to Central Khilafat Committee of India (CKC)		
(23.11.)	First Khilafat Conference at Delhi; resolved to withdraw cooperation from the Government unless Khilafat question was satisfactorily settled		
(Dec.)	Second Khilafat Conference at Amritsar; Amritsar Congress; resolved on Non-Violent Non-Co-operation		
(Dec.)	Foundation Sikh League		
(13.12)	Peace celebrations		
(24.12.)	Royal assent to the Reforms Act; amnesty (24.12.) Release of 7 internees and 11 prisoners		
1920	Elections to the Reformed Councils; boycotted by the Congress		
(Jan.) Foundation of Khilafat Volunteer Corps; foundation of Askar-e Islamia	(Jan.) demonstrations numbering tens of thousands in Moradabad, Aligarh, Kanpur, Lucknow and Meerut	(28.1.) Formation of Khandwa District Khilafat Committee	
(Feb.)	Khilafat Delegation to London, led by Muhammad Ali	(Feb.) Khilafat Committees in Nagpur, Akola, Buldana	(Feb.) Provincial Khilafat Committee Conference; resolved on Non-Co-operation (14.3.) Beginning of boycott of British goods
(19.3)	Second Khilafat Day, hartal		

Delhi	United Provinces	Central Provinces	Bengal	Sindh	NW Frontier Provinces
(19.–20.3) Khilafat Workers' Conference		(19.3.) Hartal observed	(19.3.) Hartal failure		(19.3) Complete hartal in Peshawar and Hazara Districts; Formation of first Provincial Khilafat Committee
(March) Establishment of a Hijrat Office					
(23.3) Conflict between nationalists and Imam of the Jama Masjid					
(April) Hakim Ajmal Khan renounces titles	(April) Agitation carried to small towns and villages; establishment of provincial Khilafat committees at Meerut and Lucknow				(April–Aug.) Agitation in Hazara District led by Muhammad Ishaq
	(4.–5.4.) Meeting of ulama at Kanpur, 15,000 participants				
(11.–14.4.)	CKC decides on Non-Co-operation				
(18.–19.4) Khilafat Workers' Conference					
(23.4.)	Kemal Pasha convened Grand National Assembly at Ankara				
(May)	Publication of the Hunter Report				

	(May) Branch of Khilafat Workers' Conference established in Lucknow (1.–2.5.) Khilafat conference for Oudh in Fyzabad; Hijrat, Non-Co-operation, boycott Prince of Wales		
(11.5.)	Announcement of the peace terms with Turkey		
		(May) no unrest following announcement of peace terms	
(18.5)	Beginning of Hijrat to Afghanistan		
			(May–Aug.) Intense Hijrat movement in Peshawar District
(June)	Return of Mahmud Hasan from internment in Malta		
(July)	All India Trades Union Congress founded		
(17.7.) Strike of the Workers at the Government Press		(25.7.) Provincial Khilafat Committee resolves on Non-Co-operation and boycott of foreign goods	
(1.8.)	Hartal; Khilafat Day; formal inauguration of the Non-Co-operation campaign		
(1.8.)	Death of Tilak		
(9.8.)	Order by Amir of Afghanistan prohibiting further immigration		

Delhi	United Provinces	Central Provinces	Bengal	Sindh	NW Frontier Provinces
(19.8.) Decision to boycott the flower sellers' festival at Mehrauli		(22.8.) PCC accepts Non-Co-operation			(24.8.) Call for Jihad in Hazara District; arrest of the leaders
	(26.8.) Assassination of Mr. Willoughby, Dpt. Commissioner of Kheri				
(Sept.)	Special Session of the Congress, Calcutta; acceptance of Non-Co-operation programme				
		(Sept.) Beginning of anti-liquor campaign			(Sept.–Dec.) Resignation of *lambardars* in Bannu District; strike at Islamia College, Peshawar
(26.10.) Foundation of Provincial Sikh League; raising of Sikh volunteer corps		(26.10.) Foundation provincial branch of Jamiat-ul Ulama	(Oct.) Formation of arbitration courts in Howrah and Belgachia		
			(29.10.) Madrassa College strike		
(30.10.)	Foundation Jamia Millia Islamia				
			(8.10.) Beginning of school boycott on larger scale		
(19.–21.11)	Meeting Jamiat-ul Ulama at Delhi; Non-Co-operation fatwa				

(30.11.) Death of Maulana Mahmud Hasan at Delhi		(3rd week of Nov.) Boycott of elections successful		
		(Nov.) School boycott in Jabbalpur	(Nov.) Khilafat meetings among striking mill press men	
(Dec.)	Foundation Shiromani Gurdwara Prabandhak Committee			
(Dec.)	Foundation Kisan Congress			
(Dec.) Re-imposition of the Seditious Meetings Act				(9.12.) Opening of Azad High School, Peshawar
(Dec.) Strike of the Workers of the Electricity Company				
(3.12.) Obstruction of the funeral of Abdul Ahad			(13.12.) Opening of National School in Calcutta by Gandhi	
(24.12)	Nagpur Congress; reaffirmation of Non-Co-operation resolution			
1921 (Jan.)	Visit of the Duke of Connought			
	(Jan. / Feb.) Collection of subscriptions for Central Khilafat Fund; meetings in Hamirpur, Jhansi, Kanpur, Fatehpur, Mirzapur, Benares, Etawah, Bareilly	(Jan.) Non-Co-operation in towns and larger villages; resignation titles; arbitration courts; volunteer organizations; boycott of schools and colleges mainly Jabbalpur, Nagpur	(Jan.) Incitement to the police to resign; formation of volunteer corps	(Jan.) Boycott of lawyers; foundation of village committees

Delhi	United Provinces	Central Provinces	Bengal	Sindh	NW Frontier Provinces
			(13.–20.1.) School strike in Calcutta; Government Schools temporarily closed		
		(Jan. / Feb.) Boycott of excise auctions	(Feb.) Taxi and tramway strike in Calcutta	(Feb.) Boycott movement in Sindh College	
(13.2.) Inauguration of the Tibbia College by Gandhi			(Feb.) National schools in every district	(Feb.) Internal re-organizations of Sindh Provincial Congress Committee	
			(Feb.) Jute boycott campaign. boycott of foreign clothes and alcoholic liquor	(26.–27.2) Meeting Sindh Provincial Khilafat Committee	
				(Feb.) Strike at Herman's Engineering Works, Karahci	
				(21.3.) Hartal in Karachi on the occasion of the visit of the Governor	(March) Prohibition of political meetings
					(March) Opening of National Schools in Nowshera and Ulmanza

					(13.3) Hartal in all the District Headquarters
(24.–26.3.)	Jamiat-ul Ulama declares for complete independence				
		(29.3.) Anti-liquor riot in Nagpur resulting in 9 death through police firing	(24.3) Mutiny in Rajshahi Jail	(March) Boycott of liquor licenses	
(March)	Indian Delegation to the Peace Conference				
(April) Sikh agitation			(April) opposition to Forest Department in Chittagong District	(April) Formation of volunteer associations	
(1.4.)	Bezwada Session of the AICC; resolved against introduction of Civil Disobedience				
(2.4.)	Muhammad Ali speech welcoming Afghan invasion				
	(7. – 10.4.) Khilafat conference at Meerut (10.4) Conference of Ulama in Moradabad			(6.4.) Hartal nearly complete (April) Formation of a Sabha of Artisans and Labourers (11.4.) National School opened at Hyderabad (13.4) Hartal nearly complete	
			(May) Strike in Assam Tea Gardens; exodus of the plantation workers; Steamer strike (May – July) Strike of Assam-Bengal Railway		

Delhi	United Provinces	Central Provinces	Bengal	Sindh	NW Frontier Provinces
(30.5)	'Apology' of the Ali Brothers				
		(June) Foundation of Liberal League; anti Brahmin agitation in Berar	(June) Disclosure of embezzlement of Khilafat funds	(June) Growth of anti-Non-Co-operation movement	
				(June) Picketing of liquor shops	
(8.7.)	Khilafat conference at Karachi				
				(July) Rise in political agitation due to Khilafat conference (22.7). Riot in Matiari resulting in police firing	
(28.–30.7)	Bombay Session AICC; resolved on boycott of Prince of Wales' visit; boycott of foreign clothes				
(Aug.)	Moplah outbreak in Malabar				
(Aug.)	Proscription of the Non-Co-operation fatwa				
(1.8.)	Official launching of the boycott of foreign clothes				
		(Aug.) Opening of Swadeshi shops; volunteer corps for Swadeshi propaganda	(Aug.) Movement for Arbitration Courts reaches its climax		
(Sept.) Prosecution of Maulvi Ahmad Said and Abdul Aziz Ansari					
(14.9.)	Arrest of Muhammad Ali and other Khilafat leaders; Karachi trial				

	(Sept.) Meetings of protest against the arrests in Meerut, Gorakhpur and Aligarh			
				(Oct.) Distribution of Non-Co-operation fatwa to troops in Karachi
(Nov.) Picketing of cloth shops	(Nov.) Collection of large sums for Angora fund; formation of new Khilafat committees in the Districts		(Nov.) Obstruction of settlement operations; Chaudagram: rural police ceased to work	(Nov.) Non-Co-operation movement looses momentum, Khilafat agitation gains; Collections for Angora Fund
(4.–5.11.)	Delhi Session AICC; Civil Disobedience permitted under strict conditions			
				(14.11.) Meeting Singh Ulama
(17.–21.11.)	Bombay riots in connection with boycott of the visit of the Prince of Wales			
		(17.11) Hartal observed	(17.11) Calcutta hartal; volunteer organizations declared unlawful organizations	
(18.–20.11.)	Meeting Jamiat-ul Ulama at Lahore; confirmation of the Non-Co-operation fatwa; service in the army and police declared haram			
(Dec.)	Session of the Khilafat Conference, Congress and Muslim League at Ahmedabad; Congress resolved on continuation of Non-Violent Non-Co-operation and constructive programmes.			
(Dec.) Enforcement of orders against picketing; re-imposition of Seditious Meetings Act			(Dec.) refusal to pay chaukidari tax; armed police attacked in Nilphamari bazaar	(Dec.) Foundation of Muhammadan Volunteer Corps

Delhi	United Provinces	Central Provinces	Bengal	Sindh	NW Frontier Provinces
			(24.12.) Arrival Prince of Wales; large number of arrests	(Dec.) Arrest and conviction of Jairamdas Daulatram (Dec.) Movement taken over by young Khilafatists from the Pirs	
1922 (14.1)	Non-party Conference at Bombay				
	(Jan.) Civil Disobedience in Bara Banki		(Jan.) Civil Disobedience without official inauguration; Serajganj, Tittagarh and Dhaka Districts: resistance to arrests, police opened fire;		
(31.1.)	AICC authorizes Gandhi to start Civil Disobedience campaign				
			(Feb.) Jalpaiguri; resistance to arrests, police opened fire		
(4.2.)	Chauri Chaura massacres				
(11.–12.2.)	Working Committee of Congress at Bardoli postpones Civil Disobedience; constructive programme				
(14.2.) Arrival Prince of Wales			(20.2.) Attacks and firing in Ranpur District (24.2.) Attacks on police in Chaudagram		

(24.2.)	Delhi Session AICC confirms Bardoli resolution		
(25.–26.2.)	All India Khilafat Conference at Delhi; resolution to continue Non-Violent Non-Co-operation		
(10.3.)	Gandhi arrested		
	(April) Hasrat Mohani arrested		(9.3.) Attacks on police in Chaudagram (April) Riot in Presidency Jail (April) Disintegration of the Non-Co-operation party
(June)	Civil Disobedience Enquiry Committee appointed by Congress		
		(July) National flag agitation	(July) Attack on police resulting in firing in Chittagong (Aug.) Attack on police resulting in firing in Pabna and Bakarganj
(Aug.)	Release of C.R. Das		
(11.10.)	Armistice in the Greco-Turkish War		
(1.11.)	Grand National Assembly in Turkey over the powers of the Sultan		
(Dec.)	Gaya Congress; upholds boycott on Councils		
1923 (1.1.)	Formation of Swaraj Party		
(29.1)	Turkey declares itself republic		
(3.3.)	Ablition of the Khilafat		
(May) Establishment of Swaraj Party with Hakim Ajmal Khan as President		(May–Aug.) Nagpur national flag agitation	

Delhi	United Provinces	Central Provinces	Bengal	Sindh	NW Frontier Provinces
(24.7.)	Treaty of Peace between Turkey and the Allies (Treaty of Lausanne)				
(Aug.)	Release of Muhammad Ali				
(Sept.)	Delhi Special Congress; compromise between Swarajists and No-changers				
(Oct.)	Release of Shaukat Ali				
(Nov.)	Elections of the Councils; success of the Swaraj Party				
		(Nov.) Victory of the Swaraj Party			
(Dec.)	Coconanda Congress; endorse compromise of Delhi Special Congrss				
1924 (5.2.)	Release of Gandhi				
(March)	King Husain of Hejaz proclaims himself Khalif				

Index

[illegible] the [illegible] Congress [illegible] the [illegible] number of prominent politicians [illegible] [illegible]

[illegible]

[illegible] and the other [illegible]. Meanwhile the [illegible] the washermen, water carriers and sweeper communities to pass [illegible] Swaraj Fund were also collected with moderate success.

On the 8th May [illegible] Sewa Samiti [illegible] of civil disobedience, a [illegible] which [illegible] Sewa Samiti volunteers but this was short lived. The [illegible] Sewak Mandis declined to co-operate, as the movement was political. The Seditious Meetings Act ceased to apply to Delhi on the 8th June.